D0138651

# AFRICAN AMERICAN ICONS OF SPORT

## Triumph, Courage, and Excellence

## Edited by Matthew C. Whitaker

Greenwood Icons

GREENWOOD PRESS
Westport, Connecticut · London

**Library of Congress Cataloging-in-Publication Data**

African American icons of sport : triumph, courage, and excellence / edited by
Matthew C. Whitaker
    p.   cm.—(Greenwood icons)
Includes bibliographical references and index.
ISBN-13: 978-0-313-34028-4 (alk. paper)
1. African American athletes—Biography.   I. Whitaker, Matthew C.
GV697.A1A353   2008
796.092′396073—dc22
[B]     2007052945

British Library Cataloguing in Publication Data is available.

Library of Congress Catalog Card Number: 2007052945
ISBN-13: 978-0-313-34028-4

First published in 2008

Greenwood Press, 88 Post Road West, Westport, CT 06881
An imprint of Greenwood Publishing Group, Inc.
www.greenwood.com

Printed in the United States of America

The paper used in this book complies with the
Permanent Paper Standard issued by the National
Information Standards Organization (Z39.48–1984).

10   9   8   7   6   5   4   3   2   1

For Anastacia Ami and Jackson Asante Whitaker.
Play to inspire and play to win.

# Contents

# List of Photos

# Series Foreword

Worshipped and cursed. Loved and loathed. Obsessed about the world over. What does it take to become an icon? Regardless of subject, culture, or era, the requisite qualifications are the same: (1) challenge the status quo, (2) influence millions, and (3) impact history.

Using these criteria, Greenwood Press introduces a new reference format and approach to popular culture. Spanning a wide range of subjects, volumes in the Greenwood Icons series provide students and general readers a port of entry into the most fascinating and influential topics of the day. Every title offers an in-depth look at 24 iconic figures, each of which captures the essence of a broad subject. These icons typically embody a group of values, elicit strong reactions, reflect the essence of a particular time and place, and link different traditions and periods. Among those featured are artists and activists, superheroes and spies, inventors and athletes, the legends and mythmakers of entire generations. Yet icons can also come from unexpected places: as the heroine who transcends the pages of a novel or as the revolutionary idea that shatters our previously held beliefs. Whether people, places, or things, such icons serve as a bridge between the past and the present, the canonical and the contemporary. By focusing on icons central to popular culture, this series encourages students to appreciate cultural diversity and critically analyze issues of enduring significance.

Most importantly, these books are as entertaining as they are provocative. Is Disneyland a more influential icon of the American West than Las Vegas? How do ghosts and ghouls reflect our collective psyche? Is Barry Bonds an inspiring or deplorable icon of baseball?

Designed to foster debate, the series serves as a unique resource that is ideal for paper writing or report purposes. Insightful, in-depth entries provide far more information than conventional reference articles but are less intimidating and more accessible than a book-length biography. The most revered and reviled icons of American and world history are brought to life with related sidebars, timelines, fact boxes, and quotations. Authoritative entries are accompanied by bibliographies, making these titles an ideal starting point for further research. Spanning a wide range of popular topics, including business, literature, civil rights, politics, music, and more, books in the series provide fresh insights for the student and popular reader into the power and influence of icons, a topic of as vital interest today as in any previous era.

# Acknowledgments

It has been said that debts cannot be settled unless they are first recognized publicly. It is my pleasure to acknowledge the many people who have aided me in preparing *African American Icons of Sport*, a book that could not have been published without the emotional, imaginative, and financial assistance of the following people. First and foremost, I thank everyone who committed his or her research, knowledge, counsel, and quick wit to this text. I am truly in debt to those who contributed to this volume. Their chapters have captured the dynamism of extraordinary black athletes who have embodied not only the complexity, tribulations, and triumphs of black history and life, but the strengths and weaknesses embedded in the human condition. I am deeply grateful to Elizabeth Demers, former senior editor at Greenwood Publishing, for her vision, courage, and steadfast support of this project. Working with you is an absolute delight, Elizabeth. I am particularly obliged to Kaitlin Ciarmiello, assistant editor at Greenwood Publishing Group. Words cannot express how much I have cherished your kindheartedness and attention to detail, Kaitlin.

Many of the ideas that helped frame this work were formed through dialogue and intellectual exchange with students in my Arizona State University (ASU) research seminar, titled "Playing for Keeps: Sports, Inequality and the American Dream." During the spring of 2006, students in this course gave me the opportunity to assess my thoughts and research on the intersection of race, class, gender, sexuality, and religion in the worlds of amateur and professional sports. They were an intelligent, creative, lively, open-minded, amusing, and utterly candid circle of aspiring scholars, sports enthusiasts, and athletes. This book has benefited greatly from the enthusiasm and matter-of-fact attitude of this class: Brett Caldwell, Anna Collins, Quency Darley, Nicole Del Re, Lindsay Embree, Michael Fleming, John Gray, Brett Henry, Kevin Jenkins, Jason Jourden, Kenji Kondo, Edward Limon, Garret Majlinger, Daniel Mankowski, Evan Mather, Graham Reilly, Jessica Saenz, and Sheryl Vargas.

I am especially indebted to Evan Mather and Megan Falater, two excellent research assistants, for their invaluable help throughout the publication process. Megan went well beyond the call of duty, and this book would never have been completed without her assistance and support. Brooks D. Simpson, a razor-sharp, funny, and shrewd colleague at ASU, supported this project from its inception, and even participated in it with his illuminating and timely pieces on Derek Jeter and Magic Johnson. Brooks has been a mentor and friend for 17 years; throughout this time, we have been able to enrich our friendship while witnessing the height of the Chicago Bulls dynasty, the creation of the Women's National Basketball Association (WNBA), *my* Arizona Diamondback's stirring victory over *his* New York Yankees in 2001, gold medal victories by the U.S. Women's Soccer Team in 1996 and 2004, the dominance of Lance Armstrong, the ascendancy of Tiger Woods, and the 2004 Boston Red Sox World Series victory. Our partnership has been fun and, as this book demonstrates, quite productive.

Among my peers, who are also friends, I must single out Jeremy I. Levitt. We have been friends for nearly 18 years, a friendship that began as I, a faithful admirer of his intellect and passion, was first introduced to the power of black history and life. Jeremy reached out to me and welcomed me into his world: a world colored by his principled and unsurpassed commitment to the advancement of people of African descent. Despite his persistent and questionable claims that Magic's Lakers were better than Jordan's Bulls, he is an invaluable and cherished friend and partner in struggle.

Journalist David Halberstam argues in *Playing for Keeps: Michael Jordan and the World He Made* that individuals who have preceded us always make the labor of those who follow less demanding. In this instance the enormous and ever-expanding body of literature on African American history and life, and black athletes in particular, has helped inform and buttress this study. Although a number of scholars and writers have contributed greatly to this body of literature, the following merit special recognition: Arthur Ashe, Mary Francis Berry, Gerald Early, John Hope Franklin, Douglass Hartmann, Thomas Hauser, Darlene Clark Hine, Phil Jackson, Peniel Joseph, Robin D. G. Kelley, Spike Lee, Earl Lewis, Manning Marable, Nell Irvin Painter, Arnold Rampersad, David Remnick, Sam Smith, Quintard Taylor Jr., Joe William Trotter, Cornel West, and Dave Zirin.

This book has also profited from the excellent minds and camaraderie of my colleagues at ASU: Pat Lauderdale, Keith Miller, Elsie Moore, Stanlie James, Suzanne Rios, Chris Smith, Noel J. Stowe, Norma Villa, and the stately Thomas J. Davis. I would like to add a special note of thanks to Neal Lester, whose counsel and friendship I have truly treasured. I am also deeply obliged to Peter Iverson for taking me to a number of Diamondback home games, even though my presence almost always hastened a loss for the home team.

Graduate students Elise Boxer, Monica Butler, Victoria Jackson, and Rose Soza War Soldier, all aided this project by contributing innovative perspectives and critical observations. My close friends deserve a shout out as well, especially Scott Bowman, Carole Coles Henry, Robert J. Hackett Jr., Jason Harris, Lasana Hotep, Alonzo Jones, John L. Jones, Gina Lang, Mary Radcliffe, Dan and Kristi Rutz-Robbins, and Michael A. Smart. As always, I value their encouragement, sincerity, and vivacity. My father, Michael L. Hopwood, handed down his passion for sports to me, and my mother, Covey L. Whitaker, has always encouraged my interest in academics, the arts, and athletics. Thank you for your limitless love and support, Ma. I reserve my most heartfelt thank you for my wife, Gidget, a truly phenomenal woman. We have been a team our entire adult lives, and the longevity of our union not only affirms our commitment to each other but is evidence that a loyal Green Bay Packers fan and a staunch Dallas Cowboys fan (like me) can, in fact, coexist.

# Introduction

*African American Icons of Sport* is a book that sheds light on the lives and legacies of highly successful and influential black athletes, teams, and coaches who rose above conventional stardom to come to symbolize a given zeitgeist to millions of people throughout the world. As such, it will not simply examine the rich and famous, it will explore the history and experiences of complex, multilayered individuals and groups who reflect the conflicts and contradictions of their times. It will examine the extent to which modern mass media and popular culture contributed to the rise, and sometimes fall, of the these powerful representations of tragedy and triumph, athletic excellence, individual distinction, and group excellence. In an era when black athletes are increasingly identified with ignorance, apathy, indulgence, dishonesty, and violence, some of our African American icons of sport have much to teach us about the ways in which many black athletes used their talents and opportunities to overcome not simply the obstacles others placed in their way but the struggles they faced from within. *African American Icons of Sport*, therefore, will not only speak to the achievements of distinguished black athletes, it will illuminate the possibilities of the human spirit.

The word *icon* is derived from the Greek *eikon*, meaning image. In fact, icons in the ancient world were venerated corporeal images, mammoth figures, or religious depictions. Old World icons are associated most with the art of Eastern Orthodox Christianity, but they are worth more than their value as objects. Physical representations were often sanctified during the eighth and ninth centuries, for example, and iconoclasts were those who literally ruined such renderings. In the twenty-first century, the term *icon* acquired a far more worldly meaning. Nevertheless, a secular icon often attracts its own multitude of worshippers. In modern popular culture, icons are often synonymous with symbols, such as names, faces, portraits, or even a people that are easily identified as having some well-known importance or embodying certain qualities. Indeed, many celebrities, dead and alive, have become icons. There are iconic figures in history, cinema, music, art—and in sports.

What do Jack Johnson, Jesse Owens, Muhammad Ali, Charles Barkley, and Tiger Woods have in common? Whether we admire, disregard, or deplore them, they each had some bearing on or embodied aspects of our way of life. For better or worse, they helped shape the way America is perceived, and served as role models for millions in the United States and beyond. This collection of entries explores the lives of 24 black icons of sport, one celebrated and internationally known team, and one trailblazing league that assumed iconic status in American culture and beyond.

The scholars and writers who have contributed to this text consider these icons by means of a varied assortment of viewpoints and disciplines. The interdisciplinary scholarship in this book poses and answers two very important questions: (1) What is an African American "icon" of sport? and (2) What characteristics do black athletes, coaches, and teams share that most people consider iconic? This book demonstrates that icons generally engender intense reactions in people. They frequently personify the values of particular groups and echo the influence of their time. They are often restyled or made larger by impersonation, and they often cross boundaries that exist between assorted segments of American and global society, such as those that exist between races, classes, and the sexes. The entries in this book explore the history and lives of some of the most compelling African American icons of sport by employing myriad points of view through an array of rhetorical techniques. A mixture of history, gender studies, health science, justice studies, philosophy of sport, sociology, and political science, *African American Icons of Sport* offers thoughtful analyses of some of the greatest black sports figures in history, as well as cautionary tales of suffering and sacrifice that are often overlooked in more celebrated stories of African American athletic success.

Indeed, it is in the arena of collegiate and professional sports that African Americans have confirmed what human beings can accomplish in the face of racism or in spite of it. The experiences of black men and women in American sports, in particular, are microcosms of their lives in American society. The sports world is a highly favored part of the American fabric. It would be difficult to envision the social, cultural, political, and economic development of the United States in the absence of its amateur and professional sports activity, and it would be just as hard to imagine collegiate and professional sports activity in America without the participation and contributions of African Americans.

People of African descent have been involved in American sports since their introduction to the "New World" in the sixteenth century. Initially, American sports consisted of exhibitors who used contests or physical abilities in a competitive manner as a means of amusement. Enslaved and free blacks participated in these recreational activities. Some enslaved people were permitted "holidays" by those who held them in bondage. During these holidays, they participated in ball playing, boxing, foot racing, and cockfighting. Free blacks participated in traditional contests including boat racing and horse racing.

It was the budding American interest in baseball, boxing, and horse racing that led black Americans to join their white counterparts in seeking the upward mobility, wealth, independence, and fame associated with these increasingly popular and internationalized professional spectator sports.

When professional sports were launched in America during the late nineteenth and early twentieth centuries, African Americans were almost always barred from participation. They countered by developing their own autonomous teams or pursuing their athletic ambitions in foreign countries. In his chapter on the Negro Baseball Leagues, James Coates sheds light on African American baseball players who participated in the historic professional league during the first decades of the twentieth century. A loose affiliation of segregated baseball teams, the Negro Leagues garnered standout players, such as Oscar Charleston, Josh Gibson, Cool Papa Bell, and Satchel Paige, and acquired international recognition as pioneers in professional baseball despite their segregated status.

Although the Negro Baseball Leagues eventually folded following the integration of Major League Baseball, some all-black teams remained. Chief among them were sports teams at historically black colleges and universities. The most successful coach in college football history, in fact, is Eddie Robinson. Delano Greenidge-Copprue underscores the fact that during Robinson's 56 years as head coach of Grambling State University, he became the first coach to register 400 wins. Robinson's talent, longevity, and influence on hundreds of professional football players elevated him to luminary status among African American sports figures.

Elyssa Ford illuminates the trailblazing talent of American Western icon Bill Pickett, who revolutionized bulldogging in American rodeo during the 1920s. Brian Collier demonstrates in his chapter that the Harlem Globetrotters basketball team also emerged during the 1920s as an all-black squad who transformed the game while also serving the federal government as highly regarded goodwill ambassadors to various nations. Although black people faced prejudice in team sports, the cruelest reactions to African American involvement in professional sports took place in boxing. Jeremy Levitt's chapter reveals that the renowned and notorious black boxer Jack Johnson defeated white boxing champion Jim Jeffries for the world heavyweight title in 1910, at a time when whites throughout America rioted and lynched black men with impunity. Between 1919 and the 1937, white boxers repudiated black title contenders. As Neil Wynn explains in his chapter on heavyweight champion Joe Louis, it was not until 1937 that a black boxer was formally accepted as world heavyweight champion again. Despite this troubled history, boxers such as Johnson, Louis, and Muhammad Ali embodied the perennial problems and promises that have characterized human relations in America and abroad.

James Coates, Rita Liberti, Megan Falater, and Victoria Jackson, in their chapters on Jessie Owens, Wilma Rudolph, John Carlos and Tommie Smith, and Florence Griffith Joyner, respectively, demonstrate that track and field produced many African American icons. Track and field has given opportunities to distinguished black athletes to rise to superstardom while also exemplifying black equality, the ability of human beings to overcome overwhelming odds, and the possibilities for all of us to surmount obstacles that are thrown before us externally and internally. During the late 1940s, professional sports leagues integrated gradually. Jackie Robinson broke the color barrier of Major League Baseball, becoming a symbol of athletic excellence and tempered racism in 1947 when he joined the Brooklyn Dodgers.

Integration in other sports followed. Created in 1948, the National Basketball Association (NBA) desegregated in 1949, when the New York Knicks signed Nat "Sweetwater" Clifton. As David Johns, Pat Lauderdale, Brooks D. Simpson, Mary McDonald, and Ying Wushanley establish, basketball players such as Wilt Chamberlain, Charles Barkley, Magic Johnson, Michael Jordan, and Shaquille O'Neal benefited from Clifton's breakthrough. Unlike Clifton, however, these torchbearers used their unprecedented physical abilities, unparalleled media exposure, and intense charisma to ride a wave of exposure that transcended their sport and elevated them to superstardom.

As Shawn Ladda argues in her chapter on Althea Gibson, tennis integrated when the athlete became the first African American player in the U.S. Lawn Tennis Association (USLTA) in 1950. Susan Rayl illuminates the circumstances that enabled Arthur Ashe to become the first African American to win a USLTA title in 1963. Rayl emphasized that Ashe went on to become an outspoken proponent of racial equality and the fight against AIDS. Both Ashe and Gibson won championship titles at Wimbledon, becoming the first African Americans to do so.

Racial integration in sports improved the prospects of black players and gave meaning to the liberties afforded to all Americans in our documents of freedom. African Americans have excelled in every professional sport. As Maureen Margaret Smith and Mary McDonald argue in their essays on baseball player Barry Bonds and basketball player Michael Jordan, some observers believe that Bonds and Jordan are the best players in the history of their sports. Boxer George Foreman became famous by winning the heavyweight championship in 1973, but as Scott Bowman writes in his chapter, Foreman transformed himself during the late twentieth and early twenty-first centuries into a multimillionaire entrepreneur and pitchman known by millions around the world.

The athletes in this book have been recognized not solely for their physical abilities but for their commitment to community and social justice as well. Muhammad Ali, for example, was celebrated for his physical prowess, having declared himself "the Greatest" after winning the heavyweight championship three times during the 1960s and 1970s, but his political activism elevated him to the status of icon. I demonstrate in my own chapter the ways Ali established himself as a torchbearing athlete *and* leading voice for peace and equality throughout the world. Likewise, Pero Dagbovie and Amaris J. White write in their chapter that Cleveland Browns fullback Jim Brown held the National Football League's career rushing record from 1966 until 1984, while positioning himself as a staunch advocate of black community and culture.

African American icons continue to emerge early in the twenty-first century. Indeed, Brooks D. Simpson and Rebecca A. Simpson capture the meteoric rise of Derek Jeter in their chapter on the New York Yankees star. For their part, Venus and Serena Williams have also taken the world by storm. I argue in my chapter about the Williams sisters that between 1994 and the present, the two champions often dominated the tennis world, while also making their mark on the fashion and entertainment industries. Although they routinely endured racist and sexist treatment, as champions and sisters they bore the torch of struggle carried by those who paved the way for them, while also blazing trails on which future women of color can walk and excel. In 1997, Tiger Woods, at age 21, became the first African American golfer to win the storied Masters golf tournament. As Maureen Smith details in her chapter on Woods, his accomplishments have inspired unparalleled interest in golf among African Americans and other people of color.

Together, the 24 chapters of this book remind us that the past, present, and future of sports, black people, the United States, and millions of people worldwide, are to a degree inextricably linked. Indeed, the icons examined in this text embody the complexity and dynamism that have characterized renowned leaders, the communities from which they hail, their times, and the human experience in general. These icons have not only stood at the vanguard of their sport, they often located themselves at the forefront of the struggle to secure and give meaning to freedom within the United States; some have placed themselves at the forefront of the global pursuit of justice and peace. Their athletic excellence enabled them to capture the imagination of millions, but their distinct ability to reach beyond the sports world to speak to a variety of issues and peoples through their ideals, deeds, and words, has raised them above mere celebrity to represent the spirit of our past and present.

## REFERENCES

Anderson, Terry H. *The Sixties,* 2nd edition. New York: Pearson, 2004.

Gerstle, Gary. *American Crucible: Race and Nation in the Twentieth Century.* Princeton, NJ: Princeton University Press, 2002.

Hine, Darlene Clark, and Kathleen Thompson. *A Shining Thread of Hope: The History of Black Women in America.* New York: Broadway Books, 1999.

Jay, Kathryn. *More than Just a Game: Sports in American Life Since 1945.* New York: Columbia University Press, 2004.

Marqusee, Mike. *Redemption Song: Muhammad Ali and the Spirit of the Sixties.* New York: Verso, 1999.

Miller, Patrick B., and David K. Wiggins, eds. *Sports and the Color Line: Black Athletes and Race Relations in Twentieth-Century America.* New York: Routledge, 2004.

© John Lair.

# Muhammad Ali

*Matthew C. Whitaker*

Muhammad Ali was born Cassius Marcellus Clay Jr. in Louisville, Kentucky, on January 17, 1942. Ali is one of the most highly recognized and respected celebrities in the world and many consider him to be the greatest athlete of the twentieth century. He captured America's imagination during the turbulent 1960s, evoking images of lure and loathing that turned him into an enduring icon. If raw physical ability transformed him into a three-time heavyweight champion of the world, Ali's good looks and riveting charisma captivated legions of fans that held up the champ as a modern-day hero. They also inspired revulsion in millions of Americans who saw Ali as a Janus-faced warrior who betrayed the nation through his embrace of a foreign religion and peculiar-sounding name. Ali's legacy, indeed his contemporary resonance, continues to endure, marked by a veritable cottage industry of books, memorabilia, documentaries, and movies. In fact, Ali was crowned "Sportsman of the Century" by *Sports Illustrated* in 1999 and he is widely regarded as the one of the most influential personalities in the modern era.

Ali's journey to superstardom began in 1954 when he was just 12 years old. The young Cassius Clay (named after his father, Cassius Marcellus Clay Sr., who was named after the nineteenth-century abolitionist and politician Cassius Clay) parked his bicycle in front of a Louisville department store. When he returned to retrieve his bicycle after leaving the store, it had been stolen. Angry, frustrated, and distraught, young Clay sought out a police officer named Joe Elsby Martin Sr. for help. He told officer Martin that he wanted to "whoop" whoever stole his bicycle. Martin, the coach of the Louisville city boxing program, told Ali that if he planned to "whoop" someone, he needed to learn how to fight. The following day, Ali appeared at Louisville's Columbia Gym and began his first boxing lessons with Martin.

Cassius Clay first came into public consciousness when he won the gold medal at the Olympic Games in Rome in 1960. As an Olympic coach, Martin accompanied Ali to Rome in 1960, where he competed in the light heavyweight division. Clay's medal-winning performance quickly made him the golden boy of American sports. He had grown to 6' 3" and developed an unconventional boxing technique for a heavyweight: he held his hands at his sides, rather than the standard boxing style of holding the hands high to defend the face. He relied on his height, tremendous quickness, and agility to avoid punches. Martin taught Clay to maximize his speed and grace in the ring. Even now, in fact, Ali credits Martin with teaching him how to "float like a butterfly, sting like a bee."

In Louisville on October 29, 1960, Cassius Clay won his first professional fight. The win was a six-round decision over Tunney Hunsaker, who was the police chief of Fayetteville, West Virginia. From 1960 to 1963, the young fighter amassed a record of 19-0, including 15 knockouts. The boxers he defeated included Tony Esperti, Jim Robinson, Donnie Fleeman, Alonzo Johnson, George Logan, Willi Besmanoff, Lamar Clark, Doug Jones, and Henry Cooper. Clay's victories included Archie Moore, a boxing legend who fought over 200 previous fights and trained with Clay's trainer prior to Angelo Dundee.

Clay then won a disputed 10-round decision over Doug Jones, who, despite being lighter than Clay, staggered him as soon as the fight started with a right hand. Jones continued to beat Clay to the punch throughout the fight. The fight was named "Fight of the Year" for 1963. Clay's next fight was against Britain's Henry Cooper, who knocked Clay down with a left hook near the end of the fourth round. Clay emerged victorious again after the fight was stopped in the fifth round due to a deep cut on Cooper's face.

Despite these close calls against Jones and Cooper, Clay became the top contender for Heavyweight Championship held by the fearsome Sonny Liston. In spite of Clay's impressive record, few people expected him to beat Liston. The fight was scheduled for February 25, 1964. In the weeks that preceded the fight, Clay repeatedly mocked Liston, dubbing him "the big ugly bear." During the weigh-in on the day before the fight, Clay predicted that he would befuddle Liston with his boxing skills, wear him down with his quickness, and knock him out with underrated strength. "Float like a butterfly and sting like a bee," he shouted to Liston. "Your hands can't hit what your eyes can't see" (quoted in Lois, 2006, pp. 29–30).

Clay, revealing his uncommon intelligence, lured Liston into overconfidence in his ability to defeat the top contender and utter dismay over Clay's fervor and constant agitation. Liston was unprepared for anything but a quick knockout as a result. In the opening rounds, Clay's speed enabled him to elude Liston's powerful head and body shots. He used his significant height advantage to beat Liston to the punch with his jab. By the third round, Clay was clearly winning the fight. Liston recovered somewhat in the fourth round, as Clay was temporarily blinded by a mysterious and controversial substance that was discovered on his gloves. Many believe that the material was something that was used to close Liston's cuts near his eyes, or something intentionally smeared on Liston's gloves to harm Clay.

Despite his impaired vision, Clay evaded Liston's punches until his eyes cleared up and his sight returned. Toward the end of the fifth, a re-energized Clay hit Liston with a barrage of combinations. He was in complete control of the fight by the sixth round. Liston had no answer for Ali's proficiency, agility, and endurance. Then, in a stunning turn of events, Liston refused to emerge from his corner at the beginning of the seventh round. He simply gave up. Liston later claimed that he could not continue because of an injured shoulder. Many believed that the fight had been "fixed" because of this inexplicable and shocking conclusion.

Clay was victorious, however, having overcome overwhelming odds to defeat a mysterious and seemingly unbeatable foe to win the heavyweight championship of the world. Ali raised his hands in victory, ran to the ropes in front of press row, and shouted to many who ridiculed his bombastic persona and foretold his defeat, "I shook up the world! I shook up the world! I'm pretty! I'm a bad man!" (quoted in Lois, 2006, p. 80).

Immediately after the fight, he stunned the world again by announcing that he had joined the highly controversial Nation of Islam (NOI) and changed his name to Cassius X, rejecting his surname as a remnant of colonialism and his ancestors' enslavement. He was mentored by the Black Nationalist leader and NOI minister Malcolm X, and directed by Elijah Muhammad, the mercurial and authoritarian leader of the NOI. Cassius X was soon given the name Muhammad Ali by Elijah Muhammad, who explained that the name *Muhammad* meant "worthy of all praise," and that *Ali* meant "most high."

Many people, particularly members of the media, rejected Ali's new name and snubbed his religious conversion. Howard Cosell, one of the most influential broadcast journalists in the twentieth century, was among the first prominent figures to accept Ali's transformation and new name. Ali and Cosell went on to forge a strong friendship based upon mutual respect and admiration. The adoption of Ali's new name, however, signified his new identity as a Muslim and presaged his emergence as a powerful spokesperson for and symbol of freedom, self-determination, and black pride.

Ali's conversion, coupled with his increasingly visible Black Nationalism, race consciousness, boastful personality, quickly eroded his unsolicited "golden boy" image. When he refused to be inducted into the military and serve in Vietnam in 1966, the U.S. government and millions of Americans labeled him a "draft dodger." On a warm spring morning in Houston, Texas, on April 28, 1967, Ali was among 46 young men inside a Houston military recruitment building who were completing paperwork, undergoing physical exams, and submitting themselves to an initial introduction to the mores that many U.S. Army recruits are subjected to.

The recruits were summoned individually and ordered to step forward. "Cassius Clay!" a young lieutenant barked, "Army!" Ali did not budge. "Clay!" the soldier snapped again. "Army!" Ali still did not move. The charade continued for several more minutes before another officer explained the penalty for refusing the draft: five years in prison and a hefty fine. Ali was unfazed. Finally, a soldier told Ali that he would have to draft a statement explaining why he declined to serve in his nation's army. Ali wrote quickly: "I refuse to be inducted into the armed forces of the United States because I claim to be exempt as a minister of the religion of Islam" (Ronney, 2001).

Ali stated later, quite simply, "I ain't got nothing against them Vietcong." When he made his controversial statements about the war, he made no direct link between it and racial issues. It was not until Stokely Carmichael (later Kwame Ture) appropriated Ali's comments in an effort to rally black opposition to the war that Ali began to speak of the connections between white supremacy in the United States and America's involvement in Vietnam. "Why," Carmichael asked, "should black folks fight a war against yellow folks so that white folks can keep a land they stole from red folks? We're not going to

Vietnam. Ain't no Vietcong ever called me nigger" (Bingham and Wallace, 2000). Carmichael's more reflective comments resonated with Ali, and after hearing them, Ali often told reporters and listeners that "no Vietcong ever called me nigger" when he was pressed to explain his antiwar stance.

It may be difficult for many to remember now, but the furor that greeted Ali's decision was extremely intense. It was a potent brew of naked racism, angry jingoism, and intense xenophobia. Ali received constant death threats and was menaced by cruel phone calls at home. "You cowardly turncoat black rat!" yelled one caller. "If I had a bomb I would blow you to hell." Another caller screamed frantically as she vented her anger. "Cassius Clay? Is that you? You better'n my son? You black bastard, you. I pray to God they draft you tomorrow. Draft you and shoot you on the spot!" The media was no less abusive. One editorial argued that "for his stomach-turning performance, boxing should throw Clay out on his inflated head. The adult brat, who has boasted ad nauseum of his fighting skill but who squealed like a cornered rat when tapped for the Army, should be shorn of his title" (Bingham and Wallace, 2000).

Boxing authorities granted this writer's wish. When Ali refused to serve, he was stripped of his title, sentenced to prison, and fined $10,000. Freed on appeal, he was inactive as a boxer for over three years while his case dragged on. The state of New York eventually granted him a license to fight in 1970, and the U.S. Supreme Court ruled in his favor in 1971. Despite Ali's ability to avoid jail, he had touched a plethora of nerves in the United States and became anathema to mainstream America. Ironically, it was his antiwar stance and exile that put him on the path toward his future status as a freedom fighter, spiritual champion, and international advocate of black liberation.

By refusing to respond to his given name and enter the draft, however, Ali's personal life was thrown into disarray and controversy. Professionally he struggled to keep active and to maintain his status as heavyweight champion. He was essentially banned from fighting in the United States and forced to accept bouts abroad between 1965 and 1970. From his rematch with Liston in May 1965 to his final fight against Zora Folley in March 1967, he defended his title nine times. Few other heavyweight champions in history have fought so much in such a short period.

Ali won a 15-round decision against Canadian George Chuvalo. Ali then went to England and defeated Henry Cooper and Brian London by stoppage on cuts. Ali's next defense was against German southpaw Karl Mildenberger, the first German to fight for the title since Max Schmeling. In one of the tougher fights of his life, Ali finally stopped his opponent in round 12. Ali returned to the United States in November 1966 to defeat Cleveland "Big Cat" Williams in the Houston Astrodome in three rounds.

On February 6, 1967, Ali returned to a Houston boxing ring to fight Ernie Terrell, in what was to be one of the uglier fights in boxing. Terrell had angered Ali by refusing to address him as Muhammad Ali. Terrell insisted upon calling the champion "Clay," and Ali vowed to punish him for this insult.

*Too many victories weaken you. The defeat can rise you up stronger than the victor.*

During the fight, Ali shouted at his opponent over and over: "What's my name fool? Uncle Tom! What's my name" (Remick, 1998, p. 289). Terrell suffered 15 rounds of brutal punishment. Many have argued that Ali refused to knock Terrell out because he wanted him to suffer for disrespecting Ali and his religion.

Some maintain, however, that although Ali dominated the fight brutally, he was simply unable to knock Terrell out, causing many to question even more strongly Ali's 1964 "phantom punch knockout" over Liston. After the fight with Terrell, Tex Maule argued that Ali's performance was an enthralling display of boxing skill and a troubling display of malice. Ali followed up his victory over Terrell with what many boxing analysts consider to be his most inspired performance; a virtually flawless effort in a victory against the aging Zora Folley at Madison Square Garden on March 22, 1967.

Ali's rejection of the U.S. military and his allegiance with the NOI made him a lightning rod of controversy. He became one of the era's most recognizable and controversial figures virtually overnight. He appeared at rallies with Elijah Muhammad, the leader of the NOI, declaring his loyalty to him at a time when mainstream America viewed the NOI with skepticism and resentment. This made Ali a target of fury and suspicion as well. He often appeared to provoke intense reactions with pronouncements that vacillated between support for the traditional Civil Rights Movement as embodied by Martin Luther King Jr. to outright support of separatism as personified by Malcolm X.

During the three years Ali was in professional exile (after being stripped of his title in 1967) he fought to appeal his conviction. He remained in the spotlight and supported himself by giving many antiwar and antiracism speeches on college campuses in the United States and abroad. He began to more consciously and strategically cultivate and communicate his political and religious beliefs, as well as intensify and coordinate his humanitarian activities. Despite his separation from the boxing world, he remained true to his principles, and during his exile he fashioned a new life.

Whatever the vast majority of people thought of him and his actions, he made it clear that he was sincere. His forthrightness helped him reclaim the respect of the public. His unyielding support of black rights, and the humorous, down-to-earth way in which he critiqued white supremacy and black forbearance, began to endear him to both young and old, liberal and conservative, and many across race lines. His views on the war in Vietnam began to become more widely accepted as the conflict spiraled further out of control. He devoted a great deal of time to studying Islam and making a living from public speaking. People around the globe began to listen much more closely to what he had to say, and those who were able to see past his bravado, ego, and disarming humor heard thoughtful criticisms of white racism and inequality in America and passionate pleas for black self-determination.

For example, when Ali appeared at Randolph-Macon College for Men in Virginia on April 17, 1969, to give one of 168 campus speeches he would give that year to raise legal funds for his ongoing defense against the draft, he delivered an address touting the wisdom of Elijah Muhammad and the spiritual efficacy of the NOI. Ali urged those who attended his address to educate themselves about black history and Islam, become more active in their communities, support black-owned businesses and institutions, and challenge white supremacy. After all, he noted, white people routinely associate only with each other, and they often place a "white face" on most of what they design, come into contact with, or control. "Even Tarzan, way back in Africa," he explained, "is white" (*The Catholic World*, April 18, 1969).

Many criticized Ali for making his addresses so entertaining and amusing, arguing that the seriousness of his subject was often obscured. In fact, it was Ali's ability to use humor and anecdote to put a profoundly human face, as well as a kind of pop culture polish, on black indignation and rage that enabled him professionally and made him a very effective communicator and Black Nationalist leader who inspired people of all races. Of Ali's many gifts was his ability to get others to investigate their own perceptions, beliefs, and actions. His antiwar stance and speeches that decried black marginalization motivated many young people to become outspoken on issues related to race, war, and representation. Many have argued that his actions helped ignite the insurgency of a number of black athletes, as typified by the 1968 Olympic protests involving John Carlos and Tommy Smith.

Ali made Black Nationalist ideology, Islamic teachings, and white racism transparent and uncomplicated. When asked about how he felt about whites in an interview, Ali seized the moment to discuss the limitations of white liberalism and the crafty ways in which many whites seemingly supported black progress, while engaging in actions that maintained white power and privilege. "We know that every individual white ain't devil-hearted, but that doesn't change what happens to the black man," argued Ali. "Blacks stay so far behind, so far behind that it's a shame. [Whites can maintain this system because] they are good thinkers, they're smart, they're planners. Is Martin Luther King marching and causing trouble? Okay, we'll let the blacks use the public toilets, but let's make 'em fight six months for it, and while they're fighting, we'll make another plan. The airlines [for example] will give jobs to a few black pilots and black stewardesses, but by the time they're finally hired, white folks are on the moon in spaceships" (*The Catholic World*, April 18, 1969).

Although he was truly hated by many whites early in his career, he was able to evade the damage that targeted white hatred usually brought to its subjects. He rarely said anything without a certain level of wit, and his rage, like his incessant bragging and egoism, was often mitigated by his side-splitting humor. Ali offered the public the contradictory pleasure of having to take him seriously while not having to take him seriously. He was very much aware of himself and played a game of public relations deceit as cleverly as anyone. Ali made himself the center of laughter but never the object of it. He controlled what his audiences laughed at when he made himself a source of humor. His laughter was meant to signify something other than deference—a boyish joy in his own freedom, strength, and ability to inspire, convert, and command.

In 1970, Ali was finally able to get a boxing license. Due to a loophole (there was no state boxing commission in Georgia), he was granted a license to box in Georgia. Having won his case and his "greatest fight" against the U.S. government, Ali was now living in an American society that had in some sense caught up with him. Now that he had stripped it of some of its prejudices, hypocrisy, and ignorance, he could return to what had made him famous in the first place: boxing.

In October 1970, he returned to defeat Jerry Quarry in three rounds. Shortly after the Quarry fight, the New York State Supreme Court ruled that Ali was unjustly denied a boxing license. Once again able to fight in New York, he fought Oscar Bonavena at Madison Square Garden in December 1970. Ali beat Bonavena in 15 rounds, paving the way for a title fight against the awkward and highly efficient Joe Frazier.

Ali lost a thrilling contest with Frazier, who proved to be an annoying contender. He would later win another rematch with Frazier in the legendary "Thrilla in Manila" in 1975. Ali made it clear that although he was devoting the majority of time to regaining the heavyweight crown, he would still be outspoken on issues of equality, religion, race, and representation. In the weeks leading up to his highly anticipated championship bout with the younger, presumably indestructible George Foreman (the "Rumble in the Jungle"), Ali, in his mesmerizingly megalomaniacal way, responded to questions about his form by proclaiming his strength and agility: "I rassled an alligator, I done tassled with a whale, I handcuffed lightning, and threw thunder in jail" (Bingham and Wallace, 2000, p. 252). Not withstanding his vainglorious antics, Ali possessed an acute understanding of the fight and the significance it held for millions of people, particularly people of African descent around the world. Before the fight Ali told reporters:

> I'm going to win the fight for prestige, not for me but to uplift my brothers who are sleeping on concrete floors today in America, black people on welfare, black people who can't eat, black people who have no future. I want to win my title so I can walk down the alleys and talk to wineheads, the prostitutes, and the dope addicts. I want to help my brothers in Louisville, Kentucky, in Cincinnati, Ohio, and here in Africa regain their dignity. That's why I have to be a winner, that's why I'll beat George Foreman. (Bingham and Wallace, 2000, p. 252)

Few believed that an aging Ali would defeat Foreman on October 30, 1974, in Kinshasa, Zaire. Ali's cunning (including the introduction of his famous "rope-a-dope" strategy), however, triumphed over power as he knocked out Foreman in the eighth round.

He regained more than the heavyweight championship that night, however; he recaptured the support and respect of many who had doubted and reviled him. He also transformed the respect that millions of Africans had for him into something that was more akin to worship in the eyes of many. Prior to the Foreman fight, Africans in Zaire (now the Democratic Republic of the Congo) and throughout the continent had lauded his devotion to them and their heritage, his deference to their customs, and his willingness to interact with average citizens. His defeat of Foreman, who insulted the locals by bringing German shepherd guard dogs (symbols of European colonization) with him to Zaire, refusing to leave his Kinshasa compound, avoiding contact with the everyday people of the country, and refusing to drink the local water or eat the indigenous foods, helped make Ali a symbol of African Diasporic pride, power, and prestige. The fact that he embraced Africans at a time when many people, including a great many African Americans, still grudgingly admitted that there existed a connection between the two groups, only enhanced his legendary status as an international champion of African Diasporic history and life.

For many, Ali's victory over Foreman in the ring merely opened the door to a victory that had far more important implications for people of African descent. In defeating Foreman, he had symbolically defeated much of what many black people had believed Foreman embodied at the time: a celebrated black person who maintained fame and fortune by not speaking out against white racism or actively supporting the black freedom struggle. Many people believed that it was these kinds of black heroes who undermined the fight against white supremacy and the international cause of pan-Africanism. In the minds of many, this symbolic victory would eventually overshadow his triumph over Foreman and his subsequent wins in the ring until his retirement in 1981. If his protest of the Vietnam War made him an international champion of peace, his victory in Zaire made him an international patron of people of African descent.

Ali converted from NOI to orthodox Sunni Islam after he defeated Foreman in 1975. He attributed his conversion to the shift toward Sunni Islam made by W. D. Muhammad after he gained control of NOI upon the death of his father, Elijah Muhammad in 1975. In 1975, Ali also fought Frazier in the last of their three confrontations. Ali's frequent insults, slurs, and belittling poems directed at Frazier increased the anticipation and excitement for the fight. The bout itself lasted 14 back-breaking rounds, which saw Frazier's trainer Eddie Futch refuse to allow Frazier to continue and Ali emerge victorious. Ali was so spent after the contest he said, "This must be what death feels like." This fight has been called the greatest fight of all time by many. Ali won many of the early rounds, but Frazier staged a comeback in the middle rounds. By the late rounds, however, Ali had reasserted control, and the fight was stopped due to Frazier's eyes being closed.

Neither fighter was ever the same again. Frazier would permanently retire after two more fights, and a declining Ali would struggle with many opponents from then on, aided by some controversial victories. Ali retained his title until a February 1978 loss to 1976 Olympic champion Leon Spinks. Ali fought Spinks again in a rematch in September 1978 and won a highly controversial 15-round decision over his opponent. On June 27, 1979, Ali announced his retirement and vacated the title. His retirement was short-lived, however, and on October 2, 1980, he challenged Larry Holmes for the World Boxing Council's (WBC) version of the World Heavyweight Title. Looking to set another record, as the first boxer to win the Heavyweight Title four times, Ali lost by technical knockout in the eleventh round.

Ali's health took a turn for the worse during the late 1970s and early 1980s. He was diagnosed with Parkinson's disease during this period; his motor functions then began a slow decline. He was ultimately diagnosed with pugilistic Parkinson's syndrome. Despite the apparent end of his boxing career and his deteriorating medical condition, Ali would fight one more time.

On December 11, 1981, he fought rising contender and future world champion Trevor Berbick. Although Ali performed marginally better against Berbick than he had against Holmes 14 months earlier, he still lost a 10-round unanimous decision to Berbick, who at 27 was 12 years younger and in better condition. Following this loss, Ali retired permanently in 1981, with a career record of 56 wins (37 by knockout) and 5 losses. Muhammad Ali beat almost every top contender of his era, an age that has been labeled the Golden Age of Heavyweight Boxing. Ali was named Fighter of the Year by *Ring Magazine* more times than any other boxer, and participated in more *Ring Magazine* Fight of the Year matches than any other heavyweight. He is a member of the International Boxing Hall of Fame and he tallied victories over seven other Hall of Fame inductees. He is regarded by many as the greatest heavyweight champion of all time, and one of the best pound-for-pound boxers in the history of the sport. Ali boxed with his mind in addition to his body. He is also one of only three boxers to be named Sportsman of the Year by *Sports Illustrated*, and he was a highly intelligent self-promoter, whose psychological tactics before, during, and after fights were very entertaining and effective. It was his unsurpassed skill, however, that enabled him to reach the pinnacle of the sports world and maintain his dominance for decades.

Ali's quick wit, political philosophy, religious beliefs, activism, and humanitarianism (especially after his retirement in 1981), set him apart, not only from other star athletes but also from other leaders in general. Activist Dick Gregory has said,

> I don't know anyone that has as great an impact on people as Ali. Not just black people; not just Muslims . . . he got our attention; he made us listen. And he grew within people who weren't even aware he was there. Whatever the universal God force meant for him to do, it's out of the bottle, and it isn't ever going back. Ali is inside all of us now, and because of him, no future generation will ever be the same. (Quoted in Bingham and Wallace, 2000, p. 256)

Many contemporary black iconic athletes, such as Michael Jordan and Tiger Woods, in fact, are faced with profound societal pressures to not only demonstrate excellence in their sport but also be spokespeople for ideals and causes that extend beyond the course or court. Although it appears as if much of the current generation of athletes prefers to distance themselves from issues of social justice, Ali continues, despite his declining health, to denounce inequality, racism, religious intolerance, and war.

*Wars of nations are fought to change maps. But wars of poverty are fought to map changes.*

Ali's human rights work has taken him to every state in the United States and to every continent on the globe. His most important trip, however, came in 1994 when he went to Vietnam. He made the journey to close a tumultuous chapter in his life and to bring together the families of American and Vietnamese servicemen missing since the war. He was greeted at every stop by thousands of Vietnamese who showed up to demonstrate their appreciation for his principled refusal to fight in a war against their people. This collective gesture of gratitude reflected how far Ali's influence has reached into every corner of the globe, and how his uncanny ability to mobilize multitudes, regardless of race, religion, or nationality, is unsurpassed. His distinct and unrelenting activism, empowered by his charisma and generated by his legendary athletic ability, made him one of the most recognized and influential voices of peace and justice in the twentieth century. These unique personal traits helped make him a master of the politics of popular protest. This is why Ali is so revered in the world today.

Despite Ali's failing health, he remains a beloved and active public figure. He launched the U.S. Constitution's 200th birthday commemoration. He published an oral history, *Muhammad Ali: His Life and Times* with Thomas Hauser in 1991, and he received a Spirit of America Award calling him the most recognized American in the world. In 1996, Ali lit the flame at the 1996 Summer Olympics in Atlanta, Georgia. He has lent his name and presence to hunger and poverty relief, supporting education efforts of all kinds, promoting adoption, and encouraging people to respect and better understand one another. It is estimated that he has helped to provide more than 22 million meals to feed the hungry, and he travels, on average, more than 200 days per year.

In 1999, Ali received a special one-time award from the BBC at its annual Sports Personality of the Year Award ceremony, which was the BBC Sports Personality of the Century Award. In 2001, actor Will Smith starred in a biographical film, titled *Ali*, about the champion's life. Ali received the Presidential Medal of Freedom at a White House ceremony in 2005, and the prestigious Otto Hahn peace medal for his work with the U.S. Civil Rights Movement and the United Nations. On November 19, 2005, the $60 million nonprofit Muhammad Ali Center opened in downtown Louisville, Kentucky. In addition to displaying his boxing memorabilia, the center focuses on core themes of peace, social responsibility, respect, and personal growth. Muhammad Ali currently lives on a farm near Berrien Springs, Michigan, and on an estate in Paradise Valley, Arizona, with his fourth wife, Yolanda "Lonnie" Ali.


## FURTHER READING

Ali, Muhammad, and Richard Durham. *The Greatest: My Own Story*. New York: Random House, 1975.

Bingham, Howard L., and Max Wallace. *Muhammad Ali's Greatest Fight: Cassius Clay vs. The United States of America*. New York: M. Evans and Company, 2000.

Brunt, Stephen. *Facing Ali: 15 Fighters, 15 Stories*. New York: Lions Press, 2002.

Early, Gerald, ed. *The Muhammad Ali Reader*. Hopewell, NJ: Ecco Press, 1998.

Hauser, Thomas. *Muhammad Ali: His Life and Times*. New York: Simon and Schuster, 1991.

Lois, George, ed. *Ali Rap: Muhammad Ali, The First Heavy Weight Champion of Rap*. New York: ESPN Books, 2006.

Marqusee, Mike. *Redemption Song: Muhammad Ali and the Spirit of the Sixties*. New York: Verso Books, 2004.

Remnick, David. *King of the World*. New York: Vintage Books, 1998.

Ronney, John. "Muhammad Ali: He Fought with His Fists and his Words," *U.S. News and World Reports*, August 20, 2001.

David Ashdown/Keystone/Getty Images.

# Arthur Ashe

*Susan Rayl*

He's not mentioned in ESPN's Top 100 Athletes of the 20th Century. Nor is he identified as one of the century's best by CNN or *Sports Illustrated*. A 16-member panel assembled by the Associated Press created their own list of the top 100 athletes of the twentieth century, and he was not part of this list, either. Yet Arthur Ashe was one of the most significant athletes of the twentieth century; an icon if you will, a man admired not just for his ability on the tennis court but also for his contributions as a social activist, a humanitarian, and an author.

Born July 10, 1943 to Arthur Ashe and Mattie Cordell Cunningham, Arthur Robert Ashe Jr. grew up and spent the first 16 years of his life in Richmond, Virginia, a city in the segregated South. In 1947, his father took a job as the supervisor for Brook Field Park in Richmond. The family moved to a small home on the property, which also included a swimming pool, baseball fields, and tennis courts. Mattie died in 1950 due to pregnancy complications at the age of 27. In a poignant autobiography, *Off the Court*, written by Ashe and Neil Amdur, Ashe noted that losing his mother affected him greatly. His father had a tremendous influence on him, however, and took on the role of both mother and father for Ashe and his younger brother, Johnny.

Mrs. Otis Berry, a widow in her late 50s, moved into the Ashe home and for the next 14 years helped Ashe's father raise the boys. The senior Ashe did not hesitate to discipline his sons if he felt they misbehaved. He set a good example by giving up smoking, limiting his alcohol consumption, and dedicating himself to his family. He sons accompanied him wherever he went, and with just a sixth-grade education he taught them numerous vocational skills. Nurtured and loved by their father while growing up, Ashe and his brother learned to be independent, despite the racism of the time. Ashe's father valued education and the ability to read well and instilled this in his children. When Ashe discovered a copy of *National Geographic* in a neighbor's garage, he became a lifelong fan. The Ashe family did not remain small for long, however. When he was 11, his father married Lorene Kimbrough. Ashe gained a stepbrother, Robert, and stepsister, Loretta, and the family grew close.

The all-black Richmond Racquet Club, comprising mostly well-educated and upper-income players, used Brook Field as its home court. Students from Virginia Union University (VUU), a historically black university, also used the courts to supplement the only two on campus. Ron Charity, one of the college players, spent a lot of time at Brook Field. Soon, he began to teach seven-year-old Ashe, who took to the game enthusiastically. When Charity tried to register Ashe and Sterling Clark, another young black player, for a city tournament at the segregated Byrd Park, he was turned away. Ashe instead participated in the Colored Intercollegiate Athletic Association Tennis championships held at VUU in 1953, where he met Dr. Robert Walter Johnson. Johnson was a coach who worked with Althea Gibson, a top female African American tennis player.

During the summer of 1953, Johnson and his son Bobby coached Ashe for a few weeks in Lynchburg, Virginia. Known as "Dr. J." by his students, Johnson had earned All-America status as a running back at the historically black Lincoln University and worked as a general practitioner at his own medical practice. As a member of the all-black American Tennis Association, he spent much of his free time developing top black junior players, including Ashe, on his backyard court. The Johnsons took their students to two tournaments in the summer of 1953, thereby exposing them to the world of black tennis. Bobby Johnson taught his young players tennis strategies and skills, and they had daily contests on different strokes, serves, and shots. Ashe learned to master not only the physical aspects of tennis but also social skills that would be beneficial to

> *Racism can't be overcome. It will be there for the rest of your life. There will always be people who don't like you because you're Black, Hispanic, Jewish. You have to figure out how to deal with it. Racism is not an excuse to not do the best you can.*

him, especially against white players. Similarly, Johnson impressed upon his young athletes the importance of maintaining one's temper on the court. He encouraged his players to call an opponent's shot good when in doubt and taught them to travel with food because of discriminatory policies that denied blacks the right to enter or be served in most restaurants in the South.

Ashe witnessed his first professional tennis match at about age 11. Ron Charity took several Richmond club players, including Ashe, to watch the match. The young player gained a new idol that day in Pancho Gonzales, a world-class player. Three years later, in 1957, Ashe became the first African American to play in the Maryland Boy's Tennis Championship, his first integrated event. As he played more matches against white juniors, he realized that he was not just playing a game but also challenging assumptions about black inferiorities. Though no white players ever refused to play him, racism still affected Ashe's experience in tennis. Looking for more competitive players than Brook Field Park could offer, Ashe traveled to Grant Park in Richmond but was turned away from the all-white venue due to his ethnicity. He was also denied an opportunity to represent Richmond on a five-man team against players from the West Side Tennis Club in Forest Hills, New York. Despite these challenges, by 1960 Ashe won several regional titles and was ranked as one of the top junior players in the country. The love and discipline he received from his father and relatives, as well as his first tennis instructors, Charity and Johnson, prepared him well for his future and the life he would lead outside of his hometown.

Ashe's father wanted to see his son excel in tennis. Opportunities to play winter tennis did not exist in Richmond, so in 1960 Ashe moved to St. Louis to live with Richard Hudlin, a friend of Johnson's, for his senior year of high school. The move proved permanent for Ashe. He attended Sumner High School, where Hudlin taught. Ashe overcame his shyness at this school and also earned the highest grade point average of his senior class. Hudlin, who captained the University of Chicago tennis team in 1924, also had a tennis court in his back yard. While Johnson stressed a ground-stroke game on his clay court, in St. Louis Ashe practiced on a fast and slick wooden floor at the local armory. Hudlin and white pro Larry Miller taught Ashe additional aggressiveness on the court and new techniques for his shots. At this time, Ashe also changed his grip from Eastern to Continental.

In November 1960, Ashe won his first U.S. Lawn Tennis Association (USLTA) National Interscholastic Title. Soon after, University of California at Los Angeles (UCLA) tennis coach J. D. Morgan contacted Ashe and offered him an athletic scholarship to play tennis. Ashe immediately accepted. Though he was sad about his son moving away, the senior Ashe supported the young tennis player in his decision. By his high school graduation in 1961, Ashe ranked fifth as a junior player and was named a member of the Junior Davis Cup team that traveled in the summer. Ashe achieved two firsts as an African American athlete; he was the first to obtain a UCLA tennis scholarship and the first on a Junior Davis Cup Team. At UCLA Ashe studied business administration, returning to Richmond only for family, tennis matches, and special events.

Ashe developed his own strategy for combating racism during his early years at UCLA; he planned to wait until he was established as a player before he fought racial prejudice. Though he did not receive the same invitation to play at the Balboa Bay Club, as his white UCLA teammates, Ashe declined to protest when offered the opportunity by his coach. He did not want his tennis to suffer, and agreed with Morgan that some day he would fight racism on his own terms. (Sadly, many USLTA member clubs continued to maintain discriminatory memberships until the 1980s.) Though not all black athletes or contemporary black activists shared this approach, Ashe's strategy for attacking racism reflected the thoughtfulness he brought to other areas of his life, including tennis.

UCLA took second to the University of Southern California at the National Collegiate Athletic Association (NCAA) championships in 1963. Ashe lost in the semi-finals, but he remained excited about his future in the sport. Joan Ogner, a white woman, approached Ashe after an exhibition match at the California Club in April of that year. When she learned that Ashe hoped to go to Wimbledon in the summer, she gathered $800 from men at a card game in another room to assist him with his expenses. Her act helped him realize that there were generous people from all ethnicities in the world. The night after the NCAA championships, Ashe and many of his teammates and competitors boarded an airplane to London, England, to play at Wimbledon.

Ashe faced and triumphed over limitations in London just as he did in the United States. He joined a group of lesser-known players in the "B" locker room at Wimbledon, a step down in amenities from the "A" locker room. Regardless, Ashe made it to the third round at Wimbledon in 1963, losing to Chuck McKinley in straight sets. (McKinley won the tournament that year.) Ashe also participated in a tournament near Budapest, where he reached the semi-finals. On August 1, Ashe became the first black player to be selected for the U.S. Davis Cup team. He won against Orlando Bracamonte of Venezuela in his first match. He did not have an opportunity for a second match for nearly two years, however, due to the talent of his Davis Cup teammates and the structure of the Davis Cup tournament.

News of Ashe's success followed him back to the States. He graced the cover of *World Tennis* magazine in November 1963 and finished the year as the sixth-ranked player in the United States. Outside of tennis and academics at UCLA, Ashe spent many hours talking and spending time with a wide variety of people, including foreign students. He also joined Kappa Alpha Psi, a black fraternity. His new status on campus and in Los Angeles allowed him to meet and spend time with well-known celebrities. He developed his political views while attending UCLA, admiring men such as Martin Luther King Jr., Andrew Young, Jackie Robinson, and Joe Louis. Ashe won the NCAA Men's Singles title on June 21, 1965, while UCLA won the team title. Postponing his last semester of classes, he traveled with the Davis Cup team to New Zealand in October 1965 and then to Australia afterward. He played on grass for three consecutive months, winning four tournaments and making a name for himself internationally. The following year, he graduated from UCLA.

Ashe, who inherited a family history in the military, served two years in the Reserve Officer's Training Corp (ROTC) while in college. Upon graduation in 1966, he attended ROTC basic training camp for future officers at Fort Lewis, Washington, while his brother Johnny served in the military on a second tour of Vietnam. Lieutenant Ashe then spent the next two years assisting the West Point tennis team, training for and traveling to tournaments himself, and working as a data processing officer. His Davis Cup teams lost in 1966 and 1967, but by the end of 1967 Ashe retained the number two singles ranking for the third consecutive year.

Ashe became engaged to Patricia Battles in 1967, though he ultimately called off the engagement. He was 24 years of age and wanted to travel to tennis tournaments around the world without the responsibility of a wife or family. In order to concentrate on his tennis career, he made a promise to himself to wait until he was 30 to marry.

In his first public political act, Ashe accepted an invitation to speak at Reverend Jefferson Roger's church, the Church of the Holy Redeemer, in Washington, D.C. Ashe's supervisors reprimanded him for disregarding regulations, which forbade army personnel from giving political speeches. A month later, he heard about King's assassination on the radio while traveling to New York City, and like many African Americans, experienced sorrow and disbelief. Ashe participated in the 1968 Davis Cup Tournament despite activist Stokely Carmichael's request that he boycott the event to protest South Africa's participation. The cup's first round was hosted in Richmond at Byrd Park, the segregated venue that had denied Ashe entrance when he was only seven years old. The United States easily won the initial round of the tournament, with Ashe as the lone African American on the court.

In September of that year, Ashe participated in the final match of the U.S. Open against Tom Okker of the Netherlands. The stands stood only half full,

*If a child comes to school hungry, the best school in the world won't help. You have not seen many civil rights groups marching for medical and nutrition rights for children.*

as Sunday's matches were rained out and postponed to the following day. Nonetheless, both Ashe's father and former coach Johnson attended the event. Ashe made them proud, winning 14-12, 5-7, 6-3, 3-6, and 6-3. As the only African American man to win the title, the ceremony held special meaning for Ashe, his father, and the black community because of the barriers he faced to succeed. His father came out onto the court to stand with him for the tearful, but joyful trophy ceremony. Ashe could not accept the $14,000 he earned in prize money, however, because he was an amateur player associated with the military.

As he played on the tennis circuit, the Black Power Movement sought to challenge the racism present in the United States. Ashe used different tactics, though, refusing to support a proposed black athlete boycott of the 1968 Olympics. Instead, he worked behind the scenes to fight racism in the United States and abroad. He used his U.S. Open win to talk about blacks in professional sports during his CBS *Face the Nation* television show appearance. The first athlete ever invited on the show, Ashe discussed the lack of progress made toward equal opportunity for black athletes in professional sports since the passage of the Civil Rights Act of 1964.

The U.S. team won the finals of the Davis Cup in 1968 in Adelaide, Australia. As a member of the team, Ashe toured Southeast Asia, played tennis for the troops in Vietnam, and visited hospital and military units. His visit confirmed his understanding of the world's view of racism and skin color; he believed black children needed black role models to convince them they were capable of achieving. His success also helped him create the U.S. Tennis Association (USTA) National Junior Tennis League to develop inner-city players. He knew it was tough for blacks to get into tennis, a sport controlled by whites, and hoped that the Junior Tennis League would provide some players with opportunities not otherwise available to them. In addition, he helped organize the International Tennis Players Association in 1969 and served as its treasurer.

Ashe received endorsement opportunities beginning in 1969. He displayed a good image and appeared to be "acceptable" to white Americans because of his involvement in the army and Davis Cup. He signed a contract with two sporting goods companies: Head and Catalina. In 1970, he also became the tennis director at Doral Country Club in Miami, Florida, and served as a representative for Philip Morris. The following year, he made appearances in stores for Catalina, Head, and Philip Morris and also coached at tennis clinics for American Airlines and All-American Sports.

Ashe won the Australian Open, the second of his three Grand Slam titles, on January 26, 1970. This year also marked Ashe's international "coming out" as an activist, as he called for the expulsion of South Africa from the International Lawn Tennis Federation (ITF) because of that nation's policy of apartheid.

Ashe, who became interested in South Africa in the late 1960s, equated South African apartheid to segregation in the United States. Now that he was a champion, he felt he could become more politically vocal. He also spoke against apartheid at the United Nations in 1970. He applied for a visa to South Africa in 1969 and again in 1970, but was turned down both times. He and Stan Smith, accompanied by sports writers Frank DeFord, Bud Collins, and Richard Evans, toured Kenya, Tanzania, and Nigeria in 1970, playing tennis on a goodwill tour by request of the U.S. State Department. The following year, participation on the professional circuit took him to west Africa. Ashe became an officer of the newly organized Association of Tennis Professionals (ATP) in 1971. When questions concerning the ITF's suspension policy arose in 1973, 79 members of the ATP, including Arthur Ashe, boycotted Wimbledon.

South Africa finally granted Ashe a visa in 1973. He became the first black professional to play in the South Africa Open Championships. Many in the black community, however, believed he should not go to South Africa. Ashe thought he should be able to play in the tournament held in South Africa, and likewise argued that if white South African athletes opposed apartheid publicly, they should be able to play in the United States. A well-read man, Ashe learned much about the history and politics of South Africa before he traveled there in November 1973. He demanded three conditions before he agreed to compete in the first integrated event in South Africa: (1) he would not play before a segregated audience, (2) he would not travel as an "honorary white," and (3) he would be allowed open access to all areas of the country and would not be censored. Piet Koornhof, the South African minister of immigration and sport, agreed to these conditions. As noted in ESPN's *Sportcentury* video presentation on Arthur Ashe, aired in February 2001, Ashe played for the black South Africans, many of whom came to support him. Though Ashe lost to Jimmy Connors in the final, he won the doubles with Tom Okker. He then traveled to Soweto, where he taught a tennis clinic and was welcomed by the people.

Ashe developed good and sometimes close relationships with most of the South African players, including Ray Moore and Cliff Drysdale. He admired men such as M. N. Pather, leader of the nonracial sports movement, and colored poet Don Mattera, who was under a banning order for standing against apartheid. Still, black journalists in South Africa viewed Ashe as a political tool who gave the South African government undeserved credibility. Ashe, who wanted to understand apartheid fully before repeatedly speaking against it, continued to go to South Africa each year to participate in its tennis tournament and learn more about its politics and social policies. The knowledge gained from each trip helped shape his politics and worldview. South African activists believed he could help the anti-apartheid cause by taking information about the segregationist policies back to black Americans in the United States. After the first trip in 1973, Ashe and Owen Williams established the Black Tennis Foundation in Soweto, a facility that included eight tennis courts. Ashe was one of the first athletes to call for the release of Nelson Mandela from imprisonment on Robben Island. His activism became linked with the politics of South Africa and the lives of black South Africans.

Sixth-seeded Arthur Ashe played Jimmy Connors in the finals of Wimbledon on July 15, 1975. Over the years, Ashe had developed a reputation for making it to the finals but then coming in second place. In fact, after winning the Australian Open in 1970, Ashe lost 14 of the next 19 finals, including the 1972 U.S. Open. Yet Ashe defeated Björn Borg in the World Championship Tennis finals two months earlier in May 1975 in Dallas. Despite three earlier losses to Connors, Ashe felt he wouldn't lose at Wimbledon in 1975. Just before the event began, however, Connors announced a $5 million lawsuit he planned to bring against Ashe for slander and libel. As president of the ATP, Ashe had openly challenged Connors for refusing to play in the Davis Cup or to join the ATP. Despite the pressure the news of a lawsuit brought, Ashe defeated Connors 6-1, 6-1, 5-7, and 6-4 to win the Wimbledon Men's Singles title. This victory made him the only black man to ever win this tournament. After his victory, Ashe looked toward his friend Donald Dell in the stands and raised his right fist. His only regret was that he did not see former coach Johnson in the crowd after what he described as his greatest victory.

Ashe met Jeanne Marie Moutoussamy, a photographer, in late 1976 at a United Negro College Fund benefit in New York City. He gave Moutoussamy a red rose, his mother's favorite flower, on their first date. They married on February 20, 1977, when Ashe was 33 years old. The ceremony took place at the United Nations Chapel in New York, officiated by U.S. ambassador Andrew Young 10 days after Ashe underwent heel surgery to remove bone chips. Ashe's father thought Jeanne looked just like his wife and Arthur Junior's mother, Mattie, and the two did bear a close resemblance.

Ashe continued to maintain a national public presence. He wrote an instructional series for *Tennis* magazine and a biweekly column for the *Washington Post* in the late 1970s. He also made commercials for the National Guard and became a consultant for Aetna Life and Casualty Insurance Company. He won his last tournament title in 1978 at the Pacific Southwest Championships, defeating Brian Gottfried, and played his last Davis Cup in 1978, where he set an American record for singles Davis Cup victories at 27 wins. Ashe believed that his involvement in politics had affected his play on the court, but he felt he had no choice other than to continue his role in political activism. For Ashe, being involved or doing was more important than the outcome or winning. He wanted to meet people who had something to contribute, and he wanted to make contributions to the world in ways other than through his tennis game. Tennis and his status as a top player gave him an unusual opportunity for assisting others.

Ashe suffered a heart attack in July 1979 while participating in a tennis clinic in New York and spent 10 days in the hospital. Heart disease ran in his family. In mid-December, Ashe underwent quadruple bypass surgery. Three months later, while running in Cairo, Egypt, Ashe experienced chest pains and the following month decided to retire from competitive tennis. He finished his active playing career at the age of 36 with a record of 818 wins, 260 losses, and 51 titles. Interestingly, he later served as national chairman of the American Heart Association in 1981.

Ashe's career in tennis, however, continued. He was named captain of the U.S. Davis Cup team in September 1980. For Ashe, representing the United States as captain of the Davis Cup team was the ultimate experience. He proudly wore his Davis Cup jacket, which was navy blue with red and white USA lettering. Under his tutelage, the team won the Davis Cup in 1981 and 1982. During these years, Ashe and Davis Cup team member John McEnroe maintained a challenging relationship due to their differences in personality and on-court behavior; Ashe was reserved and calm while McEnroe was outspoken and volatile. When Ashe was removed as Davis Cup captain in 1983, he continued his promotion of tennis as a commentator for ABC and HBO Sports. He also spent more of his time writing.

Ashe underwent additional heart surgery in June 1983, this time needing a double bypass. Following surgery, he felt sluggish and uncomfortable. He received a blood transfusion to increase his strength. This transfusion occurred two years before mandatory testing of blood for the HIV virus.

Ashe, who had developed an isolationist view of South Africa in the 1970s, now called for economic and political sanctions against the nation. After learning about the deaths of hundreds of innocent citizens, he no longer wished to be viewed by the South African government or apartheid opponents as an ally and in 1983 helped found Artists and Athletes Against Apartheid in order to expose apartheid to the world. Ashe protested apartheid policy outside the South African embassy in Washington, D.C., on January 11, 1985, and was arrested. Some who had earlier described Ashe as a tool of the apartheid government, now believed that he had redeemed himself through his changed views of South Africa, his 1985 protest, and subsequent arrest. When Nelson Mandela was finally released five years later on February 11, 1990, Ashe called white South African friend Ray Moore, who had denounced apartheid, to tell him of Mandela's new-found freedom. Ashe was one of the first people Nelson Mandela asked to speak with upon his release because of the tennis player's continued political work for South Africa.

The mid-1980s brought great joy to Ashe. On March 21, 1985, he was inducted into the International Tennis Hall of Fame, a validation of his skill on the tennis court. It was a momentous event that was only overshadowed by the birth of Ashe's daughter, Camera, in December 1986. She became the focus of his life, along with his writing. He completed his three-volume book, *A Hard Road to Glory: A History of the African American Athlete*, after spending hundreds of hours in research. This three-volume work was Ashe's third publication, though it was his lengthiest project, following *Arthur Ashe: Portrait in Motion*, co-written with Frank DeFord in 1975, and *Off the Court* with Neil Amdur in 1981.

A lifelong reader, Ashe stressed education over athletics. He opposed affirmative action policies, which he felt insulted the intelligence of African Americans. He also supported NCAA propositions 48 and 42, which maintained specific academic standards for athletes to gain admittance to college and eligibility requirements for athletic participation. Ashe's opinions angered many black coaches and members of the black intelligentsia, who believed college entrance exams were culturally biased and poor predictors of academic success. Ashe disagreed, however, and stated that "coddling black athletes" undermined initiative and motivation.

In 1988, Ashe suffered numbness in his right hand and was hospitalized. Tests and a biopsy of his brain tissue showed the presence of toxoplasmosis, a bacterial infection experienced by many HIV patients. Additional tests showed Ashe had, in fact, developed full-blown AIDS. He likely obtained the virus from a blood transfusion during his second open-heart operation in 1983. He encountered additional sadness when his father died of a stroke on March 19, 1989. Ashe called a press conference on April 8, 1992, with the organizational assistance of HBO, to announce he had AIDS. With the knowledge that *USA Today* had already learned of his illness, he thought it best that the news come from him before it could be reported from other sources. While HBO notified the sports media, Ashe, with the help of friend and sports journalist DeFord, prepared his statement and made dozens of calls to family and friends to notify them in advance. Following the press conference and in the face of misfortune, he forged ahead.

Ashe did not allow the public's awareness of his illness to prevent him from continuing his work. In September 1992, he protested the poor treatment of Haitian refugees by the United States and was arrested outside the White House. Three months later he once again addressed the UN General Assembly, this time on World AIDS Day. He asked the delegates to increase funding for AIDS research and education. December 1992 was also the month that *Sports Illustrated* named Ashe their 1992 Sportsman of the Year. With his life slipping away, Ashe worked hard to finish his memoirs, titled *Days of Grace*. This book included a poignant letter to his daughter, Camera, which read in part: "Wherever I am when you feel sick at heart and weary of life, or when you stumble and fall and don't know if you can get up again, think of me. I will be watching and smiling and cheering you on."

On February 6, 1993, at age 49, Arthur Robert Ashe Jr. died of AIDS-related pneumonia in New York. His body lay in state in the governor's mansion in Richmond. He was the first person to receive this honor since 1863, when Confederate General Stonewall Jackson was so honored. Over 5,000 people waited in line to pay their respects, and his funeral was attended by almost 6,000 people. Fittingly, Andrew Young, then mayor of Atlanta, delivered the eulogy for his dear friend. Ashe was buried in Richmond on February 10, 1993.

At Ashe's funeral, Young noted that the famed tennis star "took the burden of race and wore it as a cloak of dignity." Though Ashe died young and bore the scourge of AIDS, he said the most difficult thing he had to deal with in life was being a black man in American society. He wanted people to understand where he had come from and how he became the person he did. As an African American and a public figure, he knew his actions would be scrutinized, though he shielded his stress from the admiring public. A statue of Ashe, with books in one hand, tennis racket in the other, and surrounded by children was dedicated on July 10, 1996, on what would have been his fifty-third birthday. The statue was dedicated on Monument Avenue in Richmond, a street where statues of Confederate war heroes also stand. The USTA named their New York stadium Arthur Ashe Stadium in 1997. Arthur Ashe remains not only an icon of American sport but an icon of American history. His life serves as an example for future generations.

## FURTHER READINGS

Ashe, Arthur R., Jr. *A Hard Road to Glory: A History of the African-American Athlete*. New York: Amistad Press, 1988.

Ashe, Arthur, with Neil Amdur. *Off the Court*. New York: New American Library, 1981.

Ashe, Arthur, with Frank DeFord. *Arthur Ashe: Portrait in Motion*. Boston: Houghton Mifflin, 1975.

Ashe, Arthur, with Alexander McNab. *Arthur Ashe on Tennis*. London: Aurum Press, 1995.

Ashe, Arthur, and Arnold Rampersad. *Days of Grace: A Memoir*. New York: Ballantine Books, 1993.

CNN. "Arthur Ashe." CNN/SI, http://sportsillustrated.cnn.com/tennis/features/1997/arthurashe/biography.html (accessed October 5, 2006).

ESPN. "Author Ashe." ESPN Sportcentury, ESPN Classic (Bristol, CT: February 2001).

The Official Website of Arthur Ashe. http://www.cmgworldwide.com/sports/ashe/index.ph. (accessed November 5, 2006).

AP Photo/Roberto Borea.

# Charles Barkley

*Pat Lauderdale*

his nickname changed to "Sir Charles." This emerged when he made a famous television commercial dressed as a member of the English gentry on the way to a foxhunt. The commercial was not simply made in jest; many began to view Barkley as elite on the basketball court. He made a reputation for himself as a dominant rebounder, defensive player, three-point shooter, and play-maker who often inspired his team to excel.

Barkley, however, possessed a paradoxical nature, and often news headlines about him brought controversy. During a game against the New Jersey Nets, for example, Barkley spat at a heckler, unintentionally also spitting on a young girl at the arena. The media later discovered that he became a friend of the girl and her family because of his explanation and the sensitivity he expressed to them.

When Julius Erving announced his retirement from the Philadelphia 76ers, Barkley became the Sixers' star player. His celebrity status as the star led to his first appearance on the cover of *Sports Illustrated*. By the 1989–1990 seasons, he was named Player of the Year by both *Sporting News* and *Basketball Weekly*. He averaged over 25 points and 11 rebounds a game and a career high 60 percent field-goal percentage. He was selected to the All-NBA First Team for the third consecutive year and earned his fourth All-Star selection. His outstanding play continued the next basketball season, and he was chosen for his fifth straight All-Star game. In the All-Star game he led the East to a 116–114 win over the West team with 17 points and 22 rebounds, which were the most rebounds in an All-Star game since Wilt Chamberlain garnered 22 in 1967. Barkley was presented with Most Valuable Player honors at the All-Star game, and then named to the All-NBA First Team for the fourth straight year. However, his team in Philadelphia lost again to Michael Jordan's Chicago Bulls in the Eastern Conference Semi-finals, although Barkley contributed almost 25 points and 11 rebounds per game.

Barkley's final year in Philadelphia was in 1991–1992. He earned his sixth straight All-Star appearance and finished his 76ers career ranked fourth in team history in total points (14,184), third in scoring average (23.3 points per game), third in rebounds (7,079), eighth in assists (2,276), and second in field goal percentage (56.7 percent).He led the team in rebounding and field-goal percentage for seven consecutive seasons and in scoring for six straight years. After several early round playoff defeats, and with the Sixers failing to make the postseason playoffs in the 1991–1992 season with a 35–47 record, he demanded to be traded from Philadelphia. In the summer of 1992, he was traded to the Phoenix Suns.

When the 76ers traded Barkley to the Suns, he was considered the NBA's second-best player, behind only Michael Jordan. Barkley was too powerful for small forwards, and too quick for power forwards. He became an assist leader when other teams double-teamed him. An indisputably talented player, he made his teammates better.

Barkley continued to evoke controversy, though he created some intentionally. The icon starred in a controversial Nike television commercial, which

focused upon his statement, "I am not a role model."
This comment created great public debate about the
nature of role models and developed discussions with
respect to who should and should not be considered a

---
*I am not a role model.*

---

role model, especially for children. Barkley later said that he was glad that he
could help bring this topic to a public forum. Some analysts think his commercial also referred to earlier comments by former Vice President Dan Quayle,
who complained about televised "role models" after television character Murphy Brown became a single mother. Regardless of his purpose in the Nike advertisement, the cultural debate that ensued shed more light and less friction
on the issue of role models.

Barkley also continued his self-taught political education. For example, he
read *The Autobiography of Malcolm X*. He changed his political party affiliation from Republican to Democrat and stressed the importance of class and
race. Many Republicans gave us fish, he argued, instead of teaching us how to
fish. He labeled the Republican revolution of 1994 as mean-spirited, and denounced Pat Buchanan as a neo-Nazi. He maintained that public schools must
be funded through local property taxes. At the same time, his career was tar-
nished with his legal problems, which usually involved charges concerning his
physical aggressiveness off the court.

In his quest for a championship, Barkley was traded to the Houston Rockets in 1996. There he joined Hakeem Olajuwon and Clyde Drexler, two other
aging superstars. Barkley's aspirations of a championship, however, never became a reality. Endless questions about why he had never won one continue.
After retiring from the NBA, Barkley remained an integral icon of basketball
both as a popular television NBA commentator and analyst on Turner Network
Television (TNT) and as an author.

Barkley wrote several books about many subjects. His books reflect his interest in larger issues such as race, class, money, scandals, politics, and the impact
of role models on his life. In *I May be Wrong but I Doubt It*, written in 2003,
the icon attempted to stir people to think more deeply by either making them
angry or encouraging them to laugh. His next book, published in 2005 and titled *Who's Afraid of a Large Black Man?*, asserts that we must remember the
sacrifices that others have made for us. Barkley argues that people who put
their lives on the lines, both black and white, did not sacrifice so that he could
simply have mansions and expensive cars. He suggests that if he was not earning $3 million a year to dunk a basketball, most people would run in the other
direction if they saw him coming down the street. As an icon, he now focuses
more upon racial prejudice and explains why racism is the biggest cancer of his
lifetime.

Barkley's athletic success affords him access to well-known and famous people. This access, combined with his ability to get others to reveal sensitive yet
crucial information, is very important. His interpersonal skills create the opportunity to generate discussions about race and other political issues that

*Any time something bad happens to a black person because of racism, I feel it in my soul. I really do.*

might not occur without his intervention. Barkley encouraged Tiger Woods to speak about his first experience with racism, for example. Barkley stated, "I became aware of my racial identity on my first day of school, on my first day of kindergarten. A group of sixth graders tied me to a tree, spray-painted the word 'nigger' on me, and threw rocks at me. That was my first day of school. And the teacher really didn't do much of anything. . . . So I had to outrun all these kids going home, which I was able to do. It was certainly an eye-opening experience, you know, being five years old" (Barkley, 2005, p. 7).

Barkley's work provides the world with the opportunity to learn about the experiences of famous people to whom they might not otherwise have access. His conversations also provide individuals such as Woods with the opportunity to describe important experiences that they do not often share publicly.

His work also challenges abstract understandings of race. He has been asked if a black person is a phony if she or he speaks in a different way depending upon the audience. He rhetorically says no. The way he speaks around his former teammates in a basketball locker room is dramatically different from the way he might speak in other situations. Barkley's detractors claim that he is a chameleon, but his supporters consider him instead an honest diplomat. Barkley's reflexive character has helped him develop his own unique perspectives, which helps him probe deeper into controversial issues.

In his conversations with Barack Obama, the U.S. African American Senator from Illinois, Barkley stresses the importance of understanding complex reasons for the changes in race relations in the United States, especially in light of the fact that Senator Obama won his seat in a state that is overwhelmingly white. Barkley suggests that all poor people have suffered from the old divide-and-conquer strategy of politicians and others. He emphasizes that we cannot understand race and racism without understanding religion and economic factors. He agitates some people while entertaining others, much in the spiritual tradition of Muhammad Ali, Bill Russell, and Rosa Parks.

In his conversations with Reverend Jesse Jackson, the famous civil rights activist, Barkley examines the deeper reasons for racism and the continuing contradictions embedded in current times. Jackson notes that most people don't have the sense, for the most part, that slavery was the law of the land until 1865. Prominent institutions such as Yale University still have many colleges that are named after people who were either slave traders or shippers of slaves. Jackson became a role model for Barkley along with his previous ones, such as Martin Luther King Jr., Muhammad Ali, and Malcolm X.

One of the major points in his political work reveals the struggle concerning how we can make progress on important issues such as fixing our schools when we can't even get a couple of more diverse coaches hired. Barkley notes that we fight so many battles on so many fronts. Consider some of these battle fronts: His comment on the exposure of pop singer Janet Jackson's breast during the halftime show in the 2004 National Football League Super Bowl scandal is revealing. He notes that people and the media are less irate with the Bush administration for starting a war for profit than they are with Jackson for showing her breast. He suggests that we don't know what's important and what's not important, and the naked breast of Jackson is not going to traumatize anyone. His comment following the September 11, 2001, terrorist attacks on the World Trade Center and the war in Baghdad suggests that we consider the fact that Osama bin Laden and Saddam Hussein used to both work for the United States and now they're enemies. He maintains that such ignored relationships are part of the political hypocrisy in the United States.

After being asked if he had ever been in the governor's office in Montgomery, his response was a resounding no. He stressed that they don't let many black people in the governor's mansion in Alabama, unless they're cleaning. In similar situations, it would not be atypical for him to note that most of the black people that have been in the mansion have been servants of some kind. Such comments by Barkley are not simply hyperboles or images from the past; instead they reveal much of the pain of modern times.

Barkley mentions that Malcolm X described a boxer named Cassius Clay who changed his name and identity to Muhammad Ali. His point was that we should not underestimate the quality of the mind that a clown might possess. Although a clown can never imitate the wise man, the wise man can imitate a clown. Initially, many people thought Muhammad Ali was a crazy man. When they realized that he was not crazy, but instead very sane, they tried to stereotype him as a clown. Barkley has had a parallel life in this respect. He recently said in an ironic tone, concerning his daughter who is considering dating, that if he killed the first person who wanted to date her, the word would get out. He mentioned that everything gets blamed on the Clintons, especially Bill Clinton, and that Bill must have shot John F. Kennedy. There is an Internet site devoted to the irreverent yet ironic quotes of Barkley. His sense of humor and irony melded into a critical analysis of politics is reflected in his everyday life, and his words that have been published.

Barkley wants everyone to discuss critically important issues openly, such as racism and prejudice. He maintains that we as a society need conversations rather than facades of political correctness. He suggests that it is important to move people out of their comfort zones and discuss the deeper issues. He takes his own advice and writes and discusses events such as Magic Johnson's experience of being HIV-positive, the Augusta National Golf Club prejudice against women, child abuse at the hands of priests, the complex reactions to the horrors of 9/11, and why God does not have a favorite team to emphasize the importance of thinking critically, but not cynically. Thinking cynically describes the opinions of individuals who maintain that self-interest is the primary motive of human behavior, and who are disinclined to rely on sincerity, human value, or any type of altruism. Thinking critically, on the other hand, is a systematic inquiry into the conditions and consequences of a concept, idea, or theory, and an attempt to understand its potential, limitations, and dangers.

Barkley has given straightforward comments on controversial issues that do not reflect ostensible common sense and with words that often are not politically correct. Even when he reveals the truth, that doesn't seem to matter much to his detractors. They see him as making comments that he shouldn't, and he's condemned for it.

Over the past decade, he has often played in celebrity golf tournaments. Though he is a great basketball player, he is not a skilled golfer. He usually remained at the rear of the tournament play throughout the competition. Despite his poor golf game, he usually attracted the biggest crowd of any of the celebrities, including Michael Jordan, Mark McGwire, Pete Sampras, and John Elway. Barkley's ability to talk to many different types of people, his concern for their feelings, and his interest in young children help him generate interest. Security ropes separated the golfers from the crowds; Barkley told the guards to get rid of the barriers because he wanted to walk with the people.

Barkley was inducted into the Basketball Hall of Fame in 2006. Initial headlines noted that he averaged almost 12 rebounds and approximately 22 points per game in 16 NBA seasons. Barkley's teams won 50 games in a single season seven times in his 16-year career. Many analysts and observers also considered him the best player of the original 1992 Dream Team, which won the Olympic gold medal in basketball in Barcelona, and featured Barkley, Magic Johnson, Michael Jordan, and Larry Bird.

Barkley accepted his induction graciously. He communicated thankfulness, although his gift for irony and humor was present as well. He almost seemed to be a role model. He thanked his financial adviser for protecting his money, and gave advice to today's players by telling them that the money they make now needs to be saved since it might have to last the rest of their lifetimes. He also took young players to task for selfish play, and gave examples of how he thinks the game should be played. He noted that he did not finish his college education and has been arrested several times. Then he quickly pointed out that he always was acquitted, suggesting the irony behind the comments. He reminded us of the headlines from his 1993 Nike television spot, when he warned the audience that he was not a role model; he argued instead that parents should be role models. He noted that basketball has been important and significant in his life, but it's the least important thing to him now.

Charles Barkley incorporates varied dynamics into his character. He often is viewed as a recognized Hall of Fame NBA basketball player, as a moral entrepreneur with a political strategy on contemporary issues such as racism and role models in the media, and an activist against racism in the United States. His detractors identify him as a selfish, arrogant individual who employs a personal agenda to further his own success. These varied and diverse viewpoints shape him as an important person, mainly because he connects to diverse American people at different levels of interest and concern.

His current perspective on contemporary issues led him to become more of a moral entrepreneur in politics. Most political pundits claim that he does not have a chance if he were to run for governor because he has no political experience in lower levels of government. However, those pundits seem to ignore the fact that neither Jesse Ventura, a former governor of Minnesota, nor Governor Arnold Schwarzenegger of California had much prior political experience. Currently, Barkley seeks support to run for the office of governor of Alabama. He wishes to speak for those who are voiceless. He continues to emphasize the deep problems that prevent lower-class individuals from obtaining a good education. He clearly does not subscribe to the facile slogan that poor people need to pull themselves up with their own boots because he knows that many of the poor have no boots at all. He donated $1 million to help victims of Hurricane Katrina, and used the tragedies surrounding Katrina as vivid examples of the deep-rooted economic and racial problems in America.

Barkley stresses that people rarely talk about institutional problems such as racism until something tragic or revolting arises (Edwards, 1980; Lauderdale, 2005). Institutional forms of racism are particularly pernicious. They are not the ugly bigotry or racial prejudice of individuals but the existence of systemic and often covert policies, laws, and practices that disadvantage and continue to harm people emotionally, economically, and politically. This form of racism attacks specific collectives that have been racialized (falsely claimed to be of a "race" since race as a real category is a historical facade) or specific ethnic groups. Restrictive covenants, for example, ostensible race-based prejudice in housing and redlining (the practice of denying or increasing the cost) in bank lending or insurance are obvious types of institutional racism. He also believes that professional athletes often can have a greater impact through business than through athletics.

Barkley is an important public figure. His personality and intellectual searching lead him to find complicated, difficult answers. There are a number of interesting qualities that he has developed. One of his characteristics is his refusal to settle for easy or trivial questions with obvious answers, but instead look for important, hard questions with difficult answers. He usually relishes answering questions and questioning answers, often with quick introspection. Barkley also understands the importance of role models and, more important, the importance of those people who paved the way for his success. In addition, his commentary often reaches many because he communicates via irony. He recently noted, for example, that the best rapper in modern times is a white guy, the best golfer is a black guy, and the tallest basketball player is Chinese.

Barkley gives back, often with more than words, to those who helped him gain success. He bought his mother a new house, for example. He made numerous donations to the Auburn University Foundation, the Cornerstone Schools in Alabama, Leeds High School (his alma mater), Macedonia Baptist Church in Leeds, and the Minority Health and Research Center at the University of Alabama at Birmingham. These contributions were intentionally provided to schools and institutions that serve the area he lived as a child.

Barkley, with all his contradictory actions, is truly an icon. More important, his complicated nature reminds us of our own contradictory behaviors. His concern for the nation's well-being, and his willingness to demand that we continue discussing and analyzing critical issues such as prejudice, in general, and racism, religion, and poverty in particular, provide him with opportunities to improve the nation as well as each of us individually.

## FURTHER READING

Barkley, Charles. *I May Be Wrong but I Doubt It*. New York: Random House, 2003.

Barkley, Charles. *Outrageous!* New York: Random House, 1994.

Barkley, Charles. *Sir Charles: The Wit and Wisdom of Charles Barkley*. New York: Warner Books, 1994.

Barkley, Charles. *Who's Afraid of a Large Black Man?* New York: Penguin Press, 2005.

Edwards, Harry. *The Struggle That Must Be: An Autobiography*. New York: Macmillan, 1980.

Lauderdale, Pat. "Racism, Racialization and American Indian Sports." In *Native Americans in Sports*, edited by C. Richard King. New York: M. E. Sharpe, 2005, pp. 248–252.

AP Photo/Marcio Jose Sanchez.

# Barry Bonds

*Maureen Margaret Smith*

After sitting out most of 2005 due to injuries, baseball slugger Barry Bonds prepared for his return to the national pastime amid great speculation. At the start of the 2006 baseball season, he faced great scrutiny for his remarkable home run hitting and his links to a grand jury investigation of the Bay Area Laboratory Co-Operative (BALCO) and trainer Greg Anderson. Despite media attention to his alleged involvement with performance-enhancing drugs and two best-selling books detailing his controversial career, Bonds had 708 home runs and was only 7 away from passing Babe Ruth on the all-time home run list. He was also only 48 home runs away from surpassing all-time leader Hank Aaron. ESPN decided to cover the home run chase with a new reality series titled *Bonds on Bonds*, which would give the athlete the opportunity to clear his image. Even after Bonds broke the all-time home run record, the debate surrounding his legacy as a player remains in question.

Barry Lamar Bonds was born to baseball player Bobby and his wife, Pat Bonds in Riverside, California, on July 24, 1964. The young couple had been married a little more than a year when the icon was born. Athleticism ran in the family. Bobby Bonds, a baseball player who was also born and raised in Riverside, was the brother of Olympic hurdler Rosie Bonds. Only 11 days after his son's birth, Bobby signed a contract with the San Francisco Giants that included a bonus of $8,000 and guaranteed him a monthly salary of $500. He played for eight teams during his Major League career. For the first few years of Barry's young life, he, his younger brother, Ricky, and his mother lived in Riverside while his father hustled in the minor leagues. The young icon's father soon made the big league Giants squad in 1968 and moved the family north to San Carlos, located in the greater San Francisco Bay area. San Carlos was predominantly white, but Bobby's success afforded him the opportunity to live in the upscale neighborhood. His young sons spent a lot of time in the Giants locker room. Legendary outfielder Willie Mays even became honorary godfather to Barry.

Barry grew up in San Carlos. His early education began at Arundel Elementary School, but his parents transferred him to the Carey School to begin his fifth-grade studies. As a youngster, he played in the San Carlos Little League. His father, while successful on the baseball field, struggled with alcoholism off field. After 10 years of marriage to Bobby, Pat filed for divorce. She soon changed her mind and remained with her husband, however. Bobby was traded to the New York Yankees when Barry was 10 years old. Given that he played for several teams, the professional baseball player was not always around while his children grew up. After playing with the Yankees, he played with the California Angels, the Chicago White Sox, and the Texas Rangers. His family remained in the Bay area as he moved from team to team.

Barry followed in his father's footsteps by finding continued success in sports. He entered Junipero Serra High School in San Mateo, California, in 1978. There he played baseball, basketball, and football. A private, all-boys Catholic school, Serra High was known for its great athletic teams. Other notable professional athletes graduated from the school, including New England Patriots quarterback Tom Brady, former wide receiver Lynn Swann of the Pittsburgh Steelers, and baseball players Jim Fregosi and Gregg Jefferies. As the son of a professional baseball player, Barry certainly faced immense pressures from his peers and family to follow in his father's footsteps. As a sophomore, he played wide receiver on the junior varsity football team, which won the West Catholic Athletic League (WCAL) title. The next year, he suited up for the varsity, but his team ended up with a disappointing record of two wins and seven losses. His junior year was his last for football; he gave up the sport after that disappointing season. He also played basketball for three years, one year on the junior varsity and two on the varsity team.

Bonds also played baseball throughout high school. In three varsity baseball seasons, he hit .404. He even hit a stellar .467 during his senior year, when he was named a high school All-America athlete. As a freshman, he started in center field and batted lead-off for the Serra High Padres, which claimed the WCAL championship title with a record of 16 wins, 8 losses, and 1 tie. Bonds led the WCAL in home runs that year and was named second-team all-league. He attracted local media attention for his on-the-field performance. As a junior, he established himself as a legitimate baseball player headed for the next level. Scouts attended Serra games, and Bonds did not disappoint. He led the league in home runs for a second consecutive year, though his team lost in the WCAL title game. The icon's senior season numbers were impressive. He hit an amazing .467, led his team with 14 home runs and 42 runs batted in, and garnered great attention from Major League scouts. Bonds did not respond well to this extra attention. People who knew him at the time suggested that his behavior grew increasingly arrogant. He was often late for practice and let his schoolwork slide. Scouts also identified him as having an attitude problem, which limited the opportunities offered to him. Bonds graduated from high school in 1982 and committed to playing baseball at Arizona State University (ASU).

Despite intentions to attend ASU, Bonds was considered for drafting by several Major League clubs. The athlete's father, whose relationship with his oldest son was bound by baseball but strained by his drinking problems, became more involved in the student's baseball career as talk of a draft grew. Bobby announced that he would be handling his son's baseball career. This news was enough to scare away several interested teams. As a result, the San Francisco Giants drafted Barry in the second round, which the young ball player with a big ego considered an insult. Only a few weeks later, Bonds learned that he was not selected for the Northern California High School All-Star team, in large part because he spent much of the tryout in the bullpen asleep. The coaches based their decision on his growing reputation as a difficult player and teammate and failed to recognize that the young man was exhausted the day after his school prom. When the Giants offered him $70,000, his father asked for $75,000 and the Giants refused. Barry decided to follow through on his original plan to attend ASU, a college rich in baseball tradition.

Bonds played three seasons of college baseball with the ASU Sun Devils. He enjoyed great success as a collegiate athlete under head coach Jim Brock. As a freshman, Bonds started and became only the third freshman to ever start for the Sun Devils. He hit a freshman record of 11 home runs, which also led the team. That year, the Sun Devils advanced to the College World Series and finished third.

Bonds continued to play for the Sun Devils his sophomore year. He ended this season with a record of 55 wins and 20 losses, and spent much of the season ranked number one. He hit .360 with 11 home runs, 55 runs batted in, and 30 stolen bases. The following summer, he played for the Hutchinson Broncs in Hutchinson, Kansas, in the Jayhawk League. This league consisted of college players who wished to hone their skills for the next college season.

Bonds's third year with the Sun Devils proved more challenging. As a junior, he moved over to center field after teammate Oddibe McDowell left for the minor leagues. Prior to the start of this season, the team faced tough sanctions for violations of a work-study program, which cost them their 1984 Pac-10 title, 14 scholarships, and the eligibility of 5 players for the start of the season. The Sun Devils suffered on the field. For the first time in school history, the team posted a losing record, finishing with 31 wins and 35 losses. Still, Bonds performed at an impressive level, hitting .368 with 23 home runs and 66 runs batted in, earning him second-team All-America honors.

Bonds's overall athletic work at ASU was impressive as well. He was named to the All-Pac-10 team all three seasons. He hit .347 with 45 home runs and 175 runs batted in over his college career. *Sporting News* selected him to its All-America team in his final season. In addition, Bonds was named to the All-Time College World Series Team in 1996, in part because he tied a National Collegiate Athletic Association record with seven consecutive hits in the series when he was a sophomore. Despite his great statistics in college, Bonds's poor attitude plagued his team throughout his three years at Arizona State. His sophomore year, his teammates actually voted to kick him off the team. He only remained on the team because Brock changed his mind and allowed him to stay. His father appeared at games and practices, which added to his pressure and made things worse. Bonds seemed to lack the social skills necessary to get along with his teammates. They viewed him as a cocky, spoiled athlete who lived by a different set of rules. Even his on-the-field abilities did not seem to win his teammates over. After his junior season, Bonds was drafted sixth in the first round of the Major League Baseball draft by the Pittsburgh Pirates. He decided to leave college at this time and pursue his professional career in baseball.

Bonds began his professional career on a high note. He signed with the Pirates in June 1985 and received a $150,000 signing bonus prior to assignment with the Prince William Pirates of Prince William, Virginia, a Class A Carolina League. Prince William manager Ed Ott once played catcher with the Major League Pirates. Bonds played in 71 games that season and led the team with 13 home runs and a .299 average. The next spring, he was invited to be a nonroster player at Major League spring training in Bradenton, Florida. The Pirates were coming off an abysmal season with 104 losses, so in many respects they could only improve. No one other than Bonds himself expected him to make the Major League ros-

*My career is an open book, but my life is not.*

ter. He didn't make the club but was reassigned to the Triple A team in Hawaii, which placed him just one step away from the Major League team. Pittsburgh Pirates manager Jim Leyland told Bonds that he'd be called up sometime in the season; the move to Triple A was still disappointing for him. Bonds did not want to play for the Hawaii Islanders in Honolulu. He set about making sure he would be sent up to the Pirates as soon possible. In 44 games, he hit .311 with 7 home runs, 37 runs batted in, and 16 stolen bases. His efforts worked, and in May 1986 he was called up to the Major Leagues to suit up for one of the worst teams in baseball.

Bonds's early experiences with the Pirates were disappointing. His first game with the team took place on May 30, 1986, against the Los Angeles Dodgers. He went 0 for 5 at the plate and the Pirates lost 6-4. His second game, which took place the next day, did not see much improvement. He scored his first Major League hit, a double, only to be picked off at second. In his first 100 at-bats with the Pirates, Bonds only had 17 hits. He hit .223 with 16 home runs and 102 strikeouts in his rookie season, and the Pirates lost 98 games. These were not impressive numbers. Nevertheless, Bonds was much more secure in making the club as the starting center fielder during the following year's spring training. By May, however, Leyland moved the athlete over to left field and started newly acquired Andy Van Slyke in center. The Pirates also improved and won 82 games this year. Bonds hit 25 home runs and stole 32 bases. He was developing into a well-rounded baseball player; he could hit home runs, but he also had incredible speed and posed a threat on the bases.

Bonds's personal life also changed as his career progressed. He met Susann "Sun" Branco, who would become his first wife, when he was in Montreal for a series against the Expos in June 1987. Sun was a Swedish immigrant who made a living as a dancer at Chez Paree, a well-known gentleman's club in Montreal. By the end of 1987, Sun moved in with Bonds at his home in Phoenix and they were soon engaged. They married on February 5, 1988, in Las Vegas. Two years later, their son, Nikolai, was born. Bonds was becoming a baseball superstar during this time. That season, he was named to his first All-Star team. He also won his first Most Valuable Player award and his first Gold Glove award for his defensive play in left field, and led the Pirates to the postseason for the first time in 11 years. His MVP season saw him post his best numbers ever with a .301 average, 33 home runs, 114 runs batted in, and 52 stolen bases. By moving Bonds to the middle of the lineup, Leyland put him in a position to make more significant contributions to the team. Bonds and new teammate Bobby Bonilla were called the "Killer Bs" for their offensive production, though even their collective talent did not push the Pirates any closer to constant success. In the postseason, the Pirates lost to the Cincinnati Reds in the National League Championship Series. Bonds's performance in the series was abysmal, with no home runs scored and a poor .167 average. It was a disappointing ending to a terrific MVP season.

Bonds's opportunities to shine continued in the next season, however. The 1991 Pirates found their way to the postseason with a record of 98 wins and 64 losses. Bonds himself had another great year, hitting .292 with 25 home runs, 116 runs batted in, and 43 stolen bases. He finished second to the Braves' Terry Pendleton in MVP voting. In the playoffs, the Pirates faced the Atlanta Braves and hoped to avenge their prior year's poor postseason performance, as did Bonds. The Pirates and Bonds were disappointed, however. In seven games, the team lost to the Braves and Bonds failed to demonstrate his athletic skill, hitting .148 without scoring any home runs or batting in any runs.

Before the 1992 season, Bonds signed a one-year contract with the Pirates. This contract was the highest one-year deal in baseball history at $4.7 million. It also made the player eligible for free agency at the end of the season, meaning that he could then choose to play for whatever team offered him the best contract. Bonilla had already left the Pirates to play for the Mets for a hefty five-year, $29 million deal, which Bonds hoped to emulate. Both believed that white teammates including Andy Van Slyke and pitcher Doug Drabek were awarded more generous contracts than their black teammates over the years, which ultimately led both Bonilla and Bonds to decide to leave the Pirates. Though Bonilla was no longer in the lineup, the Pirates managed to win their third consecutive National League East Crown with 96 wins. Bonds had his best season ever, hitting .311 with 34 home runs, 103 runs batted in, and 39 stolen bases. He won his second MVP award and looked forward to signing a new contract that would reward him for his stellar success on the field. For the second year in a row, the Pirates faced the Braves in the National League Championship Series. Bonds fared better this year by hitting .261 with one home run and two runs batted in for the series. Though these were his best postseason statistics, they were not enough to get past the Braves. The Pirates lost game seven and the series when the lumbering Sid Bream beat a Bonds throw to home plate. This loss cemented the end of Bonds's time in Pittsburgh.

Bonds's career with the Pirates established him as one of the best players of his generation. The Pirates also improved as a team during his stay, finishing in second place in 1988 and making it to the postseason in 1990, 1991, and 1992. The athlete was a critical factor to the Pirates' success enjoyed in those years, and was so outstanding an athlete that he won two MVP awards and was named to the 1990 All-Star team. Several reasons contributed to his decision to leave the Pirates, though finances were a primary factor. Teammates signed with the Pirates for contracts in excess of $12 million, while Bonds was repeatedly denied big contracts and instead made less than $3 million despite his MVP performance. These discrepancies in pay made Bonds bitter toward the organization, so he determined to take advantage of free agency. After losing to the postseason Braves for the second series in a row, Bonds shifted his focus to signing with a new team, though contract offers proved difficult to find. Few teams were interested in the athlete for two reasons: Bonds was expensive and had an attitude with which few teammates and managers wanted to work.

Bonds did sign a contract, however. In December 1992, he signed a record $43.75 million deal with the San Francisco Giants for six years. In the process of being purchased by Peter Magowan, the Giants were mired in rumors, including assumptions that Magowan would move the team to Florida. Bonds's contract was Magowan's first deal and signaled his commitment to winning games and to the franchise. The contract was also a symbolic homecoming of sorts for the young baseball player, who would play for the same team his father had played for the first seven years of his career. At a press conference announcing his signing, Bonds explained how much it meant to him to play for the Giants organization and to play in the same outfield once occupied by his father and godfather. It was announced that he would even get to wear Mays's retired number 24 jersey and occupy his godfather's former locker. This news generated so much negative response from fans that Bonds switched his jersey to 25, which had been his father's number. A new team represented a new start for Bonds, and he did not let anyone down.

In his first season as a Giant, Bonds led the league with 46 home runs. His batting average was .336 and he accumulated 123 runs batted in, earning him a second-place finish in voting for the MVP award. With the Giants, Bonds continued to be a dominant player in the game. Bill James, an established expert of sabermetrics (the statistics of baseball), considered Bonds the best player of the 1990s. He even ranked the icon as the sixteenth best player of all time and called Bonds the most "unappreciated superstar" of his lifetime. James predicted that when people consider all of Bonds's accomplishments, he will be rated among the five greatest players in the history of baseball.

Bonds, a home-run hitter with speed and a good defensive glove, achieved two significant milestones during the 1990s. In 1996, he became a member of the exclusive 40-40 club, meaning that he had hit 40 home runs and stolen 40 bases in a single season, which is a unique accomplishment that showcased his power and speed. Only José Canseco, Alex Rodriguez, and Alfanso Soriano share membership with Bonds in the 40-40 club as of the time of this writing. That season, he also became only the fourth player to hit 300 home runs and steal 300 bases. The next year, Bonds slugged 40 home runs. Though he was reaching an age when many players begin to lose their power, he became the first member of the 400-400 club in 1998 with 400 career home runs and 400 stolen bases. That season, he hit .303, swatted 37 home runs, tallied 122 runs batted in, and won his eighth Gold Glove award. *Sporting News* named him Player of the Decade.

Following his highest home run total in 2000 (49, with a .306 average), Bonds returned to the Giants in 2001 still hoping to help his team reach the World Series. It was a remarkable year for the athlete, who spent much of it chasing

Mark McGwire's 1998 single-season home run record. Bonds hit his seventieth home run on October 4, 2001, and tied McGwire's record. He hit the record-breaking 71 the next day. Bonds ended the season with a new record of 73 home runs. This new accomplishment established him as a legitimate challenger to Babe Ruth and Hank Aaron, who sat atop the all-time home run list with 714 and 755, respectively. After his record-setting season, Bonds thanked McGwire for setting such a high goal. He reached other milestones during that season, including his five hundredth career home run on April 17. This marker made him the seventeenth Major Leaguer to join an exclusive group of athletes with over 500 career home runs. Bonds also set a single-season record for walks with 177, since many pitchers chose to give him a base on balls rather than face his slugging powers. He also set a single-season record with a slugging percentage of .863.

Bonds capitalized on his record-setting 2001 season during the off-season, when he signed a new contract with the Giants worth $90 million over five years. Expectations were high, as fans flocked to the ballpark to witness his home run hitting. Bonds and the Giants both had a terrific season in 2002. The athlete broke his year-old single-season record for walks with 198. He slugged 46 home runs. He also hit .370 to win his first National League batting title, and finished with an on-base percentage of .582, which broke Ted Williams's 1941 record of .551. On August 9, Bonds became only the fourth player in Major League history to hit 600 career home runs. In addition, the Giants made it to their first World Series since 1989 to play the Anaheim Angels. Bonds displayed an offensive show that put any concerns about his prior postseason play to rest. He set a record for the most home runs in a single postseason with eight. In the World Series, he hit .471 with 4 home runs and 13 walks, including 7 intentional walks. The Giants lost the Series, despite Bonds's work, four games to three.

Bonds's life changed personally and professionally at this time. It was very fortunate that he enjoyed such a great postseason in 2002, as he soon faced great personal problems. His father was very ill and died less than a year later in August 2003. A major highlight of Bonds's 2003 season occurred when he stole his five hundredth base to become the first player to ever hit 500 career home runs and steal 500 bases. That season he hit 45 home runs and hit .341, remarkable numbers for an aging athlete.

Bonds's life was soon disrupted by investigations into the use of performance-enhancing drugs, as well. In 2003, BALCO was investigated for providing professional athletes with performance-enhancing drugs. Bonds was called to provide testimony to a grand jury. He claimed that he had never knowingly ingested banned substances, though he may have unknowingly taken two substances that were given to him by Greg Anderson, his trainer. The two substances were "the clear" and "the cream," which Bonds said his trainer identified as flaxseed oil and arthritis cream. Anderson was indicted for supplying professional athletes with anabolic steroids. He spent three months in prison in 2005 without naming the athletes involved. Since Anderson was Bonds's trainer and the athlete's talent seemed to defy the aging process, many journalists, fans, and other baseball players suspected that he had benefited from using illegal substances. Though he did not test positive for any of the substances in question, speculation grew.

Baseball was hit hard with evidence that seemed to suggest that many players were using illegal substances. Congress asked several players to testify, including Mark McGwire, who refused to discuss his 1998 record-setting home run season. McGwire's refusal may have confirmed suspicions that he had benefited from steroids, though Major League Baseball had not banned use of steroids by 1998. Baseball officials instituted a new drug policy, though it does not test for all banned substances. Fan reaction to the scandal was mixed. Many enjoyed the monster-length home runs, drug accusations or no. Bonds claimed that his increased production was due to a new training regimen, better nutrition, and legal supplements.

Despite the rumors swirling around the athlete, Bonds continued to perform on the field with his fourth consecutive MVP season. He broke his single-season record for walks in 2004 for the second time with 232. This marked the first time a player was ever walked more than 200 times. Not surprisingly, Bonds also became the all-time leader in walks, as he broke Rickey Henderson's record of 2,090 career walks. The icon won his second batting title with a .362 batting average. He also hit more home runs, reaching number 660 on April 12, 2004, and tying his godfather's record. He hit number 700 on September 17, joining Babe Ruth and Hank Aaron as the only players to ever hit so many career home runs. Yet baseball seemed to be taking its toll on his body. His injuries added to the growing speculation about his involvement with performance-enhancing drugs. He had never enjoyed a good relationship with the media, but several heated exchanges with different journalists prior to his 2005 season made this relationship even worse. He admitted that the media had finally gotten the best of him and suggested that 2005 might be his final season. Indeed, multiple surgeries to his knee kept Bonds out of the first 142 games of the season. He returned in September to play in a total of 14 games. In that brief time, however, he hit five home runs. He ended the season with 708 home runs and Babe Ruth's total of 714 in his sights.

Press coverage of Bonds at the start of the 2006 season was overwhelming. For as many people who wanted to see him break Aaron's record, there were as many people who believed he had used illegal substances to reach his outstanding accomplishments; the latter group thought he did not deserve to break Babe Ruth's record. Two books published in the off-season added fuel to the fire. *Game of Shadows*, written by two *San Francisco Chronicle* reporters, detailed Bonds's involvement with BALCO and the grand jury investigation. Jeff Pearlman published *Love Me, Hate Me: Barry Bonds and the Making of an*

*I like to [beat] the odds. I'm not afraid to be lonely at the top. With me, it's just the satisfaction of the game [that is important]. Just performance.*

*Anti-Hero*, which gave an overview of Bonds's career in baseball, including run-ins with teammates, accounts of his alleged steroid use, and general ugliness with members of the media. Inundated with attention, praise, and criticism, Bonds indicated that the 2006 season would be his last whether he broke the record or not. To the press, he explained that he no longer enjoyed professional baseball, though he still loved the sport. His poor relationship with the media only worsened during this time period and he often refused to speak with the press after games.

Bonds did receive one opportunity to communicate through the media. ESPN created a show covering the athlete's final chase of the home run record and, in some ways, allowed him unfettered access to a media outlet that was willing to tell his side of the story. *Bonds on Bonds* aired for several weeks before it was canceled due to low viewing numbers. One early episode showed Bonds, in a weak moment, breaking down in tears in reaction to treatment from fans and reporters.

Bonds admitted that he was driven to succeed because so many people counted on him. Liz, his second wife, and children Nikolai, Shikari, and Aisha Lynn were significant factors in his decision to continue playing baseball. Much of the ESPN program showed Bonds spending time with his family and provided viewers with another perspective of the athlete.

Bonds had a very rough start to the 2006 season. Fans from opposing ballparks were ruthless when he came to bat, holding up signs and throwing syringes on the field to reference rumors of steroid use. He hit under .200 for his first 10 games and seemed unable to get into a rhythm. His first home run occurred on April 22, which was the longest streak Bonds experienced without a home run in eight years. The grand jury also continued their investigation, announcing their intent to charge Bonds with perjury and tax evasion for his 2003 testimony. (At the time of this writing, no charges have been filed.) The tax evasion charges refer to Bonds's unreported income from selling memorabilia. Bonds had used this income to buy a house for a mistress, who later testified about the events to the grand jury. Anderson was found in contempt for refusing to testify against his client and longtime friend, and was sent to jail twice during 2006

Bonds did improve his performance despite this added pressure, and as expected, this kept fans coming to the games, whether they were rooting for or against the slugger. He finally tied Babe Ruth's long-hallowed record of 714 home runs on May 20, 2006. Eight days later, he broke this with number 715 against the Colorado Rockies. Bonds appeared to be relieved to have finally surpassed Ruth. Many reporters reasoned that his play improved after this in part because the pressure to do so was gone. He was no longer viewed as the long ball threat, and pitchers rarely intentionally walked him. Yet at every at-bat at away games, Bonds still faced crowds that booed and jeered him. At home games, in contrast, he was cheered as a hometown favorite.

During the 2006 off-season, Bonds was a free agent and negotiated with several teams, though he repeatedly expressed his desire to return to the Giants and finish his career with them. Initially the Giants seemed reluctant to sign the slugger, perhaps because of the steroids controversy along with the hefty price tag it would cost them to sign him. Ultimately, they came to an agreement that kept Bonds in a Giants uniform for a one-year $15.8 million deal with an additional $5 million for meeting certain performance goals. Soon after his contract was signed, it was reported that Bonds had tested positive for amphetamines. As a result, he would be subject to further tests during the season. Bonds entered the 2007 season number two on the list of all-time home runs, only 21 shy of breaking Hank Aaron's seemingly unattainable record 755.

The 2007 season opened with Bonds hitting home runs at a pace that made it clear Aaron's record would not stand for long. Though he eventually slowed down, the crowds packed San Francisco's AT&T Park and as he approached the hallowed 755. Giants fans were given a pin that read "I was there" when Bonds hit a home run leading up to the big one. As he continued hitting home runs, there was more dialogue in regard to his connection to steroids. In a survey conducted by ESPN, 52 percent of baseball fans surveyed stated they did not want Bonds to break the record. ESPN admitted to having a difficult time locating African Americans to participate in the survey, which was relatively small. However, they did find that 46 percent of African Americans surveyed felt Bonds had been treated unfairly in his pursuit of the record, with 25 percent of Caucasians agreeing. Twenty-five percent of surveyed African Americans felt Bonds had been treated unfairly because of his race, whereas no Caucasians felt this way. When asked if Bonds should be inducted into baseball's Hall of Fame, 85 percent of African Americans surveyed said yes, with 53 percent of Caucasians agreeing. Clearly there seemed to be some disconnect between how the two racial groups interpreted his pursuit of the record. Certainly neither community can be discussed in monolithic terms, but it is worth considering the ways his skin color has impacted the multiple ways baseball fans, as well as nonbaseball fans, have viewed his performances. While Bonds has never been especially active in politics or spoken out on issues of race and ethnicity, many fans, both black and white, felt that the persecution he faced in the media and visiting ballparks were due to his race, rather than his perceived steroid usage or brash mannerisms.

As the All-Star Game approached, Bonds was selected to the National League team after a campaign by the Giants to have him be the unofficial host of the summer classic, which was held in San Francisco. Bonds was voted as a starting outfielder and reveled in the fan adoration of him in his hometown. Less than a month later, on August 4, he tied Hank Aaron's home run record-hitting number 755 in San Diego's Petco Park. Baseball Commissioner Bud Selig, who waffled all season about whether he would attend the record-breaking game, was absent but had sent a representative to congratulate Bonds for his achievement. Selig had attended a number of Giants games in the days leading up to the tying home run. Three days later, in the comfortable confines of his hometown AT&T Park, Bonds hit his record-breaking 756th home run against the visiting Washington Nationals. Though Hank Aaron did not attend, another controversial slight to Bonds, he did tape a congratulatory message that was played on the Jumbotron screen. The city of San Francisco hosted a celebration of Bonds and presented him with a key to the city. No mention of steroids was made, it was simply a celebration, and Bonds seemed to bask in the glory of the San Francisco fans who showered him with their cheers and appreciation.

San Francisco fans love Bonds for his on-the-field success as well as his off-the-field contributions to the Bay area. He has donated time and money to a number of charitable endeavors. In partnership with the United Way, he formed the Bonds Family Foundation. This organization recently started the Link'n'Learn program, which provides tutoring for at-risk youth. He contributed to efforts to build the Barry Bonds Junior Giant Field at McCovey Cove and helped dedicate the Bobby Bonds Memorial Field in Daly City. He also worked with the Make-a-Wish Foundation. In 1999, Bonds established a scholarship fund at Serra High to be awarded to an African American student. In addition, he has been active in Bay area events supporting the Police Athletic League and other groups. His lifetime connection and his loyalty to the Bay area, along with his stellar performances, including leading the team to a World Series appearance, make him a fan favorite in spite of the steroid rumors. San Francisco Giants fans, for the most part, seem to be largely supportive of their hometown player. Nationwide, Bonds does not enjoy such adulation despite his Hall of Fame numbers.

Bonds's offensive abilities in combination with his father's talent put the two athletes at the top of several father-son records. They hold the top spot for home runs, stolen bases, and runs batted in. When Bonds reached the 300-300 club, he joined his father, who was the fifth member of that group. He and his father are the only Major Leaguers to reach the 30-30 club in five seasons. In addition, the icon is only the twenty-fifth player to tally 2,000 hits and 400 home runs, and is just one of seven players to have 2,000 hits, at least 200 home runs, and 400 stolen bases.

Barry Bonds is arguably one of the greatest baseball players in history, though his legend will be debated for years to come due to suspicions of steroid use. A 13-time All-Star, 8-time Gold Glove winner, and 7-time National League MVP, Bonds only misses one accolade from his long list of accomplishments: world champion. This award may elude him as his career comes to a close. As the 2007 season winds down, Bonds will again be available to the team willing to pay him the most money. Perhaps he will again express his desire to complete his career with the Giants and take a pay cut to support the team's efforts to build for the future. It seems likely that he could choose to sign with an American League team where he could serve as a designated hitter and chase his World Series ring. Bonds's statistics speak for themselves, though there is simply no consensus on what the legacy of the icon will be.

## FURTHER READING

Bloom, Barry M. "Bonds Reflects on '01, Dad's Influence," October 5, 2005, MLB.com, http://barrybonds.mlb.com/NASApp/mlb/news/article.jsp?ymd=20051004 &content_id=1237223&vkey=news_sf&fext=.jsp&c_id=sf (accessed August 1, 2006).

Fainaru-Wada, Mark, and Lance Williams. *Games of Shadows: Barry Bonds, BALCO, and the Steroids Scandal that Rocked Professional Sports.* New York: Gotham, 2006.

Fainaru-Wada, Mark, and Lance Williams. "The Truth: Barry Bonds and Steroids." *Sports Illustrated* (March 13, 2006).

Hamrahi, Joe, with Bill James. "Being Barry Bonds." *Baseball Digest* (May 29, 2006).

Pearlman, Jeff. *Love Me, Hate Me: Barry Bonds and the Making on an Anti-Hero.* New York: HarperCollins, 2006.

AP Photo/Cleveland Browns, HO.

# Jim Brown

*Pero Gaglo Dagbovie and
Amaris J. White*

Brown excelled in sports at Manhasset, playing basketball, track, baseball, lacrosse, and football. At age 14, he became a starter on the varsity football team. Ed Walsh, Brown's high school coach and later his good friend, spoke very highly of him. During his senior year, he averaged an impressive 14.9 yards per carry as a running back. He was also a solid defensive player at the linebacker position. He earned a total of 13 varsity letters. He also received all-state honors in each sport that he played except baseball. Nonetheless, the New York Yankees recognized his talent and abilities, offering him a note-worthy minor league contract during his senior year.

While he met athletic success, Brown did not conveniently fit the stereotype of the high school jock. He was the leader of a gang composed of his athlete peers called the Gaylords, as well as a solid student; he graduated in 1953 on the honor roll. He was a popular school leader and elected the "chief justice of the high school" by his peers. Brown's athletic prowess was recognized by more than 40 colleges and universities, which attempted to recruit him. His choices were limited by his times; in the early 1950s, young blacks could only attend historically black colleges and universities or liberal white institutions outside of the South.

Ohio State University and Syracuse University showed serious interest in Brown. Following the advice of his friend Ken Molloy, he attended Syra-cuse. Molloy was an attorney and Syracuse alumnus who wanted Brown to follow in his footsteps. Surprisingly, Brown did not earn an athletic scholar-ship to Syracuse. Molloy garnered financial support from wealthy Manhasset businessmen to support Brown during his freshman year. The attorney was confident that Brown would prove himself and receive a scholarship by his sophomore year. This seemed logical, but did not happen. Like many African Americans at predominantly white colleges and universities of this era, Brown encountered a great deal of racism at Syracuse. Ben Schwartzwalder, the head football coach at Syracuse, did not like African American players. The coach vowed, prior to Brown's arrival, never to play another African American foot-ball player after his experience with Avatus Stone, an exceptional player who had refused to conform to Schwartzwalder's notions of a "good Negro." Schwartzwalder told Coach Walsh that Brown could only attend Syracuse if he obeyed 10 specific rules that applied solely to him. The rules were ridiculous to Walsh. The one that struck a chord with the coach was Schwartzwalder's decree that Brown could not date white women. Walsh refused to comply with Schwartzwalder's request, and Molloy's behind-the-scenes wheeling and dealing essentially got Brown into Syracuse.

During his freshman year, Brown did not start and rarely played for the Or-angemen. On average, he carried the ball only once per quarter for significant yardage. The student, who knew that he was more talented than the starting running backs, was not happy. He felt alienated and underappreciated. The psy-chological impact of racism on his mind at this time was profound. He developed distinct survival mechanisms and found support outside of the football program. Roy Simmons Sr., Syracuse's head lacrosse coach, embraced Brown. The basketball coach did not like Brown and refused to start the black players, even though they were arguably the most talented people on the team, but Brown befriended several black teammates. Brown and his fellow black players spent time together, often discussing the realities of being a black athlete at Syracuse. These consciousness-raising sessions represent the early stages of Brown's development into an African American athlete-activist. Nonetheless, he was not happy during his freshman year. At Manhasset High School, he was a living legend and the white community of students, coaches, and teachers embraced him. In contrast, he had very limited support at Syracuse. At the end of his freshman year, he told Walsh that he would not return to school in upstate New York. According to Brown, it was primarily Dr. Collins, the superintendent of Manhasset, who convinced him to push on at Syracuse.

The decision to remain at Syracuse proved very important to Brown. He was on the verge of becoming, in his words, a "big-time gangster." His sophomore year at Syracuse was a major turning point. He was promoted to the starting running back position after two players ahead of him on the roster became injured. He immediately proved himself and made an impact. As a sophomore, he was Syracuse's second leading rusher. During that year, he also averaged 15 points per game in basketball, ran track, and initiated his illustrious lacrosse career. He was an exemplar, even qualifying for the 1956 Olympics as a decathlete. During his junior year, he continued to excel in sports. He rushed for more than 600 yards, averaging 5.2 yards per carry, averaged 11.3 points per game in basketball, and was a Second Team All-American in lacrosse. As a senior, Brown averaged 6.2 yards per carry for a total of 986 yards. During the 1956–1957 academic year, the Orangemen were selected to play against Texas Christian University in the Cotton Bowl. Brown used this prestigious, nationally televised game as an opportunity to prove his skills and value as a potential NFL star. He played exceptionally well in this game. He ran for 132 yards, scored three touchdowns, and even kicked three extra points. He recalled that after this game, despite Syracuse's one-point loss, American football aficionados finally recognized him.

Brown also concluded his athletic career at Syracuse as a first-rate lacrosse player. In his senior year, he scored 43 goals, averaging more than 4 goals per game, and was named First Team All-American. He was the first African American to play in the North-South game. He played for half of the game, scored five goals, and had two assists in the North's 14-10 win. Though Brown started lacrosse later than he started his other adopted sports, he was truly an accomplished player. His natural athleticism and strength allowed him to excel at this additional sport. Roy Simmons Jr., former head lacrosse coach for Syracuse and the son of Brown's lacrosse coach, reflected that Brown "was a polished stick-handler" with distinctive skills who could score at will. He broke new ground by playing lacrosse at Syracuse. He was not the first African American to play lacrosse at a predominantly white college or university, but he was the first African American collegiate lacrosse superstar.

While the first NCAA lacrosse championship was held in 1977, lacrosse was being played competitively at colleges, universities, and athletic clubs in the United States beginning in the 1890s. Brown played the game when it was still an elite collegiate sport. Lacrosse at Syracuse was significant during his times, but it trailed most other men's sports in terms of participation, audience, and income generated. Between 1957 and 2004, seven African Americans, beginning with Brown, were named First Team All-Americans in Division I men's college lacrosse. Another African American would not follow in Brown's footsteps to earn this sought-after honor for more than 20 years. Brown endured racist taunts in lacrosse as he did on the football field. He confronted racism on the field directly with his skills. He also responded to his detractors on campus. During his senior year, he purchased a large red and white Pontiac Bonneville that he drove around campus and to his home lacrosse games. On one occasion, he purposely drove his new car to a home game with one of his white girlfriends by his side. He took her into the stands, went to the locker room to get dressed, led his team to victory, and then retrieved his girlfriend. Though Brown did not continue this behavior as a professional football player, the racialized and normative masculinist posturing he exhibited became central to his philosophy.

Brown graduated from Syracuse with a degree in physical education. Later on in his life he said that philosophy and logic were his favorite subjects. After graduating, he had more than a few options based upon his superior athleticism. He was seriously recruited by Major League baseball teams, by at least one professional basketball team, and even by a professional boxing promoter. Brown opted to commit himself to football. Had a lucrative professional lacrosse league existed, he might have selected lacrosse. In 1957, the Cleveland Browns selected him in the first round of the NFL draft. He was the sixth player selected overall.

Brown's first year in the NFL was extraordinary. It did not take him very long to become accustomed to professional football culture or to make a significant impact on the Browns' organization and the NFL. As a rookie, Brown played in 12 games and rushed for 942 yards, averaging 4.7 yards per carry. He scored nine touchdowns. He also played an instrumental role in helping the Browns win the Eastern Division championship. For his efforts, he was awarded Rookie of the Year. His second season in the NFL was even more impressive and the second-best year of his career. He played in 12 games, rushed for a league-leading 1,527 yards, averaged 5.9 yards per carry, and scored 17 touchdowns. In 1958, Brown was awarded the Associated Press NFL Player of the Year. The next seven years of his career were equally as impressive. The best season of his career was 1963. He rushed for 1,863 yards, averaging an incredible 6.4 yards per carry.

Brown's nine-year career with the Cleveland Browns was record-setting. He had a total of 2,359 carries and never missed a game. He played in a total of 118 games during which he was the opposing team's defense's focal point. He led the NFL in rushing in eight of his nine seasons: rushing for 12,312 total yards, 5.2 yards per carry, and rushing for 106 touchdowns. His career rushing record lasted until Walter "Sweetness" Payton broke it during his 1984 season. In 1964, Brown helped his team win the NFL championship, upsetting the Baltimore Colts 27-0. During this year, he rushed for 1,446 yards, averaging 5.2 yards per carry. In 1965, his final season, Brown earned his second AP NFL Player of the Year honor, rushed for 1,544 yards with 5.3 yards per carry, and scored 17 touchdowns. He was selected for the NFL Pro Bowl team in each year of his career.

Brown created memorable moments in professional football. Many highlight films feature his athletic talent and commemorate these moments. His teammates and opponents have distinct memories of his talent. He was especially well known for his power, speed, ability to change speeds and directions, stamina, leadership skills, and mental endurance. Countless reels of NFL film footage show Brown breaking tackles and literally carrying defensive players with him down the field. At 6' 2" and 230 pounds, Brown was indeed a formidable football talent. While he could be elusive, he did not avoid contact with opposing teams' defenses. He used his broad shoulders and free arm to punish and ward off would-be tacklers. Brown also brought a complex mental component to his game; before beginning his illustrious Hollywood acting career, he was an accomplished actor on the field. He developed the habit of routinely rising slowly after being tackled. In this way, he never let the opposition know when or if they had hurt him. He demoralized the opposing team's defense, denying them the satisfaction of celebrating moral victories. Marvin Van Peebles astutely likened Brown to the cunning Brer Rabbit character of African American folklore, a descendant of West Africa's Anansi the spider.

Brown was truly a student of football. He studied the opposing defenses meticulously. He also brought a distinct intellectual and metaphysical flavor to his game. One of his favorite books dealt with psycho-cybernetics and visualization. Before games, Brown often meditated, visualizing what he was going to accomplish during the game at hand. He explained that imagining the plays of a game made them much easier to accomplish. His status as the best player on the team (arguably since his rookie season) enabled him to exercise some power at other levels. He was instrumental in getting Paul Brown, Cleveland's head coach at the time, fired. During Paul Brown's last year as coach, Jim Brown had his least productive year. Art Modell, the team's owner, fired Paul and hired Blanton Collier, who was head coach for the Browns from 1963 until 1970. Though there are of course conflicting stories about the nature of Paul Brown's dismissal, most agree that Jim Brown spearheaded the campaign to get rid of him. The change in coaches was ideal for the icon. Collier offered him better opportunities. According to Brown, Collier allowed some members of the team to play a larger role in running the offense. In fact, Brown, in consultation with other players, called many of the offensive plays during his last year.

Brown's presence in professional football also meant that he influenced his white teammates. Like many running backs and quarterbacks, he had close relationships with his offensive linemen, especially John Wooten, Gene Hickerson, Dick Schafrath, John Morrow, and Monte Clark. Despite the unprecedented expressions of racism in U.S. sports during this time period, professional athletic teams, especially football, often served as miniature spaces of cross-cultural and cross-racial interaction. Brown, who lived in a predominantly white area from the age of eight and spent his college years at a white institution, certainly felt comfortable around white people and knew how to survive as a statistical minority. As a representative of black America, he must have altered his white teammates' views of African American culture, in turn dispelling stereotypes and breaking down artificial racial boundaries.

Brown played professional football during an era in which professional athletes did not earn millions of dollars. When he first joined the Browns, he agreed to a $15,000 contract. In Cleveland and elsewhere, he also played in all of the elements, always on natural grass and never indoors in a controlled environment. Though cross-generational comparisons between athletes are difficult to make, Brown played professional football during a time when the offenses, passing games, and overall schemes were not as complex as they are today. Sports technology made particularly large leaps in the post–Civil Rights Movement years. Simply put, opposing defenses, or "the enemy" in Brown's mind, knew that he was the centerpiece of his team's offense. The statistics demonstrate this. In his career, Brown carried the rock 2,359 times, doing so 202 times in his rookie year, the year that he had his fewest carries. In 1961, his most active ball-carrying year, he carried the ball 305 times. Whereas today's superstar athletes usually miss games here and there due to minor and major injuries, Brown never missed a game due to injury. He was extremely durable and fit. He could be compared to the best running backs of any period.

Brown's remarkable accomplishments are more clearly understood when explored within the context of race in U.S. sports and culture. Until the modern Civil Rights Movement and beyond, African Americans were systematically denied the right to cross the color line. In all major U.S. sports, blacks faced challenges. African Americans faced varied reception from the NFL before Brown began his career. Different teams had different philosophies. The Browns were progressive when viewed in comparison to some teams and a bit conservative when viewed next to others. The NFL banned African Americans from playing in 1933. Prior to this ban, many African American professional football players, including Robert "Rube" Marshall, Frederick "Fritz" Pollard, and Paul Robeson, stood out. The reintegration of African Americans into the NFL began after World War II when the Los Angeles Rams added Kenny Washington and Woody Strode to their roster in 1946. The integration of the NFL was a slow, gradual process, increasing by the 1950s, the decade that witnessed

Brown's start. The last team to integrate was the Washington Redskins, which in 1962 signed Bobby Mitchell.

Brown played football during the turbulent and reform-generating years of the modern Civil Rights Movement. Though composed of various, often competing groups, ideologies, and leaders, the primary goal of the modern Civil Rights Movement was to end the era of Jim Crow segregation. Activists in this movement focused on proving and publicizing that they de-

*I'm not interested in trying to work on people's perceptions. I am who I am, and if you don't take the time to learn about that, then your perception is going to be your problem.*

served the most fundamental citizenship rights. More than a few professional football players followed this trend. Brown and his colleagues in the 1950s and 1960s proved in the NFL that blacks were equal, if not often superior, to their white counterparts. Brown's explosive, physical running style was a raw, athletic expression of black power during the classic Civil Rights Movement. In delivering punishment to would-be tacklers, who were often white, Brown made a collective statement on behalf of black people. For many young blacks during the modern Civil Rights Movement, he became a Joe Louis of football. Black youth found dignity, respect, and strength by vicariously living though Brown as he ruthlessly stiff-armed those standing in his path.

After a season that earned him his second AP Player of the Year honor, Brown retired from the game in 1965 at the peak of his career. He shocked the sports world with his decision, which was made as he acted in the film *The Dirty Dozen*. He walked away from football, devoting more time to his bourgeoning acting career as well as his interests in race relations and the African American struggle for liberation and equal rights. During the 1960s, Brown became a committed civil rights activist. He founded the Negro Industrial and Economic Union (NIEU), later named the Black Economic Union (BEU), in Cleveland while still playing with the Browns. This new organization sought to empower black communities by having professional black athletes create African American–run businesses, urban sports facilities, and programs geared at helping youth development. Brown and others wanted blacks to get involved in economic development, self-determination, and nationalism. The organization, which was composed of young black entrepreneurs, MBAs, and black professional athletes, proclaimed as its motto: "Produce, Achieve, and Prosper." The NIEU/BEU reportedly helped more than 400 businesses get started.

Brown was also instrumental in creating a support network for Muhammad Ali when the latter athlete refused induction into the U.S. military due to his Islamic beliefs. This act may have made Ali public enemy number one, but within the African American community Ali was often embraced and celebrated for his commitment to not only his religious faith but to the ideology of Black Nationalism. Ali, then known as Cassius Clay, publicly announced his commitment to Elijah Muhammad and the Nation of Islam after defeating Sonny Liston in the boxing arena on February 25, 1964. At the time, the U.S. government considered the Nation of Islam to be one of the most dangerous

African American organizations in terms of U.S. internal security and domestic stability.

Ali and Brown were by no means strangers. Ali supported the Black Economic Union. Brown truly believed that Ali needed to be validated by those with prominent voices like his. He was not willing to abandon him due to his controversial stance. He contacted Ali and arranged for him to come to Cleveland on November 10, 1966. Among those who were present were Bill Russell, Lew Alcindor (later Kareem Abdul-Jabbar), and Brown. They spoke intimately with Ali for approximately two and a half hours. After their private meeting, Brown and his colleagues stressed their support of Ali at a highly publicized meeting with the media. Brown's support of the struggle for collective African American advancement began with his upbringing in St. Simons, Georgia, reemerged during his years at Syracuse, and entered another phase during the Civil Rights and Black Power Movements. His activities during the 1960s marked merely the early stages of his commitment to the African American struggle, however. Since then, he has worked with many reform-seeking organizations within African American communities.

Brown also committed himself in the 1960s and beyond to his acting career. His decision to devote his energies to acting may have surprised many, but it was not totally without precedent. In 1964, when the Browns won the NFL championship, he appeared in the western *Rio Conchos*. Between 1964 and 2005, Brown appeared in 45 films. His most productive decade as an actor was the 1970s, the decade of blaxploitation films. He established a new paradigm for black male actors as a physically unstoppable "black-power sex figure." Unlike any male actor before him, Brown embodied the black superhero. To his young black audiences, he was strong, serious, attractive, masculine, and mysterious. Young black men felt validated when Brown reacted violently to white oppressors. On screen, he acted out what young black men could only envision in their dreams. His action roles could have reinforced stereotypes of the black man as a brute, a buck, and a hypersexualized being. During his films of the 1960s and 1970s, Brown's typical character was both powerful and charismatic.

Brown's characters were also appealing to white America because they so often worked hand in hand with representatives of white American culture. The directors of films starring Brown recognized their growing black clientele, but did not want to alienate their white male audiences. During the black power era, Brown did not play the role of the "politically militant black man." At the same time, the empowered characters he played during the 1960s in part laid the foundation for the African American male superheroes that appeared during the 1970s.

Brown played many roles in film. In the 1960s and 1970s, he appeared in a total of 23 films. He was in 11 films in the 1980s. Since the early 1990s, Brown appeared in another 11 films. Of all his films, *100 Rifles* was one of his most controversial and significant. This western, released in 1969 and directed by

Tom Gries, starred not only Brown but also Burt Reynolds, Raquel Welch, and Fernando Lamas. Set in Mexico in 1912, Brown's character, an Arizona lawman named Lyedecker, seeks out bank robber Yaqui Joe, played by Burt Reynolds. Lyedecker and Yaqui Joe eventually unite to fight for the Indians. This film notably featured a sex scene with Brown and Raquel Welch, making this the first major Hollywood film to feature an interracial love scene. The scene certainly pushed the envelope in terms of American popular culture's acceptance of interracial sex. More than a few moviegoers responded to the film with anger, especially in the South. Though *100 Rifles* is one of Brown's most popular movies, it should not be used to define his career. Since *He Got Game* (1998), he has also worked with famous African American filmmaker Spike Lee. Brown's most recent film was *The Outsider*, released in 2005. He paved the way for African American athletes to enter the film industry.

Brown also gained notoriety after his retirement from football for his various run-ins with law enforcement. While married to his first wife, Sue Jones, the Brown household was marked by a number of domestic conflicts. In addition, during the 1960s, Brown was charged with raping an 18-year-old woman, accused of throwing his girlfriend from a second-floor balcony, and arrested for a hit-and-run car accident. In 1978, he was found guilty of assaulting a man on a golf course. In 1985, he was again charged with rape and assault, though the charges for this case were dropped. The next year, he was arrested for allegedly beating up his fiancée. In 1999, he was convicted in Los Angeles for threatening his wife. He later served less than four months in prison because he refused to receive the counseling that a judge required him to seek. Brown's alleged crimes against women raise complex questions, especially since he was raised and socialized by interconnected generations of black women. With their words and through their actions, they certainly imbued him with an authentic sense of respect for African American womanhood. How do onlookers make sense of Brown's mistreatment of women and domestic violence?

The admiration and respect that Jim Brown holds for his great-grandmother complicate analysis of his violent behavior. His relationships with other women, including his mother, can be categorized as tumultuous at best, however. The following question arises: At what point did Brown's positive relationships with women transform into relationships plagued with accusations of abuse and violence? The relationship between Brown and his great-grandmother, Nora P. Daughtry, was one of the most positive and influential relationships he experienced during his lifetime. At age eight, she died and Brown moved to New York to live with his mother. Maybe his transition to New York fostered his negative associations with women. The bond between Brown and his mother was strained from the outset. This relationship became even tenser during his teenage years, when she began to date men. Brown experienced anger and shame over her relationships with other men, which led him to confront his mother and the men she dated. Nevertheless, his mother had little desire for her son to protect her reputation, and Brown eventually moved out and into his girlfriend's house. His problematic relationships with women, and the domestic violence that has characterized his interactions with more than a few of them, test his position as a Black Nationalist and an American icon.

Hand in hand with controversy, social activism and reform also characterized Brown's post–professional football career. In the late 1980s, Brown founded Amer-I-Can. This nonprofit organization is committed to creating programs and methods to transform the lives of gang members and prisoners. The organization was launched in Los Angeles and, by the dawning of the new millennium, had expanded to a dozen other major U.S. cities. Even now Brown continues his commitment to social activism. He regularly speaks out in defense of young African Americans with whom he can sympathize. For instance, during the recent Ohio State University football program scandal, he was among the few to defend Maurice Clarett. Brown is regularly interviewed and sought out by the media to address issues of race, sports, and American popular culture.

## FURTHER READING

Bogle, Donald. *Toms, Coons, Mulattoes, Mammies, and Bucks: An Interpretive History of Blacks in American Films*. New York: Continuum, 2001.

Brown, Jim, with Myron Cope. *Off My Chest*. New York: Double Day, 1964.

Brown, Jim, with Steve Delsohn. *Out of Bounds*. New York: Kensington Publishing, 1989.

Freeman, Mike. *Jim Brown: The Fierce Life of an American Hero*. New York: William Morrow, 2006.

Gates, Henry Louis, Jr., and Evelyn Brooks Higginbotham, eds. "Jim Brown." In *African American Lives*. New York: Oxford University Press, 2004, pp. 115–116.

Lee, Spike. *Jim Brown: All-American*. Home Box Office, 2004.

Lee, Spike. *That's My Story and I'm Sticking to It (as told to Kaleem Aftab)*. New York: W.W. Norton, 2006.

Schwartz, Larry. "Jim Brown Was Hard to Bring Down." Sportscentury Biography. http://espn.go.com/classic/biography/s/Brown_Jim.html (accessed February 10, 2008).

Photofest.

# Wilt Chamberlain

*David J. Johns*

Wilton Norman Chamberlain broke records as the first player to ever score 100 points in a professional basketball game and one of only two players to score more than 30,000 points during his professional career. A towering figure at 7' 1", he is one of the greatest players in the history of the sport of basketball. He was inducted into the Hall of Fame in 1978, named one of the 50 greatest players in the history of the league, and also became the first player to be named both Most Valuable Player and Rookie of the Year in the same season (1960). He defied physical and social limitations, changing the sport in the process. Seemingly sculpted for the sport of basketball, he enjoyed more than 14 seasons as a player. During his years in the sport, rules were changed, records broken, and rivalries born. Chamberlain was an icon of the sport. He elevated the athleticism of the game, quickened its pace, and married spontaneity with superior athleticism to craft. He introduced new and more spectacular ways of shooting, passing, and dribbling the ball, for example. By changing techniques employed in the game, Chamberlain increased popular awareness of black male athletes and helped transform basketball from a sport to a cultural signifier and marketable form of entertainment. He helped revolutionize the game of basketball, and in the process engendered larger social change.

Born August 22, 1936 to William "Bill" and Olivia Ruth Chamberlain in Philadelphia, Pennsylvania, Chamberlain was not particularly abnormal or outstanding in the first few years of his life. The sixth of nine surviving children, he was closest to his younger sister Barbra. Her presence anchored him throughout his lifetime. Their father was a janitor at a publishing company who also earned additional money fixing things for his neighbors. Their mother cared for the homes and children of mostly affluent Jewish families. Hard-working and committed to their family, Chamberlain's parents greatly influenced the course of his development. From his father, Wilt inherited his competitive spirit and a love for sport. From his mother, he learned to be respectful and live with grace.

Willful and self-directed, Chamberlain developed a strong work ethic early in his life. Each of the family's children held at least one job. They pooled their money to assist their parents with household responsibilities such as paying bills, buying furniture, and purchasing food. Chamberlain took great pride in his ability to contribute to his family's well-being and never felt shame for their socioeconomic circumstances. Although he lacked natural killer instincts and a drive to be aggressive, as a child he found it difficult to sleep late. He said that he could not rest when there were dreams to be realized and money to be made.

Chamberlain's mother noted that he always wanted to be the best in everything he did. He learned to use everything he possessed to his advantage: a sharp memory that allowed him to recall numbers with ease, a physical presence that often betrayed his youth, and an ever-increasing athleticism and strength.

In his youth, Chamberlain was motivated, competitive, and amiable. He spoke with a stutter, struggled as a reader, and was placed in remedial reading classes. He worked diligently to overcome these impediments, and later in 1973 he revealed that he possessed a love of literature, a secret he kept from many throughout his life. Friends described young Chamberlain as socially and physically awkward, which

were characteristics he eventually overcame each time he stepped onto center court.

Chamberlain grew accustomed to gawkers early in life. At only nine, he easily stood at least eight inches taller than other children his age. He remembered feeling separate from the rest of the world around the age of 13, when people began to gape and ask uncomfortable and insensitive questions about his anomalous height. Though his exceptionality was often met with admiration and genuine fascination, at other times it resulted in negative criticism and stinging ridicule. He often said, "In a world filled with Davids, no one roots for Goliath." Referencing the biblical battle between David and Goliath, Chamberlain understood that in a society where the average person could not relate to the corporeal and social experiences of an African American giant, many people considered him abnormal and refused to identify with his experiences.

As a child Chamberlain thought basketball was a game for "sissies" and instead preferred track and field. He competed for George Brooks Elementary School, where he and his sister Barbra were successful athletes. He anchored the school's 300-yard shuttle relay team as a fourth-grader at the Penn Relays, a high-profile track and field competition held annually at the University of Pennsylvania. He basked in the applause and excitement of the crowd when his team won. In that moment, he vowed to become a track star. He also dreamed of winning Olympic gold as a decathlete.

Chamberlain grew to six feet by the time he was 10 years old and dedicated himself to basketball at the age of 13. His new love for basketball grew out of childhood friendships with neighborhood friends. The young men spent their summers at local Haddington Recreation Center, where they fell in love with the game. Chamberlain maintained a strong upper body, often through the various jobs he held. Strength and his naturally tall frame aided him immeasurably when he found himself playing simultaneously for several leagues and often against older, more seasoned players. He enjoyed his first taste of printed praise when *The Cobbler*, a junior high school newspaper, documented his success in sport in 1951.

At Overbrook High School Chamberlain stepped onto the center court and found himself on the front page. In the years between 1940 and 1960, no other school in the nation produced as many talented ball players as Overbrook. Few schools managed to win as many league titles and championships as Overbrook, which claimed nine public league titles in 13 years. When Chamberlain enrolled in 1951, he demanded attention on the basketball court. His athleticism not only attracted the attention of the press, it also bolstered his social life and attracted admiring fans.

Chamberlain grew confident in his abilities as a ball player and was often celebrated during parties thrown at the homes of his more affluent white school-mates. During his tenure at Overbrook, divisions between the majority Jewish students, who enjoyed wealth and a higher socioeconomic status, and poorer black classmates were blurred. During a time when the nation still struggled to find solutions to the problems of slavery, failed reconstruction, and unremitting vestiges of racism, Overbrook students were, by all accounts, close. The continued success of Overbrook's basketball team in general, and Chamberlain in particular, indisputably contributed to the overall closeness of the student body.

Chamberlain quickly established himself as a scorer at Overbrook. He averaged 31 points per game in his first season and scored 800 points in his first 16 games. Confirming his reputation as the most talented high school player in the country, he played as an All-American, a nationally recognized star athlete, in 1956. He also led Overbrook to the city championships in 1954 and 1955. He concluded his high school career with 2,252 points and foreshadowed his legendary 100-point NBA game by scoring 90 points in a game against Roxborough High School.

Unfortunately, Chamberlain fought against a demeaning nickname beginning in his first year of high school. Jack Ryan, sports journalist for the *Evening Bulletin*, dubbed the then 6' 11", 200-pound sophomore "Wilt the Stilt," a name Chamberlain utterly detested. Many black athletes of the time struggled with symbolically humiliating names given to them by the media. These names likened athletes to animals and functioned to reduce their hard work and nurtured abilities to freakish clichés that denied them humanity or sensitivity.

Chamberlain much preferred the childhood moniker "Dippy" to the Stilt. The Stilt reminded him of a crane standing in a pool of water, whereas Dippy reminded him of friends. It was a nickname given to him when someone suggested that he dip under doorways and ceilings to avoid hitting his head, which he had to do frequently. Dippy eventually evolved into the "Big Dipper," a name that captured his personality as well as his playing style. On the court, Chamberlain was physically intimidating. He also played with intensity and flamboyance, much like the grand assemblage of stars forming the Big Dipper. He had another connection to constellations as well. As a child, he loved to fall asleep while staring at the stars. As an adult, he continued to sleep under them, aided by a wooden rectangle carved from the ceiling of his Bel Air estate Ursa Major, the Latin name for the Big Dipper.

Chamberlain enjoyed a nurturing relationship with Eddie Gottlieb, basketball aficionado and founding father of the NBA, while still in high school. Gottlieb owned the Philadelphia Warriors, a charter member of the Basketball Association of America, later named the National Basketball Association of America (NBA). He helped secure summer employment for the student at Milton Kutsher's Country Club. At Kutsher's, Chamberlain formed relationships and played basketball with people who remained lifelong friends. Gottlieb's family became a second family to Chamberlain during these summers. He enjoyed meals with both Gottlieb's and Kutsher's families. These friendships were some of the intimate and enduring relationships that punctuated his life.

Chamberlain developed many friendly relationships with children. He distrusted many adults and felt wary of those interested in him only because of his fame or fortune. In contrast, he seemed at ease and unguarded with children. He developed a remarkable rapport with the 10-year-old son of his coach, Frank McGuire. He also developed a meaningful friendship with Stephanie Arizin, granddaughter of Paul Arizin, first draft choice of the Warriors in the 1950 NBA draft. Stephanie wrote Chamberlain on her own accord, requesting an autograph. He happened upon the letter three years after it was originally sent and rushed to telephone the 14-year-old Stephanie and apologize for his tardiness. The two spoke for hours. During a conversation with Stephanie's father, Chamberlain learned that she was battling a brain tumor and was given less than a year to live. He promised to stay in touch, and the two spoke almost every week for the last months of her life. This contact with children and communities reinforced his greatness as a ball player and a man.

Chamberlain set precedents and broke records even before he entered the NBA. He was the first player for whom the territorial draft was enacted when, in 1955, Gottlieb evoked the right of a team to draft players within their draft region. Essentially, Gottlieb chose Chamberlain four years before 1959, when the young player would be eligible for the draft. At the time, players were restricted from entering the NBA until the year that their peers graduated from college. Few athletes were ever as pursued by colleges and universities as he was. He received over 120 offers from schools throughout the nation. One school promised to make him a movie star while others offered free tuition, support through medical school, and other monetary rewards. In the end, Chamberlain chose to attend the University of Kansas.

Like Overbrook High School, by the 1960s the University of Kansas developed a reputation as a powerhouse in men's basketball and was known for producing some of the brightest stars of the sport. Located in Lawrence, the Division I men's basketball team at Kansas was a perennial championship contender. A significant factor in Chamberlain's decision to attend Kansas was the presence of coach Phog Allen, who is sometimes referred to as the father of basketball coaching.

The move from the heart of urban Philadelphia to Lawrence was not difficult for Chamberlain. Though he soon led the Jayhawks to the NCAA championship game in 1957, his transition to the segregated town of Lawrence was not smooth. During his visits to Kansas before enrollment, notable residents of the area, both black and white, courted him. While en route to Kansas before the start of his freshman year, however, he and teammate Doug Leman stopped for sandwiches at a diner in Lawrence, where Chamberlain was refused service because of his race. Incensed, he planned to return to Philadelphia but was convinced to stay after talking things out with Coach Allen.

Though he declared himself anything but a race rebel, Chamberlain had a way of changing things to suit his immediate needs that benefited the larger black community. Following his conversation with Allen about the incident at the diner, the coach contacted his son, Mitt Allen, a well-respected attorney, to express his disgust with the way Chamberlain was treated. The college player also leveraged his notoriety and solicited the support of university chancellor Franklin Murphy to instigate change. Following these incidents, previously segregated businesses in Lawrence went out of their way to accommodate Chamberlain because his presence would, at the very least, increase profits. When Chamberlain entered establishments after games with other black people, business owners welcomed (or at least permitted) his presence.

Chamberlain reshaped the game of basketball during his collegiate years. During his first year on varsity, offensive goal tending, for a maneuver in which a player reached above the rim to aid a shot, was made illegal. Around the same time, new rules mandated that a player's foot could not pass beyond the free throw line until the ball reached the rim, which was designed to prohibit players from jumping from the line to slam-dunk free throws. These changes were designed to decrease Chamberlain's natural abilities on the court. The most significant of these changes was the widening of the lanes around the basketball hoop, a direct attempt to move Chamberlain further away from the net and slow his dominance. Although many of these changes did very little to impede Chamberlain's play, they took a toll on his relationship not only with other players but also with the sport of basketball. He spent his professional career estranged from his white teammates and negatively portrayed in the news, believing that he was characterized as a Goliath and villain before he even entered professional basketball.

Chamberlain began many traditions at Kansas that he took with him to the NBA. He set staggering scoring and rebounding records and offered dazzling displays of athleticism and strength during games. He was praised for his endurance and speed. Nevertheless, at Kansas, he was described as a disappointment. The media scrutinized Chamberlain whenever Kansas lost and then accused him of underperforming regardless of his actual performance. Although he attracted record-setting crowds of fans and spectators and put up double-digit box scores, when the Jayhawks failed to capture the national title in 1957, the media blamed Chamberlain.

Chamberlain also received undeserved disapproval at the final NCAA game of the 1956–1957 season versus North Carolina. North Carolina's main techniques focused upon limiting Chamberlain's ability to play by forcing him away from the basket, for example. The game ended in regulation play with both teams tied at 46 points. The game went into triple overtime and with five seconds to play and North Carolina up by one point, a defender deflected a low pass to Chamberlain. North Carolina won, and the media blamed Chamberlain for the loss, despite the fact that he was named the game's MVP, scored 23 points, and accumulated 14 rebounds.

Chamberlain decided to leave Kansas early when a frustrating junior year ended with the Jayhawks' inability to reach the final game of the season. Though he enjoyed his time at school, his decision to leave early was unquestionably influenced by the prospect of becoming one of the highest paid athletes in the world and realizing a childhood dream. Professional sporting careers offered social mobility, including the capacity to earn money and support one's family. This was a compelling incentive to otherwise underprivileged black people, especially black males. Capitalizing on the opportunity to obtain financial independence, Chamberlain happily entertained conversations with representatives from the NBA after his junior year.

The rule prohibiting players from entering the NBA until the year their college cohorts graduated prohibited Chamberlain from suiting up with the Warriors until the 1959–1960 season. In the interim, the world-traveling Globetrotters contracted with Chamberlain, granting him the ultimate dream for players of color.

The Harlem Globetrotters was one of the most successful teams in the nation. Known not only for their clever ball-handling abilities but also their comedic antics, members of the Globetrotters were among the finest and most entertaining basketball players in the world. With them, Chamberlain pushed himself to develop many of the skills he soon employed to elevate the level of play in the NBA. The Globetrotters team was a national symbol for African Americans during a time when black players were just becoming a presence in the NBA. Before Chamberlain joined the ranks of celebrated black icons of sport like Jackie Robinson or lesser-known boxer Tom Molineaux, he dazzled fans and represented black America as a member of the Globetrotters. He felt comfortable with these men. Unencumbered by issues of race or different cultural approaches to the sport, he looked forward to the opportunity to travel the world in the company of friends who were also some of the most skilled players in the world. He frequently played with the Globetrotters in later summers. He looked forward to his time with them and enjoyed these experiences very much.

Chamberlain officially joined the NBA in 1959, playing for the Warriors. NBA owners struggled to increase revenues and fill seats at this time. Chamberlain was the highest paid player in the history of the sport, however, and his acquisition was expected to bring increased attention and patronage to both the Warriors and the league. Few properly estimated the impact Chamberlain would have, however. For example, as black athletes continued to integrate the sport, more black fans supported the league. During the 1960s, black audiences in urban cities like Philadelphia particularly enjoyed the sport. Chamberlain's participation undoubtedly influenced basketball's popularity in his community. Moreover, the increase in revenue and attention helped resuscitate the fledgling association.

Chamberlain made his professional debut in the NBA on October 24, 1959, in New York's Madison Square Garden, one of the most storied arenas in basketball. As at both Overbrook and Kansas, he quieted skeptics and affirmed fans with his powerful performance. Leading the Warriors to a 118-109 victory over the New York Knickerbockers, Chamberlain had officially arrived. He scored 43 points and secured 28 rebounds in that first game. He also made 9 of 15 free throws and successfully shot 27 from the field. He still holds the record for most field goals in a season with 1,597 made in the 1961–1962 season.

In his first season, Chamberlain led the league in scoring and rebounding, averaging 37.6 and 27 per game, respectively. Though players on opposing teams physically hammered him, he and the Warriors dominated the league. The team finished second in the league, winning 49 of 75 games. In the play-offs, the Warriors defeated the Syracuse Nationals, the team that had defeated them in the NBA semi-final the year before.

Chamberlain's first season was one of the most accomplished rookie seasons in the history of the NBA. He broke 8 records, averaging 37.6 points per game and scoring 2,707 points in total. He became one of only two players ever named Most Valuable Player and Rookie of the Year in the same season. He is also only one of two players from a losing team to be named the NBA finals MVP.

He fought against the league's other preeminent center, the Boston Celtics' Bill Russell, beginning in that first 1959–1960 season. Standing at only 6' 9" and weighing 220 pounds, Russell lacked the stature of Chamberlain. The two were dubbed "archenemies" by the media, which wondered aloud if Chamberlain would assert himself as the league's most dominant big man or if Russell would fortify his position as the best center in basketball.

The men first met in an anticipated fourth game against the Celtics at Boston. Critics and fans alike wondered if the Warriors could reach number one with the addition of Chamberlain. The personal competition between Chamberlain and Russell proved to be more riveting for the fans than the actual match of the teams. With his powerful shot-blocking, quick passing, and speed, Russell was credited with elevating the level of defensive play and often touted as one of the greatest defensive players of all time. Matches between the two athletes, both of whom attracted and electrified audiences with their innovative and stylish play, were marketing dreams for the league. Although the Celtics won their first game against the Warriors; Chamberlain scored 30 points to Russell's 22. Chamberlain's rookie season remains one of the most spectacular in the history of the sport.

Throughout his basketball career, Chamberlain made statistical achievements that remain unmatched. Statistically more dominant than any other player, Chamberlain averaged 30.1 points and 22.9 rebounds per game with the Warriors. During the 1961–1962 season, he averaged 50.4 points per game and played every minute of 79 of the team's 80 games. These successes did not protect him from criticism, however.

Chamberlain continued to outscore and statistically outperform Russell, though the Warriors conceded more victories to the Celtics. The media described Chamberlain as a selfish player who played too many minutes in each game out of concern for his individual stats and earning potential, while Russell was remembered, at least until his retirement, as a selfless team player who conceded personal advancement for the sake of the team. Well liked by the media, Russell's Celtics personified the championed David when juxtaposed against Chamberlain, the quintessential Goliath. Each time the Warriors lost, Chamberlain felt the wrath of fans. His reputation suffered when the Warriors lost to the Celtics in the 1964–1965 finals and the championship eluded him for the fourth time. Again he was blamed for the team's loss. Although he wanted to perform better, he was also tired of criticism from the media.

Chamberlain's nickname, in addition to unfair criticism, followed him through his career. The Stilt continued not only as a strongly disliked name but also as a symbolic representation of the ways that many perceived him. Some considered him animalistic, a sheer product of nature blessed with advantages he "unfairly" used to dominate. The name itself betrayed many of the attributes responsible for Chamberlain's ineffaceable basketball legacy. Contrary to the stoic and fragile image evoked by the nickname, he moved with what has been described as a dancer's grace. He perfected an effective fade-away jump shot and competed for the duration of nearly each of his team's games. Chamberlain also slam-dunked the basketball with such force that defenders feared that their wrists might be crushed under his weight. His physical movement dazzled spectators, attracted new fans, and strengthened the NBA as an organization. His style and effort increased the aesthetic value of the game and pushed play past simply scoring baskets. These contributions impacted the sport during a time when black players, in spite of insensitive practices such as animalistic nicknames and unspoken restrictions on numbers of them on each team, began to dominate the sport. In the process, NBA revenues soared.

Chamberlain played with the Philadelphia Warriors until 1964, even relocating with the team to San Francisco. The following season he returned to Philadelphia to play with the 76ers. Chamberlain won his second MVP during the 1964–1965 season and won the NBA championship in 1967. In 1968, after several successful seasons with the 76ers, Chamberlain was traded to the Los Angeles Lakers. Although the exact reason for the trade remains a mystery, during the Eastern Division finals, which the 76ers lost, Chamberlain said his coach told him not to shoot. Chamberlain only played 12 games in his second year with the Lakers after seriously injuring his knee. He returned the following season to won his second NBA championship in 1972. The 1972–1973 season would be Chamberlain's last.

Chamberlain's impressive but underacclaimed career remains shrouded in controversy. Though one of the most influential and individually accomplished players in the history of the sport, he often felt misunderstood and underrated. In addition, although standoffs between him and Russell were highly sensational and entertaining battles, the icon's place on the list of best players is heavily debated.

Chamberlain left many indelible marks on the game of basketball. He was the first player to score 100 points in a single game, for example. The Warriors faced the Philadelphia Eagles at Hershey Arena in Pennsylvania on Friday, March 2, 1962. In this unprecedented and untelevised event, Chamberlain broke precedent by scoring 100 points. Though uncelebrated at the time it occurred, that night stands as a testament to the capacity and might of an individual player and to the collective influence and supremacy of black athletes in the sport. After missing three shots, with 98 points in the final seconds of the fourth quarter, Chamberlain slam-dunked the basketball with 46 seconds remaining on the clock.

The 100-point game and Chamberlain's efforts in every game he played make him one of the most influential figures in the development and popularization of basketball. When he retired in 1973 after playing for the Los Angeles Lakers, he held records for scoring 31,419 points. He also held records in field goal percentage at 51.1 percent, 23,924 rebounds, and 4,643 assists. He was a four-time MVP, two-time NBA champion, NBA finals MVP, and Rookie of the Year. He never fouled out despite having played over 1,200 games. He also played more minutes than any other player in the league.

Chamberlain often reminded reporters, critics, and friends of his statistics, records, and accomplishments on the court. Though at times he intimated otherwise, he struggled as Goliath. He never received the acclaim of players such as Bill Russell and Kareem Abdul-Jabbar. He frequently questioned why the careers and performances of other players were never scrutinized as much as his or why critics failed to recall his numerous records.

Chamberlain flirted with other sports in his lifetime. After the Lakers lost the 1970–1971 NBA final to the Milwaukee Bucks, Chamberlain decided to fight championship boxer Muhammad Ali in Houston, Texas. Boxing was Chamberlain's father's favorite sport. The two shared a love for boxing, and many of the basketball star's heroes were boxing legends. The fight never took place, however, because of a purported financial misunderstanding with Chamberlain's contract. He also seriously considered playing professional football with the Kansas City Chiefs in 1966 and fell in love with the sport of volleyball during physical rehabilitation.

Chamberlain's success was not without difficulties. He complained that he was unable to live a normal life. Believing most people wanted to use him for his money, time, or endorsements, he publicly bemoaned being asked for autographs. He once said noted that the primary drawback to fame was that so many people expected so much from him. Additionally, he lamented having to live up to other people's expectations, and thus kept a close group of advisors and friends to help him avoid associating with people who might otherwise attempt to exploit him. His would often host the son of lifetime friends

Milton and Helen Kutsher. During the later years of his life, he spent time surrounded by a close-knit group of friends. Sy Goldberg and Chamberlain remained friends for decades. Over time, Goldberg acted as his attorney, business advisor, agent, and friend.

> *I believe that good things come to those who work.*

After retiring from the sport of basketball, Chamberlain found success in business, entertainment, becoming an author, and continuing to pioneer. He acted in the 1984 film *Conan the Destroyer*, authored several books, and once owned a Harlem nightclub Big Wilt's Small Paradise.

He attempted to protect his private life from the media, but he faced several instances of significant overexposure. He claimed in 1991 that he slept with 20,000 women. He later recanted the statement and said that his publishers wanted to use the line to generate interest in his second autobiography. Yet he was a brazen bachelor who loved the company of different women and was not afraid to say so. The widespread notoriety of these events contradicts personal accounts of his character offered by his family and friends. The truth likely lies between these differing perspectives. Chamberlain was a member of the Republican Party and supported Richard Nixon and Gerald Ford. Although he publicly questioned the need for all-black organizations like the NAACP, he was a member of Kappa Alpha Psi fraternity, an African American Greek letter organization, and worked throughout his lifetime to instigate social change. He supported the integration of women into professional sports by sponsoring the La Jolla Track Club. The club was renamed Wilt's Wonder Women and young girls ages 9 to 15 were coached, watched over, and encouraged by Chamberlain. Despite his reputation as a womanizer in his social life, he maintained a paternal relationship with the girls. Chamberlain also helped elevate the status of volleyball as a spectator sport and marketable form of entertainment. Becoming involved while rehabilitating an injured knee, he returned to the sport while living in Los Angeles and attracted legions of fans.

The success of Chamberlain, whose work took place alongside the burgeoning modern civil rights struggle, made possible the influx of young black athletes who would storm the gates of professional and collegiate sports programs alike. Although imperfect, Chamberlain's impact upon the sport of basketball and American society are unassailable.

## FURTHER READING

Chamberlain, Wilton Norman. *A View from Above*. New York: Random House, 1991.
Chamberlain, Wilton Norman. *Wilt: Just Like Any Other 7-foot Black Millionaire Who Lives Next Door*. New York: Macmillan, 1973.
Cherry, Robert. *Wilt: Larger than Life*. Chicago: Triumph Books, 2004.

AP Photo/Jessica Kourkounis.

# George Foreman

*Scott Bowman*

pride. Within the larger context of the 1968 Olympics, the critical issue of the individual success of any given African American athlete versus the systematic oppression of the majority of people of African descent was at the forefront of a great many minds. At question was the manner in which both white Americans and the larger global population understood the overall plight of African Americans. During this period, African Americans were experiencing disproportionate employment, arrest rates, income, homeownership (which would not include equal opportunity until some five years later), and education.

In 1968, Harry Edwards, Black Panther Party activist and sociology professor at San Jose State, was in Mexico City attempting to organize a protest by the prominent African American Olympic athletes. The protest was designed to shed light on the challenges facing African Americans in a post–civil rights era. While Foreman understood the overall message being conveyed, as well as genuinely considering participating in the boycott or some other form of protest, he felt that the protest would be contradictory to his personal success through the Job Corps. Edwards spearheaded an effort, bolstered by Tommie Smith (gold medalist in the 200-meter dash) and John Carlos (bronze medalist in the 200-meter dash), that contributed to one of the most influential protests in the history of the Olympic Games. Smith and Carlos, while high atop the medal stand, lowered their heads and each raised one black-gloved, clenched fist in the air. They were stripped of their medals and expelled from the Olympic grounds for their acts of resistance and symbolic gestures of black solidarity. Foreman responded to International Olympic Committee President Avery Brundage's repudiation of Smith and Carlos by stating that he would not fight. Nevertheless, Carlos allegedly encouraged Foreman to change his mind. This, according to Foreman, inspired him to continue fighting and eventually win the gold medal in the heavyweight division.

Under typical circumstances, Foreman's receipt of a gold medal, especially in light of the larger protests, would provide him a measure of status as an international advocate of progressive change that transcended sports. Ironically, a simple gesture in the ring diminished his ascendancy to iconic status. After he was victorious in the gold medal fight in the 1968 Olympics, the common motion by the winning boxer was to bow to the judges and spectators in each of the four directions. Prior to this act, he pulled a small flag from his robe pocket and waved it in the middle of the ring.

Under normal circumstances, an American athlete waving an American flag during the Olympics would not be improbable. However, an African American waving an American flag days after the political protests of Smith and Carlos was viewed by some members of the media and some members of the African American community as a counterdemonstration. On the one hand, Foreman's success brought forth supportive members of the dominant culture, such as Hubert Humphrey, Vince Lombardi, and even Lyndon B. Johnson. On the other hand, his return to Houston's Fifth Ward was not nearly as embracing. Foreman described visiting homes in his neighborhood that had giant posters of

Smith and Carlos, as well as interacting with Black Panther Party members that implied that he had "betrayed the cause." He felt that he was an outcast within his own community. For African Americans in the Fifth Ward, as well as other parts of Houston and the United States, Smith and Carlos had become the icons of the 1968 Olympics and the Black Power Movement, whereas Foreman's success had become an afterthought and he was viewed by many as a "sellout."

In 1969, George Foreman turned professional. In that year, he had a total of 13 fights, winning all of them, 11 by knockout. In the subsequent year, he had 12 fights, winning all of them by knockout. By 1972, he had amassed a record of 37-0, winning 34 by knockout, and did not fight past two rounds in any fight during that particular year. As a result of his efforts in the ring, he was designated the number one contender who was poised to fight the current heavyweight champion Joe Frazier. After avoiding a fight with Foreman for several months, Frazier eventually agreed to the title bout, which took place in Kingston, Jamaica, on January 22, 1973. With both fighters undefeated, Foreman scored a second-round knockout of Frazier, knocking him down a total of six times in two rounds and resulting in the infamous broadcast call by Howard Cosell, "down goes Frazier, down goes Frazier, down goes Frazier." For the second time in his relatively young life, George Foreman was a world champion. Most athletes, including many that are presented within this volume, would find iconic status simply from the accomplishments of being an amateur and professional champion; however, for Foreman, his quest for the accompanying symbolic notoriety would further elude him.

As was previously the case for Frazier as heavyweight champion, Foreman also found himself with the responsibility to face the number one challenger, Muhammad Ali. In 1967, Ali was stripped of both his championship belt and his ability to legally fight professionally in the United States, because his refused to be drafted into the Army. It took three and a half years for Ali to be reinstated. After fighting Oscar Bonavena in December 1970, Ali fought two fights against Frazier, being defeated by Frazier in 1971 (known popularly as the "fight of the century") and emerging victorious in their second fight in 1974. These fights made Ali the number one contender to fight Foreman in a title fight, known widely as the "Rumble in the Jungle."

Although Foreman was a heavy favorite (eight to one odds according to most odds makers), he was not supported by large numbers of people of African descent in America or Zaire. Although Foreman was the current heavyweight champion entering the fight, his star status was surpassed by Ali's. Ali was already an icon in 1974, as he was admired for his charisma, physical ability, and steadfast racial and political convictions. In Zaire, Foreman experienced the irony of simultaneously being the boxing heavyweight champion of the world, one of the most celebrated titles in the history of sports, while also being one of the most controversial individuals in the sport.

Many American fans, as well as African Americans, believed that the only reason that Foreman became the champion was due to Ali's controversial

*Let the other guy have whatever he wants before the fight. Once the bell rings he's gonna be disappointed anyway.*

three-and-half-year absence from the sport. Foreman achieved the pinnacle, yet at the same time was criticized for his achievements, particularly in the racially political context of the late 1960s and early 1970s, where athletes such as Carlos, Smith, and Ali were making personal and professional sacrifices in the name of their religious and political beliefs. Foreman's experiences were not much better in Zaire. He believed that Zaire was Ali's country, and most accounts of the fight and the time leading up to the fight suggest that Foreman's assessment was accurate. Whereas Ali was accessible to the Africans of Zaire and was respectful of the customs and traditions, Foreman was unobtainable and aloof. During the Rumble in the Jungle training period, citizens of Zaire greeted Foreman with chants of "Ali bomaye" ("Ali kill him") at every turn. Moreover, Foreman believed that the outcome of the fight would do little to change his status as heavyweight champion, believing he would get little respect for beating the legend and would be derided for losing. The latter of the two was Foreman's fate, as he lost to Ali in the eighth round by a strategy known infamously as the rope-a-dope. The loss furthered his fall from iconic status and plunging him into a self-described two-year depression that included womanizing, violence, and excessive spending (more than $400,000 in three months according to his brother). In 1976, after a one-year hiatus from boxing, he returned to fight four more fights, knocking out each opponent. One year later, he would fight Jimmy Young in Puerto Rico and lose a 12-round decision.

After the Young fight, Foreman claimed to be suffering from both exhaustion and heatstroke, believing that he was having a near-death experience. As a result, he believed that God was telling him to change his ways and his life, resulting in his retirement from boxing and a newfound dedication to Christianity. He subsequently became an ordained minister in Texas and inaugurated a youth center that still bears his name. Although these efforts are highly regarded, his work within Texas proved to be ordinary compared to his efforts in the ring. For most Americans, he was merely another heavyweight champion that disappeared into the obscurity often associated with retirement. Ironically, neither the iconic state of his boxing career nor the heights of his personal success would be reached for another 18 years.

Aside from Foreman's success as an ordained minister and community activist, he believed that he was coming into a clearer sense of self. This began his personal transformation toward a more widespread, iconic status that was rooted in a transformation of persona. As a young fighter, the persona that followed him was that of a cantankerous and often aloof individual. Upon his initial retirement, two major shifts of consciousness took place. First, he discovered a clearer sense of self that enabled him to make a more celebratory return to boxing. He recalled returning to the ring not because of the desire for relived fame or to exact his place in boxing history but merely to raise additional money for the George Foreman Youth and Community Center. In addition, he also believed that he could regain the heavyweight championship. Second, he embraced his ability to earn income and wealth from nonboxing methods. After retirement, the "angry George" was replaced by the "contented, beaming George," where his early trademark snarl was replaced by a trademark smile. The effects of this transformation were most noticeable in his ability to display charisma as a 37-year-old boxer, as well as his ability to obtain entrepreneurial endorsement opportunities as a spokesperson for various products and corporations.

In 1987, George Foreman announced that he would be attempting a comeback at the age of 38. Unlike many other fighters who attempted to return to the ring with unquestionably diminished physical characteristics or mental faculties, he displayed a newfound charisma and charm with which many sports fans and sports writers were unfamiliar.

Furthermore, he was seen as a refreshing change to a largely dull and uncompetitive heavyweight division. Nevertheless, when it came to the prospects of his success, the promoters, bankers, fight commissioners, and sports writers were not nearly as optimistic as Foreman. He was told that he was too old and a danger to himself based upon his age. Because he faced great difficulty finding investors and promoters to provide financial backing, he provided his own backing for many of his postretirement fights. In addition, he was initially denied a license to fight by the Nevada State Boxing commissioner's doctor, as he felt his age would play a potential role in seriously damaging Foreman's health. Eventually, he was granted his license, and his first fight was against Steve Zouski in Sacramento, California. What was most notable for this fight was that Foreman, who had spent nearly two decades fighting both the contenders and those attempting to malign his legacy, received a standing ovation. He believed it was an acknowledgment of an overshadowed legacy.

Beyond the Zouski fight, Foreman won four additional fights during 1987, nine in 1988, five in 1989, and five in 1990. During Foreman's initial four-year return to boxing, he amassed a record of 24-0, with the Everett Martin fight in Tucson, Arizona, the sole bout that was decided by neither a knockout nor a technical knockout. Although Foreman was more affable as a personality, sports writers continued to refer to the comeback as a joke.

Critics often questioned his age, his weight, his underlying intentions, and his worthiness of a title fight. Nonetheless, the bout between Foreman and Evander Holyfield, who was the current heavyweight champion (after beating Buster Douglas, who in turn had previously beat Mike Tyson) and was undoubtedly the most talented opponent of the era. In 1991, his fight with Holyfield, which went all 12 rounds, was the pinnacle of his return. Although Foreman did not win the fight, he showed that he was a worthy competitor that deserved the appropriate respect of a champion, the self-identified "people's champion," despite the rhetoric and negative characteristics by sports writers. Furthermore, he demonstrated that he was not only a draw based upon his athletic talent but was also a personally charismatic draw, as the Foreman–Holyfield fight was the highest grossing pay-per-view at that time. Foreman's self-reflection of "new George," particularly as an embraced icon, played a role in his decision to continue. After two additional fights, Foreman was given a second title shot against Tommy Morrison. Morrison defeated Foreman in another 12-round decision.

In a final attempt to regain the heavyweight championship, he inadvertently requested a title fight during the Evander Holyfield–Michael Moorer fight. Foreman attended a press conference with Holyfield in April 1994, one day before his title defense in a fight against Moorer. During the press conference, Holyfield was explaining that he intended to beat Moorer, beat Lennox Lewis (which would result in a unified heavyweight title), and fight Mike Tyson (who was considered the number one contender, yet was serving a prison term for rape). Fatefully, Holyfield did not get past the first step, as he lost to Moorer in a 12-round decision. Foreman, who was providing commentary for the fight, suggested that Moorer was unjustly given the title due to a flawed scoring system, and the exceeding control held by the primary promoters (Lou and Dan Duva). Bob Arum, another fight promoter, was speaking to Foreman shortly after the controversial commentary, and suggested that he sounded confident in his ability to defeat Moorer. Foreman concurred, and Arum arranged the fight.

The evening of the fight, Foreman recalled the large cheers and chanting of his name as he entered the ring, clearly juxtaposed to the boos and jeers received by Moorer. He reflected upon his fight with Muhammad Ali 20 years prior and the peculiar similarities and differences between the two fights. Similarly, he was the participant in a fight where the heavyweight champion was being booed and the challenger was being lauded. This time however, Foreman was the likable, iconic, celebrated fighter in the ring and Moorer was the denigrate champion. Win or lose, Foreman had achieved success in the court of public opinion, where he was viewed as an icon—not only as a boxer—but also as an individual that was successful beyond his age, his early plight of poverty, his initially rugged exterior, and his struggles for acceptance from the African American community.

By all accounts, Moorer was in complete control of the fight—until Foreman landed a devastating punch that sent him to the canvas and eventually ended the fight in a tenth-round knockout. Forty-five-year-old George Foreman defeated Moorer, resulting in Foreman being the oldest person to ever hold the heavyweight title and having the most time elapse between two heavyweight championships.

Despite the fact that he would eventually be stripped of his heavyweight titles for refusing to fight a specific contender, the iconization of Foreman as a heavyweight fighter had culminated. He had become an icon for the complete transformation of self, through both the physical ability to defy his own age in the ring and the psychological ability to discover a personal charisma that people would embrace. For the individual that had overcome poverty, a criminal past, limited education, and the challenging views of much of the larger African American community, this was the personal and professional vindication that deepens iconic status. Furthermore, unlike many other African Americans that have achieved iconic status, Foreman's boxing success came much later in life. However, the achievement that would solidify his iconic status would take place years after regaining the heavyweight title, yet have nothing directly to do with boxing.

As a boxer, Foreman made an exceptional living from the purses that were generated through his fights. With a record of 76 wins and 5 losses, as well as payouts that ranged in the tens of thousands to multiple millions, he was undoubtedly a financial earnings success. Furthermore, one rudimentary indicator of iconization is the ability to become a spokesperson—particularly for African American males. Fighters of the era such as Muhammad Ali and Sugar Ray Leonard were able to take successful and charismatic careers within the ring and transform them into lucrative product endorsement careers outside the ring. Similarly for Foreman, a likable, product-endorsing icon was constructed.

Meineke has been one of Foreman's longest and most consistent endorsement partnerships. In addition to this contract, Foreman had product endorsement deals with Salton, Thompson's, McDonalds, and KFC. Of these, Salton provided Foreman with the single greatest amount of nonboxing income and wealth. Salton is the parent company that is responsible for the creation and marketing of the George Foreman Lean Mean Grilling Machine. Foreman believes he is now better known for his grilling machines than for his boxing career.

His original deal with Salton provided Foreman and two other associates 60 percent from the grill sales (with Foreman controlling 40 percent), which represented 38 percent of Salton's $500 million in total sales. It was believed that during this period, Foreman secured more than $150 million from the sales of these grills—which included an estimated monthly compensation of $4.5 million during the height of their success. These earnings drastically outweigh the amount earned by Foreman in the ring as well as succeeding contracts offered by Salton and additional endorsement deals from other companies. In 1999, Salton bought the rights from Foreman to maintain usage of his name and selling skills for $127.5 million in cash and $10 million in stock, still representing one of the largest endorsement deals for any athlete. In addition to these monies, estimates suggest that Foreman's total product endorsing lifetime earnings are about $240 million. Finally, he has established additional entrepreneurial activities, including several motivational books, children's books, cookbooks, and biographical books, as well as a brand of big and tall clothes and motivational speaking engagements.

Having sold over 55 million grills with one's name and likeness will unmistakably establish some measure of general notoriety; however, it does not guarantee becoming an icon. In the process of becoming an icon, one must be recognized as a successful, likable African American athlete, yet also have the ability to transcend his or her race. In other words, an African American athlete reaching iconic status must, as the notable scholar W. E. B. Du Bois suggests, create a double-consciousness for themselves. On the one hand, the African American athlete must attempt to create a likable yet real persona for the dominant culture's acceptance of their iconic potential. On the other hand, they must also attempt to create real relationships between themselves and the larger African American community. Those athletes that demonstrate the greatest ability to appeal to both the dominant culture and the specific culture to which they belong will often gain the greatest praise, receive the greatest admiration, and receive the greatest compensation. For George Foreman, a long and arduous journey has led him to this status. The result for Foreman is an Olympic gold medalist, a two-time heavyweight champion, a boxing Hall-of-Famer, a financially successful businessman, an ordained minister, a motivational speaker, a father, a husband . . . an icon.

## FURTHER READING

Du Bois, W. E. B. *The Souls of Black Folk*. New York: Knopf, 1903.

Foreman, George, and Engel, Joel. *By George: The Autobiography of George Foreman*. New York: Villard Books, 1995.

George Foreman Web site, http://www.georgeforeman.com (accessed September 2006).

Mailer, Norman. *The Fight*. New York: Vintage, 1997.

McCoyd, Ed. *To Live and Dream: The Incredible Story of George Foreman*. New York: New Street Publishing, 1997.

Photofest.

# Althea Gibson

*Shawn Ladda*

A talented athlete and breaker of color barriers in tennis and golf, Althea Gibson was the first African American, male or female, to win a Grand Slam tennis event. She was the first African American to win the French Open, Wimbledon, and the U.S. Open and the first to qualify for the Ladies Professional Golf Association (LPGA).

Gibson was a gifted athlete and an individual who wanted to be seen as such rather than be judged by gender or race. Her life was filled with injustice, with Jim Crow circling her life with oppression and discrimination, but Gibson always plotted ahead.

Gibson faced the embarrassment of entering a tournament, only to learn that it was cancelled because she, an African American, was scheduled to play. She was forced to sit in the back of the bus, only permitted to use certain water fountains, excluded from lunch counters, banned from bowling alleys, restricted from locker rooms and forced to change instead in a car, not allowed a reservation at a hotel that was hosting a luncheon in her honor, and shut out of numerous tournaments. These events, and the anger and frustration they fostered, took an emotional toll on Gibson throughout her life. Fortunately, she was highly independent, strong-willed, full of survivor instincts, and a proud person. She became a champion of tennis and a professional golfer through her own determination and perseverance.

Gibson was born on August 25, 1927, in Silver, South Carolina, in a four-room cabin with the assistance of her great-aunt Mattie Davis. The family housed here included parents Annie and Daniel Gibson, paternal grandparents Junius and Lou Gibson, and five other children from her parents' previous marriages.

The town of Silver was already feeling the effects of at least three years of bad weather and limited output of crops by the time the stock market crashed in October 1929. The Gibson family made a living as sharecroppers, so the financial pressures of the time made uprooting a necessity. When Althea's aunt Sally Washington came down South from New York City for a funeral, Althea's parents decided to send their daughter to New York with Sally. It was not uncommon for families during the Depression to send loved ones to relatives that had the means to support each other. They planned to follow shortly after Althea. Daniel intended to find employment and a better financial life for the family in New York City.

While living in Harlem, Althea was known to be a rebellious youngster. She later gave the Police Athletic League Play-Street Program credit for directing her energies in a productive manner. Known in her own words as a "traveling girl" because of her energy and hard-to-sit-still nature, she enjoyed adventure. She played hooky and saw school as a place to make plans with her friends rather than learn.

Althea never enjoyed formal schooling. She attended Public School 136 for elementary school and after junior high attended the Yorkville Trade School, though she tired quickly of repairing sewing machines. Truancy officers frequently hunted her down, and she often received a scolding and beating from her father for her school absences. She was known to go to the local police precinct to ask for protection against her father when she had missed school for extended periods of time, and she spent some nights at the Society for the Prevention of Cruelty to Children. At times she would promise to stay out of trouble but soon would be back in it.

Even so, Althea described her childhood as joyful. Growing up in the Depression, she was oblivious to her family's financial challenges until she got older and realized the struggles her parents had endured. Annie and Daniel were tireless workers, always making sure that the immediate and extended family was fed. Early on in her childhood, Althea showed herself as a tough athlete. Her father Daniel, or "Dush," taught her how to box when she was young. Boxing was very popular at the time, and Dush hoped Althea might gain boxing fame. She didn't pursue this sport, but boxing definitely helped her deal with the tough neighborhood in which she lived. She defended friends and family members with her ability to fight and win.

In addition to her athletic pursuits, Althea greatly enjoyed the arts. She always enjoyed going to the movies and listening to music. Her mother enjoyed playing the piano, and Gibson loved to sing. In 1943, she won second prize in an amateur talent show demonstrating her singing ability at the Apollo Theater. Years later she stated, "I was never without a melody on my lips," and later in life she even pursued a professional singing career.

Throughout her childhood, Gibson greatly enjoyed athletics. She played paddleball with her brother within the Police Athletic League. In fact, she was the New York City paddleball champion of the Police Athletic League from 1938 to 1942. As is indicative of her life, she concerned herself with her athletic talent and playing hard and being the best she could. She wasn't concerned with who was watching her. Because of this extraordinary athletic ability, multiple individuals noticed her and wanted her (with her complete motivation) to have a chance to explore this talent. One person was Buddy Walker, a leader in the league, who supported her talents with the purchase of a few used $5 tennis rackets for her and asked her to play some of his friends. Althea was thrilled with the new challenge of tennis. She was exposed to paddleball and developed skills that would catapult her tennis development.

As Althea played at the Harlem Tennis Courts at 150th Street, with basically no tennis experience, she impressed Walker's friends as well as people who walked by the courts. One of the people impressed was a schoolteacher and a member of the famed Harlem Cosmopolitan Tennis Club, Juan Serreals, who in turn introduced Gibson to Fred Johnson, who was the amazing one-armed professional at the club, considered to be one of the best tennis coaches in the city. Johnson frequently played in singles tournaments within the American Tennis Association (ATA), an organization that sought to increase the number of African American tennis players. He was a solid player who possessed a fine coaching ability. After recognizing Althea's potential, he approached the Gibson family to offer his services to coach her. At this point she was a talented and motivated athlete who was determined to go places. But in order to do this she recognized that quality coaching and access to facilities was necessary, and thus Johnson would help her.

Althea's association with Johnson allowed her great exposure to tennis facilities and players for practice and play. Much of her tennis practice occurred at the Cosmopolitan Club, a high-class club for Harlem socialites. Johnson served as her connection to the organization as he was the club professional. He strove to teach her tennis but also wanted to give her life advice, though she was not too receptive to this aid. While she worked on her tennis game at the club, Althea continued to struggle to attend high school. She eventually dropped out.

Johnson also exposed Gibson to her first female tennis players. Rhoda Smith, for example, was considered to be a solid player. She was the first woman Althea played tennis with; her previous opponents were all men. Smith, a prominent socialite, was polished in tennis and social etiquette. She soon realized Althea's deficiencies in these areas. Gibson was a bit rough around the edges when it came to controlling her temper and minding manners on the court. Her street experience taught her to solve frustration and conflict physically rather than through communication and negotiation. Gibson first observed tennis champion Alice Marble at the club while the latter woman played a tennis exhibition. Marble was the first female player after whom Gibson wished to model her tennis skills.

Gibson entered her first tennis tournament, the New York State Open Championship, in 1942 and won the girl's singles title. No championship was held in 1943, but she won the same title in the 1944 and 1945 tournaments. Through Gibson's association with the Cosmopolitan Club, where members were from the highest class of Harlem, she was afforded connections with individuals that could help open doors for more opportunities. Again though, without her talent, none of these doors would have opened at all. A friend introduced her to boxer Sugar Ray Robinson and his wife, Edna Mae. Gibson befriended Edna Mae. She was introduced to their more lavish lifestyle, and sometimes she visited them at Joe Louis's training camp at Greenwood Lake, New York. The Robinsons also supported Althea in her tennis and music pursuits. They purchased a used saxophone for her and often subsidized travel expenses for her tennis tournaments.

In 1946, Gibson lost in the finals at the ATA national girl's championship. She nevertheless impressed two physicians, Dr. Hubert Eaton and Dr. Robert W. Johnson, who were interested in supporting and promoting promising young African American tennis players. Gibson accepted their invitation to go to Wilmington, North Carolina, to live with the Eaton family and attend high school. Without her demonstration of ability and determinedness, she would not have been noticed. She had never met the two doctors, but through her talent she once again put herself in a place to be noticed. During the summer she lived in Lynchburg, Virginia, with Dr. Johnson.

Gibson learned to like Williston Industrial High School in Wilmington, as she was elected captain of girl's basketball team and played the saxophone in the school band. Even so, returning to school was a difficult adjustment for her. She was accustomed to the streets of New York and didn't always comply with the Eaton family rules. From 1947 to 1956, she won 10 straight ATA national championships. Johnson's son and Althea won the mixed doubles tournament in all but one year from 1948 to 1955. Johnson considered her a hard but stubborn worker.

Eaton and Johnson dreamed of breaking the color line at Forest Hills and the U.S. Lawn Tennis Association (USLTA). In contrast, Gibson had no intention of being political. In fact, she argued that her athleticism and her race were unrelated. She wanted to be a tennis champion, not a politician. Prior to the late 1940s, African Americans could only participate in the ATA, while the USLTA was exclusively for white players. Gibson was on track to be the trailblazer who broke this barrier. In 1949, Althea was told that if she applied for the USLTA's Eastern Indoor Tournament, her application would be accepted. This was her moment to break the color barrier between the ATA and integrate the USLTA. She lost in the quarterfinals of the USLTA tournament but felt she had played well.

After the tournament, Gibson completed high school, graduating tenth in her class at the age of 21. She soon accepted a basketball scholarship to Florida A&M and also played on the university's golf and tennis teams. The university did not provide tennis scholarships at the time, so the admissions director offered her a basketball scholarship so that she could play multiple sports, including one that would finance her college education. Gibson excelled in tennis, but there were limited opportunities for blacks to earn college scholarships. She learned to embrace education and accepted the idea that getting a college education and tennis exposure was going to allow more options. Gibson was faced with a Tallahassee at this time that did not allow blacks to try on hats and shoes in downtown stores and no public restroom facilities existed for them. Yet she focused her attention on education and her athleticism rather than worrying about the treatment of blacks in Tallahasee.

Gibson did well in college. She majored in physical education, and many of her professors put her in leadership positions. She also was selected to lead a student disciplinary group, which was very ironic given her history of making her own rules. Often times rules were slightly bent for her at college. She was caught coming in later than curfew, smoking cigarettes, and playing pool in the men's dormitory, but the school did not supply consequences for her behavior. Perhaps officials allowed her to escape punishment because she was a few years older than other students and possessed a tough, independent nature. Fellow students described her as somewhat of a loner, possibly because of her strong focus on her athletic endeavors.

Gibson was again invited to participate in the 1950 USLTA Eastern Indoor Tournament. This time she reached the finals but lost. It appeared finally that she would get the big invitation to Forest Hills and the U.S. Open, but for some reason no invitation was arriving.

The only previous association between Alice Marble and Althea Gibson occurred years earlier when the latter observed Marble play in a tennis exhibition match. Marble had never met Gibson, but when she realized that the tournament had excluded the black player, she investigated. She soon wrote a letter critical of the USLTA's treatment of Gibson. She had learned that the powers that be, the 48-member USLTA committee, especially the Southern contingent, wanted Gibson to continue to prove her prowess in invitational tournaments. She was trapped, since she was not invited to these tournaments and consequently had no opportunity to prove her ability. Marble explained in the *American Lawn Tennis Magazine* that it was unfair for Gibson to be excluded solely on the color of her skin. Instead, the established player argued that Gibson should be judged on her tennis ability like any other player. Marble believed all players who have proved their talents deserved an opportunity. Marble's activism led to an invitation to Gibson to play in the clay court championship in Chicago. Gibson played but lost in the quarterfinals. A swirl of mixed invitations now came her way.

Some suggest that Gibson's ability to break the color barrier in tennis and her participation in the U.S. Open are even greater achievements than Jackie Robinson's advancements against segregation in baseball. Before Gibson, no African American man or woman was allowed to play in a national championship of tennis. In addition, tennis was associated with a higher socioeconomic level than baseball, so her accomplishment transcended racialized class barriers as well. The intention of this last comment is meant to place her accomplishments in perspective and on a high level in terms of not only breaking gender and color barriers but also class. In historical accounts of Gibson's life, it has been noted that she was thrust into a war simply because of race, growing up in Harlem, and her motivation to win, and this put her in contradiction with the lily-white tennis community.

Gibson made history on Monday, August 28, 1950, as the first African American in the USLTA national championships. Her match was assigned an obscure court and photographers took great liberty in flashing photos of her. Regardless, she prevailed against these setbacks, beating Barbara Knapp of England 6-2, 6-2 in her debut match. She lost the next round in dramatic fashion to Louise Brough, the defending champion of Wimbledon, 1-6, 6-3, 7-9. This match was delayed in the final set due to a thunderstorm. During the delay, the press swarmed Gibson, rattling her and ultimately preventing her from closing the match with a win.

After the loss, Gibson returned to college. From school she wrote a heartfelt letter to Marble, thanking her for her support. Evidently Marble received criticism from varying sources for her support of Gibson. Yet she demonstrated humanism and true "sportspersonship" by taking a stand with the USLTA and refusing to allow Gibson to be excluded from the national championship.

Gibson's next major accomplishment was to play at Wimbledon. Her participation there was financed through many fundraising efforts and donations. Her debut at Wimbledon was on center court, where she won her match 6-0, 2-6, 6-4.

Gibson's 1951 performance ranked her ninth in the United States. She graduated from Florida A&M in 1953 and accepted a position at Lincoln University in Jefferson City, Missouri, to teach physical education. With her teaching responsibilities, she was unable to keep up a competitive tennis playing schedule. Her ranking slowly slipped.

Nonetheless, Gibson reached a turning point in 1955. The U.S. State Department honored her with an invitation to represent the United States with Ham Richardson, Bob Perry, and Karol Fageros in a Goodwill Tennis Tour of Southeast Asia. National race relations were strained at this time, so the impetus to organize such a tour was to foster goodwill for the United States across the globe. The tour provided Gibson an opportunity to play competitively and gain some of her previous tennis form. In addition, the travel exposure, opportunities to meet different people, and belonging to an important group gave her exposure to hone some of her public relations skills. Upon returning from the international tour, Gibson continued the tour herself by traveling across the United States to play tennis exhibitions. The experience was fulfilling but stressful, as she felt great pressure to represent African Americans in a favorable way. She worried that any misbehavior or mistakes on her part would lead white people to think poorly of all African Americans.

Gibson did represent African Americans well and continued to break racial barriers. Her first Grand Slam victory occurred at the French Open in 1957, which made her the first African American man or woman to accomplish such a feat. In addition, Gibson teamed up with Angela Buxton to with the doubles championship. It was an interesting partnership between Gibson and Buxton, which lasted to the end of Gibson's life. Buxton was Jewish and Gibson an African American, both outsiders of the white establishment and both with a pervasive determination to succeed.

That same year, Gibson beat Darlene Hard at Wimbledon and Louise Brough at the U.S. Open. New York City held a ticker tape parade in her honor to celebrate these successes. *Time* magazine printed her picture on its cover. She was also named the Associated Press Woman Athlete of the Year 1957–1958 and received the Babe Didrickson Zaharias trophy.

Gibson's success continued. She won her second consecutive Wimbledon and U.S. championships in 1958 by beating Angela Mortimer and Darlene Hard, respectively. She then shocked the sports world, however, by announcing a one-year retirement from tennis. One of the main reasons she decided to step away from tennis was financial. Though her successes brought her honors such as consecutive AP Female Athlete of the Year awards, the dearth of monetary compensation left her barely able to make ends meet. She lived through poverty as a child and was hopeful that her adult life would be more financially stable. She noted many years later that this decision was hasty, since she had not figured out what to do after tennis. She later thought that a smarter idea would have been to wait until she landed a lucrative contract before making such a decision. Outside of tennis, Althea had three main goals, which

*I always wanted to be some-body. If I made it, it's half because I was game enough to take a lot of punishment along the way and half because there were a lot of people who cared enough to help me.*

relied on her financial success. She wanted to buy a new home for her family, secure a place for herself, and establish the Althea Gibson Academy to help young people.

Before deciding to temporarily retire from tennis, Gibson also faced other difficult decisions. Within tennis, she pondered whether to remain an amateur or turn professional. She also thought about pursuing singing and acting. Throughout her childhood, she always loved the movies and enjoyed singing and playing the saxophone. She had hired vocal coach James Scott Kennedy, a Long Island University professor, to help her with her voice in 1957. She sang publicly that same year at the Waldorf-Astoria Hotel in New York at a tribute to W. C. Handy, a blues legend. She was spotted by Dot Records and signed a deal that resulted in the release of an album. She was a guest on *The Ed Sullivan Show* on May 25 and July 13, 1957. These appearances were timely with the release of her album, titled *Althea Gibson Sings*, and with her win at Wimbledon. The album turned out to be a flop. When Gibson was sent the original contract from Dot Records it was for a year, but under her lawyer's advice she initialed a six-month contract. At the end of six months with poor record sales, Dot Records released her. The album's failure disappointed Althea, but she had other opportunities developing.

Gibson next entered Hollywood. She landed a role as a Southern maid in the movie *The Horse Soldiers*, starring John Wayne and William Holden. The movie was set during the Civil War and only offered her a stereotypical role. While she agreed to wear the costume, complete with a handkerchief on her head, she refused to speak some of the dialogue because she thought it demeaned black women. With the release of her album and her role in a Hollywood movie, she hoped to find other opportunities in the movies and music. Unfortunately, no other offers came. Gibson released the first of her two autobiographies, titled *I Always Wanted to Be Somebody*, in 1958.

Gibson continued to participate in athletics despite her retirement. She provided sports commentatorship, appeared in television advertisements, and endorsed products. Her three favorite topic areas for interviews and lectures were education, sports, and fitness. She received a contract to endorse Tip Top Bread from the Ward Baking Company. She was also in advertisements with Fageros to promote "The Bat" tennis racket, which was manufactured by Harry C. Lee. She also was a sports correspondent for the *London Evening Standard*. Though she came out of retirement from tennis in 1959 to participate in a goodwill tour of Latin America and the Caribbean, she did not defend her U.S. Open or Wimbledon titles.

Gibson continued to grapple with her decision about turning professional. She could remain an amateur tennis player, but the lack of financial rewards offered to amateurs limited this option. She also realized that turning professional perhaps wasn't possible with the color barriers that still existed. Country clubs might hesitate to hire an African American woman, since her presence might anger white clientele.

Controversy surrounded Gibson in 1959 when she did not respond to a racist incident in a manner that met the African American community's expectations. Ralph J. Bunche, an African American Nobel laureate and the undersecretary for Special Political Affairs at the United Nations, was refused membership at the West Side Tennis Club at Forest Hills. Gibson responded to the situation by stating that she would still play and watch matches at Forest Hills. She also said that she had no desire to gain membership herself. Her African American supporters were outraged that she didn't condemn the club's treatment of Bunche. Her comments were consistent with her politics, however. Throughout her career, she distanced herself from race. She wanted to be judged as a great tennis player rather than as an African American player or a female one.

Many fighting against racism wanted Gibson to use her competitive and stubborn nature to also join the cause directly. They wanted to see her embrace an activism role like Rosa Parks or Martin Luther King Jr.

Gibson also faced controversy about her status as an amateur player. While participating on the Pan Am Games U.S. tennis team, a team of amateurs, Gibson spoke out about becoming a professional, which complicated her amateur status. The controversy subsided a month later when she signed a professional contract with Abe Saperstein, promoter of the Harlem Globetrotters. Gibson was paid $100,000, far more than the $30,000 paid to Karol Fageros, the second highest paid female in tennis.

As a professional tennis player, Gibson joined the Globetrotters tour from November 17, 1959, to its end in April 1960. She and Fageros played exhibition matches either before the basketball game or during half time. Both women had an entertaining spirit; Fageros, who was perceived to have a model figure, wore underwear that were gold and flashy. Following the success of the tour, Saperstein offered an extension to both players to participate in a foreign tour. The women turned him down, figuring they could eliminate the middleman and make more money themselves. They underestimated the power of the name of the Globetrotters, however, and the actual overall risks of playing without a contract. Overnight they were broke.

The Globetrotters experience, however, was one that Gibson saw in some ways as a relief. She considered herself fortunate to have the opportunity to work with other black people, because she did not have to keep herself so guarded among them. Like many other black people, Gibson wore a mask with white people; she could remove this mask when she played with the Globetrotters.

Gibson responded to the Globetrotters' financial difficulties by turning her sights on her golf game and becoming a member of the LPGA. She believed golf would allow her to continue to work as an athlete and thought it was a good

*In sports, you simply aren't considered a real champion until you have defended your title successfully. Winning it once can be a fluke; winning it twice proves you are the best.*

challenge for her. Though she only learned the sport in college, it took her only three years to qualify. She became the first African American member of the LPGA. During her first six years on the tour, she played every tournament and often traveled across the United States by driving to keep her expenses down. Her highest golf earnings were $5,567, which she earned in 1966. Her accomplishments in tennis far exceeded those in golf, but she definitely contributed to the sport of golf by breaking color barriers and serving as a role model for women. She also helped integrate numerous courses. Her LPGA performance spanned 171 tournaments with her lifetime golf earnings reaching about $25,000. Her highest ranking was twenty-seventh in 1966 and her last year of competition was 1977. Her best showing at a tournament was a tie for second place at the 1970 Immke Buick Open. This tie was an amazing feat, given that she started playing the game as an adult.

Gibson returned to her earlier passions when she reached her forties. She wrote her second autobiography, titled *So Much to Live For*, in 1968. She also began playing tennis again during the same years that she played with the LPGA. She decided to give tennis one more try to see if she could become a champion again. The sport of tennis finally allowed amateurs and professionals to play together in 1968. Tennis matches offered prize money, which meant that it now provided more opportunities to earn money than golf. Billie Jean King, who described her relationship with Gibson as one of the most important friendships of her life, organized the Oakland Pro Invitational in February 1969 and invited Gibson. Though Gibson was older, she remained competitive. She continued to play in tournaments, including mixed doubles with Arthur Ashe at the 1973 U.S. Open. She also played Chris Evert in the S & H Classic in Fort Lauderdale, Florida, losing 6-1, 6-2.

The reality was that Althea had aged and was unable to regain her ranking. This was another disappointment that was compounded by her inability to make money through tennis or other endeavors. She attributed these financial difficulties, to a certain degree, on the impact of gender and color in sports. In other words, she identified herself as a tennis player and had others done the same, she would have experienced a more lucrative life. Rather she was seen as a black female tennis player who was consistently marginalized and unable to reap the benefits as her male counterpart. In addition, she often said she was born too early. Race limited endorsements and other opportunities to earn money, but she continued to use her athletic talents. In her sixties, Gibson attempted to become the oldest active member of the LPGA.

Through her retirement from both tennis and golf, Gibson provided public service to others. She sounded the message of the importance of education and sports to schoolchildren. A resident of New Jersey, she served as director of the Essex County Park Commission in her state. She also oversaw Pepsi-Cola's national mobile tennis project, which provided traveling tennis equipment to inner cities. In addition, she served the New Jersey Governor's Council on Physical Fitness and Sports. Unfortunately, she was terminated from this position in 1992 due to fiscal cuts. This loss was yet another disappointment, but with her strong will Gibson continued forward. She spent her last years living quietly, requesting few visitors. She died on September 28, 2003, of complications following respiratory and bladder infections.

Without a doubt, Gibson dealt with issues of race, gender, and class as she strove to be a successful athlete. She shied away from recognizing her identity as a force that affected her experience in sports, however. Althea wanted to always be seen as a great tennis player, rather than as a female tennis player, a mannish female tennis player, an African American tennis player, or a working-class tennis player. She was proud and wanted to earn respect from being judged on her talent and not on her identity. Perhaps today she receives less notoriety because much of the media focus has been on gender and race as compared to her true athletic talent alone. In other words, Gibson wanted to be seen as a great athlete, without being identified as a black female athlete. The media continues to marginalize female athletic talent, more so than gender or race. Our society is threatened by strong athletic women more so than gender and race, thus the media reflect this attitude.

Growing up in a lower-socioeconomic level household had a tremendous effect on Gibson's life. She struggled with financial stability until her last days. She complained that she was born too early, since tennis did not become a lucrative sport for players until she was past her athletic prime. Throughout her life she faced numerous financial setbacks, but she always persevered through these times. She also contributed to causes important to her, despite her financial difficulties. The New Jersey Performing Arts Center, for example, stands on a property she purchased for such a purpose.

Gibson also battled formal education during her childhood, adolescence, and early adulthood. She missed many days of school and struggled to continue her education. She dropped out of high school and only found a niche when she reentered school at Williston Industrial High School. That Gibson graduated tenth in her class and then graduated from Florida A&M with such little academic preparation is quite an accomplishment. Upon graduation, she accepted a college teaching position at Lincoln University. These struggles helped her value and treasure her education.

Althea won her first Grand Slam event in 1956, but no other African American followed in her footsteps until Arthur Ashe won a Grand Slam event 12 years later. The third African American to win a Grand Slam was Serena Williams at the U.S. Open in 1999. Althea's back-to-back Wimbledon titles would not be repeated until Venus Williams did so in 2000 and 2001. Gibson's success in tennis is remarkable in part because so few African Americans have followed in her footsteps in the last five decades.

Gibson's awards are numerous. She was inducted into the Lawn Tennis Hall of Fame, Black Athletes Hall of Fame, Florida Sports Hall of Fame, New Jersey Sports Writers Hall of Fame, International Scholar-Athlete Hall of Fame,

International Women's Hall of Fame, and was one of the first six inductees in the International Tennis Hall of Fame. She received eight honorary degrees. Gibson also received the National Collegiate Athletic Association's highest award, the Theodore Roosevelt Award, in 1991. She was the first woman to receive this award from the NCAA. Florida A&M University named Althea Gibson, class of 1953, the athlete of the century. She was also named one of the top 100 greatest female athletes by *Sports Illustrated*. Tennis courts were named after her at Manning High School near her hometown of Silver, South Carolina, at the Family Circle Tennis Center in Charleston, South Carolina, at Florida A&M, and at the Branch Brook Park in Newark, New Jersey.

Her legacy is strong. It includes a foundation to provide opportunities for youth to transform their lives through sports. She broke color barriers and gave others opportunities. She was a proud woman who lived with quiet dignity. She didn't want people to see her as an aged woman but rather as a strong athlete, so she secluded herself in her last days so that few could see her grow old.

She valued the importance of education, trying hard, and the arts. Her accomplishments allowed her to fundamentally change two sports and consequently offer new opportunities to those who followed her.

## FURTHER READING

Biracree, Tom. *Althea Gibson*. New York: Chelsea House Publishers, 1989.

Davidson, Sue. *Changing the Game: The Stories of Tennis Champions Alice Marble and Althea Gibson*. Seattle: Seal Press, 1997.

Festle, Mary Jo. *Playing Nice: Politics and Apologies in Women's Sports*. New York: Columbia University Press, 1996.

Gibson, Althea, and Ed Fitzgerald. *I Always Wanted to Be Somebody*. New York: Harper & Brothers, 1958.

Gibson, Althea, and Richard Curtis. *So Much to Live For*. New York: G. P. Putnam's Sons, 1968.

Gray, Frances Clayton, and Yanick Rice Lamb. *Born to Win: The Authorized Biography of Althea Gibson*. Hoboken, NJ: John Wiley & Sons, 2004.

Lansbury, Jennifer H. "The Tuskegee Flash and the Slender Harlem Stroker: Black Women Athletes on the Margin," *Journal of Sport History* 28:2 (Summer 2001): 233–252.

Schoenfeld, Bruce. *The Match: Althea Gibson and Angela Buxton*. New York: Harper-Collins Publishers, Inc., 2004.

Photofest.

# The Harlem Globetrotters

*Brian S. Collier*

As a collective, the Harlem Globetrotters are the soul and wit of world basket-ball. The organization is more than a team; it is a spirit that permeated sport, entertainment, and eventually race to become a humanitarian force that goes on to become goodwill ambassadors to the world. At a modern Globetrotters game, audiences are awed by the showmanship, basketball talent, and hilari-ous on-court antics and jokes the team uses as part of the evening. The team developed as a truly American art form. The players and the team took bits and pieces from all sorts of Americana, including other all-black basketball teams to become a sensation that travels the United States and the world using bas-ketball and humor to entertain and spread goodwill.

Sports in the early part of the twentieth century served as a vehicle for assimilation to Americanism and American ideals. Even settlement houses like Jane Addams's Hull House fielded immigrant sporting teams. To this end, neighborhood club sports took on an extremely local flavor with team names that carried some sort of local identifier. Team names like the Hebrews, Ter-rible Swedes, and Celtics were common in the 1920s for club sports teams. No sport had greater club roots in the 1920s, however, than the fledgling sport of basketball.

Basketball's very creation is rooted in local club tradition. As an employee of a Christian Club, James Naismith's job over a 14-day period was to invent a game that allowed students from a club to gain physical exercise without hav-ing to go outdoors during the cold winters of Springfield, Massachusetts. The game of "basket ball" was a quick sensation throughout cold climates around the country.

In the early part of the twentieth century, local ethnic club teams played low-scoring matches in nearly every imaginable indoor venue throughout the United States. Some local teams played in dance halls as a means to get crowds in the doors as an exhibition before the evening's dancing began. According to team lore and three quarters of a century of propaganda, the Savoy, a dance hall, was where the first game by the players who became the professional Harlem Glo-betrotters played. The team's relationship to the Savoy dance hall in January 1927 is questionable. The Savoy story, perpetuated in encyclopedias and films, is not possibly true because the Savoy Ballroom was not even in operation in January 1927, when the Globetrotters allegedly played there as the Savoy Big Five. Indeed, the Big Five did play basketball at the Savoy, but not until later in 1927.

The members of the Savoy Big Five originally hailed from Chicago. The team's three core members were former Wendell Phillips High School basketball standouts from that school's heavyweight basketball division. In the 1920s, basketball was broken into weight classes so smaller players would have a chance at success without having to play against much larger players. The core players from Wendell Phillips were Tommy Brookins, Randolph Ramsey, and Toots Wright. They played with other teams and clubs throughout the

South Side of Chicago and also possibly with the Giles Post American Legion tour of Wisconsin, where they were promoted as former college players.

The Savoy Big Five eventually disbanded. Incongruities involving the team's pay led some of the original members to create another team. They invited former Phillips players Willis "Kid" Oliver, Inman Jackson, Bill Watson, and their former coach, Bobby Anderson, to form a team called the Globe Trotters. At least for a short time, the team was named the Tommy Brookins Globe Trotters. There may have been more than one team named Globe Trotters playing games against local white teams in the Midwest at this time.

It was not easy for a team made up of African American basketball players to get games against local white teams around the Midwest in the 1920s. African American teams faced even more challenges finding games against local white teams that paid money. The Globe Trotters consequently sought out a "white face" who could help them get games. They found Abe Saperstein, a man who had arranged games for some Negro Baseball League teams in white towns in the region. Saperstein is one of the most controversial and important figures in the history of the Harlem Globetrotters and basketball. His motives and business practices, beginning with his first contact with the Globe Trotters, were unorthodox at best and immoral and racist at worst.

Since the team Saperstein led came to represent America throughout the world, it is only fitting that he was born on July 4, 1902. However, Saperstein was not an American, but a Polish Jew born in London as parents Louis and Anna tried to escape czarist Russia's imperial reach. The Saperstein family eventually made its way to Chicago. Saperstein's father obtained a tailoring job after posing as a non-Jew in the Ravenswood area of the Windy City. They were one of the only Jewish families in the neighborhood in which they lived and worked. Abe, like other immigrants, sought out sports as a way to both assimilate and prove himself to his Irish and German neighbors.

While Saperstein's athletic abilities were not sufficient to gain him entrance to the world of sports, he possessed other talents that enabled him to help the Globe Trotters and other teams. He was only good enough at sports to land himself jobs coaching local club teams. However, even as a young man, he was incredibly affable and had a great memory for names. These attributes helped him get side work as a booking agent for Negro Baseball League teams when these teams needed someone to travel ahead of them to arrange games and venues in white towns. A good memory, a love for sports, an outsider status, and a tireless knack for salesmanship made Saperstein very good at getting games. This was just what Brookins and the Globe Trotters needed when they decided to go from town to town barnstorming to play basketball.

Brookins's Globe Trotters agreed to pay Saperstein 10 percent of their take as their booking agent. Saperstein told the team he would need $100 in expenses to travel to the countryside of Wisconsin and Michigan so that he could arrange their first games. The team voted to give him the $100, though

playing the renowned Globe Trotters of Harlem. When the games did not go the way of the hometown crowd, the Globe Trotters had something else to offer: extreme athletic prowess. The Globe Trotters featured talent that was virtually unknown and rarely seen in small towns. Their wins were capped off with extremely good sportsmanship and bits of athletic showmanship during the early years.

While the team was successful, their financial earnings remained limited due to the Depression. The team worked hard, playing 150 games in just one season. Sixty-one of these games were played on consecutive nights, and some were played outdoors and in the rain. While the Globe Trotters made some money during the Depression, Saperstein managed the team's affairs shrewdly. When the team had enough money to get a second car for equipment, he bought another used Model T. He also changed the team's name from the New York Harlem Globe Trotters to just the Harlem Globe Trotters to save money on the extra two words when telegram costs increased. Saperstein also assumed more than a booking agent role during the Depression years. In 1934 he announced that the players would no longer share the profits from the team, but rather that they would be paid a flat rate of $7.50 a game. This shifted the team from a collaborative effort between Saperstein and the players to a team owned by Saperstein.

The change did not go unchallenged. Team star Runt Pullins, along with George Easter and Fat Long, had serious problems when Saperstein changed his role to team owner instead of coach, manager, and driver. These problems manifested themselves most notably with the exodus of one of the team's biggest stars, Pullins, and along with him went Long and Easter. Not only did Pullins leave the team over Saperstein's ownership grab, he also decided to form his own Globe Trotter squad using the same name. The country suddenly had at least two (and likely many other) Harlem Globe Trotter teams. Saperstein, who considered Pullins a former employee, did not enjoy the competition Pullins created with a second team. Most of the white towns did not know that there were two different teams and often did not know which team they had contracted to play. On at least one occasion, Runt Pullins showed up with his squad of five Globe Trotters and stole the evening's game and pay away from Saperstein's Globe Trotters. The feud between Saperstein and Pullins came to an end because Saperstein was able to convince the white-controlled Amateur Athletic Association (AAU) that his team was the only one on the barnstorming circuit that was purely amateur. The AAU's pseudo-sanctioning of Saperstein's team meant that teams that played against the "Original Harlem Globetrotters" as Saperstein began calling them were under no threat of losing their amateur credentials. Those teams who played other barnstorming units that might be construed as professionals, such as Pullins's team, could lose their amateur status.

Sports during the Depression era were largely about promotion, especially self-promotion. This was an area where Saperstein excelled. As the self-titled team owner, he began talking more often with sports writers as a promotional measure, but he added outright fabrications about the team and his own accomplishments. Lies were a major part of sports in this era in America, as was racism. The white owner's hyperbole indeed embodied both as he spoke about men with whom he once shared beds, rooms, and car space. He now considered these men to be his employees.

*At first we like to show our dominance and then we entertain you from there. We say we're basketball players first and entertainers second.*

This change in his relationship to the team brought out the worst in his own attitudes and speech about the African American players. For example, he claimed that his team's African roots made them "natural entertainers." He also forbade players from interracial dating, but he himself had a number of African American girlfriends.

Beyond Saperstein's racist claims, the Globetrotters were often described as a continuation of minstrelsy. In minstrel shows, blacks are degraded for the amusement of whites. This criticism of Saperstein's Globetrotters extends from the 1930s, when the owner alternated between claims that he told the team to use humor as a way to sell seats to claims that he has to keep the team from just doing humor and remind them to play ball. This criticism remains the hardest legacy for the Globetrotters to shake. It indeed has elements of truth in it, as at various times the team does use humor, and particularly humor aimed at black stereotypes, such as speaking with a Southern dialect or worse, to garner laughs.

Like the Globetrotters themselves, their performance was complicated. Comedian Bill Cosby made two important points about this criticism. He claimed that Globetrotter humor is only funny because the team is backed up by tremendous sportsmanship and athleticism. In essence, the team uses humor to defuse situations where an all-black team comes into a white town and sorely defeats its local heroes. Cosby also argued that the team does not fit the pattern of minstrelsy. If the Globetrotters of the present day are minstrels, then who are the Washington Generals, the all-white team that travels and plays against the modern Globetrotters team, in the minstrel show? The Washington Generals serve as the straight men for most of the Globetrotters' jokes. No minstrel show continually perpetuated gags against whites, which means that the Globetrotters' performance is not a true minstrel show.

While the Globetrotters' name was associated with showmanship throughout the Depression era, the Harlem Rens became increasingly known for their on-court basketball prowess. Saperstein knew that his team needed to play and beat the Rens in order to prove his claims about the Globetrotters' abilities. Building a team capable of beating the Rens and promoting a game of that magnitude were just the kind of challenges that Saperstein enjoyed. The first meeting between the Globetrotters and Rens took place as part of the *Chicago Herald*'s World Pro Championship series in Chicago in 1939. Few sports fans realize it, but basketball permitted on-court integration at the professional

> *I wanted to be the best comedic basketball player of all time.*
> George "Meadowlark" Lemon

level, or what might be considered the semi-professional level in modern times, whenever the Globetrotters played. Until the Globetrotters faced the Rens, the mainstream media paid little attention to black teams. Once the two teams faced each other in the semi-finals of the world championship game, however, everyone took notice. While Saperstein's promotions stole away the Rens' place in history as one of the greatest teams, in 1939 they secured a place in the record books by defeating the Globetrotters and silencing Saperstein, albeit only for a few months.

The loss in Chicago indeed was hard for the Globetrotters, but it set Saperstein on a mission to rebuild them. His plan to rebuild involved Toledo's Sonny Boswell, one of the best pure shooters in basketball. Boswell's shooting and height made the 1940 Globetrotter team even better than their third-place 1939 counterparts. In Chicago's 1940 World Professional Championship game, no team, including the Rens, were a match for the Globetrotters. The Globetrotters and Rens played in front of the largest audience ever amassed for basketball up to that time.

The world championship victory opened promotional doors to Saperstein and the Globetrotters. The victory gave the team a chance to play against the 1940 College All-Stars. The College All-Star team received far more attention from the white media than the Globetrotters until the game actually took place in Chicago's Coliseum. This game was an epic battle that went into overtime before the All-Stars won what was described by many in attendance as the greatest sporting spectacle there would ever be. What was more impressive was the world record–setting attendance of 20,583 fans. The number of fans in attendance was impressive, but so was the fact that the crowd was racially mixed. Saperstein felt that despite the loss, this game was "the night we came into our own."

The Globetrotters continued to find new players. While Saperstein worked with the team, he never stopped working as a booking agent for the Negro Leagues. His work as a booking agent for baseball gave him access to black communities and also a network for scouting athletic talent. His connections are exactly why Reece "Goose" Tatum, a very good baseball player from Alabama, came to play basketball. Tatum took the performance and humor of the Globetrotters to a new level and expanded the team's repertoire. He was an imposing spectacle at 6' 3", with a wingspan of more than 7' 3". His comedic timing and on-court gags also made him one of the most lovable Globetrotters of all time. While he clowned around on the court, he also learned the game of basketball to become a fantastic player.

The war brought out Saperstein's best improvisational skills. While World War II stopped many sports teams from meeting their regular demands, Saperstein saw the war as an opportunity to expand the reach of the Globetrotters by booking games at military bases around the country. The games also gave him a means to circumvent rationing rules on gasoline, oil, and rubber, which were supplies that a traveling team needed. The concessions made for the team during the war were few. Many of the Globetrotters were drafted and sent to bases where they ended up playing on segregated military base leagues. When players were drafted, Saperstein simply found more players, brought old players out of retirement, and found a way to field teams. When Goose Tatum was drafted, his absence left a real hole in the show portion of the team's routine. Saperstein filled this hole with Bob Karstens, a professional white player from Iowa. The Globetrotters integrated professional basketball by first playing Saperstein and then more prominently featuring Karstens.

The Globetrotters regrouped at the end of World War II. Saperstein capitalized on his sports connections by hiring Satchel Paige to run and coach one of the Globetrotter farm teams and four-time Olympic gold medalist Jesse Owens to manage the business affairs of Saperstein's Kansas City Stars. At half time of many of the games, Owens performed track and field demonstrations as part of his contract. The runner's relationship with Saperstein also led him to degrading exposition events, where he ran against a horse and at other times a dog. Saperstein also expected Owens to give speeches about the 1936 Olympics, Hitler, and Owens's experiences in Berlin. Owens delivered these speeches with patriotic overtones at a time when in his own country, even as a national hero, he was treated with disrespect because of his race.

Racial issues also plagued the Globetrotters as the team began actually trotting the globe. They traveled to Hawaii, Cuba, Puerto Rico, Canada, and Mexico to play. It was not uncommon for the players to be treated better abroad than they were at home. In many areas of the United States, they were still expected to drink from separate water fountains, eat from the back doors of diners, and sleep any place but a town's only hotel. The team was not universally discriminated against at home. Yet these black players, like other African Americans, found their social status limited by every ugly image of segregated Jim Crow America when they were not performing on the basketball court.

Globetrotter players were not welcome in the newly formed, segregated professional basketball leagues. Though Marques Haynes, Nat Clifton, and Ermer Robinson were widely heralded as the greatest basketball players on Earth, they were not welcome to play in these leagues. Segregation in basketball was of course a great absurdity in post–World War II America because the Globetrotters had already played white teams for nearly 20 years by this time. Yet the professional leagues simply could not imagine white audiences paying to see black players play basketball. This racial assumption gave Saperstein the kind of promotional opening he loved. He immediately hounded the Basketball Association of America (which later joined with the National Basketball League to become the National Basketball Association) to allow the Globetrotters to play against the Minnesota Lakers, the league champion team.

The Globetrotters not only played a game with the Lakers, they defeated the team. The win against the Lakers in 1948 was celebrated throughout the

Chicago South Side as a victory for African Americans everywhere. Many in white America argued that the win was simply a fluke or that the Lakers had not taken the clown princes of basketball seriously enough to win. White fans clamored for a rematch immediately. Saperstein wanted to capitalize on the excitement from the first game and managed to schedule a rematch for the following year. Again the Globetrotters were victorious. In the second game with the Lakers, the Globetrotters not only won, they were able to get a lead commanding enough that they began doing "the show." Fans loved their performance. Even more important, movie newsreels filmed both the 1949 game and the team's showmanship. As a result Americans watched a few seconds of the Globetrotters before their featured presentation at movie houses around the country. This game gave the Globetrotters free built-in nationwide marketing.

As the various all-white professional basketball organizations floundered, they turned to the Globetrotters for help. Organizations asked Saperstein to have the team play on the front half of a bill, hoping the crowds would stay to see a second game. At one such event, the Globetrotters played college all-stars from Loyola, DePaul, Marquette, and Notre Dame. This event created the College All-Star tour, in which the Globetrotters played against college all-stars. They played 18 games in three weeks on this tour and covered over 9,000 miles. The tour exposed fans across the country to both college players and the Globetrotters, thus building modern professional basketball. The tour also became the foundation, in Saperstein's mind, for other tours across Europe, Asia, and the world. Saperstein hired a secretary, Marie Linehan, to help him organize tours around the world and because of her outstanding organizational skills, the team was able to truly travel the globe.

The Globetrotters integrated and infused the world with basketball. The team entertained and played for Eva Perón, Pope Pius XII, and royalty throughout the world. In many countries, their visits were treated like official head of state visitations. The Globetrotters became not just ambassadors of basketball but actual goodwill ambassadors. The U.S. State Department did not hesitate throughout the Cold War era to use the team's fame and goodwill as a way to ease tensions. The team's calming effect on world problems cannot be overstated. Simply put, national problems waited if the Globetrotters were in town. This is a stunning notion considering that in the United States the Globetrotters athletes were not always treated as full citizens. In 1951 the team traveled to Berlin, Germany. On this trip, Jesse Owens returned to Berlin's Olympic Stadium, where he had earned four gold medals in 1936. As Owens sat on the sidelines and more than 75,000 people watched from the stands, the players brought their combination of athleticism and humor to Germany, and their presence along with Owens helped heal their national wounds from World War II.

National Basketball Association (NBA) team owners finally broke the color barrier of modern basketball by recruiting and drafting three black players. Globetrotters Nat "Sweetwater" Clifton and Chuck Cooper were two of the first players to integrate the organization. The owners initially feared Saperstein's reaction to this draft, since it meant that he lost players to the NBA. They worried that he would not play the Globetrotters in the front bill of their games, but they eventually decided that if they had the best players in their organization, then the fans might come just to see NBA games, Globetrotters or no. In typical Saperstein style, the Globetrotters owner did not deal with Clifton's departure for the NBA with grace, style, or fairness.

Yet the team's allure wore thin by the late 1970s and early 1980s. The NBA now provided much of the spectacular play that used to be unique to the Globetrotters. Many NBA players openly admitted that they got their ideas from former Globetrotter greats. The NBA provided Globetrotteresque play, which televisions streamed into living rooms around the United States. This competition was hard on the Globetrotter organization. To remain innovators, the team hired Olympic star and Kansas University player Lynette Woodard in 1985 as the first female "professional basketball player." Even Woodard's charisma and appeal could not save the organization. By the early 1990s, many people thought the Globetrotters would be sent out to pasture as a relic of a time gone by.

## Notable Globetrotters:

Hubert "Geese" Ausbie, Tommy Brookins, Wilt Chamberlain, Bill Cosby, "Wee" Willie Gardner, William "Pop" Gates, J. C. Gipson, Robert "Showboat" Hall, Charles "Tex" Harrison, Connie Hawkins, Marques Haynes, Carl Helem, Inman Jackson, Jackie Jackson, Mannie Jackson, Bob Karstens, Junius Kellogg, John "Jumpin' Johnny" Kline, Meadowlark Lemon, Bob Joe Mason, Fred "Curly" Neal, William "Kid" Oliver, Bernie Price, Reece "Goose" Tatum, Govoner Vaughn, Frank Washington, Lynette Woodard, and Walter "Toots" Wright.

## Honorary Globetrotters:

Henry Kissinger, Whoopi Goldberg, Nelson Mandela, Jackie Joyner-Kersee, Kareem Abdul-Jabbar, Bob Hope, Pope John Paul II, and Rev. Jesse L. Jackson.

Fortunes changed when the most important Globetrotter of all time returned to resurrect the team. Mannie Jackson played for the team in the early 1960s before becoming a multimillionaire through hard work in the business world. In June 1993, the world learned that Jackson owned the team, which made him the first African American to own a major sporting franchise. He was also the first Globetrotter since Tommy Brookins to have control over the team's destiny.

The team continues to perform, play, and reach audiences to the present day. Jackson recently explained that he is proud of the Globetrotters' legacy and ability to build cultural bridges. Others have noticed these bridges as well and provided the Globetrotters with awards and honors from around the world.

Through laughter and sports, the Globetrotters communicate beyond language, beyond conflict. When asked if the Globetrotters would persevere in this new modern age, Jackson compared the team to fine art, which remains relevant even as its audience changes. Though its specific meaning might change, it nonetheless remains beautiful and important. As the mesmerizing Globetrotter soundtrack "Sweet Georgia Brown," whistled by Brother Bones, pulses in the background, the Globetrotters remain one of the original American art forms.

## FURTHER READING

Biography. *The Harlem Globetrotters: America's Court Jesters*. A&E Television Networks, 2005.

Boskin, Joseph. *Sambo: The Rise and Demise of an American Jester*. Oxford: Oxford University Press, 1988.

Christgau, John. *Tricksters in the Madhouse: Lakers vs Globetrotters, 1948*. Lincoln: University of Nebraska Press, 2004.

Green, Ben. *Spinning the Globe: The Rise, Fall, and Return to Greatness of the Harlem Globetrotters*. New York: Amistad, 2005.

Kline, Johnny. *Never Lose: From Globetrotter to Addict to Ph.D.: An Autobiography*. New York: Papa Joe's Book Company, 1996.

Kuska, Bob. *Hot Potato: How Washington and New York Gave Birth to Black Basketball and Changed America's Game Forever*. Charlottesville: University of Virginia Press, 2004.

Rhoden, William C. *Forty Million Dollar Slaves: The Rise, Fall and Redemption of the Black Athlete*. New York: Random House, 2006.

Sharman, Jay, Mike Sear, David Houle, and Mannie Jackson (executive producers). *Harlem Globetrotters: The Team that Changed the World*. Burbank, CA: Warner Bros., 2005.

Thomas, Ron. *They Cleared the Lane: The NBA's Black Pioneers*. Lincoln: University of Nebraska Press, 2002.

Courtesy of Brooks Simpson.

# Derek Jeter

*Brooks D. Simpson with
Rebecca A. Simpson*

Sometimes it seems as if Derek Jeter has it all. The soft-spoken shortstop of the New York Yankees combines charisma with humility as he strives for excellence on the baseball diamond capped by clutch play and championship success. Upon his arrival in the Big Apple, he slipped comfortably into Yankee tradition, exuding an urbane style not seen in pinstripes since Joe DiMaggio. He always seems to be making the right play at the right time, igniting rallies with his bat or his base running, or snuffing them out with his fielding. A heady ball player, he maintains an enthusiasm for playing the game that barely conceals his deeply competitive nature. He deflects individual accolades by reminding everyone that it is all about winning, and carries himself in such a way that you believe it. He fields questions about baseball and his own life as effortlessly as if they were routine ground balls, deflecting the ravenous appetite of a New York media machine that has chewed up many a player at the slightest misstep. Jeter's knack for the big play, his sense of the moment, his awareness of who he is and where he is, seem as much a part of him as his smile and the twinkle in his eye. His shortcomings are obscured by his aura of confidence; he wears his celebrity with ease, although he is careful to preserve it. With an almost fanatical deliberateness, he has set out to live the life he imagined for himself. He is well aware of what it means to be Derek Jeter.

Born in Pequannock, New Jersey, on June 26, 1974, Derek Sanderson Jeter is the son of Charles and Dorothy Jeter. He owes his name to his mother's fondness for hockey player Derek Sanderson, who had just joined the New York Rangers that spring. There was some irony in the selection, for Sanderson sought the spotlight, craved publicity, and led a flamboyant life off the ice that far exceeded his on-ice skills. His namesake would follow a different path. The Jeters soon moved to West Milford, New Jersey, and then to Kalamazoo, Michigan, when Derek was four. Young Jeter returned frequently to New Jersey to visit his grandmother. When he was six, she took him to Yankee Stadium. The impact was electric: Jeter made it clear that he was determined to play shortstop for the Yankees some day. In seventh grade he turned his room into a Yankees shrine, complete with jersey and cap hanging on the wall. The following year he set down his dream of wearing the pinstripes in a school essay assignment.

The Jeters moved to Michigan so that Charles Jeter could pursue his Ph.D. in psychology at Western Michigan University. He eventually went into social work. Charles and Dorothy drew notice for the way they raised their children, instilling in them a sense of responsibility, monitoring their progress in the classroom, and encouraging Derek's athletic pursuits. The Jeters made clear their expectations and their priorities, even as they were supportive of their children's interests and encouraging them to achieve their goals. In Derek's case, the ultimate goal remained playing baseball for the Yankees, although he also played basketball for several years.

Kalamazoo was not exactly an ideal breeding ground for Major League Baseball talent, largely because of the late springs and cool weather. Jeter graduated from tee ball to Little League; he made the Kalamazoo High School varsity baseball team his first year out. Hitting over .500 his last two years in high school, Jeter gained national attention, winning player of the year awards from the American Baseball Coaches Association, Gatorade, and *USA Today*. Among his earliest fans was former Major League pitcher Hal Newhouser. The former Detroit Tiger hurler made the drive to Kalamazoo several times to watch the young shortstop in action. This was not merely the sentimental musings of an aging veteran: Newhouser scouted prospects for the Houston Astros. When the 1992 draft came around, however, the Astros opted instead for infielder Phil Nevin. The Yankees, holding the sixth pick, selected Jeter. He soon signed a contract for $7 million that included support to attend the University of Michigan, although in the end Jeter spent less than a year in college.

The 1992 season proved trying for the new draft pick. He batted a paltry .202 in Class A ball after going hitless in his first 14 at-bats in the Gulf Coast League for rookies. Indeed, he opened his professional career by striking out the first two times he batted and making an error that cost his team his first game, so there was nowhere to go but up. The following year, he advanced to Class A Greensboro, where he was recognized as the most outstanding prospect in the South Atlantic League despite making a whopping 56 errors: he batted .295, with 5 home runs and 71 runs batted in. Clearly evaluators looked beyond the statistics in making their evaluation. In 1994 Jeter made his way up the minor league ladder, rising from Class A Tampa to Class AA Albany before arriving at the Yankees' top minor league club, the Class AAA Columbus (Ohio) Clippers. Batting .344 with 5 home runs, 68 runs batted in, and 50 stolen bases, he seemed just a step away from the Major Leagues. *USA Today, Baseball America*, and *Baseball Weekly* all named him Minor League Player of the Year. The Yankees called Jeter to the Major Leagues in May 1995 to replace injured shortstop Tony Fernandez. He played a handful of games and collected his first Major League hit before returning to Triple A Columbus to continue playing minor league baseball. By year's end, it was apparent that he was ready to make his Major League debut.

Jeter happened to make the Yankees roster at an ideal moment. The banning of George Steinbrenner from supervising Yankees operations in 1990 (ironically, given Jeter's fondness for Dave Winfield, commissioner Fay Vincent banned Steinbrenner indefinitely for paying someone to provide him with negative information about Winfield) offered Yankees management an opportunity to rebuild the once-proud franchise without Steinbrenner's meddling. By 1993 the team was competitive; the following year it was leading the American League's East Division when a strike cut short the season. In 1995 the Yankees made the playoffs in the first season featuring three divisions and a wild card entry (the Yankees were the wild card), only to lose to Seattle in a gripping five-game series. The secret was to combine developing from within, cultivating talent through the farm system, with a more reasoned acquisition of ball players through free agency and trades. Jeter, center fielder Bernie Williams, catcher

Jorge Posada, and pitchers Andy Pettitte and Mariano Rivera were given the chance to develop instead of being shipped away in trades for aging stars past their prime. Although Steinbrenner returned to baseball in 1993, he showed far more restraint than before, and his episodic explosive interventions were fewer in number and far less severe in impact.

The 1995 playoffs marked a moment of transition for the franchise. Don Mattingly's first appearance in postseason play also proved to be his last bow as a ballplayer. Long the darling of New York fans, the first baseman had slipped in recent years from what had been brilliant superstar play. He chose to sit out the 1996 season as he thought over his options; also departing the Yankees was manager Buck Showalter. That meant that the Yankees lacked both a manager and a fan favorite. Joe Torre, a former Major League player whose career on the field was far better than his previous stints as a manager, took over in the dugout, and his first big decision was to name Derek Jeter as his starting short-stop for the 1996 season. Joining Jeter for their first seasons in New York were first baseman Tino Martinez and catcher Joe Girardi; they would fill out a lineup that featured Williams, outfielder Paul O'Neill, and third baseman Wade Boggs. Martinez would bear the burden of replacing Mattingly at first, while Jeter would get the opportunity of replacing "Donnie Baseball" in the hearts of the fans. That Martinez and Jeter soon became fast friends and worked out together in the off-season simply added to the story.

Not everyone thought that Jeter was ready for prime time. Some advisors pushed for a veteran to man the shortstop position. A few suggested that Jeter's future was as an outfielder. But Jeter had his advocates within the Yankees or-ganization, including Torre and former Yankees shortstop Gene Michael. The rookie personified the term *intangible*. One minor league manager who faced Jeter's team in 1994 remembered that Jeter played to win. His talent was so great that those unfamiliar with the game and those who did not pay close at-tention might fail to notice the many ways that he contributed to his team. Notice of Jeter prevailed: it was time to give the kid a chance.

Jeter opened the 1996 baseball season as the Yankees starting shortstop. He homered on opening day against the Cleveland Indians in a 7-1 New York win. During the next few months, as the Yankees made their way to first place and then fought off challengers, his modest demeanor, evident confidence, and flair for the timely play drew attention. Perhaps his first golden moment, however, happened in the first game of the league championship series against Balti-more. Batting in the eighth inning with the Yankees trailing by a run, Jeter launched a fly ball to the short but high fence in right field. As Baltimore right fielder Tony Tarasco prepared to make the catch, a young fan named Jeffrey Maier reached over the fence and tried to glove the ball, and it went into the stands. The umpires ruled it a home run, despite protests from Baltimore about fan interference, and the Yankees went on to win that game and eventually the series; in the ensuing World Series, the Yankees came back from two games down to beat the Atlanta Braves and claim their first championship in 18 years.

It was a promising initial campaign: for the season Jeter hit .314 with 10 home runs, 78 RBIs, and 14 stolen bases, a performance that earned him American League Rookie of the Year honors.

Jeter slipped slightly in his sophomore season, and so did the Yankees, who lost to Cleveland in the 1997 playoffs. The following year, however, both player and team rebounded. Leading the American League in runs scored (127) while batting .324, Jeter made the All Star team. The Yankees won a total of 125 games during the season and postseason in capturing their second World Series in three years. New York's dominance continued during the next two years, as the team added two more World Series titles, the second coming against their cross-city rivals, the New York Mets. In that confrontation, sometimes styled the Subway Series, Jeter batted .409 with two home runs and carried off MVP honors, just as he had during that previous summer's All Star game.

Four World Series championships in five years, a .324 postseason batting average during that period, three All Star game selections . . . it was the perfect melding of team and player, capped by the MVP performance on the 2000 World Series. It wasn't that Jeter had the best statistics; other American League shortstops, notably Seattle's Alex Rodriguez and Boston's Nomar Garciaparra, had numbers that more than stood up alongside Jeter's production. Nor was his play flawless: in several postseason series he had not always performed as well as the cumulative record shows, and he had a tendency to strike out more than one might like (averaging over 100 strikeouts a season). But there was something about Jeter's ability to perform under pressure, with the spotlight on him, and to do so with a cool style and grace and without self-serving boasting that cultivated his reputation. Playing in New York, with all the media attention, certainly did not hurt, but unlike some other players, Jeter responded to that challenge, and although he was surrounded by a collection of fine ball players, somehow he stood out. It did not hurt that every year Yankees management did what it could to bring over new players, including such stars as pitchers David Wells and Roger Clemens, as well as an assortment of once-great players who could still contribute. And Yankees management also made sure to lock Jeter up for years to come when he signed a 10-year contract for $18.9 million prior to the 2001 season.

Even though the Yankees repeated once more as American League champions in 2001, it was obvious that key players were playing their last season in Yankees pinstripes, including O'Neill, Martinez, third baseman Scott Brosius, and second baseman/outfielder Chuck Knoblauch. In a year marked by the terrorist attacks on September 11, baseball proved one way for New Yorkers as well as the nation to deal with their grief. That year that Yankees played the Arizona Diamondbacks in the World Series. After falling behind 2-0 at Arizona, the Yankees returned home and won three straight games, including two extra-inning contests in which they were behind by two runs and down to their last

*I'm not going to tell you that you should want to be like me, because everyone should want to be their own person.*

strike in the ninth inning. After Martinez tied the fourth game with a two-run blast in the waning hours of Halloween, it was left to Jeter, who stepped to the plate in the early hours of November 1, to hit the game-winning home run, earning him the nickname "Mr. November." However, the Diamondbacks won the series in seven games, with the deciding hit, a single, falling just behind a drawn-in Jeter. Although many fans recall his heroics in game 4, Jeter batted a mere .148. The dramatic home run provided his only run batted in of the entire series. Part of that was due to the aftereffects of an injury he suffered in the first playoff round versus Oakland, when he pursued a foul ball into the stands.

Between 2002 and 2006, the Yankees made the postseason every year as winners of the American League's East Division, yet every year they suffered disappointment in the postseason. Each year the Yankees went into the off-season determined to acquire the superstar who would prove to be the final piece of the puzzle, but securing the services of Jason Giambi, Alex Rodriguez, Randy Johnson, and Gary Sheffield proved not enough. As bad as it was to lose the 2003 World Series to the Florida Marlins, even more painful was the 2004 American League Championship Series, when the Yankees squandered a 3-0 series lead against the arch-foe Boston Red Sox, who went on to win their first World Series since 1918. Ironically enough, Jeter's personal statistical performances in many cases went up during these years. He secured three Gold Gloves at shortstop (although some wags might attribute that to Rodriguez's move to third base when he joined the Yankees in 2004), played in three more All Star games, and finished year after year among the league leaders in batting average and runs scored. Not even being named captain of the Yankees in 2003, a position previously filled by several legendary players, including Lou Gehrig, Thurman Munson, and Don Mattingly, could make up for the dearth of championships.

Ironically, during these years Jeter's celebrity status skyrocketed. Commercial endorsements, including Nike, Avon, Gatorade, VISA, Ford, several video baseball games, and numerous other products made Jeter an ever-present celebrity and by 2006 brought him some $7 million in annual compensation. *Sports Business Journal* in 2005 judged him the most marketable athlete, and he remains a top celebrity, so much so that he could even spoof his popularity with female fans while hosting NBC's *Saturday Night Live* in 2001. Although his personal life is subject to much media scrutiny, only snippets of rumors about his dating life surface, and Jeter skillfully handles inquiries before they become probing. David Cone remarked in 1999 on the athlete's age, explaining that Jeter's success had no comparison. Other players in similar situations, Cone included, had made mistakes that spoiled the chance to have an even better career. Jeter, in contrast, did not let the fame get to his head.

As the 2007 season opened, Jeter boasted a lifetime .317 batting average as well as those four World Series rings and a shelf filled with awards. He was in the prime of his career: with 2,150 hits he was well on his way to the magic

3,000-hit mark. But Jeter would say that such accomplishments pale in comparison to team achievements, and in the case of the New York Yankees that means World Series victories. In 119 postseason games over 11 seasons, Jeter batted .314 with 17 home runs, 48 runs batted in, and 85 runs scored; in six World Series appearances spanning 32 games, he has a .302 batting average with 27 runs scored but a mere 8 RBI, suggesting that it is the timeliness of his performances that has left such an enduring impression in the minds of fans. It remains to be seen whether Yankees management will be able to provide him with the sort of surrounding cast that will make a return to championship glory.

Not everyone uncritically worships Derek Jeter. His fielding has occasioned some intense debate among baseball observers. Some decry his lack of range and anticipation when he positions himself; supporters can rely upon a catalog of memorable plays, including cases where Jeter dove into the stands behind third base at Yankee Stadium—and came up with the ball. By now his dash deep to the hole to his right, followed by a heave to first, has become something of a trademark play. One scout noted that it was difficult to understand how Jeter could manage such successful plays. Perhaps most memorable was the play that took place during the 2001 American League Divisional Series against the Oakland A's. With the Yankees down two games and on the brink of elimination in the best of five series, Jeter dashed between home and first, caught an errant outfielder's throw on the run, and in one motion flipped the ball backhanded to catcher Jorge Posada, who then tagged an Oakland runner about to cross the plate. Called "the Flip," the play still stuns veteran baseball observers, yet Jeter says he was simply doing his job backing up the play. Others disagreed. Infielder Luis Soto argued that the play was a once-in-a-lifetime possibility.

Still, there is something hard to define about Derek Jeter. Writer Charles C. Euchner observed that the Yankee shortstop succeeds because of his personality. His serious, controlled personality combines with his power to create amazing plays on the field. Just as notable is his self-confidence, amounting to a sort of arrogance even he admits to having. Jeter "doesn't just think he's going to kick your ass," Sojo told a reporter; "he knows it." Even in his intensity, however, Jeter realizes the nature of what he's doing. Teammate Scott Brosius explained that Jeter understood that he was playing a game. But it is never just a game with Jeter, as another iconic moment suggested. In June 2004, against the Boston Red Sox, Jeter dove headfirst into the stands after a foul ball, and, although bloodied, came up with it. Thus "the Dive" joined "the Flip" as well as several postseason home runs as signature Jeter moments, combining determination, intelligence, and timeliness—all now trademarks of the Yankees shortstop.

One of Jeter's other trademarks is his fluid racial identity. At first glance it is not easy to determine his racial identity. He watches with amusement as people try to define him. The son of an African American father and a white mother, he has always been aware of prejudice. As a young man he noticed how store-keepers followed him around, keeping an eye on him. It was left to his mother to explain to him that they were afraid that he might steal something because they regarded him as black. "Don't let someone else's ignorance dominate you" was the lesson he learned from such experiences. He explained that his response to someone else's action, rather than the action, would determine the extent of damage caused. Nor were things always peaceful in Jeter's extended family. His father was reluctant to accompany his son to New Jersey on visits to his mother's family because his father-in-law was less than enthusiastic about the decision Dorothy had made in marrying an African American.

Jeter himself has always defined his racial identity as "black and white." He considers himself biracial, and identifies as both black and white. Rarely is he identified as a black player. His race became a public issue in 2005 when reporters learned that Jeter had been the target of hate mail for dating white women, with one letter-writer calling him "a traitor to his race" and promising that Jeter would be "shot or set on fire" if he continued to date white women. Jeter downplayed the incident. But he was well aware that the very people who cheer him on the field might react differently to him as just another person. He explained that how he feels about someone does not depend on their racial identity. He also understood that this was not the case with every one of his fans.

Race emerged again in a different way when Yankees third baseman Alex Rodriguez openly wondered why he had become the target of such intense criticism in New York. Noting that several other players (who happened to be white) seemed to evade such scrutiny, Rodriguez pondered why he was singled out. He suggested that his criticism was caused by his attractiveness, his racial identity, his financial success,, or because he played for a certain team. Yet the same things could be said of Jeter, whose salary was high enough to excite envy.

The comment also highlighted the growing estrangement between two close friends, even if the media appeared to make more of it than might have been there. In the late 1990s, Rodriguez, Jeter, and Garciaparra stood together as the game's best shortstops, players who combined offense and defense. The relationship between Jeter and Rodriguez began to fray after the Seattle star signed with the Texas Rangers for a whopping $252 million over the next decade. In various interviews Rodriguez noted that Jeter lacked Rodriguez's power and defensive prowess; moreover, Jeter was surrounded by great players, he asserted, relieving him of the pressure of being the leader, the key man in the lineup.

Understandably, Jeter did not take too kindly to those remarks, but at the time they seemed to be of little significance. However, when Rodriguez joined the Yankees in 2004, it was not altogether clear how the two players would coexist. Rodriguez volunteered to defer to Jeter in the field and play third base, although he was a Gold Glove–winning shortstop who many observers suspected might be a better fielder than Jeter. Moreover, usually Rodriguez's power and run production exceeded that of his new teammate. Yet before too long Rodriguez began running into troubles of his own that merely accentuated the difference between the two players. Along with the Yankees, Rodriguez collapsed in the 2004 ALCS against the Red Sox, failing to produce in some key situations. His postseason troubles continued the following two years, overshadowing an MVP season in 2005; in 2006 his troubles in the field increased the pressure on him to perform.

Although he was team captain, Jeter distanced himself from Rodriguez's troubles, causing some observers to wonder whether he was leaving the other man to fend for himself. How Jeter handled matters became a point of controversy as writers debated his merits as 2006 MVP (he finished second in the balloting). The following spring Rodriguez felt compelled to admit to reporters that his relationship with Jeter was not what it had once been. Jeter sidestepped another potential controversy by refusing to offer any detailed explanations of his own, merely insisting that what was important was how the two played on the field and how they both wanted to win. Nor would he respond to former teammate Gary Sheffield when he remarked that Jeter "ain't all the way black." Sheffield discounted Jeter's efforts to explain manager Torre's treatment of Sheffield, an African American outfielder, by telling Jeter that "you don't feel what other people feel," in part because of his racial identity.

Given his father's background in social work and the efforts of his boyhood idol Dave Winfield to help kids, it came as no surprise when Jeter followed the same path of exercising social responsibility through involvement in the community. During his rookie year he decided to establish a foundation to assist young people to turn away from drugs and alcohol in favor of living healthier lifestyles. The result was the Turn 2 Foundation, a play on words for a term describing a double play, with the additional meaning that the foundation also offers a place for youth to turn to for assistance. Jeter wanted to take advantage of his popularity and reputation and use it as a means to raise awareness among young people about making the right choices in life. Serving the youth of New York City and Kalamazoo, Michigan, the foundation sponsors baseball clinics, physical fitness programs, cultural enrichment programs, and education programs. It offers several scholarships to support the pursuit of its programs.

Jeter is also conscious of his status as a role model. "I'm not going to tell you that you should want to be like me, because everyone should want to be their own person," he remarks in his 2000 book, *The Life You Imagine*, "but I assure you that it's fun to be me." Nevertheless, he is quite aware of the image of his image as a role model. Charles Jeter, pointing out that parents as well as children wear Jeter jerseys and T-shirts, told his son that this meant the parents approved of how Derek conducted himself on and off the field. Jeter is very protective of that image. To be sure, he can make fun of himself: after Steinbrenner declared that his prize shortstop might do well to spend less time out on the town during the off-season, the two men collaborated on a credit card commercial that featured Jeter promising to behave before he set out on another night out. But he can also be very guarded and protective of his privacy, although always in a calm way. Jeter argued that much of his need for privacy

*If I was a doctor instead of a Yankee, I'd still be very cautious in the way that I lead my life. I'd still be careful whom I surrounded myself with, I'd still try to stay out of trouble, and I'd still have good morals. The protective wall that I build around me might be slightly thinner, but it would still be in place.*

had little to do with fame. He explained that, even as a doctor, he would behave cautiously and morally. Such a stance adds to his mystique, but it also suggests just how deliberate and structured it is. Derek Jeter is very much aware of what being Derek Jeter entails.

Charles Jeter is irritated by assertions that his son leads a perfect life, as if he almost fell into it. Those people, according to Charles, are unaware of the difficulties Derek faced as a youth. Just because it looks easy doesn't mean it was easy. The Yankee admits he doesn't let his guard down and chooses his situations carefully. *The Life You Imagine* is as much an advice book as it is an autobiography. In it Jeter shapes the narrative of his story around 10 principles or life lessons that will help young readers achieve their own dreams. In its way, the format of the book suggests just how integral image and role modeling is to Jeter's identity and sense of self.

Derek Jeter is in the prime of his baseball career. He remains among the leading hitters of the game, and he has worked hard to improve defensively. Although the Yankees have declined from their reign as World Series champions during the early part of Jeter's career, they remain a competitive team. Jeter now finds himself advancing past some of the all-time greats in Yankees history and Major League history as he establishes his own place beside the legends of the game. It remains to be seen whether he is equally adept at continuing to manage his image as a smooth, stylish, accomplished performer with the knack for performing with grace under pressure and the degree to which he can use his awareness of being a role model to bring others along his path to greatness.

## FURTHER READING

Chadwin, Dean. *Those Damn Yankees: The Secret Life of America's Greatest Franchise.* New York and London: Verso, 2000.

Euchner, Charles. *The Last Nine Innings.* Napierville, IL: Sourcebooks, 2006.

Jeter, Derek, with Jack Curry. *The Life You Imagine: Life Lessons for Achieving Your Dreams.* New York: Three Rivers Press, 2000.

Maiorana, Sal. *A Lifetime of Yankee Octobers.* Chelsea, MI: Sleeping Bear Press, 2002.

Onley, Buster. *The Last Night of the Yankee Dynasty.* New York: Ecco, 2004.

Sherman, Joel. *Birth of a Dynasty: Behind the Pinstripes with the 1996 Yankees.* New York: Rodale, 2006.

Stout, Glenn, and Richard A. Johnson. *Yankees Century.* Boston and New York: Houghton Mifflin, 2002.

AP Photo/Kevork Djansezian.

# Earvin "Magic" Johnson

*Brooks D. Simpson*

Earvin "Magic" Johnson remains in the minds of many the epitome of basketball athleticism with his style, flair, and smile. Over the years, he built upon his impressive résumé as a player by reaching out into other endeavors, sometimes by choice, sometimes by fate. As a basketball player he was perhaps best known for his ability to raise the level of his teammates' play; in his business and charitable activities he has sought to improve opportunities for people. Many people attribute the growth of the National Basketball Association (NBA) to the renewed interest that he, along with Larry Bird and later Michael Jordan, brought to the game. He remains an iconic figure in the world of professional sports, and now he thoughtfully employs the opportunities offered by his celebrity.

Born August 14, 1959, in Lansing, Michigan, Earvin Effay Johnson Jr. was the fourth of seven children. "I grew up in the kind of black family that people today worry is disappearing," Johnson recalled in the opening sentence of his 1992 autobiography, *My Life*. Lansing, he added, was "a stable neighborhood of working people." Earvin Sr., his father, worked in the local General Motors plant and augmented the family income with second jobs, including pumping gas and collecting trash. His mother, Christine, supplemented the family income as a school custodian and working in a cafeteria. They had migrated to Michigan from the South, and occasionally the family took trips to Mississippi, where the elder Johnson described the world of Jim Crow segregation. Later in life, when Johnson encountered unthinking racism, he would check his temper by recalling his father's observation that "we shouldn't forget those people had come a long way." He bonded with his fifth-grade teacher, Greta Dart, who with her husband, Jim, looked after Johnson and, as he later observed, taught him to spend time with white people.

The Johnson household was managed by parents who believed in hard work and discipline as essential to raising a family with love. Johnson absorbed the lessons. He did chores to earn money, including cleaning out the offices of two of Lansing's more successful black businessmen. He dreamed of one day having an office and a lifestyle just like theirs. Although he adored his mother, he found her embrace of the Seventh-Day Adventist Church entailed too stifling a lifestyle, and he remained a Baptist with his father. Father worked with son on playing one-on-one basketball, with the father playing hard, fouling his son, never letting up, as he urged him to develop a complete game.

From an early age, Johnson loved basketball He adored his hometown Detroit Pistons, and could not get enough opportunities to play. "No matter what else I was doing," he later recalled, "I always had a basketball in my hand." By the time he entered high school, his skill was evident. Observers noted that he played the game with a certain flair and charismatic style. At Everett High School, his stellar play earned him the nickname of "Magic." Sportswriter Fred Stabley Jr. gave him this title while recounting a performance where the teen scored 36 points, grabbed 16 rebounds, and dished out 16 assists in one contest. In his junior year, he scored 54 points against Sexton

High School, then a record for Lansing schools. He led Everett to the Class A state championship in his senior year with a record of 27–1, averaging just under 29 and 17 rebounds per game.

Entering Michigan State University in 1978, Johnson impressed observers. As a freshman, he averaged 17.0 points, 7.9 rebounds, and 7.4 assists per game. Coach Jud Heathcote noted that the new team member helped his fellow players improve their games. Teammate Terry Donnelly was amazed by how Johnson could find his teammates and get them the ball, noting that he could put the ball in teammates' hands when they didn't believe it was possible. Johnson's

*That first game, I was so excited and so nervous that I ran out of the court leading my team out. I'm trying to be cool but not show that I'm so excited. By the time I get down there, I'm about to lay it up . . . the first layup, I trip and stumble and started rolling.*

skills brought results quickly. Michigan State claimed the Big Ten conference title and finished the year with a 25–5 record. He won All-American honors in his sophomore year as he spearheaded the Spartans' drive to a National Collegiate Athletic Association (NCAA) championship with slightly improved personal statistics. In the finals Michigan State faced upstart Indiana State, led by top scorer and playmaker Larry Bird. The highly anticipated match drew a record number of television viewers. The game resulted in a 75-64 win for Michigan State, with Johnson winning Final Four MVP honors. It was a foregone conclusion that he would turn pro at the season's end.

The Los Angeles Lakers, using the draft choice they obtained in a trade with the New Orleans Jazz in 1976 as compensation for the free-agent signing of Gail Goodrich, chose Johnson first overall in the 1979 NBA draft. It was Lakers owner Jack Kent Cooke's last major decision before selling the team to Dr. Jerry Buss. Johnson's acquisition proved essential in restoring the Lakers to the ranks of the NBA's elite franchises. The restoration had already involved several years of rebuilding, commencing with the acquisition of center Kareem Abdul-Jabbar in 1975. The rookie brought his trademark enthusiasm to professional basketball, beginning with his first game. His excitement so overtook him during this game that he tripped before finishing his first layup. Teammates laughed at the mistake caused by his zeal. Abdul-Jabbar later tried to get the rookie to dampen his enthusiasm after he celebrated his first win as a Laker, but Johnson remained ebullient throughout the season.

Playing power forward with the additional skill set of a guard, Johnson quickly became a contributor. His influence was not limited to his play, however. His excitement was contagious, and helped his entire team find new enthusiasm for the game. This quality was even more important when coach Jack McKinney went down due to a bicycling injury, leaving Paul Westhead to take over.

Johnson left his distinctive mark on the 1979–1980 playoffs. The Lakers won the Pacific Division and blew through the Western Conference playoffs to the finals, where they confronted Julius Erving and the Philadelphia 76ers.

After splitting the first four games, the Lakers took game five due to a heroic performance from Abdul-Jabbar, who scored 40 points despite spraining an ankle. Up 3-2, the Lakers readied to travel to Philadelphia without their dominant center. Johnson boarded the plane, settled in the seat traditionally reserved for the absent Abdul-Jabbar, and announced, "Never fear, E. J. is here." As game time approached, the rookie had an idea: Why not have him start at center? What followed was astonishing. Although he jumped at tip-off, it would be misleading to say that Johnson simply replaced Abdul-Jabbar; rather, as Westhead recalled, he was an omnipresent force on the court. Scoring 42 points, gathering 15 rebounds, dishing out 7 assists, with 3 steals and a blocked shot, Johnson led the Lakers to a 123-107 victory. The performance became the stuff of legend, including claims that he won the game single-handedly, which neglected the contributions of his teammates. The decision to name Johnson the MVP of the finals also seemed to overlook his teammates. Several people, including Abdul-Jabbar and even Johnson, thought this honor should have gone instead to the sidelined center. "This one's for you, big fella," Johnson told the cameras as the Lakers celebrated. It was a wonderful beginning for the rookie. Rival Larry Bird, now a Boston Celtic, beat him out for Rookie of the Year honors, however.

Johnson's second year proved far more trying. He missed much of the regular season due to a knee injury. The Lakers bowed out in the opening round of the playoffs to the Houston Rockets, who eventually succumbed to Bird's Celtics. During the summer of 1981, however, Johnson again made news when the Lakers signed him to a 25-year personal services contract for $25 million, a contract far more astonishing for its length than for the dollars involved. Fully recovered from his injury and well rested, Johnson stormed back in the 1981–1982 season, as did the Lakers. Coach Westhead attempted to install a half-court offense featuring Abdul-Jabbar, replacing the fast-breaking attack under which Johnson had flourished. Dissatisfied, Johnson finally demanded to be traded, but Buss preferred instead to fire Westhead, replacing him with assistant coach Pat Riley. "It's show time again," Johnson smiled, using the phrase that would come to characterize the team's play. Although Johnson was unpopular with fans for forcing the issue with Westhead, their resentment soon faded as the Lakers rolled through the season and the playoffs, beating Philadelphia once more in the finals with Johnson securing his second playoff MVP award.

Turnabout proved foul play for the Lakers in 1982–1983. Once more they tore through the regular season and the Western Conference playoffs, only to run into a Philadelphia team that at last was ready for a challenge. The Sixers had acquired center Moses Malone, who could hold his own against Abdul-Jabbar. This time it was Philadelphia who prevailed in a stunning four-game sweep. Johnson's magic seemed to take a tumble, at least for a moment. Now that Erving had his ring, however, the league and its fans were ready for what was next: a rematch of the 1979 NCAA tournament game pitting Johnson against Larry Bird, this time featuring Johnson's Lakers and Bird's Celtics. Given the fine players on both teams, too much was made of the Bird-Johnson rivalry, but it proved to be marketing magic as the NBA grew in popularity. Once more the Lakers marched through the schedule and made their way through the playoffs. This time the Celtics, led by season MVP Bird, responded in kind, and at last the dream was a reality.

Johnson's Lakers had already won two titles to the one won in 1981 by Bird's Celtics when the two faced off for the first time in the postseason in 1984. In a hard-fought seven-game series, the Celtics prevailed and Bird was named finals MVP. For Johnson, the series was a disaster, as his poor play contributed to several Boston victories. Boston's Kevin McHale taunted him by calling him "Tragic" Johnson. Taking the loss hard, Johnson heard the criticisms of his play. He took critics' comments to heart, internalizing them and determining that he should improve his game. The following year was, at long last, the Lakers' turn to beat Boston, with the clinching game taking place at Boston Garden. It marked the fourth straight year Johnson played in the finals. That the Lakers had lost the previous eight finals confrontations between the two teams dating back to the days of Bill Russell and Jerry West (the first came when the team was based in Minneapolis) made the triumph all the sweeter. Somehow the fact that Bird once again won the regular season MVP was not quite as important as it might have been otherwise, although it still inspired Johnson to press onward. Johnson noted that waiting an entire year was simultaneously inspiring and challenging

In retrospect, these two finals were key to the development of the NBA. The league struggled in the later 1970s. The absorption of several teams from the competing American Basketball Association did nothing to rescue it from the doldrums of fan interest. Television ratings were so bad that games were regularly aired on a tape-delayed basis. The league tinkered with its schedule to try to capture better television ratings. While this reduced the number of tape-delayed games, ratings did not significantly improve for several years. Either Bird or Johnson appeared in the finals between 1980 and 1983, and Erving also played in three of those finals, but it was not until Bird and Johnson faced each other for the first time in the postseason in 1984 that ratings really improved. Until then Celtics/Lakers confrontations happened only twice a year during the regular season. Memories of previous playoff battles between the two teams during a period of Celtics dominance quickly faded. Moreover, CBS, which televised the NBA nationally, began to promote telecasts as clashes between stars as well as teams. In such an arena Magic Johnson was sure to draw his share of attention.

Johnson had been linked with Bird ever since they played each other in the 1979 NCAA championship game. During that season, it had been Bird and his upstart Indiana State team, not Johnson's Michigan State squad that attracted public interest and contributed to the large viewership for the 1979 Final Four tournament. The 1979 championship game offered Johnson a chance to perform in front of a large audience. Over the next four years, while Johnson's teams won more games, Bird received more attention, despite winning only one championship. Bird may have received this attention due to an East Coast bias in media coverage, including television's preference to broadcast games played in the Eastern and Central time zones. Some of this attention came from the reputation Johnson gained as a selfish and spoiled superstar in the aftermath of the Westhead firing, leading fans to favor other players. Still more of the attention given to Bird sprung from a desire among some fans not to give Johnson his due because he twice led teams that were denied NBA championships to sentimental favorite Julius Erving of the Philadelphia 76ers. Finally, two other issues worked in Bird's favor: He played for the legendary Boston Celtics, and he was white. Some observers even called him "the great white hope," making explicit the racial reason for his popularity. In contrast, Johnson was one of a pair of superstars alongside Abdul-Jabbar. He shared media attention with his center, just as he had to share the spotlight in the finals with Erving.

Still, the Bird-Johnson comparisons were present and waiting to be exploited. Much was made in the media of the supposed contrast in their playing styles, with Bird portrayed as a hard-working, team-oriented rural boy while Johnson was described as all-flash and Hollywood with his razzle-dazzle play and effervescent smile. Johnson claimed MVP honors in the playoffs, but by 1984 it was Bird who had won a regular season MVP and Rookie of the Year honors. In truth, their playing styles were more alike than different, since passing was key to their games. Yet Bird's passes, sometimes delivered with a great deal of flair, were never described with the "showtime" imagery associated with Johnson's no-look deliveries. The Celtics were remembered as East Coast, workmanlike, unselfish players. Many of the Celtics players were white, although the team had their share of African American players, including center Robert Parish and guard Dennis Johnson. The Lakers were known as West Coast celebrities whose "showtime" label bespoke basketball as entertainment and individual performances from a number of African American players. The play of Kurt Rambis, a white player on the Lakers team, only cemented this racialized conception. Rambis took the court complete with black-rimmed glasses, emphasizing his gawkiness and the contrast in styles supposedly delineated by race. These descriptions helped casual basketball fans, who did not understand the game, become interested in clashes between the Lakers and the Celtics. Along with the all-too-real rivalry between Bird and Johnson, these artificial contrasts helped propel the NBA toward widespread popularity. The stereotypes both concealed and revealed realities that no one really wanted to discuss. The Bird/Johnson contrast could only add to the rivalry between the two men by forcing it to carry a certain amount of societal baggage.

The NBA was not the only institution to emphasize the rivalry between the players. Basketball sneaker-maker Converse played upon the Bird/Johnson contrast in a 1984 commercial. It opened with Bird practicing alone on a court just off a road in the middle of the countryside in French Lick, Indiana. Suddenly a limousine pulls up. Johnson emerges in uniform and challenges Bird to play one on one. The irony became richer than the commercial symbolism that exploited their differences. Shooting the commercial helped foster a friendship between the two men. Yet it reaffirmed the rivalry and the stereotypes upon which it was based. Johnson explained, "I was the city slicker, the Hollywood-type of guy and he was this down-home guy. He was this guy from the back of the woods. He was a hardhat player, a hard worker and I was this flash . . . a lot of flair." The comparison was distorting. Johnson implied as much in a 1984 interview in reflecting on how he had adjusted to life in Los Angeles. "It wasn't as easy a transition for me to live out here as people thought," he remarked. "I'm still a Midwestern country boy. I like the outdoors. I like to go off by myself to a lake and relax. I miss things such as the picnics we used to have back home. You don't seem to have those family-type situations out here as much." Johnson even admitted that "Magic" was an on-court persona that did not necessarily reflect what he was all about off the court. "Magic" is in fact a personality he donned to do well in basketball. "Magic" demands excellence of himself and his team. His off-court persona, in contrast, is far more mild and quiet. Johnson uses both personalities, and believes that both are responsible for his successes in basketball and life.

Friendship with Bird in no sense dampened the rivalry; it may have enriched it. Johnson judged his successes against those of Bird. When Bird made a great shot, Johnson wanted to make a great shot as well. Nevertheless, the rivalry was bigger than that. It proved essential to marketing the NBA on television, ending the days of delayed telecasts and buried contests. Johnson commented that he and Bird thrived upon their competition, improving their games as well as the sport of basketball as they attempted to outshine one another.

The Lakers failed to defend their title the following season in 1984–1985, with Boston reclaiming the crown against the Houston Rockets, who had defeated the Lakers in the Western Conference finals. This served as a prelude for the 1986–1987 season, which may well have been Johnson's finest performance at the height of his prowess. Averaging a career-high 23.9 points per game with a league-leading 12.2 assists, he took over from Abdul-Jabbar as the Lakers' dominant player. He finally won his first regular season MVP and was the first guard to do so since Oscar Robertson in 1964. The always competitive Johnson observed that Bird had already won the award three times. For the third time in four years, the Lakers battled in the finals against Bird's Celtics, the defending champions. Up 2-1 in the fourth game of the series, played in Boston Garden, Johnson astonished fans, television viewers, and players. In the closing seconds of the game, with the Celtics up 106-105, he took the inbound pass, moved toward the foul line, released a sky hook—Abdul-Jabbar's trademark shot—and found nothing but net as he capped a furious fourth quarter comeback to allow the Lakers to take a commanding 3-1 lead in a series they eventually won in six games. Johnson secured his third playoff MVP with his performance. "Magic is a great, great basketball player," Bird graciously re-marked. "The best I've ever seen."

In many ways, the 1986–1987 season marked the beginning of a major shift in Johnson's career. He was now the brightest star in the Lakers' constellation. At long last his regular season play gained the recognition it deserved. It would also be the last time that the Lakers and Celtics played together in the NBA finals during the Johnson-Bird era. Johnson's fourth NBA championship bettered Bird's three rings. Before long it was evident that the Celtics were in decline, with the Detroit Pistons and the Chicago Bulls emerging as the dominant powers in the Eastern Conference. Johnson consequently shined on his own. In 1987–1988 he added his fifth ring as the Lakers, spurred on by Riley, became the first team to repeat as NBA champions since the Celtics had accomplished the task in 1968–1969. This time, however, the Pistons, Johnson's boyhood team, were the Lakers' opposition. They put up quite a fight, extending the match to seven games. Given the Pistons' reputation as "bad boys," this time there was no doubt as who the good guys were, at least in the eyes of many fans. Johnson fought through a bout with the flu that lasted over several games to keep the Lakers going.

Riley spoke of a three-peat for the Lakers in 1988–1989, but it was not to be. Although Johnson garnered his second regular season MVP award, the Lakers proved to be a year older and the Pistons a year better when the two teams clashed again in the finals. Whatever doubt remained that it was the Pistons' year vanished when Johnson went down with a hamstring injury. The Lakers lost in four straight. The season proved to be Abdul-Jabbar's farewell to the league. If Abdul-Jabbar had never won a championship without world-class guards Oscar Robertson or Johnson, neither Robertson nor Johnson could win a championship without the big guy with the sky hook. This interdependence became evident the following season, when despite yet another regular season MVP award, Johnson found only frustration once more when the Phoenix Suns upset the Lakers, snapping a string of three straight appearances in the finals.

Matters did not improve the following season. Johnson led a players' rebellion that resulted in the ouster of Pat Riley as coach. That spring the Lakers, now directed by Mike Dunleavy, managed to reach the finals once more, although they played the role of spectators as Michael Jordan and the Chicago Bulls clinched their first NBA championship. The torch had been passed to a new generation.

Johnson realized that things were changing, both on and off the court. For years there had been stories of his relationships with women, which usually were no more than one-night stands. In August 1991, however, he finally proposed to longtime girlfriend Earlitha "Cookie" Kelly. Within weeks, Kelly learned she was pregnant. As he prepared for fatherhood and the opening of the 1991–1992 season, Johnson had a physical. The results of his exam came back on October 25, 1991. For weeks afterward, no one could explain why he was not participating in preseason contests. Eventually the season began, and still Johnson was not playing. Why?

On November 7, 1991, the eve of what was to have been his thirteenth season in the NBA, Johnson announced that he had tested positive for HIV. As a result, he was retiring from basketball. The news stunned fans. In a tribute to Johnson, fans voted him to the 1991–1992 All Star team. This was the twelfth time he had been named to the mid-season contest; only in 1981, when he was injured, was he not selected. Johnson chose to suit up, and in a startling performance, scored 25 points and was named the game's MVP, the second time he had been so honored. Ironically, 1991–1992 also proved to be Larry Bird's last year in the NBA.

Johnson was determined not to be sidelined by his condition. In the summer of 1992 he joined a spectacular lineup of players, all but one an NBA star, to form the U.S. men's Olympic basketball team. It was the first time professionals were allowed to participate in Olympic competition, and the results were predictable. The United States won the gold medal in convincing fashion and the players became known as the Dream Team. Encouraged by his performance, Johnson considered making a comeback but chose to stay retired after the conclusion of the preseason.

At first, Johnson tried to remain active in basketball with the Lakers. He replaced Randy Pfund as coach in April 1994, but he was unable to prevent the team from missing the playoffs and declined to continue as coach. He chose to make a comeback as a player for the 1995–1996 season. Playing power forward for the Lakers, Johnson demonstrated flashes of his former skill, although he averaged less than 30 minutes playing time per game. After the Lakers lost in the first round of the playoffs, he retired from the NBA again, this time for good. In years to come he would take to the court for short spurts, including two stints with European teams that he also owned.

Johnson thus called it quits on a marvelous career. He had five championship rings, three regular season MVP awards, and three playoff series MVP awards. Although his regular season totals were curtailed by his premature retirement, he still left his mark on the record book, with 11.2 assists per game during the regular season and a playoff career total of 2,346 assists. He was selected to appear in 12 All Star games, and only his injury in 1980–1981 may have prevented a thirteenth selection. Both the Lakers and Michigan State honored him with statues outside their arenas in 2001. The Professional Basketball Writers Association established the Magic Johnson Award, given to the player who best combines on-court excellence with cooperation with the media. Yet it was his commitment to winning and his enjoyment of the contest that proved most memorable. He keeps in touch with the game, playing the occasional exhibition or appearing as a commentator on national broadcasts.

Even as he slowly let go of basketball, Johnson moved into other fields of endeavor. For all the attention paid to his 1981 contract and subsequent negotiated basketball contracts, he made far more money in business since retirement

*"Everyone looks at me and still sees basketball," he noted in 1999, "but I run my companies. People who don't know me may not believe that. But if they come in here and want to do some business, they'll find that out fast enough."*

from basketball. He was not always successful, however. Especially embarrassing was *The Magic Hour*, an ill-fated talk show that lasted two months. His efforts to educate other people about HIV and AIDS proved far more lasting and important. During his retirement announcement, he declared that he intended to be a spokesman addressing and educating people on the issue. He made good on the pledge. He worked with Arsenio Hall to produce an AIDS awareness video called *Time Out*. He also appeared with Linda Ellerbee on a television special for kids. At the same time, his activity became something of an education experience. At first some NBA players were reluctant to come into contact with him and questioned the wisdom of his comebacks. Other players met the challenge and the whispers head on, hugging Johnson and showing their support, both in NBA contests and during the 1992 Olympics. He established the Magic Johnson Foundation, a nonprofit charitable group that supports community organizations to help children and young people, as well as to educate children and adolescents about HIV/AIDS. As part of this educational effort he wrote *What You Can Do to Avoid AIDS* in 1996.

The Magic Johnson Foundation proved but a first step in Johnson's efforts to revitalize and assist challenged communities. Bearing the slogan "We are the communities we serve," Magic Johnson Enterprises became a way for Johnson to engage in numerous activities. The organization focused upon education, development, opportunity, and uplift through entertainment. For example, Johnson Development Corporation sought to revitalize urban areas by constructing entertainment complexes, frequently anchored by a movie theater bearing Johnson's name, restaurants, and retail centers. Johnson also partnered with Canyon Capital Realty Advisors to establish the Canyon-Johnson Urban Fund to assist in funding revitalization efforts. He has worked with AMC to build movie theaters, with Starbucks to open over 100 coffee shops in a joint venture, with Burger King and T.G.I. Fridays to establish franchises in various urban areas, and with 24 Hour Fitness to construct fitness centers. He branched out into producing shows for television and has also invested in the music industry. He bought into a Los Angeles–based bank to help finance these varied ventures. Johnson is not simply a name or an absentee investor, however. He takes pride in his business acumen and is quick to point out that he personally runs his companies. He brings the same desire to business that he brought to the basketball court.

In all these activities, Earvin Johnson maintained what may be the signature theme of his basketball career—he makes those around him better. He sets up some to score on the court and prepares others to succeed in life. What may seem to some to be simply magic is in fact the result of hard work and deep thought. Johnson may have come to America's attention as a basketball player, but the imprint he made on American society transcends its foundation.

## FURTHER READING

"American Express Magic Johnson 2004 All Star Game Tribute." http://www.nba .com/allstar2004/magic_tribute.

Johnson, Earvin, with William Novak. *My Life*. New York: Random House, 1992.

Lazerby, Roland. *The Show: The Inside Story of the Spectacular Los Angeles Lakers in the Words of Those Who Lived It*. New York: McGraw-Hill, 2005.

Magic Johnson Enterprises. http://magicjohnsonenterprises.com.

"NBA @ 50 interview." http://www.nba.com/history/players/magic_johnson_nba50_ pt1.html, and http://www.nba.com/history/players/magic_johnson_nba50_pt2.html.

Library of Congress.

# Jack Johnson

*Jeremy I. Levitt*

Jack Arthur Johnson, nicknamed the "Galveston Giant," was the best heavy-weight boxer of his generation and arguably in the history of boxing. He was the first African American heavyweight champion of the world, holding the title between 1908 and 1915. His boxing record was exceptional, including 113 official fights with 79 wins (44 by knockout), 12 draws, and 8 losses.

Johnson was not only an African American sports icon but perhaps more important, an American social icon who used boxing and fervent individualism to challenge white supremacy in the United States and beyond. He challenged the philosophy and practice of racial superiority of whites over nonwhites as expressed through state-sanctioned violence and the repressive control of America's sociopolitical, legal, and economic system. He was one of the country's most well-traveled, wealthy, and successful citizens. Johnson's life and legacy unveiled the myth of white superiority and consequently threatened the foundational premise upon which white supremacy rested. He single-handedly forced whites throughout the world to confront their racist misconceptions of blacks and defied the character of race relations in the United States; Johnson is consequently one of the most famous, infamous, and influential figures of the twentieth century.

Jack Johnson was born in Galveston, Texas, to Henry and Tina (Tiny) Johnson on March 31, 1878, one year after the remaining Union troops withdrew from the former Confederacy. Johnson's parents were born into slavery: Henry was born on a plantation in Maryland or Virginia in 1838 and was known for amusing his masters as a feared bare-knuckle exhibition boxer, and Tiny was born in North or South Carolina. Although the exact year of her birth is not known, she was younger than Henry.

Henry Johnson served in the U.S. Army's 38th Colored Infantry as a civilian teamster servant and likely as a carpenter during the American Civil War. He later worked as a bar porter, school janitor, and a supervising school janitor in Galveston's East School District. Tiny Johnson was a housewife who washed clothes to supplement the family's income. Despite the fact that they were illiterate, Henry and Tiny worked together to ensure that all of their children had at least five years of schooling and lived as law-abiding Christians. Henry settled in Galveston in 1867, but it is unclear when Tiny did.

Johnson had eight siblings, but only five lived to be adults. He had four sisters, including older sisters Lucy and Jennie, younger brother Henry, and adopted brother Charles. As the eldest brother, Johnson assisted his father with his janitorial duties and earned 10 cents and a new pair of red socks each week for riding along with and watching the milkman's horse-drawn wagon on Saturday mornings.

Galveston was the largest city in Texas and among the most prosperous in the country. It was a progressive city for blacks because there was gainful employment, and longshoremen were paid the same as whites, $2 a day, which was significant in 1877, particularly for African Americans that were lawfully considered property only 10 years prior. The city was said to have a Northern optimism that did not manifest in acute racial tension, although racial segregation and inequality were a fact of life. There were no laws prohibiting black and white children from playing together, though the city's school system was segregated. It was on the streets, alleys, and docks of Galveston where Johnson befriended white children, joined racially mixed gangs, and ate, fought, and slept at the homes of whites. His experiences led him to respect but not fear whites. From his childhood, he had a naturally high opinion of himself that could not be destroyed by racism.

As a youth Johnson was often beaten up by neighborhood bullies and teased because he was physically frail and a bit cowardly. His older sisters often protected him from them until one day his mother threatened to beat him if he did not learn to defend himself, which led him to dismantle one of the older and tougher neighborhood bullies. His new-found fighting prowess gave him enormous confidence and quickly earned him a reputation as a hard-hitting tough guy.

Johnson dropped out of school after the sixth grade to work on Galveston's docks and later held various menial jobs as sweeper, porter, and baker's assistant. He went to Dallas in search of employment, working at a racetrack caring for horses and then as an apprentice to a man named Walter Lewis, who owned a business that painted carriages. It was Lewis who sparked Johnson's interest in boxing by encouraging him to spar with friends for fun, which the young man took to with great ease. While Johnson appeared to be on course with his training in the profitable carriage painting trade, he sought more.

Johnson traveled to New York at the age of 16 with less than a nickel in his pocket as a stowaway on a cotton steamer, in search of Steve Brodie, an Irish immigrant saloonkeeper who became famous in 1886 for claiming to have jumped off the newly constructed Brooklyn Bridge. Johnson was, however, discovered aboard by the ship's captain and forced to earn his fare by shoveling coal and peeling potatoes. When the steamer landed in New York, he concocted a phony suicide plot to jump overboard referring to himself as a "worthless colored boy" with no family or friends, thereby appealing to the sentiments of white passengers, who filled his cap with money. It was Johnson's natural inclination to adapt to adverse circumstances and manipulate black/white power relations that separated him from most blacks.

Johnson does not appear to have ever found Brodie but his independence, drive, and confidence took him to Boston to track down Joe Walcott, a famous West Indian welterweight boxer also known as the "Barbados Demon." Johnson worked in a horse stable to support himself and eventually met Walcott. His interaction with Walcott and idolization of other black greats such as Isaac Murphy, a famous jockey, and Marshall "Major" Taylor, a nationally recognized bicycle racer, taught him that blacks could excel in sports irrespective of America's Jim Crow system.

Upon returning to Galveston in 1894, Johnson worked in a custodial capacity for a boxing gym. Here he seemed to develop and refine his boxing skills.

By the age of 16 he was extremely well built, standing 6' tall with a powerful frame, muscular arms and legs, and immense hand and foot speed. Johnson tested his prowess by challenging members of his gang and others. The critical incident that appears to have given him the confidence to become a boxer is when he beat an older, bigger, and rugged man named Davie Pierson, who accused Johnson of snitching on him after the two were arrested for playing craps.

Johnson earned his living fighting on the docks and in the alleys, clubhouses, and private boxing clubs in the area from 1895 to 1898, ultimately entering the world of the Battle Royal. The Battle Royal was a blood sport where around four to eight (or more) blacks, sometimes blindfolded or tied together, would pulverize each other in a ring for the amusement of an all-white audience until the last man stood. The winner collected the change thrown into the ring by onlookers. To many, Johnson became the king of the Battle Royal. His experiences as a black fighter in a racist and segregated society provided him with the ring experience that prepared him for national prominence. In March 1899, Johnson turned 21 and was keen to leave Galveston. After a brief marriage to Mary Austin, an African-American childhood friend, his thirst to become a national prizefighter led him to Springfield, Illinois.

Too many, Johnson was the best boxer that has ever lived. Although as previously noted, his boxing record consisted of 113 official fights with 79 wins (44 by knockout), 12 draws, and 8 losses, it was the era in which he boxed, his flamboyant style, and raw power that allowed him to become a giant among men in the annals of history. Unlike the boxers of today that fight no more than 10 rounds, Johnson routinely fought 20.

His professional career began in 1899, and by 1915 he had conquered the boxing world. His stellar career, however, was almost derailed by early losses and personal tragedy. While traveling to Chicago, Johnson's train stopped in Springfield, where he disembarked in search of a meal. He was immediately spotted by Johnny Conner, a former fighter turned saloon owner and promoter, and was offered room and board and an opportunity to win $50 if he participated in a Battle Royal. Desperate for money, Johnson accepted and pummeled his opponents before a crowd including journalists and boxing promoters. His performance created a buzz and landed him a fight with John "Klondike" Haynes in Chicago.

Although Johnson had fought for money since 1895, it was not until May 5, 1899, when he made his debut at the Howard Theatre in Chicago against Haynes that his professional career began. The Haynes bout was a far cry from fighting strongmen on the docks of Galveston. Johnson was defeated by a body blow in the fifth round and had his $10 purse withheld for allegedly quitting the fight, forcing him to beg its promoters for money to buy food. He had no job, income, or home in Chicago, making him homeless and desperate; he moved between the residences of friends and homeless shelters. After fighting in Indiana and skipping out on his landlord in Chicago, Johnson traveled to

Pittsburgh, New York, and New Haven, sometimes fighting and other times working as a trainer. He eventually returned to Galveston and reconnected with white childhood friend Leo Posner, who was matchmaker for the Galveston Athletic Club. Johnson solicited Posner to organize fights for him while he sought out a manager and spent his spare time moonlighting as president of the Twelfth Ward Republican Club in Galveston.

Posner organized a fight between Johnson and Bob White, an experienced heavyweight and top fighter in Texas, which ended in a 15-round decision for Johnson and earned him $100 and wide respect. He quickly became regarded as one of the top black fighters in the region, at times fighting as many as twice per week. On May 1, 1900, he fought his first white opponent, an Australian fighter named Jim Scanlon. Johnson knocked him out in the seventh round and seemed to relish the opportunity to defy the baseless theory of white supremacy by knocking whites out in the ring.

Soon after the Scanlon fight, Johnson took on and defeated Jim McCormick and Horace Miles and battled Haynes to a 20-round draw. He became stronger with each fight and developed into a gifted boxer; however, his career was put on hold when, in September 1900, Galveston was devastated by America's worst hurricane and natural disaster to that point. The hurricane killed over 8,000 people and displaced tens of thousands and obliterated about 70 percent of Galveston, including the home of Henry and Tiny Johnson. Johnson was deeply affected by the hurricane and its impact on Galveston—he served as a part of a black crew that assisted in both the relief and clean-up efforts. The hurricane also created a heightened incentive for him to generate money for his family.

He took on a promoter from Dallas by the name of A. Busch, who organized a few fights for him in Tennessee. Johnson fought his old foe Klondike and eventually found his way into the ring with Joseph Bartlett Choynski, a boxing icon and the first Jewish American athlete to rise to international repute. Although by 1901 Choynski was past his prime, white promoters were keen to keep Johnson from rising in the ranks too quickly and believed Choynski was the right antidote to their problem. On February 25, 1901, Choynski and Johnson fought in Galveston, and Johnson was knocked out in the third round. Both men were arrested in the ring and taken to jail by five Texas Rangers for prizefighting or fighting for financial gain, which was a felony in Texas punishable by two years in state prison. Oddly enough, they were placed in the same jail cell for 24 days, during which time Choynski taught Johnson invaluable boxing lessons. On March 8, 1901, a Galveston grand jury chose not to indict the fighters, and the county sheriff immediately released them and advised them to leave town before the state attorney levied additional charges against them. Johnson went to Denver, Colorado, and joined a boxing club named Ryan's Sand Creek House. He sparred with a string of fighters while in Denver.

Mary Austin visited and temporarily lived with Johnson in Denver and even accompanied him to California, then the boxing capital of the country.

He linked up with several fight managers and promoters and eventually settled with Frank Carillo, a hard-nosed Mexican American who dabbled in several professions including the saloon, racehorse, and dogfight businesses. He
temporarily settled in Bakersfield and chose to live in the white part of town
against the community norm of segregated living. Johnson viewed himself
above the color line. He fought and lost a decision to Hank Griffen, son of a
former slave, on November 4, 1901. Following this loss, He took several menial jobs until he had a rematch with Griffen in Oakland that December resulting in a draw.

Johnson next fought Frank Childs to a draw in Chicago and proceeded to
knock out several no-name fighters in New England, Texas, and California. It
was not until he fought Jack Jeffries that Johnson became recognized and even
vilified by America. Jeffries was the younger brother of heavyweight champion
Jim Jeffries, who was renowned for refusing to fight black boxers. Johnson's
fight with Jack took place on May 16, 1902, in Los Angeles, and the prefight
media blitz was replete with racial stereotypes and slurs. Johnson, who predicted he would knock Jeffries out 50 seconds after the fifth round began, was
not fazed by the frenzy and appeared in pink ring wear. The packed building
cheered for Jack Jeffries and hissed at Johnson. From the onset, Johnson toyed
with Jeffries and, just as he predicted, knocked him out in the fifth only to roll
him over and fan him in front of the white boxer's champion brother, whom
Johnson said that he could "lick," too. This victory over Jack Jeffries and several subsequent fights made him a household name.

Johnson then fought George Gardner, another well-known white fighter, for
20 rounds in October 1902, barely squeezing out the decision. Carillo, Johnson's corner man, who allegedly placed a significant bet on the fight, brandished
a gun and threatened to shoot his boxer if he lost. If this were not enough pressure, the media and white spectators castigated him whenever he faced a white
opponent. He nevertheless had a great deal of pride, a strong mind, and little
fear of people, particularly white men. On December 5, 1902, he fought Fred
Russell, a boxer trained by Jim Jeffries (who wanted revenge on Johnson for
dismantling his brother) known to be a dirty fighter. Russell ended the bout
by punching him in the genitals, causing Johnson to collapse in the ring. While
whites wanted to see Johnson fall, many were offended by Russell's dirty tactics and rushed the ring only to be repulsed by police. Johnson was awarded
the victory on a foul.

After firing Carillo for stealing funds, Johnson signed on with Tom McCa-
rey, a bookmaker and poolroom owner from Los Angeles who immediately
arranged for Johnson to fight Denver Ed Martin. Martin was called the black
heavyweight champion because no white champion was willing to fight him.
Johnson defeated Martin by decision in front of 4,000 spectators to become
the black heavyweight champion of the world; however, Johnson would not
be fulfilled until he defeated Jim Jeffries for the white heavyweight championship. Jeffries used race as a justification to avoid Johnson. Although Johnson
won a $1260 purse in the Martin fight (which is equivalent to $25,000 today),

he was eager for a big-money fight that could yield $10,000, which he needed to fuel his flamboyant lifestyle that included numerous cars, clothes, and women. Johnson was one of the first Americans to own a Winton automobile manufactured by the Winton Motor Carriage Company. He was an avid driver.

After the Martin fight, Johnson became increasingly frustrated that the top white boxers refused to fight him. Nevertheless, he continued to box, hoping that one day his mastery in the ring would generate public outcry for a championship match with one of the white greats. Between 1903 to October 1904, Johnson traveled and won half of his fights by knockout and the rest by decision. His October 27, 1903, fight with Sam McVey in Los Angeles earned him $2796, which was his largest payday to date. The fight improved his image with the media and was the most profitable boxing event Los Angeles had ever hosted. The Johnson-McVey fights were so popular and profitable that their handlers scheduled another bout on April 24, 1904, in San Francisco, where Johnson jeerfully toyed with McVey and angered the crowd. Some fans were so incensed with his cat and mouse game with McVey that they flipped lit matches on his back, threatened his life with racial slurs, and attempted to assault him in the ring. Johnson responded by throwing the contents of his spit bucket at them and bolting out of the building. His masterful defeat of McVey caused the media to discuss his readiness for Jim Jeffries.

Johnson met and entered into relationships with two black prostitutes from Philadelphia, Clara Kerr and Etta Reynolds, in the summer of 1903. While his relationship with Reynolds was of limited duration, he developed a long-term relationship with Kerr and lived happily with her for about two years. Johnson moved to Chicago with Kerr and made Chicago his base of operations. However, when Kerr allegedly had an affair with William Bryant, one of Johnson's childhood friends, the boxer lost all faith in black women. Following his fallout with Kerr, Johnson suffered a loss in the ring, where race played a significant role in a decision against him.

Johnson fought Marvin Hart, a top white Kentuckian contender for the heavyweight title, in San Francisco on March 28, 1905. Hart was an avowed white supremacist; prior to the bout he openly hurled racial insults at Johnson, who responded by calling him a coward to his face. Although both men fought valiantly, Hart won the bout in a controversial decision by the fight's promoter and self-appointed judge, Alex Greggains. Jim Jeffries attended the bout and relished the outcome. After the Hart fight, Johnson went on a rampage, fighting 12 more times in 1905, winning the majority of bouts by knockout and losing one match in November in the second round for a foul.

The racist commentary of sports writers, bloodthirsty spectators who reveled in the notion of a white boxer defeating Johnson, and the dirty tricks of opponents in these fights revealed that Johnson was at the epicenter of a sick society and sport. In his 1905 fight against Sandy Ferguson, Johnson punished and embarrassed the white hope so badly that the boxer kneed Johnson in the genitals three times to the roaring approval of his fans, causing him to collapse. When the referee declared Johnson the winner on a foul, Ferguson and

*The search for the "white hope" not having been successful, prejudices were being piled up against me, and certain unfair persons, piqued because I was champion, decided if they could not get me one way they would another.*

his spectators started a riot, though Johnson managed to slip away. The Ferguson incident was reminiscent of the bout with Russell; white men unable to defeat him in the ring sought to castrate him as slave owners did on plantations to keep their "black bucks" in check.

After his July 24, 1905, bout with Joe Grim, Johnson moved back to Los Angeles with Kerr, with whom he had reconciled. His life took yet another turn for the worse, however, when Kerr unexpectedly departed with what little money he possessed; she left him broke in the heart and pocket book. Taken together, these events deeply affected Johnson, who swore never to settle with other black women. In the year that followed he cleansed the heavyweight division while waiting feverishly for a bout with a white heavyweight champion. Johnson hired Sam Fitzpatrick as his new manager and even traveled to Australia with Alec McLean to show films of their fights and take on any contenders.

Johnson arrived in Australia on January 24, 1907, with great fanfare. He was an enigma to the Australians, who respected him as one of America's leading boxers but unsurprisingly shared the same racist attitudes toward blacks as white Americans. After he defeated Peter Felix, Australia's "colored champion," for the colored heavyweight title of the world on February 19, he dismantled Australian Bill Lang, another white hopeful, before 20,000 spectators on March 4. Johnson made plans to leave Australia, but not before having an affair with a white Australian woman from a prominent family. He was also arrested for physically assaulting McLean, who had filed a beach of contract claim against Johnson for failing to pay him a debt. He was forbidden from leaving Australia until the claim, which was decided in McLean's favor, was adjudicated that April.

Johnson returned to San Francisco in May, but had enormous difficulty finding anyone credible to fight, as the white heavyweight contenders stayed clear of him. He managed to muster two fights before getting what ultimately was one of his most strategic fights with ex-champion Bob Fitzsimmons, one of the hardest hitting heavyweights in history. Fitzsimmons fought Johnson on July 17, 1907, in Philadelphia, only to suffer an embarrassing knockout in the second round. Johnson's victory and public persona as a fearless and independent black man were celebrated by blacks all over the country and elevated the boxer to the status of an icon.

While Johnson fought nearly 30 more challengers over 12 years, his bouts with Tommy Burns in December 1908 and Jim Jeffries in July 1910 were the most important of his career and collectively the single greatest blow to white supremacy in the first half of the twentieth century. While his standing in the boxing world was at an all-time high, his fights with Burns and Jeffries would not occur for six more fights and another year and a half.

After defeating six other boxers in 1907 and 1908, Johnson and Fitzpatrick lobbied for a match with Burns, the Canadian world champion. Though they followed him to France to argue their case, Burns would not fight Johnson. He refused to fight a black boxer for less than $30,000 and berated Johnson with racial slurs in the press. An Australian promoter raised the capital for a fight between Burns and Johnson, however, offering $30,000 to the former and $5,000 to the latter. Johnson was not happy about receiving one-sixth of the amount of Burns but nonetheless agreed to fight in Sydney on December 26, 1908.

As Johnson entered the ring, 20,000 white Australians jeered at him in a seamless epithet of racial slurs; they did not come to see Johnson win but rather Burns thrash the black aspirant. Johnson was used to such abuse and walked down the aisle to the ring undaunted, cheery, and shaking his head with confidence. When Burns entered the stadium he received a standing ovation from the crowd. He also earned roaring cheers when he refused to shake Johnson's hand before the fight. Johnson pulverized Burns once the fight began, sending him to the canvas in the first and second rounds. With a smile on his face, he methodically talked to and beat Burns round after bloody round. He could have knocked out the champion in the first round but wanted to demonstrate his fighting skills to the world. Johnson made a mockery of his opponent by speaking to the press while pummeling him, only to knock him down a third time in the seventh round. His clinical handling of Burns was a silent retort to the widely held view among whites that blacks were weak in the stomach, yellow under pressure, and unintelligent in the ring. Johnson was holding Burns up and beating him by the thirteenth round to the utter dismay of the crowd, who called for the police to stop the fight. Burns wanted to continue, though in the fourteenth round he was so badly beaten that the police stopped the fight and the referee declared Johnson the victor. The victory created a numbing quiet as the stunned audience left the stadium. After defeating Burns, Johnson visited the grave of Peter Jackson, the black Australian heavyweight champion whom former white American world champion John L. Sullivan refused to fight on racial grounds for the world heavyweight championship that Johnson now held.

Johnson's victory sent shock waves of hope and pride into blacks in the United States and beyond and acute fear into white Australians and their Anglo-Saxon brethren in the United States. Many commentators responded with praise for the legal constraints on nonwhite immigration to Australia and de jure segregation in America. The triumph caused some sports writers to wish that there had never been a Slave Trade and that Johnson had remained in the trees of Africa. Even though Johnson was American, white Americans were indifferent to his world championship victory and had hoped that the white Canadian would defeat him. They feared the new champion's victory would empower and embolden blacks with racial pride—an unacceptable proposition given America's racial caste system. In contrast, Black America reveled in Johnson's

*They have inspired me to attainment and they have balked me; they have caused me joy and they have heaped misery upon me; they have been faithful to the utmost and they have been faithless; they have praised and loved me and they have hated and denounced me. Always, a woman has swayed me—sometimes many have demanded my attention at the same moment.*

victory, making him the most famous and respected athlete in that community.

After his fight with Burns, Johnson and his white girlfriend Hattie McClay traveled to Vancouver, British Columbia, where the boxer was prohibited from staying in white-only hotels, to fight Victor McLaglen. He defeated this boxer in the sixth round on March 10, 1909. His flamboyant lifestyle, combined with his alleged "marriage" to McClay, engendered significant attention. Interracial marriage was an aberration in Canada and America; in fact, thousands of black men were lynched or murdered for even the insinuation of relations with white women. Notwithstanding, he didn't care about the social status quo and continued to publicly enjoy the company of other white women, such as Belle Schreiber, after parting ways with McClay. When Johnson defeated a string of boxers in 1909, the media pressure on Jeffries was too great and purse too big to allow race to continue to serve as a cloak of avoidance.

Shortly thereafter, Johnson fired Fitzpatrick and hired George Little, a Chicago businessman who ran a brothel among other enterprises, to be his new manager. Johnson lived lavishly, spending money on his women companions, such as McClay, who reappeared, Schreiber, and another prostitute named Etta Terry Duryea. Even Kerr reappeared, claimed to be his wife, and sued Johnson for $406 she was allegedly owed. Finally, after years of ducking Johnson, Jeffries agreed to fight him. The fighters met on October 29, 1909, at New York's Albany Hotel, negotiated terms, and gave promoters until November 30 to submit their bids. George Lewis "Tex" Rickard, a successful businessman and casino owner, approached Johnson offered a $101,000 purse, which was the biggest offer in boxing history and worth nearly $2 million today, as well as two-thirds of the film rights to be split between the boxers. Rickard partnered with another promoter named Jack Gleason to avoid controversy after learning that Jeffries had secretly signed on with that promoter. Johnson agreed without consulting Little, as did Jeffries through his manager Samuel Berger. Both men received a $10,000 advance and the fight was set for July 4, 1910.

In the months preceding the bout, Johnson and Jeffries traveled on the road touring with various vaudeville shows and other carnival tours, while Rickard dealt with the politics of finding a venue for the fight. It was supposed to take place in San Francisco, but California Governor J. N. Gillette barred it for alleged moral and political reasons. Rickard moved the fight to Reno with the blessings of Nevada Governor Denver S. Dickerson. The run-up to the fight was filled with excitement, rumors, racial tension, heartbreak, scandal, and violence, particularly for Johnson. He created a love quadrangle with McClay, Schreiber, and Terry, resulting in feuds among the women. He also engaged in a violent skirmish with a taxi driver who refused him service, pulled a gun on Sam Langford for threatening him, beat Schreiber after a domestic dispute, and was arrested for beating a man in a bar who insulted him. For his part, Jeffries made a considerable sum on the road but grew weary from all of the hype surrounding the fight. The pressure of being the "Great White Hope" wore him down to point where he wanted to quit touring; however, he readily accepted the role of the great white redeemer.

The contest between the so-called colored heavyweight champion of the world, an interesting title given that Johnson already defeated white champion Burns in Australia, and the "champion of champions" who had retired several years earlier was the biggest news in the nation and people from around the world tuned in to hear the fight via radio broadcast. The country's racial division was reflected in blacks' support for Johnson and whites' support for Jeffries. Americans did not consider this an ordinary fight but rather a clash of the races: a test to determine whether white subjugation of blacks was a natural right or arrangement of limited duration.

As Johnson walked into the ring for the fight, the majority of the nearly 30,000 spectators hissed and hurled racial slurs at him reminiscent of the Burns fight. Jeffries's entry into the stadium was met with the thunderous roar of nearly all those in attendance, who firmly expected him to dismantle Johnson. When the fight began, the boxers spent the first few minutes feeling one another out, and by the second round Johnson seemed to have had his opponent's number. He did a lot of talking and smiling while seeming to dominate Jeffries with uppercuts. The white boxer retaliated with insults, powerful body blows, and head shots, which by the fourth round had cut open Johnson's mouth. Nevertheless, Johnson incrementally wore Jeffries down in rounds 5 through 15 while the crowd became more incensed with the cavalier and masterful way he dismantled the former white champion. By the middle of the fifteenth round, Jeffries was bloodied with a broken nose, swollen-shut eyes, and other cuts. After Johnson knocked Jeffries down several times, white spectators began shouting racial epithets and demanding that Jeffries's corner not allow Johnson to knock out the white boxer. Soon after, Jeffries's camp threw in the towel, ending the fight. Rickard declared Johnson the winner.

Black Americans celebrated throughout the country, and whites responded with ugly and pernicious violence. White citizens and police throughout the country openly spat on, beat, burned, lynched, and shot black Americans in an orgy of violence that resulted in the murder of at least 30 blacks with hundreds more severely wounded. The most detestable acts of violence occurred in the neighborhood of San Juan Hill, an area in the West 60s in Manhattan. A group of whites set a building in this neighborhood on fire, and then tried to prevent the black occupants from escaping. A black man riding on a streetcar who cheered for Johnson was assaulted by a white passenger. In Wheeling, West Virginia, a black man who drove the same type of car as Johnson was pulled from his vehicle by a group of whites. The driver was hung. Further south, several black people were killed or injured in Uvalda, Georgia, after a group of white men shot their weapons through a black construction camp.

The victory meant more to blacks than any since Emancipation; however, Johnson was aware that too much chest pumping would only exacerbate the violence and dissuaded blacks from doing so while at the same time cautioning whites not to be uncivilized. He attended celebration parties all over the country, but Chicago was where he had the biggest following. He deposited his $101,000 purse in the First Trust and Savings Bank in Chicago and bought new cars and clothes and even shared some of his purse with his old friends in Galveston. He was on top of the world, but soon the world would be on top of him.

The media characterized Johnson as a black villain throughout his career due to his "ethnic cleansing" of great "white hopes," his ability to shatter white America's machinations about black inferiority, and his fearless and cavalier attitude toward life, including his fancy for white women. After defeating Jeffries, Johnson became the most famous sportsman in the world. He achieved what he had always wanted: iconic status. However, it was also his win over Jeffries that spurred the wagons of white supremacy rolling. He became the target of public and private discrimination. Nowhere was this more apparent that through the law. Fifteen states and the District of Columbia banned the distribution of the Johnson versus Jeffries fight for fear that the imagery of a black man legally pummeling a white man would threaten America's segregated status quo. In response to the fight, Congress also banned the interstate transportation of fight films in 1912. Johnson's victory and fiercely independent and boastful character infuriated white American society. He was the world champion in the manliest of sports, bold and defiant of white authority and custom, and a role model for other blacks. His example scared whites in America and beyond.

While Johnson became a soft target of local police for speeding, even going to jail for 25 days in San Francisco as perhaps the first black man to be racially profiled while driving, his real troubles began after he badly beat Terry Duryea, his lover. For most Americans, black and white, it was bad enough that he publicly courted white women, but to beat one bloody 55 years before Emmett Till was lynched for allegedly making an overture to a white woman, and then publicly marry her was too much for most white Americans to stomach. This was also the case in Britain, where Johnson traveled to fight British heavyweight Billy Mills in 1912. British Home Secretary Winston Churchill barred the bout, however, fearing that any interracial fight resulting in a loss by Mills could destabilize white rule in the colonies in the same way that racial violence ensued after the Jeffries bout.

Upon returning to the United States, Johnson fought Jim Flynn on July 4, 1912, in New Mexico and defeated the "white hope" in the ninth round after police stopped the bout. Soon after, he opened a saloon called Café de Champion on the South Side of Chicago, which was a major hit in the city. Johnson was the champion of the world and a prominent businessman. However, his life took a serious turn for the worse when Duryea, who was abused by Johnson and shunned by blacks and whites, committed suicide in September. Scrutiny of him heightened when, within a month of Duryea's death, he had an affair with an 18-year-old white woman, Lucille Cameron, against the wishes of her mother. On October 18, 1912, Johnson was arrested and charged with the abduction of Cameron, but was thereafter released on bail to the displeasure of the crowds of whites who jeered for him to be lynched.

Johnson was charged for violating the 1910 Mann Act (also known as the White Slave Traffic Act), a federal act adopted to combat the sexual exploitation of white women, which made it a felony to "knowingly transport or cause to be transported, or aid or assist in obtaining transportation for, or in transporting, in interstate or foreign commerce, any woman or girl for the purpose of prostitution or debauchery or any other immoral purpose." Cameron refused to testify against Johnson, so the government was forced to drop its case. The two married soon after, to the utter dismay of Americans, particularly whites. Their marriage was condemned by local, state, and federal politicians and engendered venomous reactions from the governors of New York, Pennsylvania, Ohio, and Georgia, among many others. Immediately, antimiscegenation laws were introduced in 10 of the 20 states that permitted interracial marriages, and not fewer than 21 such bills were introduced in Congress.

Humiliated by its inability to prosecute Johnson, the government aggressively investigated him and coopted Belle Schreiber, who was scorned by Johnson years earlier, to testify against him. Her testimony enabled the government to obtain an indictment against Johnson for violating the Mann Act. He was charged with transporting Schreiber across state lines for sexual use, engaging her in prostitution, and sexual perversions or physical abuse, the latter of which was later dropped by the government. On May 7, 1913, the case went to trial in the U.S. District Court of Illinois and an all-white male jury found him guilty of the sexual use and prostitution charges. The judge sentenced Johnson to a $1,000 fine and one year and a day in prison. The U.S. Court of Appeals for the Seventh Circuit, however, took issue with the District Court's ruling, reversed the prostitution conviction, and remanded for resentencing the sexual use charge, though not before Johnson fled the country. He and Cameron escaped to Paris through Canada, arriving there in June 1913.

Johnson spent seven years living as a fugitive and fighting in England, Paris, Spain, Mexico, and Cuba, among other places. During this period he fought 13 opponents, losing only one bout to Jess Willard in Havana on April 5, 1915. In February 1916, while in England, he was ordered to pay a $1,100 fine for slugging his manager and was banned from England under the Alien Restriction Act. With the exception of the United Kingdom, Johnson was generally treated well in Europe and traveled with vaudeville shows to make a living. World War I made the continent an inhospitable place for him, however, forcing him to move to Latin America. After his friend and business partner Mexican President

Venustiano Carranza was assassinated in May 1920, Johnson was forced to leave the country. He returned to the United States on July 20, 1920, surrendering to federal marshals in California. He later reappeared in District Court in Chicago and was resentenced to one year in prison and sent to Leavenworth penitentiary in Kansas.

Johnson was released from prison in July 1921 and greeted as a hero by scores of blacks. Lucille divorced him in 1924, and he married a third white woman. He took on nine professional fights out of financial desperation over the next seven years, losing only two in 1928. He lived out his life as reluctant national and international hero to blacks all over the world, only to be killed on July 10, 1946, on U.S. Highway 1 near Raleigh, North Carolina, after crashing his Lincoln Zephyr on his way to New York to see Joe Louis and Billy Conn fight on July 19, 1946. He was 68 years old.

The boxer's relentless pursuit of excellence shattered and changed the world of sports and America's racist sociopolitical order. Jack Johnson was a maverick revolutionary. He transformed not only the world of sports, particularly boxing, but also American society. He is not simply an African American sports icon; he was one of America's leading sports and social icons in the early twentieth century. No other athlete or social activist during his era or since has provoked the minds and stirred the social consciousness of people while simultaneously exemplifying mastery of a craft. He defied all odds to become the indisputable heavyweight champion of the world and publicly defy social casting. He wore the clothes, drove the cars, dated and married the women, and knocked out the people inside and outside of the ring as he wanted.

Johnson's fearless brand of individualism, courage, and defiance of America's racist sports and sociopolitical orders were inimitable. He was an individual rights activist, which wittingly made him a civil rights pragmatist. He achieved what few in world history who faced systematic tyranny and violence could; he employed an apolitical philosophy of nonviolence using the weapons of hard work, excellence, and individualism to combat, invalidate, enfeeble, and dismantle a vicious sociopolitical and legal order, in this case American white supremacy. Johnson did not allow America's social status quo to define him; rather, he redefined it.

## FURTHER READING

Ardell, Jean Hastings. "Baseball Annies, Jack Johnson, and Kenesaw Mountain Landis: How Groupies Influenced the Lengthy Ban on Blacks in Organized Baseball," _Nine_ (Spring 2005): 103.

Deardorff, Donald, II. "World Boxing Champion Jack Johnson, Contemptuous and Irritating, Taunted Whites," _St. Louis Journalism Review_ 8:3 (October 1995).

Evans, Art. "Joe Louis as a Key Functionary: White Reactions towards a Black Champion," _Journal of Black Studies_ 16:1 (September 1985): 95–111.

Gilmore, Al-Tony. "Jack Johnson and White Women: The National Impact," *Journal of Negro History* 58:1 (January 1973): 18–38.

Johnson, Jack. *In the Ring and Out*. Chicago: National Sports Publishing, 1927.

Ward, Geoffrey. *Unforgivable Blackness: The Rise and Fall of Jack Johnson*. New York: W. W. Norton, 2004.

AP Photo/Kirthmon Dozier.

# Michael Jordan

*Mary G. McDonald*

> *I realize that I'm black, but I like to be viewed as a person, and this is everybody's wish.*

Player of the playoffs. Perhaps the most famous image of this win was a picture of him crying tears of joy and relief while clutching the championship trophy after securing the final victory against the Lakers.

Jordan and the Bulls would continue their dominance the next season earning a 67–12 record with Jordan averaging over 30 points per game and anchoring the Bulls defense. The Blazers would eventually fall to the Bulls in the finals with Jordan earning MVP accolades once again. The Bulls would go on to complete a three-peat against the Phoenix Suns to capture the 1992–1993 title while Jordan, who averaged over 41 points during the playoffs, also became the first player ever to win three consecutive championship MVP trophies.

Fans not only followed and praised Jordan for his athletic prowess, however. Nike advertisements also played a significant role in creating an enticing persona, which fueled the athletic mythos of the icon. Indeed, Jordan himself recognized the power of advertising. He explained that Nike's advocacy made him a dream. Even the NBA learned to promote appealing personalities and enticing images of physicality by following Nike's lead. While the NBA and Nike offered slightly different constructions of Jordan, with Nike positioning the athlete more stylishly, the similarities between the institutions' images are unmistakable; both show him as a certifiable nice guy, the All-American boy next door, while also highlighting his entertaining athleticism.

Jordan was active in creating the image his fans enjoyed. His athletic talents provided him with the opportunity to create his own persona, while also changing the institution of the NBA. Jordan's success on and off the court helped shift the possibilities available to other professional basketball players to earn higher salaries and product endorsements.

Clearly part of Jordan's appeal has been his expressive style of play. According to cultural critic Michael Eric Dyson, Jordan's physical expressiveness is best described by the Air Jordan moniker seen on his signature line of Nike shoes: "head moving, arms extending, hands waving, tongue wagging and legs spreading." As Dyson suggests, this style and grace are comparable to other historical expressions of African American culture, including jazz and rap. Jordan's ability to slam the basketball is, then, a form of cultural resistance to white power structures, given that his style is an expression of bodily ingenuity and creativity.

His style remains one of his most important contributions to the NBA. There is no question that his ability to dunk and be creative with the basketball is his own unique hallmark. The icon's expressive playing style and creativity in making improvisational movements toward the basket accounts for the moniker Air Jordan, his famous nickname and the name given to his Nike sneaker line, as well as other nicknames, including "His Airness."

Though Jordan has crafted an extraordinary talent, the intense focus on his body by Nike and the NBA demonstrate America's continued obsession with the physical capabilities of the male body. Despite women's continued presence in sport, dominant constructions of athletic masculinity legitimate myths of male physical superiority, which is often misunderstood as easily equating to male social superiority.

Fascination with the male body is complicated, however, by race. American history includes histories of white preoccupation with the physicality of black bodies. Rooted in social Darwinist thought, this focus presumes that African Americans are physically gifted, closer to nature, and less civilized than whites. Stereotypical interest in black bodies has been used by whites to justify racist treatment from the advent of slavery to the dismantling of social welfare programs in contemporary times.

Advertisements featuring Jordan offer examples of this interest in black bodies, and the icon's in particular. For example, the famous Nike "Jordan flight" commercial was first broadcast in the spring of 1985. In it, Jordan plays on a blacktopped basketball court with the Chicago skyline in the background. He slam-dunks the basketball against the sound of jet engines revving up for flight. He then remains suspended, as if airborne, with his legs apart for the final 10 seconds of the commercial. This image is an apparent testimonial to both his incredible athleticism and the alleged power of the black and red Nike athletic shoes on his feet. A voiceover asks, "Who said man was not meant to fly?" This commercial offers an affable Jordan as the quintessential natural athlete, for as the extraordinary claim suggests, he can literally fly through the air.

The NBA also followed the lead of Nike. The institution had difficulties generating interest in its games through the 1970s, but by the mid-1980s, it developed a strong promotion machine. By promoting games as unique entertainment events with stylized play and appealing personalities, the NBA reinvented itself and moved away from its 1970s image, which was linked with racist images of African American players as undisciplined and deviant. A key element of the NBA's resurgence lay in the league's ability to appease white audiences by distancing itself from mythical associations of urban blackness that connoted an uncontrollable and undisciplined style of play and carried the stigma of assumed drug abuse.

The NBA focused upon players such as Michael Jordan in order to align itself with qualities including patriotism, heroism, wholesomeness, racial harmony, moral pureness, and a disciplined physicality. Though this attention to Jordan and other black athletes seemed somewhat positive, it remained based in stereotypical assumptions; this revision of black masculinity, created by white-controlled institutions such as the NBA, was designed to evoke pleasure rather than conjure fear or disdain. Jordan's tremendous basketball skills allowed many fans of all races and backgrounds to embrace and praise black talent and achievement. Jordan's talent was sometimes used, however, by organizations such as Nike and the NBA to sell their products and ideas about athleticism and black athleticism in particular.

Additionally, the NBA and Nike reinforced beliefs about black bodies by promoting Jordan as someone who was, according to critic David Andrews, "seemingly born to dunk." His corporate sponsors encouraged a cultural pre-occupation with black physicality, though they did so in ways designed to in-duce, in the words of one social commentator, "desire without evoking dread."

In the midst of this marketing, Jordan remained a force to be reckoned with on the court. In 1988, he won the NBA's slam-dunk contest in Chicago before a capacity hometown crowd during the All-Star festivities. To win the contest, Jordan took off from the foul line and then covered a distance of 15 feet at an elevation high enough to meet the 10-foot-high basket with a forceful jam.

Jordan's political voice did not imitate those of predecessors such as Tommie Smith, John Carlos, or Muhammad Ali. In many ways, he was a willing corpo-rate pitchman as much as he was a star athlete. His participation in advertise-ments for Nike and the NBA stands in stark contrast to the vision of African American athletes as outspoken critics of the white establishment. Jordan cer-tainly had myriad reasons to work with these institutions, preferring to serve as a role model for the ideas of racial tolerance, dedication, hard work, and achievement. His decisions and the ways in which advertisers and the NBA represented him are also, in many ways, a reflection of the political atmosphere in which he lived and played ball.

From a moralizing and corporate-friendly atmosphere, Jordan first emerged. It would be a mistake, however, to assume that he actively supported many of the regressive social policies of the times. Indeed, his philanthropy work (such as establishing a Chicago Boys and Girls Club in his late father's name) suggests an awareness of many inequalities that continue to impact the poor in general and poor African Americans in particular do need redress. Still, the relentless promotion of his wholesome persona and ability to secure large endorsement deals speaks to the many of the issues of the times in which he lived.

Before he ever played a game in the NBA, Nike signed Jordan to a then un-heard of $2.5 million five-year endorsement contract. Nike's Air Jordan sneaker line generated $125 million in its initial year. He not only received support from the Nike corporation, however. With the assistance of agent David Falk, in this corporate-friendly era the athlete eventually inked endorsement deals with such notable U.S. financial icons as McDonald's, Coca-Cola, Chevrolet, and Wheat-ies. By the end of the millennium, Jordan helped generate over $10 billion in profits for his sponsors and, as one commentator observed, created a different type of athlete: "the one-man corporate powerhouse."

In this historical moment, icons of success, particularly black ones, were additionally promoted by conservative voices. Again, regardless of their own personal views on justice and equality, individuals such as Jordan, Oprah Win-frey, and Bill Cosby symbolically revealed, according to many conservatives, that the achievement of the American dream was open to everyone of good character, regardless of race, creed, sex, or class. This uncritical promotion of the American dream fails to account for large social structures that still keep many from achieving financial and psychological security. In marketing Jor-dan, Nike particularly mobilized this emotionally salient sensibility of rugged individualism by promoting him as, in Nike CEO Phil Knight's words, "the ultimate 'Just Do It' athlete." One particular print advertisement is emblematic in this regard. Featuring a meditative Jordan, the advertisement's accompanying text tells of a Jordan who failed frequently only to succeed.

While this advertisement reaffirms the long-standing American celebration of rugged individualism, it also articulates a conservative message. In an era famous for attacks on the welfare state, often halfhearted enforcement of civil rights laws, and the scapegoating of the poor, this ad suggests that success is a matter of individual will, rather than the domain of the privileged.

Advertisements depicting Jordan evolved over time, however. Nike recruited noted filmmaker Spike Lee to promote him via an aura of affability and intimacy. Shot in black and white, Lee's Nike ad campaign secured Jordan's status as a talented "regular guy." This pairing, known as "The Spike and Mike Show," was described as one of the best ad campaigns of 1991. Lee played the character of Mars Blackmon, a bike messenger transported from the film *She's Gotta Have It* into this series of Nike ads. In one advertisement in the series, Blackmon calls Jordan "Money."

Concurrently with Nike, the NBA marketing machine and commercial sponsors also continued to force new and different meanings around Jordan's athleticism and the slam-dunk. Where once the dunk stood for the apparently undisciplined flamboyance of the playground and of African Americans, it now represented success and expression. Players such as Jordan assisted the NBA in actively promoting this movement as yet another example of the spectacular entertainment and expressive personalities of the NBA. This marketing strategy received a great boast when Jordan, along with several NBA superstars, such as Charles Barkley and Larry Bird, again participated in the Olympics in 1992. As a U.S. Olympian, he again won a gold medal with the heavily marketed Dream Team in Barcelona.

Jordan also expressed himself through the written word by coauthoring his own book in 1993. *Rare Air: Michael on Michael* is a testimony to the athlete's off-the-court persona as a dedicated family man who is committed to the tough, macho world of sport, yet apparently interested in the responsibilities and comfort of family life. Photo after photo offers a window into Jordan's familial bliss and his status as a concerned husband and caring father to his young family. One particular photo features a bare-chested Jordan holding his infant daughter Jasmine, who is clad only in a diaper. It is a salient image, one that highlights the contrast of Jordan's strong, muscled body with the tenderness and innocence of his daughter.

Notably, that book was dedicated to the memory of his father, James, who was tragically murdered in the summer of 1993. Initial speculation that the death was somehow linked to Michael's gambling activities was quieted with the arrest and arraignment of two North Carolina teenagers, Larry Martin Demure and Daniel Andrea Green. Jordan's close relationship with his father was well chronicled during his career, and thus it is no surprise that he was despondent over his father's death. He was also angered over the unfair media allegations that somehow his own high-stakes gambling activities might have contributed.

While many speculated that his subsequent brief retirement from professional basketball on October 6, 1993, in order to play minor league baseball was the direct result of his grief over his father's death, Jordan emphatically stated that his father's death had nothing to do with his choice.

While James Jordan's death proved that son Michael's fame could not shield him from tragedy, many other representations show more celebratory images. *Rare Air* is filled with numerous pictures documenting many of the warm and engaging experiences of his own family life with his wife Juanita (the Jordans subsequently filed for divorce in late 2006) and his young children, Jeffrey, Marcus, and Jasmine.

What is most interesting about this book is that it challenges stereotypes about the black family while also reinforcing traditional gender roles. The Jordan family's bliss offers an enticing vision of black success and consumer comfort, countering conservative suggestions that black families are "in decline," inherently pathological or all poor. The icon's off-the-court image as a concerned father and his publicly stated belief that, "from a husband's point of view, I've got to improve," project a wholesome image.

This vision counters negative assumptions about black male athletes, including those of masculine force, hypersexuality, and deviance. Yet these sanitized images of Jordan are built upon traditional gender expectations, domestic bliss, and consumer comfort. Read from this perspective, Jordan's family values may still participate in a conservative project in regard to U.S. families even as they defend the image of American black families.

Jordan's basketball career continued to soar throughout the 1990s. He changed the fate of the Bulls. He led the once hapless team to two three-peats, that is, six NBA titles in 1991, 1992, 1993, 1996, 1997, 1998. He exhibited dramatic flair in helping his team secure the 1996 title on Father's Day. In an obvious tribute to his deceased father, James, Jordan later explained that winning the title on Father's Day "makes it even more special. There's no way to really describe it."

Jordan retired from the Bulls (again) in 1999. In an attempt to revitalize the franchise and mentor the team's young players, he came out of retirement from a career as the Washington Wizards president of player operations and minority owner to play again. He played with the Wizards from 2001 through 2003. He had helped the Washington team achieve modest success, but his competitive style apparently also managed to upset some of the team's players and executives. In a stunning move, Wizards owner Abe Pollin declined to rehire Jordan or allow him to regain his status as a Washington owner once he retired as a player from the Wizards in 2003. Jordan would eventually find his way back to the NBA as an owner of the Charlotte Bobcats.

Despite the setbacks with the Wizards, during his tenure as a player Jordan won the championship's Most Valuable Player award in each of the finals in which he played. In 1996, he was named one of the 50 greatest players in NBA history. He truly earned this honor. He averaged over 30 points per game during his 15-year professional career and was also named the league's MVP in 1988, 1991, 1992, 1996, and 1998. He was a 10-time All-NBA First Team selection (1987–1993, 1996–1998), was selected to the NBA All-Defensive First Team nine times (1988–1993, 1996–1998), and won the Defensive Player of the Year award in 1988.

> *I've missed more than nine thousand shots in my career. I've lost almost three hundred games. Twenty-six times, I've been trusted to take the game winning shot and missed. I've failed over and over again in my life. And that is why I succeed.*

Jordan fared just as well in the advertising world. He garnered high marks on the industry's Q scores, which rate celebrity credibility, recognition, and appeal. Over the years he has pitched products for Nike, Coca-Cola, McDonald's, MCI long distance telephone service, Wheaties, Hanes Underwear, Gatorade, Rayovac batteries, and Bijan cologne, among numerous others. In 1998 alone, he reportedly earned $45 million in endorsements, including $16 million from Nike in addition to his $34 million professional basketball salary.

Due to the global reach of the NBA and Nike, Jordan's iconic status continues to generate complex cultural meanings both within and outside of the United States. His life and basketball persona have touched geopolitical spaces including Poland, New Zealand, and across the Black Atlantic. As one study has revealed that for Poles, particularly for Poland's youth, living in a postcommunist nation, Jordan represents the achievement of the American dream. The basketball player's commercialized persona has served positive ends in New Zealand, paradoxically helping generate wider interest in all sports, particularly assisting in the rejuvenation of traditional New Zealand sporting activities. He also signifies black accomplishment, resolve, and pride to members of the Black Diaspora living across the world, thereby igniting hope and the possibility of a brighter future for people of color across the globe.

While Jordan serves as a transnational symbol whose meaning varies according to local histories, his ascent to the status of cultural icon coincided with the ascent of particular neoliberal, conservative ideologies within the United States. His All-American persona and reputation as a hard-working African American athlete who allegedly transcends his race have served contradictory but ultimately regressive ends. On the one hand, the vision of Jordan as an exceptional pitchman and athlete provides a compelling image of black achievement, which in turn counters lingering racist stereotypes of black men as incompetent and dangerous. Yet the celebrated image of the icon as a rugged individual simultaneously reinforces historically specific policies, which disproportionately harm people of color by suggesting that success is merely a matter of personal determination, rather than an issue affected by structures of opportunity. What may be most telling is not only Jordan's status as a great athlete and endorser, but also the ways in which representations of the icon rely upon, reinforce, and at times contradict the tenor of the times.

Even after his playing days are now (apparently) over, Jordan continues to receive social and economic rewards and connect to important trends of the day. *Forbes* magazine in 2006 still ranked him among the top 30 sport endorsers in the United States. Additionally, thanks largely to the Nike Jordan brand, which earned over $500 million in sales, he reportedly garnered $32 million in endorsements between June 2005 and June 2006. The athlete's 2005 book, titled *Driven from Within*, additionally sold well over 100,000 copies in its first year of release. Jordan also became part owner of the NBA's Charlotte Bobcats in 2006.

Jordan remains a powerful figure for a variety of reasons. Merely listing these accomplishments fails to explain what these achievements mean and why he apparently has meant so much to diverse groups of people and economic interests. Cultural critic Michael Eric Dyson is among several social commentators suggesting that Jordan's global appeal is a testament both to his own agency in crafting a tremendous athletic talent and salable public persona, as well as to the convergence of a variety of cultural needs, economic practices, and discourse.

As the Jordan phenomenon reminds us, the meanings of sporting and advertising performances can never be contained within the courts, playing fields, or even the athletic careers of particular celebrities. The backlash of Reaganism offers one important context from which to understand the significance of Michael Jordan. Yet because the cultural process is fluid, there is no guarantee that this specific version and vision of Michael Jordan will remain etched in history forever. Indeed, cultural analysis suggests that particular figures are linked to a variety of meanings, and power relations and interpretations may shift over the course of time. Jordan is a complicated, instructive, and powerful African American icon who challenges us to embrace alternative knowledge and the progressive possibilities that critical engagement offers.

## FURTHER READING

Andrews, D. L., ed. *Michael Jordan, Inc.: Corporate Sport, Media Culture and late Modern America*. Albany: State University of New York, 2001.

Andrews, D. L. "The Facts of Michael Jordan's Blackness: Excavating a Floating Racial Signifier." *Sociology of Sport Journal* 13:2 (1996): 125–158.

Dyson, Michael Eric. "Be Like Mike?: Michael Jordan and the Pedagogy of Desire." *Cultural Studies* 7:1 (1993): 64–72.

Halberstam, David. *Playing for Keeps: Michael Jordan and the World He Made*. New York: Random House, 1999.

Jordan, Michael, and David Halberstam. *Driven from Within*. New York: Atria, 2006.

Jordan, Michael, and W. Iooss. *Rare Air: Michael on Michael*. New York: Harper Collins, 1993.

McCallum, Jack. "The Desire Is Not There," *Sports Illustrated* 79 (1993): 28–35.

McDonald, M. G. "Michael Jordan's Family Values: Marketing, Meaning and Post Reagan America." *Sociology of Sport Journal* 13 (1996): 344–365.

McDonald, M. G., and D. L. Andrews. "Michael Jordan: Corporate Sport and Postmodern Celebrityhood." In *Sport Stars: The Cultural Politics of Sporting Celebrity*. D. L. Andrews and S. J. Jackson, eds. London: Routledge, 2001, pp. 20–35.

Norment, L. "Michael and Juanita Jordan Talk about Love, Marriage, and Life after Basketball." *Ebony* 47 (November 1991): 68–76.

AP photo/Eric Risberg.

# Florence Griffith Joyner

*Victoria Jackson*

Florence Griffith Joyner, the reigning world record-holder in both the 100- and 200-meter dashes, embodied athletic and personal excellence. A renaissance woman in her own right, Griffith Joyner is an icon of sport for more than her status as "the world's fastest woman"; she is celebrated for her ability to overcome adversity and for her talents on and off the track. Indeed, former USA Track and Field President Patricia Rico argued that Griffith Joyner "was a living legend. Flo Jo and track and field were synonymous. I don't think you could have one without the other. We entered a new era with Flo Jo on the scene, particularly for women. She was dynamic out there, very sophisticated. She put a new twist on women's competitive sports" (Knight).

Griffith Joyner earned her nickname "Flourescent Jo," or "Flo Jo," because of her flashy, handmade uniforms and her unique, confident style. She was also revered as a role model for young girls who came of age in the 1980s, often called "Title IX babies." After the passage of the landmark legislation declaring equal opportunity for girls and women in education, including athletics, thousand upon thousands of young girls across America hit the courts, playing fields, and tracks of their communities. Flo Jo, more than any other female athlete, showed the possibility of being both competitive and athletic as well as glamorous and feminine. She, more than any other sports legend, influenced an entire generation of girls and women to take pride in their athletic bodies and to appreciate them for their beauty, strength, and power.

Florence Delorez Griffith was born the seventh of 11 children to Robert, an electronics technician, and Florence, a seamstress, on December 21, 1959. After her parents divorced, "Dee-Dee," as she was called, and her siblings lived in a housing project in the Watts district of Los Angeles. Their mother and their grandmother, Gertrude Scott, a beautician, raised the children and encouraged them to be creative and confident individuals. Tough love was a good descriptor of the two women's parenting style. Television was prohibited during the school week, so the children became big readers. Books were scattered throughout the household, and the straight-A student flourished in a home of reading and learning. Poetry was Griffith's favorite genre, and she always kept a diary including her poems, writings, dreams, and desires.

Even in her childhood, Dee-Dee proudly stood out among her peers with a strong identity and self-confidence atypical of prepubescent girls. In elementary school, she owned a boa constrictor that she named Brandy because she was tired of the family dog and its fleas. Brandy grew to five feet in length, and Griffith enjoyed saving her sheddings in order to paint designs on the skin. Her individuality made her different from her peers. Griffith also applied her artistic talents to fashion design and beauty at a young age. She designed and constructed outfits for her Barbie dolls with her mother, and earned a popular status among many of her peers since she did all the neighborhood kids' hair and nails. At the same time, conformity was not a part of Dee-Dee's vocabulary. The young girl kept to herself and seemed to sometimes exist in her own little world, immune to ridicule. Reflecting on her childhood, Flo Jo stated while in the prime of her athletic career, "I was very quiet, always. But in kindergarten I would braid my hair with one braid straight up. I'd go all day like that, and when kids teased me, I'd just laugh with them" (Moore, "Very Fancy, Very Fast"). The confidence and strong identity in self that developed in young Dee-Dee, nourished by her supportive mother and grandmother, were the building blocks of the world's fastest woman.

Griffith's athletic success also began at quite a young age. She participated in sporting events sponsored by the Sugar Ray Robinson Youth Foundation in 1965 at the age of seven. In her first year of competitive athletics, she won a gold medal at the Jesse Owens National Youth Games. Despite the experiences of her parents' divorce and growing up in the projects, one could already see in young Dee-Dee the makings of a driven, special individual. However, she continued to face a series of obstacles in life; perhaps the process of overcoming adversity is what made her an Olympic champion and world record-holder.

After graduating as a star scholar-athlete from Jordan High School in Los Angeles in 1978, Griffith attended California State University at Northridge to pursue a degree in business. Despite earning a 3.25 GPA in her first year, financial problems forced her to drop out and work as a bank teller. Cal State assistant track coach Bob Kersee convinced her to return to the university, helped her apply for and gain financial aid, and began working with the young athlete to develop her sprinting skills in the 200-meter dash. When Kersee accepted an assistant coaching position at the University of California–Los Angeles in 1980, Griffith followed her coach, even though UCLA did not offer a degree in business. Her reluctant decision to follow her athletic dreams at the expense of her desired degree in business proved difficult. Reflecting on the transfer, in 1988 Flo Jo stated, "It kind of hurts to say this—I chose athletics over academics" (Moore, "Very Fancy, Very Fast"). A woman who sought to develop both her mind and body, the ambivalence revealed in her comment demonstrates her goal-oriented nature and her desire to be the best in all areas of her life.

Griffith thrived as a scholar athlete at UCLA; she and her teammate, heptathlete Jackie Joyner, led a star-studded Bruins squad. In 1982, Griffith won the 200-meter dash at the inaugural NCAA women's outdoor track and field championships at Brigham Young University in Provo, Utah. Her collegiate record-setting time of 22.39 seconds ensured her a place among the world's most promising young sprinters. The following year, although failing to defend her national crown in the 200 meters by placing second to Merlene Ottey of the University of Nebraska at Kerney, she competed in four events to help UCLA secure back-to-back team titles in a close race with the University of Tennessee and Florida State University. She added another NCAA gold in a different event, winning the 400-meter dash in a record-setting 50.94 seconds. Griffith still holds UCLA school records in the 200- and 400-meter dashes.

Following the 1983 track season, Griffith and Joyner continued to train with their UCLA coaches in preparation for the 1984 Olympic Games. Both women

*There's no substitute for hard work. . . . I have the medals to prove it!*

earned silver medals in their respective events; Griffith, hampered by a hamstring injury, placed second to Valerie Brisco-Hooks. She ran a personal best time of 22.04, but Brisco-Hooks's 21.81 set a new Olympic record. The loss devastated Flo Jo, who made a decision to take some time off from training to work as a secretary in a bank. She also returned to two of her lifelong passions, working at night as a hair stylist and designing children's books by day. Friends and family teased her, and she was rumored to have gained close to 60 pounds during her break from training, but they were not troubled by her sudden change in direction. Rather than moping about and feeling sorry for herself, Griffith decided to pursue her other interests and develop her many other skills.

Unfortunately, her experience is far from uncommon in the world of elite track and field competitors. With the Olympics cycling over a period of four years, the down time after an Olympic year proves to be difficult for many world-class athletes, especially those who participate in sports that are less popular in their respective countries. In the United States, significant popular interest in track and field only comes in Olympic years. Elite athletes find themselves struggling to continue strenuous, time-consuming training schedules while also having to work additional jobs to support themselves financially. Many individuals walk away from the sport, while others, like Griffith, return to training and competing after being encouraged by a coach or a close friend to pursue their dream of winning an Olympic gold medal. In 1986, Bob Kersee and Al Joyner, Jackie's brother and 1984 Olympic triple-jump gold medalist, convinced Griffith to return to track and field to prepare for the 1988 Seoul Olympics. That same year, Bob Kersee and Jackie Joyner married, and 20 months later Florence Griffith and Al Joyner tied the knot. These four athletes created an American track and field dynasty.

In the moments immediately following the Olympic trials second round of the women's 100-meter dash, television commentators Marty Liquori and Bob Hersh were speechless. Liquori finally broke the silence as he stammered in disbelief, "It can't be! No one can run that fast!" Florence Griffith Joyner's time on the scoreboard read an unbelievable 10.49 seconds. Had the timing system broken? Was the race wind-aided, with wind speeds over two meters per second, which would therefore make her ineligible to break the world record? More important, did a woman really just break 10.5 seconds in the 100 meters? Impossible! As the commentators struggled to make sense of what just happened on the rock-hard Mondo track in Indianapolis on that hot July day, at-home television viewers watched the race rerun repeatedly, and fans who had witnessed the event sat dumbfounded and awed by the spectacle. The anemometer read that the wind was less than two meters per second, declaring the race legal, and the timing system appeared to have functioned normally. After a delay, the meet officials certified the race results; Flo Jo had just become the fastest woman in the world, breaking Evelyn Ashford's old world record by nearly three-tenths of a second.

Perhaps Griffith Joyner's outfit and style contributed to the disbelief in the stands and among the commentators and home viewers. Dressed in an electric purple bodysuit with one leg bare, a turquoise bikini brief, and long orange, black, and white fingernails, Griffith Joyner looked more like a cartoon image than an actual person as she stormed down the track. The second half of the race only contributed to this fantasy-like quality; she ran virtually even with her competitors over the first half of the race, and extended her lead by what seemed to be an impossible margin (over 4 meters) over only the last 50 meters. The contrast between her one purple-clad leg and her bare one worked to accentuate her already gigantic and powerful stride length and turnover. With her hair free and blowing in the breeze generated by her gazelle-like speed, and her costume-like uniform, Griffith Joyner appeared more superhero than human.

Her postrace interview added to her mysterious, iconic nature. Her soft, yet rich and comfortably confident voice provided a marked contrast to her flashy, flamboyant clothing. She explained the race as if she knew in advance what the rest of the world was still struggling to comprehend. Downplaying the remarkable nature of her feat, Griffith Joyner, who earned the nickname Flo Jo through this flamboyant trials performance, backed up her performance with a time of 10.61 seconds in the final; had her 10.49 record been recalled, her time in the final still would have broken Ashford's world record.

Sports writers who reflected on Flo Jo's magnificent performance recognized immediately the momentous nature of the feat. Covering the Trials, Kenny Moore wrote,

> How could this converted 200-meter runner, in only her fourth serious 100 meters, take a huge .27 of a second off the world record? That's two-and-a-half times the slice Ben Johnson cut from the men's 100 record last year with his watershed 9.83. According to projections based on past improvements, no woman was supposed to reach even 10.65 until the year 2000. (Moore, "Getup and Go")

In fact, the projections proved correct: only Marion Jones has broken 10.7 seconds in the nearly two decades since Griffith's 10.49. He also pointed out that Griffith Joyner's time was faster than both Ben Johnson's 100 meters the previous day in a qualifying round and O. J. Simpson's personal best as a member of a world record–setting relay team! 

Flo Jo headed to the Olympics in Seoul, Korea, to compete in four events: the 100 meters, 200 meters, and as a member of both the 400- and 1600-meter relays. She earned gold in both of her individual competitions, breaking the world record in the 200 meters in both the semifinals and the finals, setting a new mark of 21.34 seconds. Her third gold came as she anchored the 400-meter relay; she picked up her fourth medal, a silver, by running a leg of the 1600-meter relay. The world's fastest woman broke world records in two events in less than three months and returned to the States packing a whole lot of Olympic hardware. Flo Jo also reinvigorated interest in her sport at a time when track and field's profile was sinking. Her unorthodox style and flamboyant racing outfits stole newspaper headlines and magazine covers. Reflecting on her career, she described how running filled her with excitement, made her feel free, and allowed her to express herself. Her self-confidence came from the cumulative effect of learning from every race that she had run—whether she won or lost. An incredibly driven and perseverant person, willing to endure pain and overcome obstacles, Griffith Joyner achieved her goals and dreams.

Flo Jo's year was 1988; she finished it with prestigious recognition, earning the title of Associated Press's Female Athlete of the Year, U.S. Olympic Committee's Sportswoman of the Year, and the Sullivan Award (given to the nation's most outstanding amateur athlete). Perhaps she knew something that no one else did as she was competing in the Olympic Games, as she would soon retire from the sport at the height of her career. Knowing, perhaps at a subconscious level, that she was going to win, she enjoyed each moment of every qualifying round and race, which enabled her to fully embrace the Olympic experience. Writing about her performance in the 100-meter Olympic final, Moore noted, "Her smile began growing at seventy meters, even as she roared away. By 90 meters it was a glorious grin. By 95 she had her arms up celebrating. At 100 the clock stopped at 10.54. . . . With that smile she beamed out all the sensations of her joyfully relaxed mastery in a way more evocative than any eye-popping outfit" (Moore, "Go, Flo, Go"). With the benefit of hindsight, it becomes obvious that Griffith Joyner enjoyed every moment of her Olympic victories because she knew that they would be both the climax and the last moments in her competitive track and field career. Reflecting on the 1988 Olympics nearly a decade later, she recollected in an interview, "Twenty meters before I got to the finish line I was so overwhelmed with joy. I knew that I was going to win the gold medal because I didn't see anyone else close by. I thought, 'My God! The race is about to be over and I'm going to finally win a gold medal—my first gold medal in the 100 meters" (Hatch and Hatch, p. 48). Only an elite athlete perfectly in tune with her mind, body, and spirit can have that type of awareness and clarity while in the act of making history.

In February 1989, Griffith Joyner retired from her sport, naming acting, designing, modeling, and writing as areas of interest that left her little time to train. Trying to justify why she would retire at the top of her game and perhaps frustrated by her decision, many individuals both inside and outside track and field raised drug accusations to explain both her incredible feats and her abrupt decision to retire. These individuals apparently chose to ignore the hard evidence: Griffith Joyner passed all 11 of her drug tests in 1988. She was clean as a whistle and always vehemently denied she had done anything unethical, citing determination, the ability to endure incredible amounts of pain, and hard work for her achievements. Flo Jo's reflections on her Olympic gold medal achievement illustrate her sense of accomplishment and should allay the skepticism of critics. The award was the fulfillment of a dream. Her strong sense of identity, self-worth, contentment, and accomplishment told her that it was time to move on to other talents in her life. She had endured 20 years of pain and hard work to achieve her dreams, and she accomplished them with style and flair.

> *It was a twenty-year dream. At that moment I knew everything was worth it. I felt so happy inside that I had it won I just had to let it out.*

Many athletes at the top of their games possess a strong sense of self and confidence in their unique identity. Flo Jo became the embodiment of a new ideal in American womanhood: a woman who could be both beautiful and physically fit, both feminine and powerful. With her revealing outfits, her long hair loose and flowing, and her three-inch artistically manicured nails, Flo Jo brought style and sexuality to women's athletics. Although girls and women who participated in "feminine" sports that emphasized grace, beauty, and performance, such as gymnastics, figure skating, and cheerleading, benefited from media coverage and popular support, those who competed in traditionally male sports associated with power, strength, and aggression found coverage and support lacking. Stereotypes plagued women who competed in these sports in the United States; many were considered to be lesbians or asexual, or to have "something wrong" with them that motivated them not to conform to American ideals of womanhood.

Girls and women in America entered sports participation in record numbers after the passage of Title IX. These athletes revised American ideals as they demonstrated that athletic success and femininity could exist together; moreover, physical fitness and a healthy lifestyle became central components of what made up the new American woman.

Title IX did not provide identical opportunities to all American women, however. This legislation and the expansion of girls' and women's opportunities in sports benefited white women of privileged backgrounds more than it helped those of color and lower socioeconomic status. As a black female, Flo Jo is an icon of sport for more than her athletic prowess; she is a role model for the girls of America, especially African American girls, who wish to become the best in their area of talent and to go after their dreams.

Flo Jo demonstrated that female athletes need not be humble. Her confidence was not cocky or arrogant; rather, she exuded a radiance that an unfortunate number of female athletes and women in general lack. For example, she painted three fingernails red, white, and blue and a fourth gold, to reinforce her goal of Olympic gold. Reflecting on her success after the Games, she boldly stated, "There's no substitute for hard work. . . . I have the medals to prove it!" Her confidence came from her strong sense of self and pride in her identity, which were instilled in her by her mother and grandmother from birth. A goal-oriented and driven person, Flo Jo had confidence and self-awareness that allowed her to achieve and also enjoy her successes in life.

As a volunteer and woman of service, Griffith Joyner remembered her roots and recognized her responsibility from her position of celebrity and privilege to always help others. In 1989 she became spokesperson for the American

Cancer Society, the Multiple Sclerosis Foundation, and Project Eco-School. Four years later, President Bill Clinton appointed her as co-chair of the President's Council on Physical Fitness and Sports (PCPFS) with Tom McMillen, a star basketball player, Rhodes scholar, and U.S. Congressman.

During their joint tenure, Griffith Joyner and McMillen developed an adult fitness program and established the Silver Eagle Award to promote fitness among seniors. The two leaders also helped develop a three-year advertisement campaign focused on youth fitness titled, "Get Off It!" and later, "Get Up, Get Out." Finally, they supported the decision to make available in the Spanish language all health-related materials produced by the PCPFS. The Clinton administration dramatically expanded the programs of the PCPFS, thanks in large part to the hard work and dedication of American activist-athletes Griffith Joyner and McMillen. In his eulogy of Griffith Joyner, Clinton commented on the athlete's service and commitment to community. "Though she rose to the pinnacle of the world of sports," he stated, "she never forgot where she came from, devoting time and resources to helping children—especially those growing up in our most devastated neighborhoods—make the most of their own talents" (Noden).

Drawing from her significant body of experience in volunteerism and service work, in 1994 Flo Jo and her husband, Al, started the Florence Griffith Joyner Foundation for Disadvantaged Youth. The nonprofit organization encouraged young people to apply the lessons learned from participation in athletics to their lives in general, including school, family, friendship, and community. The Joyners and their staff worked with inner-city children to provide them with opportunities they might have lacked otherwise, just as the Sugar Ray Robinson Foundation activities in the Watts neighborhood of Los Angeles provided Griffith Joyner with opportunities during her childhood.

As a renaissance woman, Griffith Joyner demonstrated that athletes are not one-dimensional and can be successful on and off the track. After 20 years devoted to strenuous training and competitive athletics, she turned to fully embrace her other talents and interests, including acting and modeling, designing, and writing. Indeed, she pursued each of these passions. Flo Jo had a holistic sense of self-improvement and developed skills that utilized both her body and her mind. She embodied a philosophy that many athletes, especially those in individual sports, strive for, a philosophy that celebrates a well-rounded lifestyle. Though she always sought out new challenges and projects, Griffith Joyner seemed even busier in retirement than she did in her years as an elite athlete. In addition to running the foundation with her husband and contributing to other volunteer organizations, she managed to write 33 children's books (one for each of her nieces and nephews) and a book on exercise and nutrition for adults titled *Running for Dummies*. She continued to design clothing for herself, her family, friends, and for sale; in 1989 she helped design the Indiana Pacers basketball uniforms and logo for the 1989–1990 season.

She also jumpstarted her own nail company, FloJo Nails, selling nail art including paints, stencils for designs, artificial nails, and glitter.

A natural performer, Griffith Joyner recognized her true calling in retirement as she found herself pulled toward the big screen. She acted in films and television series (both in the United States and abroad), made celebrity appearances on game shows, participated in documentaries and made-for-television specials on sports, worked as a sportscaster covering track and field, and produced as well as acted in educational programs for youth. In conjunction with *Ebony* magazine and the American Medical Association, she worked on a documentary titled *A Guide to Healthy Living for African Americans*. She also participated in *A Crash Course on Calcium* for the National Dairy Council, and with SmithKline Beecham Pharmaceuticals she acted in *"Protecting Our Kids": Against Childhood Diseases through Vaccination*. In perhaps her best-known educational documentary, Griffith Joyner worked with Arsenio Hall and others to produce *The Flo-Jo Workout: Mind, Body, and Spirit*, which introduced young aspiring athletes to her holistic and healthy lifestyle philosophy. For Flo Jo, her life was seamless; there were no boundaries separating career, volunteerism, and recreation; those were simply manmade, constructed categories with artificial divisions.

After 1988 and retirement from track and field, Griffith Joyner's number one priority became her family. Following the examples set by her mother and grandmother, she concentrated on being a mother to her first and only child, Mary Ruth, who was born in the fall of 1990. The Joyners were like three peas in a pod—a close-knit family that cherished its fortunes and dedicated itself to helping others. They also embraced their large extended family, spending time with many nieces and nephews, aunts and uncles, and brothers and sisters. Finally, for the Joyners, family also included the even larger extended family of American track and field. They fully embraced life and surrounded themselves with loved ones.

On September 21, 1998, Florence Griffith Joyner passed away in her sleep in her Mission Viejo home. The official cause of death from the sheriff-coroner's office included three causes: positional asphyxia, epileptiform seizure, and cavernous angioma of the left orbital frontal cerebrum (a brain abnormality discovered during autopsy and a signifier of repeated seizures). At the time of her death, Flo Jo was only 38 years old. She was a legend who died young, before her body began to decay and before other athletes could relieve her of the title of world's fastest woman. Iconic Florence Griffith Joyner will always be remembered for her power, beauty, and incredible speed.

Today, the many memorials and articles on Florence Griffith Joyner separate her athletics from her postathletic talents. This dichotomous interpretation, however, does not truly describe or provide a full understanding of the woman she was. Flo Jo's strong sense of self included athleticism as a central component; she continued to work out after retirement because being physically fit was a fundamental part of who she was and because she simply enjoyed it. The world's fastest woman had no problem heading out to the local high school in a sweat suit to jog a few laps around the track, much like any other recreational runner. She expressed herself through her flamboyant style and confident attitude in order to be true to herself, not to be unique or different, or to grab others' attention and headlines. The way she carried herself with grace, power, confidence, and dedication inspired a generation of young women to pursue their athletic aspirations and to do so without shame or fear of sacrificing their femininity. Griffith Joyner never forgot her roots; she recognized her responsibility from her position of privilege to always help others. She was a renaissance woman and a true champion in all aspects of her life, both on and off the track.

## FURTHER READING

Aasang, Nathan. *Florence Griffith Joyner: Dazzling Olympian*. Minneapolis: Lerner Publications, 1989.

Griffith Joyner, Florence. *Running for Dummies*. Foster City, CA: IDG Books, 1999.

Hatch, Robert, and William Hatch. "Florence Griffith Joyner." In *The Hero Project: How We Met Our Greatest Heroes; Two Teens, One Notebook, Thirteen Extraordinary Interviews*. New York: McGraw-Hill, 2006.

Knight, Athelia. "Track Star Griffith Joyner Dies at 38." *Washington Post*, 1998. http://www.mmjp.or.jp/amlang.atc/di&legends/flojo/aboutflojo.htm (accessed October 28, 2006).

Koral, April. *Florence Griffith Joyner: Track and Field Star*. New York: F. Watts, 1992.

Moore, Kenny. "Getup and Go: Florence Griffith Joyner's Dramatic Garb Made Her a Colorful Blur as She Smashed the World Record in the 100 Meters at the Olympic Trials," *Sports Illustrated* (July 25, 1998). http://sportsillustrated.cnn.com/olympics/features/joyner/flashback2.html (accessed October 14, 2006).

Moore, Kenny. "Go, Flo, Go: Florence Griffith Joyner Did Just That in Blazing to Victory in the 100 Meters," *Sports Illustrated* (October 3, 1988). http://sportsillustrated.cnn.com/olympics/features/joyner/flashback3.html (accessed October 14, 2006).

Moore, Kenny. "Very Fast, Very Fast: U.S. Sprinter Florence Griffith Joyner Is Certainly Eye-Catching—If, That Is, You Can Catch Her," *Sports Illustrated* (September 14, 1998). http://sportsillustrated.cnn.com/olympics/features/joyner/flashback1.html (accessed October 14, 2006).

Nagel, Rob. "The Joyners." *Epic Lives: One Hundred Black Women Who Made a Difference*. Detroit: Visible Ink Press, 1993.

Noden, Merrell. "FloJo Lived Her Life in Fast-Forward," *Sports Illustrated* (September 22, 1998). http://sportsillustrated.cnn.com/olympics/features/joyner/flojo_noden.html (accessed October 14, 2006).

# Joe Louis

*Neil A. Wynn*

Joe Louis was the world heavyweight boxing champion from 1937 until 1949 and one of the few internationally known African Americans during that period. While his boxing achievements made him a hero for black Americans, his undoubted prowess in the ring and his unassuming public demeanor, combined with his military service during World War II, established him as a famous international figure. Through his achievements Louis had a significant impact on race relations at a pivotal moment in American history and was a crucial transitional figure between the era of Jack Johnson and Muhammad Ali.

Joe Louis was in many ways a classic example of the American rags-to-riches story, the "poor boy made good" by overcoming poverty and racism to achieve national and international fame. Like the other great African American sporting figure of the 1930s, Jesse Owens, he was born the son of sharecroppers in Alabama in 1914; also like Owens, his grandparents had been enslaved. Named Joe Louis Barrow, he was one of eight children. When he was about two, his father, Monroe Barrow, was committed to a state mental institution after being diagnosed with schizophrenia; his mother, Lillie, later married Patrick Brooks. Monroe Barrow was assumed to have died when his son was four, but was found alive in a hospital for the Negro Insane in Mount Vernon, Alabama, in 1937 by the press. He died 18 months later.

In 1926 the family followed Brooks to Detroit. Louis dropped out of school at the age of 17 and worked in a number of laboring jobs, delivering ice and coal, because he struggled at school. He also worked for a while in the Ford Motor Co. He began boxing in his early teens, however, and fought his first amateur fight in 1932. Having mistakenly dropped the name Barrow in filling out the amateur registration forms, he became known thereafter as Joe Louis. After winning 50 of his 54 contests, in 1933 he won the National American Athletic Union light heavyweight title. In all, Louis fought 58 amateur bouts, lost 4, and won 54, 43 of which were by knockout and 7 on points.

In 1933 John Roxborough, a black businessman, took over Louis's management and persuaded the former lightweight boxer Jack "Chappie" Blackburn to become his trainer. They moved Louis to Chicago where Julian Black, a successful real estate man, joined the management team. The three schooled Louis in how to conduct himself inside and outside of the ring. Aware of how hard it would be for a black boxer to succeed in a white-dominated sport, and also wishing to distance Louis from the controversial legacy of Jack Johnson, Roxborough laid down seven rules for his boxer to follow:

1. Never be pictured beside a white woman.
2. Never go into nightclubs unaccompanied.
3. No "soft" fights.
4. No fixed fights.
5. Never gloat over a beaten opponent.
6. Always appear impassive and expressionless in front of press photographers.
7. Always live clean and fight clean.

When Jack Johnson visited the Louis training camp in 1935, Louis's entourage quickly turned him away. In addition, Blackburn warned Louis how hard it was for an African American to win contests if they were to be decided on points, and he told his protégé to aim for knockouts and a clear victory whenever possible. Louis followed all of these rules faithfully, particularly in the ring. With a roaming style and deadpan expression, he would move forward relentlessly, constantly jabbing before unleashing his powerful blows to body and head. Afterward he was respectful to the losers and polite and courteous to the press. He was by nature rather shy and reserved, due in part to a slight speech impediment, and this often made him seem taciturn, even a little surly.

In July 1934 Louis turned professional. After winning his first fight, his purse was $59. Eventually he would win prize money in the thousands. In 1935 Louis was able to write a check for $269 and send it to the welfare board to repay relief payments made to his family seven years earlier. He won all of his 12 fights in 1934 and after 6 more victories in 1935, Mike Jacobs, a New York boxing promoter, assumed the promotion of Louis's fights. Louis fought his first fight in New York City at Yankee Stadium on June 25, 1935, when he faced former heavyweight champion Primo Carnera. He knocked out the tall Italian (he was over 6' 6") in the sixth round. The fight assumed political and racial overtones as commentators drew references to the Italian attack on Ethiopia and Carnera's association with the fascist regime of Benito Mussolini, but this was a minor episode compared to what would come later in another fight.

Louis went on to fight and knock out three other contenders for the heavyweight title: King Levinsky, Paulino Uzcudun, and former heavyweight champion Max Baer. Writing in the *New York American*, famous sports reporter and writer Damon Runyon described the blow that felled the Spaniard Uzcudun in the fourth round as "the swiftest and most explosive" he had ever seen. It was the ferocity of his punches that won him the nickname of the "Brown Bomber." In his fight against the well-liked Baer on September 24, 1935, Louis demolished his opponent, knocking him down twice in the third round before knocking him out in the fourth. Baer said that the audience had not paid enough to see his execution, when he was asked why he did not get up and fight on.

On June 19, 1936, Louis faced another former heavyweight champion, the German Max Schmeling. Louis was overconfident and did not train properly for the bout. Schmeling claimed to have spotted a weakness in Louis's performance as a result of poor preparation. Louis was caught repeatedly by punishing right-hand blows, and was knocked out in the twelfth round as a result. He made his comeback on August 18, when he knocked out Jack Sharkey in the third round. After a number of relatively easy fights including those against Al Ettore, Jorge Brescia, Eddie Simms, Steve Ketchell, and Bob Pastor, he was matched against James Braddock (known as the Cinderella Man due to his comeback and defeat of Max Baer in a major upset in 1935) for the world heavyweight championship ahead of Schmeling.

On June 22, 1937, in front of a crowd of 45,000 at Comiskey Park, Chicago, Louis came back from an early knockdown to knock out the favorite

*Once that bell rings you're on your own. It's just you and the other guy.*

Braddock in the eighth round and win the heavyweight title. Writing in his autobiography, Louis later recalled that Braddock was one of the bravest opponents he ever fought. By beating him, the22-year-old Louis became the youngest heavyweight champion in history (in 1956 Floyd Patterson, 21, became the youngest champion, and then Mike Tyson, 20, in 1986); he was also the first black heavyweight champion since Jack Johnson almost 30 years earlier.

Louis won the first defense of his title against Welshman Tommy Farr on August 30, 1937, on points after 15 hard rounds. He won his next two fights against Nathan Mann and Harry Thomas easily with knockouts in the third and fifth rounds, respectively. Despite these victories Louis clearly felt he still had something to prove after his defeat by Schmeling, and this gave their eventual rematch in 1938 a special edge. However, it assumed a much greater significance than simply one of personal satisfaction. On both sides of the Atlantic the fight was presented in terms of competing ideologies and races, with Schmeling representing Nazi Germany and Louis standing for the hope of liberal democracy and racial equality.

Adolf Hitler, the Nazi leader, had praised Schmeling's achievement in 1936 and welcomed the boxer home with a celebratory lunch. The regime had represented Louis's defeat as a triumph for Nazism and a German victory. Hitler had clearly been angered by the success of Jesse Owens and other black athletes in the U.S. team at the 1936 Berlin Olympic Games. In 1938 more than 2000 Germans traveled to the United States to watch the rematch, and publicity had strong political, national, and racial overtones. One story suggested that President Franklin Roosevelt met Louis at the White House and on feeling the boxer's muscles remarked, "We need muscles like yours to beat Germany." However, some historians question whether this meeting ever took place (Louis had met FDR in 1935), let alone whether the president ever made such a comment. Nonetheless, the contest clearly was seen as more than a boxing match. When it came to their fight on June 22 in New York, Louis wasted no time and dispatched his opponent in just over two minutes in the first round before an audience of over 70,000 and thousands more listening to the match on the radio.

Where rioting among angry whites had followed Jack Johnson's defeat of Jim Jeffries in 1910, Louis's victory was greeted with wild celebrations in the streets of Harlem and elsewhere among the African American population. Now, too, most white Americans celebrated the fact that the champion's title was still held by an American; additionally, many saw the fight as a triumph for democracy. For many Americans Louis had effectively dealt the myth of white supremacy a serious blow, but for African Americans he had helped undermine racial stereotypes and become one of greatest heroes of all time—the subject of songs, poems, and articles singing his praises. Later writers such as Maya Angelou and Black Nation of Islam spokesman Malcolm X recalled the inspirational significance of Louis for African Americans. So powerful was his image that Martin Luther King Jr. recalled that the last words of a young black man about to die in the gas chamber were "Save me, Joe Louis."

Despite this great success, Louis had to overcome considerable resistance among followers of boxing whose views were still determined by race. White boxing press commentators often made clear racial references when describing Louis, or suggesting that his ability or ferocity came from the jungle. Some writers described him as a ruthless, ferocious, unmerciful killer, a savage and primitive, a dark destroyer, even a wild—but magnificent—animal. Others mocked his shuffling style or suggested that his speech impediment (a slight stammer) and reserved public manner reflected a lack of intelligence or laziness. Even when he was recognized as champion, at least one reporter could lament that nothing could be done about it, while another said patronizingly that if he was a Negro at least he was "our Negro." However, Louis's skill could not be denied, and in 1935 he had already been voted boxer of the year. Still, the negative attitudes only changed gradually and they have continued to linger into the twenty-first century.

In 1939 Louis knocked out four successive challengers for the title: John Henry Lewis, Jack Roper, Bob Pastor, and Tony Galento; he had four more successful fights in 1940, three (against Johnny Paycheck, Al McCoy, and his second fight against Arturo Godoy) by knockouts. Some of these fighters were regarded as in the "bum of the month" category, but the first fight against Godoy had gone the full 15 rounds before Louis won on points. The fight against Galento, marked by some bitter personal animosities, was fierce even though it ended in the fourth round. In 1941 Louis knocked out four more fighters and then beat Louis "Buddy" Baer (brother of Max Baer). Baer actually knocked Louis out of the ring in the first round, but the champion responded and knocked the challenger down three times in the sixth. He won when Baer failed to come out for the seventh round. There was some suggestion that Baer had been hit after the bell. Louis then went on to face Billy Conn on June 18. Conn was the light-heavyweight champion and was quick and clever in the ring. After 12 rounds he was clearly ahead on points, but in the thirteenth round Louis knocked him out. Louis successfully defended his title once more that year, defeating Lou Nova with another knockout in the sixth round.

Following the Japanese attack on Pearl Harbor in December 1941, Louis fought Buddy Baer again in January 1942 and won in the first round. In a gesture that received enormous publicity despite the absence of any fanfare on his part, Louis gave most of his winnings, some $47,000, to the Navy Relief fund. Louis also made a positive impact with his much-quoted after-fight comment that America would win the war and "We all got to do our part, and then we'll win. 'Cause we're on God's side." The press now hailed Louis as the best boxer ever, a "credit to his race," to boxing, and now a national hero. His iconic status was ensured the following day when the champion enlisted in the U.S. Army as a private like any ordinary person, rather than accept a commission, and was sent for training at Camp Upton, New York. He fought one defense of his title on March 27, 1942, when he faced Abe Simon in a rematch. Simon was knocked out in the sixth round and afterward Louis donated his purse to the Army Emergency Relief Fund. He had also paid $3000 to provide seats for servicemen.

Louis was promoted to sergeant in August 1942 and staff sergeant in 1944, yet his role in the army was largely public relations, boosting morale by making special appearances with other black boxers George C. Nicholson, Walker Smith (better known as Sugar Ray Robinson), and George J. Wilson, visiting men in the hospital, and fighting exhibition bouts for service personnel in bases in the United States and Europe. In all, he fought 96 exhibition matches during the war. He also featured in war posters and in a film, *This Is the Army*, with future president Ronald Reagan in 1943. The 1938 Schmeling-Louis fight was also used in the propaganda film *The Negro Soldier* (1945) to highlight the differences between Nazism and American democracy (although in reality Schmeling was not a Nazi and actually fell afoul of the regime after his defeat in 1938). A full-page photograph of a helmeted Louis thrusting a bayonet was featured in *Negroes and the War*, a popular Office of War Information booklet. In recognition of his patriotic work, Louis was awarded the Legion of Merit by the army in 1945.

Although seen as the epitome of loyalty and an outstanding representative of both "his race" and country by many observers, some African Americans felt he should do more to protest against discrimination. Although the war brought several advances in race relations—an executive order forbidding discrimination in defense industries, the creation of the Fair Employment Practices Committee, the widening of military service to include African Americans in the Air Corps and all areas of the navy—the armed forces were still segregated. African Americans in the army were concentrated in noncombat roles, and black servicemen faced constant abuse and violence both within the military and from civilians. Race riots across the country in 1943, particularly those in Detroit and Harlem, pointed to the increase in racial tension during the war.

Clearly no outspoken critic of America's failings on race, Louis nonetheless made some attempt to effect change. He refused to appear before segregated army audiences, and he also spoke on behalf of Jackie Robinson when he was excluded from camp baseball and football teams. Louis lobbied on Robinson's behalf to help secure him a place in officer training. While on tour in Britain, he protested when he was turned away from a theater that had been segregated on the order of the U.S. military and gained admission as a result. After the war he spoke out in support of army veteran Isaac Woodard who was assaulted and blinded by a white policeman. Louis was reported to have said that having fought for "the American cause," America was going to have to give African Americans their civil rights, too.

If Louis's role during the war helped win greater acceptance for African Americans and could be seen as part of the wider move toward inclusion that saw the beginning of integration in baseball with Jackie Robinson joining the Brooklyn Dodgers in 1947, and the beginning of the desegregation of the U.S. armed forces the same year, there was still a long way to go. In spite of everything, old prejudices persisted even with regard to boxing: racist Senator Theodore Bilbo of Mississippi could still say in 1945 that he thought prize fights between Negroes and white men were among the most disgraceful things in American life.

Bilbo's attitude notwithstanding, Louis returned to the ring for an eagerly awaited rematch against Billy Conn on June 19, 1946. Before the fight Conn indicated that he would outrun the champion, to which Louis replied with the famous remark, "He can run but he can't hide." In the event, Conn had lost much of his speed, and Louis knocked him out in the eighth round. An audience of 45,000 people who paid almost $2 million for the privilege watched the fight. However, despite his share of the receipts and his considerable previous earnings, Louis was now facing difficulties as a result of financial irresponsibility and developments in his personal life. These problems were to dog his postwar career.

Louis had married Marva Trotter, a secretary from the black newspaper the *Chicago Defender*, only hours before his fight with Max Baer in 1935. Boxing, however, kept the couple apart much of the time, and Louis also had many affairs with women, including one with singer Lena Horne and another with actress Lana Turner. Like several other successful boxers of the day, he went to Hollywood in 1936 to act a part based on his own life in *The Spirit of Youth*, and like many successful sportsmen, he also enjoyed the attentions of attractive women. Eventually Marva filed for divorce 1941; she and Joe publicly reconciled but then divorced in 1945. Although they remarried in 1946, Louis owed Marva a considerable amount in alimony; he also owed over $250,000 in back taxes. He and Marva finally divorced again in 1949. They had two children, Joseph and Jacqueline, but it is clear that Louis was not particularly a family man.

In addition to his debts to his ex-wife and the IRS, Louis was the victim of his own generosity and spendthrift lifestyle. He had a penchant for expensive suits, fine cars, and race horses; he lost money playing golf and gave money away to friends and relatives. Through much of the 1930s he had provided thousands of dollars in financial backing for the Brown Bombers softball team made up of old friends from Detroit; he invested money and lent his name to friends' business ventures ranging from the Brown Bomber Chicken Shack and Joe Louis Restaurant, through the Joe Louis Milk company and the Joes Louis Insurance company. Most of the businesses failed, and Louis lost a small fortune. He also borrowed heavily from his promoter and manager, both of whom allowed him to spend without control, but made sure they were repaid before he settled his tax bills. In addition, income tax had been levied even on the fights where he had donated money to the army and navy, and by 1950 he owed the IRS over $200,000 in back taxes; by 1957 this had risen to over $1 million.

*Every man's got to figure to get beat sometime.*

These debts kept Louis fighting beyond the point he should have retired. He fought Tami Mauriello in September 1946. After almost being knocked down himself, Louis won in the first round with a knockout. The champion then spent the rest of year and the early part of 1947 touring Mexico and Central and South America fighting exhibition matches to raise money. The trip barely covered his expenses. In 1947 he was matched against a black challenger for the title, "Jersey" Joe Walcott. Although many people regarded Walcott, who was older than Louis, as a has-been, the fight on December 5 in Madison Square Garden, New York, went the full 15 rounds. Louis was twice knocked down but won on a disputed split decision. The two men fought an unimpressive rematch on June 24, 1948, and Louis won with a knockout in the eleventh round. He announced his retirement immediately afterward.

Faced with a huge tax bill in 1950, at the age of 36 Louis decided to make a comeback and faced another African American, the "Cincinnati Cobra" and now reigning champion, Ezzard Charles. Louis was badly beaten and lost on points after 15 rounds. Despite this defeat, he carried on boxing, and he managed eight victories against reasonable opponents before facing Rocky Marciano on October 26, 1951, in Madison Square Garden. After being knocked out in the eighth round, Louis finally retired for good. He had only lost 3 of his 66 professional fights, and he had won 49 by knockouts. He had also captured the affection of both the boxing press and the American people.

Life after boxing proved difficult for the ex-champion. After a brief tour to entertain troops in Japan and Korea, he found employment for a while in advertising, working for the Louis-Rowe Publicity Agency. As his tax liabilities increased, Louis became a professional wrestler to earn more, and also performed briefly in a circus. The wrestling ended with two broken ribs and damage to his heart. In 1955 Louis married the owner of a New York beauty salon, Rose Morgan, but their marriage ended three years later. In 1959 he married a Los Angeles lawyer and the first black woman to practice law in California, Martha Malone Jefferson. Public sympathy and congressional intervention led the IRS to reduce their demands on Louis, but Martha who persuaded the tax authorities that her husband no longer had earning power and was not worth pursuing for back taxes. She and Louis moved to Las Vegas in 1966 and he found work in Caesars Palace as a greeter and debt collector.

Sadly, in later years Louis became a heavy drinker and addicted to cocaine; his erratic behavior as a consequence led to his brief hospitalization in very public circumstances in 1970. In 1977 he suffered a massive heart attack and was subsequently confined to a wheelchair. He was supported through illness and declining years by show business friends, including Frank Sinatra and Sammy Davis Jr. With this help, Louis was still able to attend some public functions and on April 11, 1981, he received a standing ovation from the crowd before the championship fight between Larry Holmes and Trevor Berbick. He died the next day. On the special instructions of President Ronald Reagan, Joe Louis was buried in Arlington National Cemetery on April 21, 1981.

By the time of his death, many people regarded Louis as a rather pathetic remnant of a bygone era; in contrast to someone like Muhammad Ali, whom he criticized publicly both for his religion and for his style of boxing, Louis appeared to some black commentators especially as an Uncle Tom figure. However, although he did not play any part in the Civil Rights Movement of the late 1950s and 1960s, the reality was that through his astonishing achievements he helped win acceptance for black sportsmen and furthered the cause of racial integration in a period when the existing racial attitudes were being questioned by war and the ideological conflict with Nazism and then communism. In holding the world heavyweight champion's title for 12 years, and in recording so many wins by knockout, he established a claim to be one of the greatest boxers of all time. Louis's fights against Carnera, Baer, and Braddock, his second against Schmeling, and first against Conn, are still recognized as classics. Muhammad Ali certainly acknowledged publicly that Louis had been a great boxer if not the "greatest" (a title he reserved for himself), and he entertained the ex-champion at his camp in 1976.

Louis was not just an inspiration and model for other black athletes; he was also a heroic symbol for the whole African American population in the period of the Great Depression. His boxing achievements challenged the racial orthodoxy of the day and directly questioned ideas of black inferiority. At a time when black men were still being lynched, he beat whites openly and fairly and overcame the prejudices of many of his countrymen in the process. His actions during the war provided further cause for black pride and a potent emblem of national unity. In recognition of all his achievements, Louis was awarded the Congressional Medal of Honor in 1982 and was the first person to be inducted into the International Boxing Hall of Fame in 1990.

## FURTHER READING

Bak, Richard. *Joe Louis: The Great Black Hope*. New York: Da Capo Press, 1998.

Capeci, Dominic J., and Martha Wilkerson. "Multifarious Hero: Joe Louis, American Society and Race Relations during World Crisis, 1935–1945." *Journal of Sport History* 10:3 (Winter 1983): 5–25.

Hietala, Thomas R. *The Fight of the Century: Jack Johnson, Joe Louis, and the Struggle for Racial Equality*. Armonk, NY: M. E. Sharpe, 2002.

Louis, Joe. *Joe Louis, My Life*. New York: Harcourt Brace Jovanovich, 1997.

Margolick, David. *Beyond Glory: Joe Louis vs. Max Schmeling, and a World on the Brink*. New York: Alfred A. Knopf, 2005.

McRae, Donald. *Heroes without a Country: America's Betrayal of Joe Louis and Jesse Owens*. New York: HarperCollins, 2002.

McRae, Donald. *In Black & White: The Untold Story of Joe Louis and Jesse Owens*. New York: Simon & Schuster, 1997.

Mead, Chris. *Champion Joe Louis: A Biography*. New York: Charles Scribner's Sons, 1985.

Sklaroff, Lauren Rebecca. "Constructing G.I. Joe Louis: Cultural Solutions to the 'Negro Problem' during World War II." *Journal of American History* 89:3 (December 2002): 958–983.

AP Photo/Charlie Riedel.

# Negro Baseball Leagues

*James R. Coates*

From the early years of the formulation of the American colonies to the late 1960s, America was virtually two dual societies: one black and one white. They were separate and totally unequal. Black society was left with inferior products in housing, jobs, and education, though one area in which black society did not believe it was deprived was in its leisure endeavors. Foremost among American culture's outdoor sporting endeavors was the grand old game of baseball. Black society's thirst for the game was answered by the creation of the fast-paced, slick fielding, show-boating, entertaining Negro Baseball Leagues. These leagues lasted until the 1950s, and the games they played were attended by blacks and whites.

The topic of blacks in American society predates the founding of this nation. Race was also a major issue within black society, as blacks even disagreed over the term they wished to use to describe themselves. This debate has included terms such as *colored*, *Negro*, *black*, and *African American*. Participants of the first black baseball leagues referred to themselves as "colored," which is consequently the term used to identify these players in this chapter. From around 1911 until the mid-1950s, players in these baseball leagues described themselves as "Negro," so that term is used to relate to the leagues during that time period.

The first baseball league for colored players was developed in the mid-1880s. It should be noted that Negro League Baseball was always open to white players. In other words, these leagues were technically integrated. Most baseball leagues were integrated until the late 1880s, when the color line was formally drawn, segregating professional mainstream baseball leagues to only whites.

Many teams participated in the leagues during those early years, including the Pittsburgh Keystones, the Cuban Giants of Trenton, New Jersey, the Gorhams of New York, the Lord Baltimores, the Boston Resolutes, and the Norfolk Red Sox. Other areas that had early teams were Philadelphia and Louisville. The first black professional baseball team was organized in 1885. The Argyle Hotel of Babylon, a resort hotel built in 1882 in Long Island, New York, actually sponsored the team, which was composed of the black waiters working at the hotel. The team players served as an attraction for the guests of the hotel and played nine games their first season. They played against the best white teams of New York City and Long Island, winning six games, losing two, and tying one during that early season. The members of this successful team were Ben Holmes on third base, A. Randolph on first, Ben Boyd on second, William Eggleston as shortstop, Guy Day as catcher, Milton Dabney in left field, Charles Nichols in right, and George Parego, Frank Harris, and R. Martin as pitchers.

Other players found success on the field as well. Sol White, a baseball player and historian of the Colored Base Ball Leagues, held remarkable records himself. Standing 5' 9" and weighing 170 pounds, he participated in the mainstream white leagues for five seasons before the color line ban around 1888. He never batted below .324 during his years in the mainstream leagues. He was also advertised as the only player with a college education; although White attended Wilberforce University for a couple of years, there is no evidence that he obtained a degree. The advertisement about his education was about a particular league, since Moses "Fleetwood" Walker played for three years at Oberlin College in Ohio in the late 1860s before playing professionally as White's contemporary.

Other accounts claim that the team sponsored by the Argyle Hotel actually consisted of players from three semi-pro black teams: one from Washington, D.C., called the Manhattans, and the Keystones and the Orions from Philadelphia. The newly combined team was named the Cuban Giants. According to the other account, any duties performed by these men as waiters, bellhops, or porters, were purely coincidental to their primary responsibilities as baseball players.

The early years of the Colored Base Ball Leagues were dotted with short-lived teams, players of questionable skills, poor attendance at times, and poorly financed ownership. Some owners and promoters actually put local town players in uniforms to compete against true professionals who traveled through the area. Ambrose Davis, who owned the Gorhams of New York, was the first African American owner of a salaried black team. He was also one of the owners who jumped at the opportunity to buy up the outstanding talent pool on a team that was folding. On occasion, he gobbled up the best players on a team that consistently beat his squad. After the Cuban Giants badly beat his Gorhams in two consecutive games, Davis signed the better players of the Giants to contracts that were more lucrative on his own team, even though it was the middle of a baseball season. He brought George Stovey, Clarence Williams, Frank Grant, and White from the Cuban Giants to his Gorhams. Each of those black players had experience playing in the white professional leagues. Stovey, along with Moses Walker, formed one of the first black batteries in white professional baseball, with Grant pitching and Walker catching. Walker is noted as the first black player in professional baseball.

The Giants remained a popularly used team name through the early years of the Colored Base Ball Leagues. In some cases, a city might have two teams with the name Giants. There were the Cuban Giants (later named the Genuine or Original Cuban Giants), the Cuban X-Giants, the Chicago Columbia Giants, the Chicago American Giants, the Leland Chicago Giants, the Philadelphia Giants, the Brooklyn Royal Giants, and the Page Fence Giants. The name Giants also remained popular with the teams that comprised the Negro Leagues from the 1920s to the 1950s. The reasons for the name's popularity with the Negro League teams are probably varied. One theory, though, suggests that the name was used in imitation of the National League's extremely successful and popular New York franchise. Regardless of the names used to identify the teams, the Cuban Giants of the Argyle Hotel remained a force throughout the era of the Colored Base Ball Leagues, ultimately serving as the progenitor of the Negro Baseball Leagues.

Members of the Colored Base Ball Leagues lived during a notably difficult time in the history of the United States. They performed at a time and era when a black person's life was considered of little value to many in the majority white society. This era, known historically as "the Progressive era" in the United States, saw African American citizens markedly separated from the rest of society via legal court sanctions. The U.S. Supreme Court ruled that segregation was indeed legal with its decision in a Louisiana railroad-car case, *Plessy v. Ferguson*. The ruling in this case legally separated blacks from the rest of American society for nearly 60 years. Yet despite these social impediments, black society participated fully in the great American pastime of baseball. Social movements, including the Niagara movement, Booker T. Washington's industrial education movement, and the formation of the National Association for the Advancement of Colored People (NAACP), challenged the limitations black people faced. Although they were separate from mainstream leagues, the Colored Base Ball Leagues provided entertainment and diversion for African Americans during this tumultuous time. The early years of Colored Base Ball provided the foundation of what became the glory years and folklore of baseball in black culture, "The Negro Leagues!"

As the twentieth century began, and segregation in the United States became more entrenched, African American society paralleled white America. Black America developed a mass communication system through the Associated Negro Press. This news service linked the sporting and educational worlds of black society. The Associated Negro Press writers were talented and operated within a world that lent little credence to the white world that surrounded them. As one reporter of the time argued,

> There was no white world as far as the black world of that time was concerned . . . We were not even aware of the white world in the sense that it meant anything of consequence to the world in which we lived . . . Our heaven and our glory was in Harlem; not at Harvard, but at Howard and Lincoln, Clark and Morris Brown, Tuskegee and Alabama State, and finally Florida A&M and other schools west of the Mississippi, Wiley and Grambling. All joined in possession of the black world. Nobody cared about Georgia Tech, nobody worried about Auburn. Nobody even worried about Notre Dame. We had our own. We had our Howard Bisons. We had our Golden Tuskegee Tigers, and that was the thing the black press wrote about. These were the things that we celebrated and that marked the Headlines that made the black press important. And of course the Beautiful verses and beautiful lines of men like Langston Hughes and Countee Cullen. (Hogan, p. 8)

The communication system and outlet to African American society and culture was alive and well. The Associated Negro Press helped provide national exposure for the Negro Baseball Leagues of the twentieth century.

The Negro League Baseball teams provided some of the leisure and downtime relief available to the black educated middle class and elite of the era. The Negro Baseball Leagues provided far more than pure entertainment to the community, just as the Associated Negro Press offered more than just communication.

## List of Professional Negro League Baseball Teams

| | | |
|---|---|---|
| Algoma Brownies | Columbus Buckeyes | Nashville Elite Giants |
| All Nations | Columbus Elite Giants | New Orleans-St. Louis Stars |
| Argyle Hotel Athletics | Cuban Giants | New York Black Yankees |
| Atlanta Black Crackers | Cuban House of David | New York Cubans |
| Atlantic City Bacharach Giants | Cuban Stars East | New York Gorhams |
| Baltimore Black Sox | Cuban Stars West | New York Harlem Stars |
| Baltimore Elite Giants | Cuban X-Giants | New York Lincoln Giants |
| Birmingham Black Barons | Dayton Marcos | New York Lincoln Stars |
| Brooklyn Eagles | Detroit Stars | Newark Browns |
| Brooklyn Royal Giants | Detroit Wolves | Newark Dodgers |
| Chicago American Giants | Ethiopian Clowns | Newark Eagles |
| Chicago Columbia Giants | Harrisburg Giants | Newark Stars |
| Chicago Giants | Harrisburg-St. Louis Stars | Page Fence Giants |
| Chicago Leland Giants | Havana Red Sox | Pennsylvania Red Caps of New York |
| Chicago Union Giants | Hilldale Daises | Philadelphia Giants |
| Chicago Unions | Homestead Grays | Philadelphia Stars |
| Cincinnati Buckeyes | Houston Eagles | Philadelphia Tigers |
| Cincinnati Clowns | Indianapolis ABCs | Pittsburgh Crawfords |
| Cincinnati Tigers | Indianapolis Athletics | Pittsburgh Keystones |
| Cincinnati-Indianapolis Clowns | Indianapolis Clowns | St. Louis Giants |
| Cleveland Bears | Indianapolis Crawfords | St. Louis Stars |
| Cleveland Browns | Jacksonville Red Caps | St. Paul Gophers |
| Cleveland Buckeyes | Kansas City Kansas Giants | Stars of Cuba |
| Cleveland Cubs | Kansas City Monarchs | Toledo Crawfords |
| Cleveland Elites | Long Branch Cubans | Toledo Tigers |
| Cleveland Giants | Louisville Black Caps | Washington Black Senators |
| Cleveland Hornets | Louisville Buckeyes | Washington Elite Giants |
| Cleveland Red Sox | Louisville White Sox | Washington Pilots |
| Cleveland Stars | Memphis Red Sox | Washington Potomacs |
| Cleveland Tate Stars | Milwaukee Bears | Wilmington Potomacs |
| Cleveland Tigers | Mohawk Giants | Zulu Cannibal Giants |
| Cole's American Giants | Monroe Monarchs | |
| Columbus Blue Birds | Montgomery Grey Sox | |

*Age is a case of mind over matter. If you don't mind, it don't matter.*

Satchel Paige

In the face of hardening segregationist policies, the leadership of the educational elite within the African American community, led by W. E. B. Du Bois and others, launched efforts to reaffirm, reconstruct, and build black American culture. This awakening is described as the Harlem Renaissance. This renaissance took place in all aspects of black society, and entrepreneurs and investors of Negro League Baseball redesigned and restructured their product as well. The end result of their efforts was the Negro Leagues.

Negro League Baseball entered a new era of prosperity and change beginning in 1920 until its demise in the 1950s. Rube Foster founded the Negro National League of baseball. Foster, acting in a role similar to that of a commissioner, ruled this league until it matured. The league became very successful. A second league, called the Eastern Colored League, was organized in 1923. From 1924 to 1927, the two leagues played four Negro World Series. The Eastern Colored League folded in 1928, however, and most of the teams returned to playing on an independent status. Foster became ill and died in 1930. The league he founded folded in 1931 due to lack of leadership and difficulties caused by the Depression. Problems with ownership and appropriate funding shifted some teams from one city to another, which also meant that these teams had to change their names. (See the sidebar.) The Great Depression deeply affected the black community, causing additional stress and struggle in a community that already fought racism. Money for leisure activities, such as paying to attend a baseball game, was just not readily available for most blacks. Most Negro League teams survived this era by moving back and forth across the country, playing games in one town or city after another. This system of movement became known as barnstorming.

Stability returned to Negro League Baseball when, in 1933, Gus Greenlee established the second Negro National League. An East–West All-Star game developed with the advent of this new league. This yearly game surpassed even the Negro League World Series in popularity through attendance and fan interest. From the mid-1930s to the late 1940s, legends of the players and some of the teams of these leagues grew and became lore. The pitching of Satchel Paige and the home-run hitting of Josh Gibson were two of the many celebrated tales.

In mainstream Major League baseball today, the names of Cy Young, Ty Cobb, and Babe Ruth reign as legendary. In the Negro Leagues, Paige (real name Leroy Robert Paige), Cool Papa Bell (real name James Thomas Bell), and Gibson served as heroes. In fact, many in the black press referred to Babe Ruth as the white Josh Gibson. The legends of men like Paige, Bell, and Gibson made the Negro Leagues what they were. Paige, for example, pitched until he was 61 years old. Born on July 7, 1906, in Mobile, Alabama, he pitched his last three innings of professional Major League baseball for the Kansas City A's of the American League in 1965. He pitched his last season in 1967 for the

Indianapolis Clowns of the Negro Leagues. Paige's glory years lasted from 1926 to 1950 when he played with the Negro Leagues. He pitched over the years for the Chattanooga Black Lookouts, Birmingham Black Barons, Baltimore Black Sox, Cleveland Cubs, Pittsburgh Crawfords, Kansas City Monarchs, Santo Domingo, Santo Domingo All-Stars, Newark Eagles, Mexican League, Satchel Paige's All-Stars, New York Black Yankees, Memphis Red Sox, Philadelphia Stars, Chicago American Giants, and the Indianapolis Clowns.

> *They used to say, "If we find a good black player, we'll sign him." They was lying.*
> Cool Papa Bell

Paige was an important figure throughout the majority of the Negro Leagues' duration. One tale of his athleticism describes a game he pitched against Gibson's team. Paige, a right-handed pitcher, had never pitched against Gibson in a crucial game-on-the-line type of situation. He intentionally loaded the bases in the last inning to bring Gibson to the plate. Gibson struck out on three pitches. He finally received an opportunity to pitch in the white Major Leagues in 1948. In 1971, he was inducted into the National Baseball Hall of Fame. He died on June 8, 1982, just before his seventy-sixth birthday. No player epitomizes the lore and legacy of the Negro Leagues more than Satchel Paige.

Josh Gibson similarly symbolized the lore of the Negro Leagues through his power hitting. He was born on December 21, 1911, in Buena Vista, Georgia, and played in the Negro Leagues from 1929 to 1946 as a catcher. The primary teams for which he played were the Homestead Grays and Pittsburgh Crawfords. He also played two years in the Mexican League and one year in Santo Domingo. Gibson's batting ability riveted crowds who came to see him play. He hit with an individual swing that reliably produced home runs.

Tales of Gibson's power hitting were second to none in baseball. He was credited with hitting home runs completely out of Yankee Stadium in New York, Griffith Stadium in Washington, D.C., and a stadium in Pittsburgh. These feats led reporters to cover the Negro Leagues. Wendell Smith of the *Pittsburgh Courier* and Sam Lacy of the *Baltimore Afro-American Ledger* reminded readers that Gibson may not have had any hitting equals. Not even Babe Ruth hit as well as Gibson! There were always discussions in the black community as to who actually hit more home runs, Ruth or Gibson. One thing is for sure: no player, other than Satchel Paige, received more notoriety in Negro League accounts than Gibson. He died on January 20, 1947, of a stroke. Gibson was inducted in the Baseball Hall of Fame in 1972. At that time, he was only the second player from the Negro Leagues to be so named.

James "Cool Papa" Bell, hailed as the fastest man to ever play baseball, played in the Negro Leagues from 1922 to 1950. He was born on May 17, 1903, in Starkville, Mississippi. He played for the St. Louis Stars, the Detroit Wolves, the Kansas City Monarchs, the Homestead Grays, the Pittsburgh Crawfords, the Memphis Red Sox, the Chicago American Giants, the Detroit

Senators, and the Kansas City Stars. He also spent time playing for teams in Mexico and Santo Domingo. His fame came from his speed, which is one of the most admirable qualities an athlete can possess in the eyes of many African Americans. Even athletes of large stature with extreme strength and power must be swift. Bell had speed to spare. Stories exist of him scoring from first base on a bunt by Satchel Paige while they played against a group of white Major Leaguers. Bell was said to twice have hit the ball to the shortstop in a game and beat the throw to first base; the person playing shortstop against Bell was said to be Jackie Robinson, who in 1947 became the first black player to play in the modern Major Leagues. This also gives some perspective of the quality of the skill level and play in the Negro Leagues. Though Robinson received an opportunity to play in the white Major Leagues, many other players from the Negro Leagues who were considered to have better physical skills never got a call or were well past their peak playing days.

Bell, a centerfielder, was a switch hitter and threw left-handed. The best, albeit exaggerated description of his speed was that he was able to turn off the light switch and be in the bed before the room got dark. In his 25 years of Negro League participation, Bell was credited with a .341 lifetime batting average. In exhibition games against white leagues, he is reported to have batted a .391 average. Bell died on March 7, 1991, in St. Louis, Missouri.

The talent of these three men demonstrates why the play of the Negro Leagues was of such high quality. Accounts of their talent also show the thrills and enjoyment that fans would experience and come to expect upon attending games played in these leagues.

Another aspect of Negro League Baseball that is very rarely spoken about is its female ownership. At a time when most of America truly thought that women did not belong in such arenas, women owned teams in the Negro Baseball Leagues. For example, Effa Manley was the owner of the Brooklyn Eagles, turned Newark Eagles, from 1935 to 1948. At that time, she was the only female owner of a team in baseball. A white woman raised in a household with a nonbiological black father, she was very well received in Negro League Baseball circles. She was well ahead of her time for involvement in such business ventures. Players under her contract included Larry Doby, an infielder who was the first black player in the white American League division, playing with Cleveland the same year that Jackie Robinson played with the Brooklyn Dodgers, pitcher Don Newcombe (who later played in the Major Leagues with the Dodgers and won the National League's Cy Young and MVP awards in 1956), and infielder/outfield Monte Irvin, who also was selected to baseball's Hall of Fame. Manley's reign as owner of the Eagles and her dealings with other owners earned her induction in baseball's Hall of Fame in 2006.

Though segregation prevailed in American society, African Americans forged ahead with all aspects of their lives. In some areas, like baseball, they produced a product so outstanding that white society on many occasions spent their leisure funds attending Negro Baseball League games. As social customs began to change, so did changes to racial custom and institutions. Black baseball ended as Major League Baseball integrated. In many ways, the Negro Leagues began to decline when Jackie Robinson joined the Dodgers. Despite this demise, the Negro Baseball Leagues remain a vital part of American baseball. The history and glory of the Negro Baseball Leagues are stored and still collected in their museum in St. Louis, Missouri, primarily through the efforts of John "Buck" O'Neill, a former player and lifelong historian of the leagues. O'Neill himself was on the 2006 baseball Hall of Fame ballot, though he was not selected and passed away a few months after the balloting. The Negro Baseball Leagues' greatest ambassador has passed, but he leaves a lifetime of glorious history for all to cherish.

## FURTHER READING

Brashler, William. *Josh Gibson: A Life in the Negro Leagues*. New York: Harper and Row, 1978.

Hogan, Lawrence D. *A Black National News Service: The Associated Negro Press and Claude Barnett*. Rutherford: Farleigh Dickinson University Press, 1984.

Holway, John. *Blackball Stars: Negro League Pioneers*. West Port, CT: Meckler, 1988.

Holway, John. *Black Diamonds: Life in the Negro Leagues from the Men Who Lived It*. West Port, CT: Meckler, 1989.

Holway, John. *Voices from the Great Black Baseball Leagues*. New York: Da Capo Press, 1992.

Peterson, Robert W. *Only the Ball Was White*. New York: McGraw-Hill, 1984.

Riley, James A. *The Biographical Encyclopedia of the Negro Baseball Leagues*. New York: Carroll & Graf, 1994.

Robinson, Frazier "Slow." In Paul Bauer, *Catching Dreams: My life in the Negro Baseball Leagues*. Syracuse, NY: Syracuse University Press, 1999.

Ruck, Rob. *Sandlot Seasons: Sport in Black Pittsburgh*. Urbana: University of Illinois Press, 1987.

AP Photo/David Zalubowski.

# Shaquille O'Neal

*Ying Wushanley*

Shaquille Rashaun O'Neal, born on March 6, 1972, in Newark, New Jersey, is considered the most physically dominant and one of the best centers in the history of the National Basketball Association (NBA). A powerful player who stands 7' 1" and weighs 325 pounds, O'Neal helped lead the Los Angeles Lakers to three consecutive NBA titles and the Miami Heat to one between 1999 and 2006. He became an instant sports celebrity when he joined the NBA in 1992, and has also pursued hobbies as a rap singer and screen actor with noticeable success.

O'Neal's first and middle names, Shaquille Rashaun, mean "little warrior" in Arabic. Yet the future basketball Hall of Famer is best known as "Shaq," a name that epitomized his unstoppable physical power and dominance on the basketball court. Teams playing against him often had to apply special strategies in order to diminish his impact on the game's outcome. One such method is "Hack-a-Shaq," initially invented by Don Nelson, coach of the Dallas Mavericks, to hinder the scoring ability of the Chicago Bulls during the 1997–1998 season. Nelson determined that the use of an intentional foul on a low-percentage free-throw shooter of the opposing team could help a team gain scoring advantage. The strategy ultimately became well known for its application again Shaq and his Los Angeles Lakers in 1999.

O'Neal was one of two sons and two daughters of Philip Harrison, a career serviceman in the municipality of Newark, New Jersey, and the U.S. Army, and Lucille O'Neal, also an employee of the city of Newark. His biological father, Joe Taney, abandoned the family shortly after Shaq was born. Responding to media's inquiry into Taney's role in his life, Shaq responded that biological fatherhood is not the same as true fatherhood. He explained that he had not seen his real father in over two decades, and did not expect to see him any time soon. Harrison, on the other hand, is O'Neal's true father because, in O'Neal's own words, "He's the one who raised me and made me what I am today."

During the 1970s the United States experienced its worst economic performance since the Great Depression. Increasing inflation and unemployment drove millions of Americans into poverty. Lack of employment opportunities in Newark forced Harrison to seek alternate employment. In order to better provide for his family, Harrison joined the U.S. Army and became a career serviceman in the military. Frequent relocation from base to base was the norm for military life. It also became a major part of O'Neal's childhood. But traveling was never fun for the young boy; frequent relocation simply deprived him of forming any lasting friendships. Often a stranger in a new place, he was eager to make friends with his peers. He would do anything to attract attention, such as pulling the school's fire alarms. His tactics won him more reprimands from school authorities than friendships. O'Neal was regularly teased by his peers about his Islamic name, unusual height, and big shoe size. Agitated and enraged, he would easily lose his temper and resort to his fists in self-defense. Fistfights may have stopped the verbal insults from his agitators from time to time, but it never prevented him from staying away from trouble at school, with peers, and in everything associated with growing up as a super-sized adolescent.

Bad experiences were transformed into good lessons, however. Living on military bases taught O'Neal one of the most important principles in life: discipline. Harrison was a very strict enforcer of this principle. "You learn things as an army brat that you don't even know you're learning," O'Neal recalled in his autobiography. "If you screw up . . . you face the consequences. With my dad, there was no, 'Well, we'll let it go this time.' He didn't let anything go. And gradually, you learn how to behave, how to respect authority." O'Neal possessed great physical potentials for basketball. But it was discipline that would make him stand out among his talented peers in the sport.

Concerned about his behavioral problems, his parents encouraged him to take up dancing and to play sports, although he showed little natural athletic talent. Their intention was to channel his abundant energy into something constructive through physical activities, discipline his social behavior, and structure his time through organized sports. Their plan worked. Not only did O'Neal stop fighting after taking up dancing, he was also very good at it. His big body did not hinder his coordination.

When he was in the sixth grade, his family relocated again with Harrison's service transfer, this time to Fulda, West Germany. Interestingly enough, O'Neal's basketball career began on an U.S. Army base in Germany. Attending a basketball clinic for youngsters given by Dale Brown, the head coach at Louisiana State University (LSU), O'Neal caught Brown's attention with his imposing 6' 8" body frame and shoe size of 17. The LSU coach was nearly speechless when O'Neal approached him for advice at the end of the clinic. "How long have you been in the army, soldier?" Brown asked. "I'm not in the army," replied O'Neal. "I'm only 13." Brown must have felt like he had been slam-dunked without any notice. He was only more shocked when he learned that O'Neal was not even on the base's high school team (Fulda American High School), allegedly because his feet were too big and his movements too slow and clumsy. All that made a lasting impression on Brown, who immediately urged Harrison to eventually enroll his son at LSU and play basketball for the famed Tigers.

In 1987, Harrison was transferred again, this time back to the United States to San Antonio, Texas. At age 15, O'Neal entered Robert G. Cole Junior-Senior High School in the fall and also joined its basketball team as a junior. It did not take long for him to impress his coaches, teammates, and his opponents. If he was ever a clumsy and slow mover on the basketball court, by the time he entered Cole High he had transformed himself into a dominant force in the game. In the two years since the Brown clinic in West Germany, O'Neal's co-ordination had caught up with his extraordinary physique. In addition, he grew out of his troublesome stage and became a role model in self-discipline and hard work, both on and off the basketball court.

His efforts paid off. Not only was his 6' 10" and 250-pound body a towering presence on the court, but his quickness, agility, and basketball skills began to impress people. Every opposing side of Cole High would double- and triple-team him, but O'Neal was unstoppable. In his very first varsity basketball season, he led Cole High on an undefeated regular season record, only to encounter their only loss in the Texas State Class AA Regional Finals. O'Neal had himself to blame for the defeat. With five seconds left in the game, he missed two crucial free throws, ending his team's chance for the state championship. When a taller, stronger, and more mature O'Neal returned to his senior season, he led his team all the way to the state championship title. During his two years at Cole High from 1987 to 1989, he averaged 32 points, 22 rebounds, and 8 blocked shots per game, and his team achieved a 68–1 record. O'Neal also set numerous scoring and rebounding records and grew to his adult height of 7' 1".

O'Neal's performance earned him a spot on the *Parade* High School All-America team, and he was named the most valuable player (MVP) in two prestigious postseason tournaments, the McDonald's All-Star Classic and the Dapper Dan Classic. By then, he had become one of the most sought-after high school players in the country. Every college and university wanted to enroll him, but few had a chance. In fact, the competition to recruit O'Neal was over before it even got started. He signed a national letter of intent before his senior season to attend LSU over basketball powerhouses such as the University of North Carolina at Chapel Hill, the University of Arizona, the University of Kentucky, Duke University, Indiana University, the University of Michigan, and the University of California–Los Angeles.

Three major factors secured O'Neal's choice of LSU. First, he liked the location of the university with its main campus in Baton Rouge. Although it was nearly 500 miles from San Antonio, where his parents lived, it was closer than most other schools, so his parents could come and see him play at home games. Second, O'Neal preferred the style of play in the Southeastern Athletic Conference, to which LSU belonged. He believed that this conference fostered dirty, hard play in contrast to the safer, easier play of the Atlantic Coast Conference. Third and possibly the most important factor was his connection with LSU head coach Dale Brown. Ever since their first meeting at the basketball clinic in West Germany, Brown had stayed in touch as he promised, giving the young player advice and encouragement as he became a more skilled player and grew into manhood. The LSU coach also earned the trust of O'Neal's father with his honesty and straightforwardness in dealing with the family.

O'Neal enrolled at LSU in the fall of 1989 and began to play big-time college basketball. Under the tutelage of Brown and a much more sophisticated management and training system than his high school had provided, he blossomed. As a first-year freshman of the team, he took action in every one of the 32 games of the season and averaged a respectable 13.9 points per game. But as one of the "Twin Towers," a nickname he shared with his seven-foot teammate

Stanley Roberts, O'Neal received more attention for his ability to rebound and block shots. He averaged 12 rebounds per game and set a conference record of 115 blocked shots. However, he would not be the star of the LSU team that season. This honor belonged to his teammate Chris Jackson, the superb sophomore point guard of the Flying Tigers. A shooting machine with a season high of nearly 28 points per game, the 6' 1" Jackson was elected First Team All-America at the end of the season. Jackson forfeited his last two years of college eligibility and moved on to play professional basketball in the NBA. In 1991, Jackson converted to Islam and changed his name to Mahmoud Abdul-Rauf. Meanwhile, Stanley Roberts also left the team because of academic problems, leaving O'Neal the burden of carrying the LSU Tigers but also a stage upon which to shine on the national scene.

O'Neal was ready for both when the 1990–1991 season arrived. He had trained extremely hard during the off-season. At 18 years of age, his body was stronger and better toned, his skills more refined and more versatile, and his mind more determined. He became the driving force of the LSU squad. When the season ended, he had left his mark in the history of college basketball. He doubled his scoring average from the previous year with 27.6 points per game. He increased his rebounding average to 14.7 per game, leading the nation in that category. He was selected the NCAA Division I Consensus First Team All-American and was named Player of the Year by *Sports Illustrated*, the Associated Press, and United Press International. Despite his personal achievement, however, his crucial leadership to the team was greatly limited when he suffered a hairline fracture to his leg late in the season, forcing him to be sidelined for four games. Had he stayed healthy, the LSU Tigers would likely have won the SEC tournament and become a formidable contender for the NCAA championship title.

O'Neal contemplated turning professional after this season, but his parents persuaded him to stay in college to complete his degree. The 1991–1992 season was not the most memorable for him and LSU fans. Despite his personal achievements—being selected the NCAA Division I Consensus First Team All-American the second year in a row and leading the nation in average blocked shots—O'Neal found that the cohesiveness of his team had disintegrated. Selfishness often overshadowed the importance of teamwork and the college game became less enjoyable. For many rival teams, beating LSU meant stopping O'Neal, and they would try everything to accomplish this. As he recalled, "On every play I got double-teamed, triple-teamed, quadruple-teamed, fouled, hacked, handcuffed, and assaulted." In a game against the University of Tennessee, he was fouled so hard while attempting a dunk that he lost his cool. He broke the grip of the defender who was still hanging on to him and swung his elbow. Although neither of them threw a punch, their teammates and even coaches got into a big fight on the floor. O'Neal was subsequently suspended from the following game, which LSU lost to the University of Kentucky.

*Me shooting 40 percent at the foul line is just God's way to say nobody's perfect.*

The Tennessee game was a turning point on O'Neal's career path. The college game was not fun any more, and it was becoming too dangerous for the player who could not be stopped by conventional basketball tactics. Suddenly, staying at LSU did not seem an option any longer, nor would it make any sense. On April 3, 1992, immediately following the NCAA tournament, O'Neal held a press conference to announce his decision to enter the NBA draft. He explained that he had committed himself to the game, but that he believed that he should stop anything that no longer felt fun. He was ready for his career in the professional rank, and no one would argue against his decision, not even his education-oriented parents.

On June 24, 1992, O'Neal was drafted first overall by the Orlando Magic, an NBA expansion team that commenced in 1989. The Magic signed him to a seven-year, $40 million contract, making him by far the highest-paid rookie in any sport. When he arrived in Orlando, the central Florida city best known for Disney World, thousands of Magic followers turned out to welcome him. Many of them were driven by the hope that he would be a savior for their team, which had lost more than 70 percent of its games in the previous three seasons. O'Neal would not disappoint these fans or the franchise that had never experienced a winning season.

In his first year with the Magic, O'Neal helped the team end its losing streak with a 41–41 record. The team only missed the playoffs because the Indiana Pacers had the same record in the conference and edged the Magic via a tie-breaker formula. O'Neal led the team in scoring with 23.4 points per game. He also set the team scoring record with 1,893 points and led the NBA in field goal percentage (.562). He was voted NBA Rookie of the Year and selected to start in the All-Star game as the first rookie to do so since Michael Jordan in 1985.

If 1992 was the turning point of fortune for the Orlando Magic when it acquired O'Neal, its fortune increased dramatically the following year when the team brought in the talented rookie point guard Anfernee "Penny" Hardaway from Memphis State University. Enhanced by Hardaway's brilliant assistance and sharp shooting, the Magic soon rose to prominence in the Eastern Conference. The Magic ended their regular season with a team record of 50 wins and went to the playoffs, only to be defeated 3-0 by the Indiana Pacers in their first ever postseason series. O'Neal improved his game scoring average to 29.3 points. He also set a new team season scoring record with 2,377 points and again led the NBA in field goal percentage (.599). Following the NBA season, O'Neal won the gold medal as a member of the U.S. Olympics team and the MVP award at the 1994 World Championship of Basketball.

Aside from his basketball accomplishments, O'Neal was equally successful off the court. He signed multimillion-dollar endorsement contracts with Pepsi and Reebok, touring the world as a representative of his commercial sponsors, recorded a song with the Brooklyn hip-hop trio Fu-Schnickens, and released his debut album, *Shaq Diesel*, which sold more than one million copies. He also co-starred with Nick Nolte and teammate Penny Hardaway in the Paramount film *Blue Chips*.

O'Neal's career with the Magic reached its peak in 1994–1995. After winning a record 57 games in the regular season, the Magic continued its upward surge during the playoffs. It defeated the Boston Celtics 3-1 in the first round. In the Eastern Conference semifinals, the Magic conquered the Chicago Bulls which contained his Airness, the freshly out-of-retirement Michael Jordan. The Magic continued to claim its first conference title by defeating the Indiana Pacers 4-3 in the best-of-seven finals. But the Magic lost its steam in the NBA finals, beaten in four straight games by the Western Conference Champion Houston Rockets.

For O'Neal, it was a season full of high marks. The third-year veteran led the league in scoring average, field goals attempted, field goals made, and total seasonal points. The Magic's sweeping defeat in the NBA finals, however, made him realize that in order to win a championship both he and the team would need to mature physically as well as mentally.

In 1995–1996, the Magic set a franchise record of 60 wins (.732) during the regular season and entered the playoffs for the third year in a row. After defeating Detroit and Atlanta in the first two rounds, the Magic faced the Chicago Bulls again, a team it beat only a year before in the conference semifinals. But this time the Magic was no match for the Bulls, led by superstar Jordan, who by then had reestablished his total dominance of the game. The Bulls swept the Magic in the conference finals and went on to win the first championship of its second triple-crown.

The Magic's repeated failure to capture a NBA title sealed O'Neal's departure from Orlando. In 1996, he signed a seven-year, $120 million contract with the Los Angeles Lakers. At this stage, he wanted an NBA championship ring more than anything else and believed the Lakers was the team that could realize his dream. He turned down a larger contract offer from the Magic because he wanted to join the Lakers so badly. No one was going to make him change his mind.

O'Neal's contract paid immediate dividends for the Lakers in the 1996–1997 season, leading the team to a 56–26 record, its best effort since 1990–1991. He averaged 26.6 points per game, finishing third in the league in blocked shots (2.88 per game) and fourth in field goal accuracy (.557). Injury, however, kept him out of nearly 40 percent of the games. The Lakers, after beating the Portland Trail Blazers in the first round of the playoffs, were defeated by the Utah Jazz in the Western Conference semifinals. For O'Neal, his turn to capture the NBA championship title was yet to come.

The following two seasons were trying for O'Neal and his teammates. They were young, dynamic, and talented, but lacked experience and sophistication when they were needed the most. In 1997–1998, the Lakers posted its best seasonal record of the decade with 61 wins and cruised all the way to the

*I want to be strong, dominant. Like Wilt Chamberlain.*

however, Van Gundy resigned abruptly from his head coach position, citing personal reasons. He was succeeded by Pat Riley, president of the Heat and one of the greatest coaches in NBA history. It was only two years before that Riley "fired" himself after a very disappointing season and gave Van Gundy the head coach job. The sudden shuffle in the Heat's front office led to speculation that the legendary Riley had been planning to replace Gundy to give himself a chance to relive his glorious past of being the master at the helm and steering the team all the way to the championship title.

In Greek mythology divine intervention often accompanied the extraordinary accomplishment of Greek heroes. Such supernatural assistance is not scientifically recorded in modern sport, but having Riley as its head coach (despite his motive) was the closest thing to divine intervention the Miami Heat could have possibly received. Riley soon proved to his fans and critics that he was the right man at the right time to lead the Heat as its head coach. After a remarkable 52–30 regular season, the Heat went on to defeat Chicago, New Jersey, and Detroit to claim its first conference title and advanced to its first NBA finals in franchise history. The Heat faced the Dallas Mavericks, also a first-timer, for the championship title. After losing the first two games in the series in Dallas, with an embarrassing blowout in the second match, the Heat was declared all but finished by many critics and odds makers. To their dismay, the Heat came alive in the last minutes of the third game in Miami, led by a resilient and superb Wade. This game was the turning point. Miami won that match and the following three in a row to become the third team in NBA history to win the championship after being down 0-2. Wade went on to win the NBA finals MVP award.

Despite his below-average performance due to injury, O'Neal finished the season leading the NBA in field goal percentage, joining Wilt Chamberlain as one of only two players to lead that category nine times in league history. The championship was also his fourth title in seven seasons and fulfilled his promise to the people of Miami in July 2004 when he vowed to "bring the title home."

In his 14 years with the NBA at the end of 2006, O'Neal has compiled one of the most impressive career records in professional basketball. He earned All-NBA honors in each of his first 14 seasons and was named NBA finals MVP three consecutive times in 2000–2002. He was named one of the 50 Greatest Players in NBA history in 1996, the youngest player to earn the honor.

Outside of basketball, O'Neal has accomplished what few professional athletes could have even imagined. He has starred or appeared in a dozen feature movies and commercials; produced six of his own music albums, including the aforementioned *Shaq Diesel* (1993) and *Shaq Fu: Da Return* (1994), which have sold more than 500,000 and 1 million copies, respectively. He has written two autobiographies, *ShaqAttaq!: My Rookie Years* (1993), with Jack McCallum, and *Shaq Talks Back: The Uncensored Word on My Life and*

*Winning in the NBA* (2001). He also has authored a children's book, *Shaq and the Beanstalk and Other Very Tall Tales* (1999). He has been featured on numerous television shows, magazine covers, and in video games. With his impeccable NBA records, his remarkable achievements in the entertainment industries, his highly desirable marketability for commercial sponsors, and his charismatic personality, especially among the younger generation, O'Neal has become one of the most recognizable sport and cultural icons in the world.

## FURTHER READING

Eichhorn, Dennis. *Shaq*. Seattle: Turman Publishing, 1995.

O'Neal, Shaquille. *Shaq and the Beanstalk and Other Very Tall Tales*. New York: Jump at the Sun, 1999.

O'Neal, Shaquille. *Shaq Talks Back: The Uncensored Word on My Life and Winning in the NBA*. New York: St. Martin's Press, 2001.

O'Neal, Shaquille, and Jack McCallum. *ShaqAttaq!: My Rookie Year*. New York: Hyperion Books, 1993.

Sullivan, Michael J. *Sports Great Shaquille O'Neal*. Berkeley Heights, NJ: Enslow, 1998.

Taylor, Phil. "Unstoppable," *Sports Illustrated* (June 4, 2001).

Ungs, Tim. *Shaquille O'Neal*. New York: Chelsea House, 1996.

# Jesse Owens

*James R. Coates*

Born in abject poverty in the American South, Jesse Owens rose to become one of the true icons in the world. He became known not just in the world of sports, but was renowned for his humanity and friendship endeavors in many parts of the world.

At the height of his fame and glory, Owens won four gold medals in the 1936 Berlin Olympic Games, setting or tying the Olympic or world record in all four events. His athletic success during the games' uncertain and tense international political climate was amazing, especially when compared to the historic statistics of the Olympics at that time.

On September 12, 1913, Oakville, Alabama sharecropper Henry Cleveland Owens and his family awaited their twelfth member. Emma Fitzgerald Owens delivered that new family member, who was named James Cleveland Owens. James, called J.C. by his family members, was the tenth of the eventual eleven children in the family. While Henry worked as a sharecropper, Emma took in other people's clothing for sewing and ironing to help with extra money in the household. Jesse, like most of the other children in the house, picked cotton to help with the household income. The family of four girls, seven boys, and parents lived in extreme poverty.

Illiteracy was the normal ingredient for sharecroppers of Henry Owens's generation throughout Alabama and most other regions of the South, and he was no exception. Due to their illiteracy, most sharecroppers never used money for food, even when shopping at the grocery store in Oakville. The sharecroppers' inability to read, write, or do math did not help them. Henry and Emma made sure that their children would not meet the same fate of illiteracy that captured their existence. With the laws of the nation changing, openly allowing for all children—including African Americans who were previously excluded from formal education in some states—to be educated, the Owens couple stressed the importance of reading and a formal education to their children.

Jesse admitted that he was the only one of the boys who did not help with much of the hard work during those sharecropping days. It was not because he was too young or small, it was because of his illness. Each winter he became sick with pneumonia, and at least twice believed he was close to death. His family consequently kept him away from the hardest tasks. Emma was the person given credit by Jesse for pulling him through those terrible periods of illness.

Henry Owens decided that his life would have to change, if not for himself, at least for his wife and children. He summoned his family and told them of his intent to move them to the North. The new environment of the North was a very strange one for Jesse. The family moved from an environment where the races were isolated from one another to one that was open and free by comparison. Jesse now attended a school with white children. While living in Oakville, he could barely go to school, and attending school with white children was simply out of the question. Many of the white students that he went to school with may have been new to the city and country themselves, but they nevertheless were white and in the same schools—this was a totally new experience for

Jesse. Integrated schooling was not a possibility open to him in Oakville. He also wore clothing that covered his body. This was new, as he always wore either secondhand clothing that had belonged to his older brothers or clothing that was so worn that they were more rags than anything. With the Northern climate of Cleveland being much colder than that of the Southern climate of Oakville, clothing that covered more of the body was appropriate. Along with his shyness, Jesse's desire to please his teachers and other adults led him to allow himself to be called Jesse rather than J.C., because he didn't want to cause a problem.

> *I always loved running—it was something you could do by yourself, and under your own power. You could go in any direction, fast or slow as you wanted, fighting the wind if you felt like it, seeking out new sights just on the strength of your feet and the courage of your lungs.*

Jesse's participation in athletics was to change the world in which he lived. He was able to obtain a high school education and then receive a scholarship to one of the largest colleges in the country. This opportunity came at a time when segregation was still the law of the land. While attending Fairmont Junior High School in Cleveland, Jesse met the man who would become his coach, mentor, and longtime friend, Charles Riley. Owens learned a great deal about life, including good manners, as well as track and field from Riley.

During his senior year, Jesse ran a time of 9.4 seconds for the 100-yard sprint and ran the 220-yard sprint in 20.7 seconds. His 100-yard dash time tied the national record and placed him on the national scene. His times gave him national acclaim and recognition. After graduating from high school, he accepted an offer to attend Ohio State University in the fall of 1933. According to Jesse, "There were no athletic scholarships at Ohio State University then, not even if your marks had been good, nor even if you'd learned how to use your legs to become the world's fastest human the year before" (Owens, *Blackthink*, p. 14). He also worked part-time to make ends meet and asked that his father be given some type of employment by the university.

Owens's popularity was very evident from the beginning of his career at Ohio State. By 1935 he had come into national prominence. The National Intercollegiate Championships of that year left no doubt that he was no longer just a national figure but was well on his way to world acclaim. The fans attending the championships, held at the University of Michigan, saw him break five world records and tie another in about an hour's time. All of this was done while he was injured; he had wrestled with one of his fraternity brothers and strained a back muscle and sustained other bruises and injuries. On May 25, 1935, he was hurting so badly that he couldn't properly warm up for his sprints or field events. Only moments before the 100-yard race did his back pain subside enough to allow him to participate.

His performance was truly amazing. His times and distances were 9.4 seconds in the 100-yard sprint and 26' 8.25" in the long jump, setting a world record that remained unbroken for 25 years. This was also his only attempt in the long jump for the day. In the 220-yard straight-away sprint, his time was 20.3 seconds, also a world record. He won the 220-yard low hurdles in 22.6 seconds—another world record. That day in track and field was truly amazing for the fans, the sport of track and field, and Jesse himself.

On July 5, 1935, Jesse Owens married Minnie Ruth Solomon. The wedding took place in the living room of Minnie's parents' home in Cleveland. The newlyweds also were to spend their wedding night there. From this partnership three children were conceived, all girls. Gloria Shirley Owens (Hemphill), the oldest, was born on August 8, 1935. Beverly Owens (Prather) is the middle daughter, being five years younger than Gloria. The youngest is Marlene Owens (Rankin). These girls were raised to be strong and independent individuals.

The year 1936 saw a few amazing activities that appeared to be sporting events but turned out to be far more political and social in nature than they were athletic. Jesse's accomplishments were among these activities. Joe Louis (boxing), Max Schmeling (boxing), and Marty Glickman (track) were participants in other activities that year that made sports become more political than it had been before.

Jesse, along with all of the U.S. athletes competing in the Olympics, had to deal with Avery Brundage. Brundage would soon become the president of the U.S. Olympic Committee and one of the most powerful men in track and field worldwide. He was also reportedly a Nazi sympathizer during the time that Hitler's Aryan supremacy doctrine was propagandized by the Nazi Party.

Jesse faced a number of competitors at the 1936 Games. Eulace Peacock, the only person to regularly have beaten Jesse in the 100, was unable to pose a threat because of injuries. Neither Peacock nor Ralph Metcalfe, Jesse's main competitor in the 100-meter run, were threats in the long jump. Peacock was injured and did not make the Olympic team at all. Metcalfe placed second to Owens in the 100-meter trials final and was a part to the team traveling to Berlin. Owens, having set four world records and tied at least one other, was talked about and sought after by the press more than any of the other American track and field athletes. Metcalfe and Eddie Tolan were also known because of their participation in previous Olympic competitions. In fact, before Owens broke the world record in the 100-meter sprint, the record was held by Metcalfe and Tolan. The Berlin Games, however, represented the first time the world press personally meet this new reigning record holder of five world marks.

At this time, Hitler and his Nazi Party ruled Germany with a propaganda machine seldom seen anywhere. The major premise of this propaganda was that of Aryan supremacy and the notion that Germans were the master race. This political ideology encompassed all aspects of life, including athletic superiority. In fact, various reports remarked that Hitler claimed the American team had to bring "black auxiliaries" to compete against the superior Nazi Aryan team. Further, the official Nazi newspaper slurred the African American team members. The newspaper account also suggested that an assistant to Foreign

Minister Joachim von Ribbentrop complained to Martha Dodd, daughter of the U.S. ambassador to Germany William E. Dodd, that black athletes were not even human.

The early part of the 1936 Olympic Games began just as Hitler and others knowledgeable about worldwide track and field competition expected they would. The Germans dominated their competitors before home crowds that placed 110,000 people in attendance at the stadium. While blacks had participated in the modern Olympic Games almost from their inception, support for their inclusion came mainly from European nations. The 1932 Los Angeles Games were the first to have any significant number of African Americans participate. Most everyone knew of the black athletes the Americans brought, and some of those athletes (Owens, Metcalfe, and Johnson) held or were performing at world or Olympic record times and distances, but they would be considered no threat, by reporters, track and field officials, and many athletes, to the Aryan athletes assembled by Hitler and his propaganda machine.

During the first day of competition, Hitler observed the early success of the German athletes. He summoned these early victors, reported to be Tilly Fleischer and Hans Woellke, to his personal box at the stadium and congratulated them publicly. This public greeting was also done for a victorious Finnish athlete. Next to win a gold medal at those Games was Cornelius Johnson, an African American high jumper. Though Hitler was known to arrive and depart from the competitions at approximately the same time each day, he decided to leave the rest of that day's competition before any congratulatory offers could be extended to Johnson. Explanations and rumors about his early departure were plentiful. One explanation stated that he arrived and departed on a set schedule each day, and on the day that Johnson won his gold medal it was time for the Fuhrer's departure when the medal presentation ceremony was to take place. It was also rumored that he left because he would not publicly congratulate a black man due to his dislike of Jews and blacks. The rumors soon twisted to the notion that it was Jesse Owens who was snubbed by Hitler. The rumors persisted so long and were published by so many news organizations that many believed it to be true. Owens's comments also left readers believing that he indeed was the person slighted by Hitler. In truth, if anyone was snubbed, it was Johnson. However, make no mistake about it, Owens's performance at the 1936 Olympic Games was a major blow to Hitler's Aryan supremacy doctrine as well as to the racial arrogance of the United States.

Owens, being the most noted of the African American track and field participants, was clearly the favorite of the people in attendance. Jesse performed from August 2 to 9 and did extremely well. At the Berlin Games Jesse Owens won the 100-meter sprint, tying the Olympic record of 10.3 seconds. In one heat, he actually broke the world record with a time of 10.2, but this time was disallowed because of the wind speed at his back. He also won the 200-meter sprint, setting a new Olympic record of 21.1 seconds; won the long jump, setting

*The battles that count aren't the ones for gold medals. The struggles within yourself—the invisible, inevitable battles inside all of us—that's where it's at.*

a new world and Olympic record with a leap of 26 feet, 5.25 inches; and was a member of the world and Olympic record-setting 400-meter relay team with a time of 39.8 seconds.

The U.S. 400-meter relay team was quite controversial, despite its success. According to reports, the coaches pulled the sprinters of the team together on the day of the relay and told them there would be changes to the team. The original members of the team were Glickman, Stoller, Foy Draper, and Frank Wykoff. Head coach Lawson Robertson of the University of Pennsylvania told the sprinters he had heard rumors that the Germans were holding their best sprinter back for the 400-meter relay, so he and the other coaches decided to make changes so the best possible team was on the track. Of course, this was not an accurate statement—in head-to-head competition Glickman and Stoller beat Draper and Wykoff—but Robertson used this excuse to justify the changes. He removed Glickman and Stoller, both Jews, from the team and replaced them with Owens and Metcalfe, both African Americans. In the eyes of Hitler, the black man was only slightly less offensive to himself and the Nazi Party than was the Jewish man. With Robertson's changes, the U.S. team had given Hitler exactly what he had been looking for: a way to prevent Jewish athletes' participation in the Berlin Games.

This particular coaching maneuver meant that Owens was able to win his fourth gold medal at those Games. Of course, the two removed runners were not happy. Neither were Metcalfe and Wykoff truly happy when they reminisced about the incident many years later. One fact remained, however, that Brundage, Robertson, Cromwell, and Hitler could not hide: Jesse Owens.

Fatigued from all the post-Olympic competitions the athletes were asked to participate in throughout Europe, along with receiving very little rest, having no money, and being homesick for his wife and child, Owens decided not to take part in any further post-Olympic competitions on the advice of his coach and mentor, Larry Snyder. Instead he made plans to return to the United States to take advantage of several reported financial opportunities presented to him.

Brundage, now president of the Amateur Athletic Union (AAU) and American Olympic Committee (AOC), had his assistant, Daniel Ferris, announce that the AAU was suspending Owens from all further amateur competition in the United States. Snyder and Owens insisted that the AAU had no right to force participation from athletes who did not sign agreements to participate in such competitions. According to AAU guidelines, participation could only be demanded from athletes who had already signed agreements to do so. The AAU for its part said that Jesse was insubordinate and did not fulfill his obligations because he did not participate in the post-Olympic meets as required by the contract agreement with the AAU.

When Owens returned to the United States, he had to face the press and its questions about his suspension and the reported snubbing they believed he received from Hitler. As uncomfortable as it might have been, he answered the questions to the best of his ability. His major new dilemma was in what direction he should take his life. He was reportedly offered significant sums of money to appear with different entertainers, white and black. His decisions included whether to turn professional, go back to college, take one of the entertainment offers, or try to be reinstated with the AAU. Surprisingly he received a great deal of verbal support from the press in the form of articles and radio commentary, but nothing tangible. Many of these reporters, along with members of the National Collegiate Athletic Association (NCAA) felt that the AAU was indeed manipulating the Olympic athletes, especially Owens. The AAU received all the financial rewards, while the athletes received nothing for themselves. The NCAA and the AAU were at major odds with one another by this point in their existence. Any support Owens received from the NCAA and Ohio State must be looked on with a very critical eye, because these institutions did not typically follow through with their offers to athletes. With the exception of Larry Snyder, the main interest of the university's personnel was in the windfall that would be reaped by them if Owens were to return to school to participate in the track and field program.

In the meantime Jesse lived life to its fullest. Since he had just returned to the United States, he was participating in one parade after another, most of them in his honor. He and his wife received gifts and accolades from city officials, friends, and well-wishers. Shortly after returning to New York to be in a parade honoring all of the returning American Olympians, Jesse signed a contract with professional agent Marty Forkins.

He soon found out that almost all of the offers for financial reward that he received while in England from various sources were either bogus or reneged. Two that remained open to him were from members of the African American community: one from a vaudeville entertainer, and the other from Wilberforce University, a historically black college and university located in Ohio.

The IRS placed a lien on Jesse's income for back taxes in 1938. By that time he had also ventured into a number of other endeavors, including managing a barnstorming basketball team, managing a regional softball team, racing against professional baseball players, taking part in vaudeville acts, opening a dry cleaning business, and of course having a foot race with heavyweight boxing champion Joe Louis. Owens's athletic endeavors brought fame and fortune, to some degree, to his life. They also brought swindlers and problems with the government. As anyone who's had any encounters with the IRS will attest, you know who won such high-profile disputes with the government. Jesse did not prevail against the IRS.

Owens's introduction to the black athletic revolution occurring in the United States and elsewhere during the 1960s took place on the international stage of the Olympics. His reaction to the tactics utilized and the platform chosen (the Olympics) to bring attention to black athletes' plight was not unusual. In fact, many segments of the African American community, including the athletes themselves, disagreed on the appropriateness of the tactics used by each arm of the Civil Rights Movement. The major difference was that the athletes' rejection of Jesse came on the world stage of the Olympics, and from a chief organizer of the movement, Professor Harry Edwards. Most others from the African American community who disagreed with the revolution did so in anonymity. No one from the African American community would have accepted the insults from Edwards. To be blunt, Edwards was not the only American, black or white, to direct insults at Owens. Several others took the time and effort to put their beliefs about his behavior in writing, addressing him as "boy," "slave," and an Uncle Tom. Jesse weathered those indignations with his usual class and dignity, and later came to understand some of the rationale being used by the "Black-thinkers" for their revolutionary actions.

Many individuals, African Americans and whites, did not give credit to Owens for his community involvement, which included working with youth and building what might be deemed positive relationships between the races in America. Jesse worked with underprivileged youth on a regular basis as a board member of the Chicago Boys' Club. At times this organization served as many as 1,500 young people. He also worked for over five years as the Sports Specialist of the State of Illinois Youth Commission. He was America's Ambassador of Sports, a position to which he was appointed to by officials from the U.S. State Department. He even served as special representative of President Dwight Eisenhower to the 1956 Olympic Games hosted by Australia.

After returning home from the 1936 Games and dealing with various personal difficulties, Owens traveled extensively on behalf of both public and private entities. He made motivational speeches to professional organizations, business meetings, church functions, parent teacher organizations, and youth groups.

In addition to working as an ambassador and consultant, Owens also had a track and field athletic competition named in his honor. In 1976, President Gerald Ford presented him with the highest civilian honor, the Medal of Freedom. President Jimmy Carter presented him with the Living Legend Award in 1979.

After his death, Owens's family and friends created the Jesse Owens Foundation (JOF). The organization's goal is "to promote the development of youth to their fullest potential." The organization was also established to "perpetuate the ideals and life's work of this Olympic champion and humanitarian." The establishment of the JOF has served as a great resource for research on and about Jesse. In addition, the JOF has provided funding to assist more than 350 college students. The scholarships for educational funding are allotted through the Ruth and Jesse Owens Scholars Program at Ohio State University, which helps with funding for students who accept admission to that institution.

Jesse Owens is one of the true icons of sports, no matter what era or which athletes he is measured against.

## FURTHER READING

Baker, William J. *Jesse Owens: An American Life*. New York: Free Press, 1986.

MacAloon, John J. *This Great Symbol: Pierre de Coubertin and the Origins of the Modern Olympic Games*. Chicago: University of Chicago Press, 1981.

Mandell, Richard D. *The Nazi Olympics*. Urbana: University of Illinois Press, 1987.

Owens, Jesse, with Paul G. Neimark. *Blackthink: My Life as Black Man and White Man*. New York: William Morrow and Company, 1970.

Owens, Jesse, with Paul G. Neimark. *I Have Changed*. New York: William Morrow and Company, 1972.

Rurup, Reinhard. *1936 The Olympic Games and National Socialism*, 2nd edition. USZ, Wien: Institute F. Sportwissenschaften, 1996.

Sears, Edward S. *Running through the Ages*. Jefferson, NC: McFarland, 2001.

THE NORMAN FILM MFG. CO.
PRESENTS

BILL PICKETT
WORLD'S COLORED CHAMPION...IN
'THE BULL-DOGGER'
Featuring The Colored Hero of the Mexican Bull Ring
in Death Defying Feats of Courage and Skill.
THRILLS! LAUGHS TOO!
Produced by NORMAN FILM MFG. CO.
JACKSONVILLE, FLA.

Photofest.

# Bill Pickett

*Elyssa Ford*

As Garth Brooks sings in "The Rodeo," rodeos, cowboys, and cowgirls are icons and heroes of the American West. These reminders of the country's great rural and ranching past tie Americans to our heritage. Often, rodeo queens with curled blonde hair or tough "good ol' boys" from Texas represent the rodeo and cowboys, but racial minorities also played an important role in the development of the rodeo. Blacks, Native Americans, native Hawaiians, and many immigrant groups performed with the Wild West shows and competed in championship rodeos in the 1920s.

Though not commonly known as a home to cattle and cowboys, Hawaii held an international rodeo competition in 1903. A few years later, several of Hawaii's top cowboys competed in the 1908 Cheyenne Frontier Days rodeo. Native Hawaiian Ikua Purdy won the World's Steer Roping Championship, and two other Hawaiians placed in the top six. Many Native Americans participated in Wild West shows, and others, including Tom Three Persons and Jackson Sundown, won fame and world titles in bronc riding in the 1910s.

Though these men and many others competed with and won contests against white cowboys, an African American man named Bill Pickett was one of the most well-known rodeo performers in the early twentieth century. As the lone representative from rodeo in this collection—one of the earliest and most iconic American athletic events—Pickett emerges as not only an impressive African American man from this time in our nation's history but also as one of the most important early cowboys in rodeo.

An active competitor in rodeos and a performer in Wild West shows from the 1880s until the 1930s, Pickett was an important black figure. He participated in these rodeos at a time when racial discrimination against African Americans kept many black performers away from athletic and sporting competitions. More than just a participant in these rodeos, though, he actually invented and popularized one rodeo event—bulldogging. Today known as steer wrestling, bulldogging entailed leaping from the back of a racing horse onto the back of a running steer. The cowboy grabbed both of the steer's horns, jumped to the ground, and twisted the steer's neck up. To still the steer, the cowboy bit it on the lip or nose and then pulled the animal to the ground.

As with other rodeo events, bulldogging originated from ranch work. This work, however, was done by dogs, not men. These cattle dogs, often part bulldog, located stray cows in the brush. To keep them still, the dog bit the cow on the lip. The pain caused the cow to stay in place or fall to the ground until a cowboy arrived to rope it. As legend has it, Pickett saw these animals "bulldogging" and wondered if he could do the same. At only 5' 7" and 145 pounds, he quickly mastered the technique. Like bronc riding, which came from breaking wild horses on the ranch, bulldogging soon appeared in rodeos. He was famous as the creator of bulldogging and successful in his career—he bulldogged around 5,000 steers—and the event quickly became popular. In the 1920s women competed in bulldogging, and the event continues today as steer wrestling as a mainstay in rodeos.

Pickett's grandmother came to Texas as a slave belonging to the Barton family from South Carolina. They arrived in Texas in the 1850s and settled near Austin. The Picketts used this last name, not that of their owners, and worked with cattle and horses in the area. They lived with the Bartons until they were freed after the Civil War. Pickett's father, Thomas, was born into slavery but freed when he was young. He and much of his family stayed near Austin after they were freed. Thomas married Mary Gilbert, who was of mixed race heritage (African American, Native American, and white), in 1870. Shortly after their marriage, Willie M. Pickett was born in either 1870 or 1871. Though given the name Willie, he was known as Bill from a young age.

With 13 children, Thomas moved the family closer to Austin and grew vegetables to sell in town. Despite this and the other odd jobs he worked, the family made very little money. Like other poor, black children in the area, Bill attended school through only the fifth grade, when he dropped out to work. As a boy and young teen, he gained experience with cattle and horses when the cattle drives came through Austin from south Texas on the way to Kansas City. In fact, it was common to see herds of cattle moving along Congress Street, the major thoroughfare in Austin. Pickett learned to read horse and cattle brands and watched the cowboys to learn how to ride and rope. After practicing his bulldogging technique, he supposedly demonstrated it for a group of cowboys struggling with a calf. Despite their taunts, Pickett succeeded in subduing the calf and impressing the cowboys, who spread the story of the young bulldogger across Texas. Regardless of whether that story is true, Pickett certainly used his horse and cattle skills in exhibitions and local competitions to earn money. By the age of 15 or 16 he worked on nearby ranches as a cowboy and competed in local riding events.

In the late 1880s, the Pickett family moved to Taylor, Texas, a small town about 30 miles outside of Austin. Bill continued to work on ranches and compete in local competitions. From 1889 to possibly 1893, Pickett earned $5 per week feeding and working the cattle on the nearby Williamson County ranch. During this time, he met Maggie Turner, the daughter of a former slave and white plantation owner. They secretly dated and then married December 2, 1890. Early in the marriage, Pickett picked cotton in the fall and hunted during the winter to support the family. He still continued to compete in local rodeos, riding in the first fair/rodeo held in Taylor in 1888. The couple had nine children over the course of their lives. Though Pickett wanted to teach

*The steer longed into the arena . . . Pickett's horse plunged full speed after it. [Pickett] leaped from the saddle. He turned a complete somersault along the length of the steer's back, flying out and down over the curved horns . . . to fasten his teeth in the side of the steer's mouth. With sheer strength he dragged the running behemoth's head to the tan-bark, thrust its horn in the ground, and forward momentum threw the steer hocks over horns in a somersault of its own.*

Bill Pickett Invitational
Rodeo Website

his children to ride horses and compete in the rodeo, his two sons died young. His daughters did not compete, but they loved to hear about their father's experiences in the rodeos and Wild West shows. Active in the local Baptist church, Pickett juggled his position as a deacon with his home life, ranch work, and performing schedule.

Since the introduction of cattle and horses to the Americas, people have ridden horses and raised cattle. Both in the wild and on ranches, cowboys and cowgirls needed the necessary skills to work with and control these animals. Breaking horses and roping cattle were part of the daily lives of ranchers in the Western United States. Work, however, did not reign supreme at all times. Rides on the range could become horse races, and cowboys often gathered together on the weekends to hold informal roping and riding competitions. Thus, the very real skills used on the ranch became the popular events in the rodeo. Steer roping, bronc riding, and horse racing can all be seen in modern-day rodeos even though most of the competitors have never worked on a ranch or used these skills for anything other than competition.

Today we often think of rodeo, along with baseball, as the quintessential American athletic event, but Mexican ranchers and cowboys actually worked with cattle, rode horses, and held rodeos long before whites moved to the Western and Southwestern United States. Very similar to the Western rodeo in the United States today, the Mexican rodeo or the *charreada* began as horse and cattle-handling skills were used in weekend competitions. Events such as bronc riding, bull riding, and roping appeared in the charreada and later in the Western rodeo. Unlike the Western rodeo, which focuses very specifically on riding and roping skills, the charreada included an emphasis on the cowboys' Spanish and Mexican cultural heritage. Therefore, not only did the cowboys, or *charros*, compete in these events, they did so often without monetary compensation and with a focus on bravery and patriotism. Today, this emphasis on cultural heritage remains with a strict dress code for performers and with the inclusion of many events unique from the Western rodeo, such as reining maneuvers, a female group performance, and trick roping events.

Once whites arrived in the American West, they quickly combined their own equestrian skills with the Mexican rodeo to create the Western rodeo that we know today. Because the first rodeos were informal and held on local ranches, the exact location and date of the first rodeo are unknown. Prescott, Arizona, claimed to be the home of the world's oldest rodeo in 1888, but Pecos, Texas, also tells of an early rodeo held in 1882. A bronc rider was crowned champion in 1869 in Deer Rail, Colorado, and an early wild bronc riding competition was held in Cheyenne, Wyoming, in 1872. Regardless of the exact time and place, rodeos quickly appeared throughout the American West. Small rodeos held for local cowboys along with large national competitions arose during the 1890s, and by the 1920s rodeo was internationally known. The three major rodeos in the United States and Canada—the Cheyenne Frontier Days in Wyoming in 1897, the Pendleton Round-Up in Oregon in 1910, and the Calgary Stampede in Alberta, Canada in 1912—all opened before 1920 and attracted cowboys and cowgirls from the United States and Canada. Though white riders were most common, Hawaiians, Native Americans, and African Americans also competed at these rodeos, often winning.

As ranching and rodeoing emerged in the American West, Bill Pickett grew up in Texas and started working with horses and cattle. In the late nineteenth century, Pickett worked as a cowboy on ranches near Austin and opened a business with his brothers. The Pickett Brothers Broncho Busters and Rough Riders lasted for several years and advertised itself as a company that specialized in breaking wild horses and taming wild cattle. Little is know about this business, but soon thereafter Pickett became well known for his bulldogging technique. He worked part-time on Lee Moore's ranch, and Moore started taking him to fairs and rodeos, sometimes performing alone, at other times with his brothers. By 1900, he traveled in Texas, Arizona, and Colorado to perform in rodeos. Pickett finally decided that Moore took too large a cut of the winnings and allowed Dave McClure to schedule rodeo performances in 1903. His exposure increased dramatically with McClure, and he even performed at the 1904 Cheyenne Frontier Days.

Though Pickett actually invented, performed, and perfected the bulldogging technique, it could be said that McClure was responsible for much of his success. At this time in American history, blacks were not permitted to compete in rodeos in some places, and many whites would have refused to compete with a black rider. To bypass this racial prejudice, McClure gave Pickett the nickname "Dusky Demon." Though he still encountered much racism in his travels, this name allowed Pickett to compete in places in which he might not otherwise have access. Despite this racism and the limits placed on him, he still reached a rather surprising level of popularity. In the 1910s and 1920s, a time when many blacks in the country lived in fear and danger from Jim Crow laws, newspapers like *Harper's Weekly* published popular and positive accounts about Pickett and his rodeo exploits.

On one of his rodeo trips in 1905 in Fort Worth, Texas, Zack Miller from the 101 Ranch saw Pickett perform and invited him to move to the Miller Ranch in Oklahoma. The Miller family started the 101 Ranch in the 1890s, and it soon grew to 110,000 acres, 250 employees, 100 horses, and even a herd of buffalo. Pickett came to the ranch and performed in a big Western show there later that year. From this point until his death in 1932, he used the 101 Ranch as a base for his family, traveled in Wild West shows and rodeos around the world, and bulldogged over 5,000 steers.

Though his first exposure to travel and performance came in the rodeos, the Wild West shows promoted Pickett to a more visible level and increased his popularity. Buffalo Bill Cody created the first Wild West show in 1882 and soon ran the most well-known and most popular show in the country. For the first performance in Nebraska, the show drew applications from over 1,000 cowboys and included prizes for roping, shooting, riding, and bronc breaking.

After the overwhelming success of this show, Buffalo Bill designed a traveling Wild West show that combined certain stereotypical elements of the West like buffalo, cowboys, and Indians into a popular entertainment form, bringing the "true" West across the United States and into Europe and Australia.

At this time in American history, circuses and big over-the-top shows were popular. Wild West shows certainly fit this mold with their stage-coach runs, Indian attacks, and shooting tricks. Unlike circuses, though, Wild West shows were able to speak more directly to the American imagination. As Frederick Jackson Turner declared the end of the Western frontier in 1893 with the last of the Indian wars and the disappearance of unruly towns of the "wild" West, the Wild West shows created by promoters like Buffalo Bill kept that image alive and brought it to people far outside Western America.

Shortly after Buffalo Bill's initial success, other Wild West shows appeared. Pawnee Bill Lillie ran the largest competitor, and by 1893 his included over 300 performers and 200 horses. While Buffalo Bill's show featured sharp-shooter Annie Oakley, Pawnee Bill's major attraction was May Lillie, her-alded as "Champion Girl Shot of the West." Zach Miller and his brothers created their own Wild West show, the Miller 101 Ranch Show, in 1905. They, too, featured a female performer. This time, though, it was bronc rider Lucille Mulhall. A riding phenom rather than a shooting champion, Mulhall previously performed with her family's Mulhall Wild West Show. Given the title of the first cowgirl by President Teddy Roosevelt around 1900, Mulhall was one of the most well-known early cowgirls. However, she was not the only star of the Miller 101 Ranch Show. After seeing Pickett in Texas, the show also featured the Dusky Demon and his unique bulldogging technique.

First performing for the show only part-time, the Miller brothers offered him a full-time position in 1908. Starting at a wage of $8 per week, Pickett toured with the Wild West show and worked on the ranch during breaks. He moved his family to the ranch in 1908. The large family had to live in two tents until a two-room lean-to house could be built. Only there for a short time, Pickett moved his family to Ponca City, a short distance away, so that his children could attend school. Billed as "the greatest sweat and dirt cowboy that ever lived, bar none," he lived away from his family for much of the year and constantly risked his life to bulldog steers. The travel, low wages, danger, and separation worried his wife. They were apart for so long and lived in separate locations even when he was at the ranch, and many of the other cowboys did not know that Pickett was married and had a large family.

One of the most memorable and strange events in Pickett's life occurred not long after he joined the Miller brothers' Wild West show. After traveling in the United States and Canada in 1908, the brothers decided to send part of the show, including Pickett, home to the ranch while the rest continued a tour in Mexico. A period of political unrest engulfed Mexico at that time, as a struggle between longtime president and dictator Porfirio Díaz and opponent Francisco Madero. The show consequently attracted only a small audience, lost money every day, and received fines for many offenses. The government fined the show if it opened late or if an advertised performer failed to appear. Pickett appeared on the printed program from the tour in the United States and Canada, but he now was at home in Oklahoma. This meant the Miller brothers paid fines each day because of his absence. In order to avoid losing more money, the brothers sent for him to join the tour in Mexico.

*He [Pickett] was exploited in a way. He was black and yet he was unique in what he did. But then in those days, all black athletes were exploited in one way or another.*
Bill Pickett Invitational
Rodeo Website

When he arrived, a group of Mexican bullfighters watched the show and paid particular attention to Pickett and his bulldogging, as it was the closest event to bullfighting. With a very different understanding of bulls in the Mexican bullfight versus the American rodeo, the bullfighters believed the American cowboys were disrespecting the bull and viewed bulldogging as a lesser and easier sport than bullfighting. Joe Miller, one of the Miller brothers, heard the criticisms and challenged the bullfighters to a bulldogging competition. At the appointed time, though, the bullfighter failed to appear. Still upset about the comments, Miller declared that Pickett could and would bulldog any bull chosen by the Mexican bullfighters. Miller said that it was not hard to fight a bull and that bullfighters were not any braver than the American cowboys. This offended many Mexicans because bullfighting was their national sport.

On the day of the event, Pickett had to remain in the ring with the bull for 15 minutes and be in direct contact with the bull for 5 of those minutes without actually bulldogging it. Though left out of Miller's bargain with the bullfighters, he agreed to the competition because he, too, believed that he was better than any bull. If he succeeded, Miller would win 5,000 pesos; if he lost, the bullfighters would cover his funeral expenses. With a coffin to the side of the arena, Pickett and his beloved horse Spradley entered the arena and were greeted with many boos. As the bull appeared, Pickett saw that the Mexican fighting bulls differed structurally from the Texas cattle. He attempted to change horses in order to keep Spradley out of danger, but Miller's derogatory comment about bullfighting had incensed the crowd. They thought Pickett was backing out of the competition and refused to make any concessions for his horse.

During the event, the bull gored Pickett's horse in the hindquarters. The crowd grew angry and threw items into the arena. A glass bottle hit Pickett, breaking three of his ribs and cutting him. After 38 minutes, 7 and a half of those in contact with the bull, he left the arena. They won the bet against the bullfighters, but they did not win supporters among the Mexican people. The members of the show waited more than two hours to leave the arena, only able to leave after the angry crowd dispersed. Despite the severe injuries to Pickett and his horse, both recovered and continued to appear in rodeos and Wild West shows.

After this life-threatening trip to Mexico, Pickett's family moved from Ponca City to the 101 Ranch in 1910. This allowed the family to spend more time together, even though he continued to travel across the United States and to international locations. While in the United States, his bulldogging technique changed because of pressure from animal rights proponents. He no longer bit the lip of the steer and instead just flipped it on its back. This technique is still used today in rodeos. Biting the lip of the animal was still the traditional and the popular technique.

In the winter of 1913–1914, Edward Arlington, a stock owner and partner in the 101 Ranch Show, formed a group of performers from the 101 Show and Buffalo Bill's show to travel to South America. After a long journey by ship from New York, the group appeared in Argentina, Uruguay, and Brazil, among other places. Despite an outbreak of smallpox on the ship, the death of several group members, and the killing of all their horses because of disease, the trip was a success. The group performed up to three times a day in order to accommodate everyone interested.

In these performances outside of the United States and away from the reach of animal rights activists, Pickett was able to bite the steers' lips when bulldogging. The trip to Argentina was a different and liberating experience for him because the nation's racial climate was different from that in the United States. He spoke openly with people in Argentina and experienced certain rights, like the ability to eat in restaurants and walk freely in the streets. Widely popular among Argentinean audiences, Pickett spoke some Spanish and sometimes performed in the costume of an Argentinean cowboy.

After returning from South America, Pickett traveled with the Miller Ranch Show to New York and performed to large crowds in Madison Square Garden. The group then went to England and performed twice a day. Despite popularity with the audiences and a successful performance for the royal family, Pickett faced intense criticism from animal rights activists. Even though he returned to his U.S. technique of just flipping the steers, he was arrested after the first show. Zach Miller bailed him out of jail and then paid a fine of $25 after each show so that Pickett could continue bulldogging during their stay in London. Despite the problems from local police and the animal rights activists, the visit was a success, with Pickett even bulldogging a wild Scottish Highland steer.

Following this success and that of Buffalo Bill's Wild West Show tour of Europe, Miller also planned a European tour. The outbreak of World War I, however, forced him to cancel the tour and return to the United States. After the canceled tour, Pickett was getting older but continued to work on the Miller 101 Ranch and perform in rodeos. A silent movie was filmed on the ranch in 1914 and 1915. Pickett and other cowboys appeared in the film and also worked on it. He later starred in his own film titled *Bull-Dogger*. One of the few blacks to appear on the big screen at this time, he never became a movie star and was not well known for his film work. After filming the movie, he traveled to rodeos again in 1915. In this season he both bulldogged and rode broncs. During this time of international and domestic travel between 1913 and 1915, the Miller brothers' show experienced the biggest seasons in its history. The show and its performers took up over 30 railroad cars when they traveled, and between 1908 and 1916 the show netted a profit of $800,000.

Throughout this success, Pickett struggled as he aged. By 1917 he was 47 years old and became injured more frequently. Joe Miller died from carbon monoxide poisoning in 1927. In 1929 George Miller died in a car accident, and Pickett's wife died after a short illness. This left him largely alone because his daughters had long since grown, married, and moved away. Like Pickett, the 101 Ranch also suffered. With the deaths of George and Joe Miller, the management of the ranch fell to Zack Miller and Joe's two sons. Though they struggled to maintain the ranch, the Great Depression hurt them. The business was in debt by 1931, and the Millers lost control of the ranch.

Likewise, the Miller brothers had to close their Wild West show in 1931 because of declining popularity and monetary losses. This crushed Pickett, but he stayed at the ranch to help the brothers. Along with the Miller brothers, he still lived and worked on the ranch even though it was under new ownership. In March 1932, he fell off his horse in a roping accident, and another horse kicked him in the head. After 14 days in a coma at a hospital in Oklahoma, Bill Pickett died on April 2, 1932. Buried on the 101 Ranch, he survived many hundreds of steers, a bull goring in Mexico, and racial discrimination across the country. By the time he died, he had forever changed the world of rodeo.

Over 200 friends, fans, and supporters attended Pickett's funeral. Former competitors and well-known personalities like Will Rogers remembered him fondly, but Pickett had to wait much longer to receive wider recognition. Though a celebrity during his life and the only known inventor of a rodeo event, he still encountered racism while he was alive and after his death. Because of his race, he was barred from some rodeos, and the Miller brothers' show was not permitted to perform in some towns if he was listed on the program. This animosity against black athletes continued for many years.

Finally in 1971, 40 years after his death, Bill Pickett was inducted into the National Rodeo Cowboy Hall of Fame, the first black to be honored. More recently, the U.S. Postal Service featured him on a stamp, Fort Worth raised a statue of him, and his hometown of Taylor, Texas, named a school after him. Probably the most important tribute, however, is the Bill Pickett Invitational Rodeo. Begun by Lu Vason in 1984, the rodeo attracts over 13,000 visitors every year and is the country's only touring black rodeo. With this rodeo, Pickett's name and accomplishments live on, but so do the many unheard and unknown black cowboys and cowgirls who worked on ranches and competed in rodeos through the late nineteenth and into the twentieth centuries.

## FURTHER READING

Bill Pickett Invitational Rodeo Website. http://billpicketrodeo.com/web/pages/pickett
  .htm.

Hanes, Bailey. *Bill Pickett, Bulldogger: The Biography of a Black Cowboy.* Norman:
  University of Oklahoma Press, 1977.

Johnson, Cecil. *Guts: Legendary Black Rodeo Cowboy Bill Pickett.* Ft. Worth, TX:
  Summit Group, 1994.

Massey, Sara. *Black Cowboys of Texas.* College Station: Texas A&M University Press,
  2000.

Sanford, William and Carl Green. *Bill Pickett: African-American Rodeo Star.* Springfield,
  NJ: Enslow Publishers, 1997.

# Eddie Robinson

*Delano Greenidge-Copprue*

*Long after I left Jackson I started to come back in the summer to pick cotton. It wasn't so much for the money. I wanted to use the hard work as a way to build up my body to get ready to play football. The other pickers couldn't understand me then. But I was using the remnants of slavery and sharecropping to my advantage instead of being used by others.*

Eddie Robinson coached football at Grambling State University for 56 years and is one of the most important coaches in the history of college football. He combined an entertaining personal style and organizational box-office appeal with technical excellence on the field. He was the first coach ever to win over 400 college football games, and after his retirement, he was enshrined in the College Football Hall of Fame. While he was an icon by any measure of the word, his achievements transcend the game of football to become significant contributions to African American struggle for civil rights.

Robinson was born on February 13, 1919 in Jackson, Louisiana, to Frank and Lydia Stewart Robinson. His father was a third-generation sharecropper, and his mother was a domestic worker. When he was eight years old, his family moved to the larger city of Baton Rouge, where Robinson's father was able to escape a life of sharecropping and provide broader opportunities for his family. Those early years in rural Louisiana, however, left their mark on Robinson, teaching him the value of a strong work ethic. As he recalled:

> Long after I left Jackson I started to come back in the summer to pick cotton. It wasn't so much for the money. I wanted to use the hard work as a way to build up my body to get ready to play football. The other pickers couldn't understand me then. But I was using the remnants of slavery and sharecropping to my advantage instead of being used by others.

Robinson learned from his parents and grandparents the value of hard work, and this early lesson would help him discover at a young age what would become one of his life-long passions—football.

McKinley High School football coach Julius Kraft captivated his imagination and served as a role model. Recalling the first time he ever saw football practices, Robinson explained his admiration for the coach and his status. The players referred to Kraft as "sir" and "coach," and he reciprocated by encouraging and complimenting them. Yet the coach also expected great things from the players. Kraft's charisma and discipline later became trademarks of Robinson's own coaching career. McKinley's football players wore jackets and ties on their visits to see younger students of the community, modeling professionalism off the field as well as on the field, where discipline and hard work were founding principles. Watching Kraft and his team, Robinson knew he wanted to be involved in football.

He followed through on his desire and played football in high school and college. He played running back at McKinley for Kraft. He later majored in English and played quarterback at Leland College in nearby Baker, Louisiana.

During his junior and senior years at Leland, he worked as an apprentice assistant coach under Coach Ruben Turner. He led his college to an 18–1 record during his apprenticeship. This experience proved invaluable, as Turner helped Robinson study football and see the game as a player and, more important, as a coach.

What should have been a world of opportunity closed before Robinson's eyes after he earned his bachelor's degree in 1941. Though he'd proven himself a capable leader in an eight-year football career, few venues provided him a chance to show his leadership skills. The first job he landed after graduation involved shaking weevils out of sacks of corn at the Kambuck and Burkett Feed Mill. The pay was hardly enough to live on, so at nights he worked on an ice wagon to help make ends meet. With new wife Doris in his arms, he learned firsthand what a college degree and black skin could earn him in a racist society: indignity. He was never one to complain, however. He always did what he needed to do, letting his actions speak for him, never losing sight of his dreams.

Robinson did create one opportunity for himself. Earning 25 cents an hour and enduring Louisiana summer heat and weevils on his body, he welcomed an interview for a better job. Ralph Waldo Emerson Jones, the president of the Louisiana Negro Normal and Industrial Institute of Lincoln Parish, was looking for someone to take his spot as football coach. While the interview between Prez, as Jones was called, and Robinson was about football, the recent graduate's expertise with baseball landed him the job. Over the course of a casual conversation about great Negro League players, Prez challenged Robinson to a hitting contest, declaring that he could strike Robinson out. Robinson accepted the challenge, and just before throwing a fastball, Prez hired him.

The interview, it turned out, was about character rather than football. The character Robinson showed during his interview by challenging Jones with a blend of spirit and collegiality earned him the job. Before meeting Robinson, Jones had conducted a background check on him, asking neighbors and men in the local barbershop about his character. He was interested in knowing what kind of person Robinson was. The job wasn't restricted to football strategy or technique; the job would be to build men of character through football.

Robinson gained the head coaching job at Grambling, and with no experience as a head coach, he attended the coaching clinic at Northwestern University. Coaches, black and white, from programs big and small, studied all aspects of football at the clinic. As a former quarterback at Leland, Robinson was already familiar with some of the plays run by Northwestern, for the Leland system borrowed from them. He built upon this knowledge at the clinic, consulting with legendary Northwestern football coach Lynn "Pappy" Waldorf. Robinson would remain a life-long student of the game, attending clinics whenever he could. He earned a master's degree from the University of Iowa in 1954.

As the train rumbled back to Grambling before his 1941 inaugural season, Robinson had designed a system for his school, which blended what he'd learned from Turner and Waldorf. He was ready. At Grambling Station, however, Robinson was brought back to reality by Prez. His employer explained that the primary focus of his first season should be to learn to coach, not win football games. These words seemed a lukewarm vote of confidence at best. This advice rang true during those early days of Grambling football because Robinson had so small a pool of students from which to forge a football team. In 1941, Grambling enrolled 175 students, only 40 of whom were male, providing the new head coach with just enough players for a college football team.

At a small school with a limited budget and big dreams, Robinson wore multiple hats during his first year at Grambling. For $63.75 a month, he was charged with coaching football, maintaining the fields, taping the players, and writing the game summaries for the local paper. He coached basketball during the winter and baseball during the summer. Throughout the year, he also taught physical education. At times, Robinson and his Tigers went into the community, helping repair houses and harvesting crops on farms.

Robinson's age, as well as his inexperience, influenced his coaching. Some of the players on his team were older than the 21-year-old head coach. His early struggle for authority was compounded further because just the previous season he had played against some of the players he now coached. His new position charged the football team with tension; in less than one year, he changed from the team's rival to its coach. Morale also wavered as the team opened the season with five straight losses. After the fifth loss, Prez's words seemed to carry prophetic weight, since it seemed that Robinson might not win one game the whole season. He was learning to coach, at least, which meant that he began to manage players and their personalities.

Robinson improved his team by cutting the older players who were undermining his efforts. The younger remaining players, with allegiance to their young coach, began to execute his system. Team morale improved. Once his words took on a type of hard truth on the football field, and once his players began to see that the head coach understood football down to the physics of bodies colliding, the team responded favorably to his instruction. Their trust in Robinson led to Grambling's first victory under him on November 15, 1941. The team soundly defeated Tilliston in Austin, Texas, 37-6. After an 0–5 start, Grambling split its final six games, finishing with three wins against eight losses. Future prospects ran high, although these prospects were tempered by the attacks on the U.S. naval base at Pearl Harbor and the looming menace of war.

While World War II waged abroad, Robinson and his players built upon the momentum they gained in the 1941 season, executing with precision and intensity through the entire 1942 season. They finished the year undefeated at 8–0, making that squad the last team to be unbeaten, untied, and un-scored-upon in college football. While they shut down opposing offenses, the war overseas shut down the Grambling program for two years, as Grambling men left the campus and the football field for the battlefront and uncertainty.

Robinson had no college football teams for the 1943 and 1944 seasons, but he coached the football team at Grambling High. This position gave him the chance to work with Paul Younger, one of the greatest athletes ever to play football. Younger earned the nickname of "Tank" for the way he leveled opposing defenders who attempting to tackle him. In his junior year of high school, Younger played both sides of the ball with unrelenting intensity. In his senior year, Grambling High won the north Louisiana high school championship. The high school team, however, was denied the chance to play for the Louisiana state championship when Xavier Prep, the south Louisiana champion and an all-white team, refused to play against them in a winner-take-all state championship game. As Robinson explained, "Blacks and whites weren't about to compete against each other in Louisiana in the 1940s." But that time was inching closer.

Although World War II stopped football at Grambling for two years, the service his players provided was consistent with Robinson's wider view of collegiate football. He and many others considered the war to be a battle against prejudice. It was only fitting then that his Grambling men should take up arms against Nazi Germany and the ideology of the master race. Robinson envisioned football as a vehicle toward social change, and World War II provided his players with a worthwhile battle to fight. These young men had a war on their hands and their job was to fight for freedom, despite the racism they faced in the United States. The Grambling players in combat for a cause greater than themselves were a source of pride for the team's head coach. He later explained:

> We knew America was not perfect for blacks, but we began to read about Hitler's plans for the master race. If America lost the war, then whatever rights blacks had won would likely be lost. We joined the war effort with full force and pride. The history books are filled with stories of our contributions. I am proud of them to this day.

The Grambling Tigers made a strong return to football after the war. Robinson's team compiled nine wins against only two losses in 1945. The 1945–1948 Grambling teams also featured the powerful running of Younger. During his four seasons at Grambling, Younger compiled 60 career touchdowns, then an NCAA record, and in 1949 became the first player from a historically black college to play in the National Football League. Preparing Younger for the next level, Robinson told him that many other black athletes depended upon him. If Younger failed, other black athletes might never have an opportunity to play professionally. Guided by Robinson's expertise, Younger set touchdown records while running out of the backfield. He also broke tackles on fields across the land and had a stellar professional football career, becoming a five-time Pro Bowl player and gaining berths in both the college and pro Football Halls of Fame. Robinson and Younger both helped put Grambling and black college football on the map.

Robinson's coaching encompassed the game of football, but he also challenged his students' conceptions of themselves. He insisted that his players look beyond the confines of their own campus and beyond the idea that they attended a historically black college. He asked them to accept the idea that they, too, were Americans. Many of them did not believe that they were entitled to the same opportunities and privileges available to other Americans. Robinson's words bring us flush against one of the major debates of the twentieth-century African American and American struggle for civil rights.

African Americans held different opinions about their place in American society. At the turn of the twentieth century, former slave–turned-author, college president, and political leader Booker T. Washington endorsed the philosophy of separate but equal as a means of ensuring the development of black culture economically, socially, and politically. Coming out of the crippling bonds of slavery, African Americans, he argued, did not have the societal infrastructure in place to compete with whites. It would take time for them to develop institutions for their communities. So he promoted a practice known as accommodation, which promoted the social segregation of whites and African Americans as the latter group created community institutions: In a speech in 1895, he explained, "In all things that are purely social we can be as separate as the fingers, yet one as the hand in all things essential to mutual progress" (Washington). Though Washington described "mutual progress," his argument masked the reality that blacks and whites would live in separate and unequal worlds, which preserved the status quo. W.E.B. Du Bois, a Fisk- and Harvard-trained economist, historian, novelist, and sociologist, promoted competition in contrast to Washington's philosophy. Du Bois believed in directly engaging and working alongside whites. Robinson combined the philosophies of Washington and Du Bois, using the platform of the historically black college as a means of promoting both racial and national pride.

Along with using football as a means toward righting the social and moral wrong of racism, Robinson recognized the importance of expanding Grambling's program beyond northern Louisiana. His vision of the school was similar to that of Jones, who sought to make Grambling for blacks akin to what Notre Dame was (and remains) for Catholics: a source of pride. The college had nothing less than national and international aspirations, which was no small feat for a small school in a town of some 5,000 people.

Robinson pushed Grambling to interact with white colleges and universities. To increase the exposure of the football program, he encouraged the school to join the Southwestern Athletic Conference (SWAC). This conference featured all-white schools and brought Grambling before the eyes of a wider audience. Grambling eventually earned 17 SWAC championships or co-championships in the Robinson era. Along with expanding the school's reach in college football,

Robinson contributed meaningfully to Black America and wider U.S. sports culture with the development of his football "classics."

With the help of Grambling sports information director Collie Nicholson, Robinson made the phrase "Grambling football" part of the consciousness of Black America and the nation. Robinson and Nicholson instituted what they called "classic" games. Classics were staged in major cities throughout the United States to attract the attention of black athletes to the Grambling program and to put the school on the national landscape of college football. The classics showcased black talent from a historically black college. This marked a shift from the paradigm of professional football recruiting practices, in which black players from predominantly white colleges were traditionally given the nod over black players from historically black colleges. In some seasons, Grambling had as few as two home games because of the classics. The football program attracted a national audience through the classics, however, which benefited the players, the university, and Black America. The games also offered fans and scouts the opportunity to see talented players, some of whom went on to have All-Pro and Hall of Fame careers in the NFL.

The classics offered Robinson's team many opportunities to reach new audiences. Grambling played its first classic in 1955 against Florida A&M in the Orange Blossom Classic. The game attracted 48,000 fans, the largest crowd before which Robinson's team had ever played to this point; Grambling's home stadium could accommodate only 2,000 fans. The game signaled to Robinson that there was indeed an audience for black college football, if venues were made available. In 1956, Robinson began sketching what he called the Sugar Cup Classic. He imagined this classic as a game between Grambling and another black school in Tulane Stadium, which could accommodate 80,000 fans. The Sugar Cup, as he explained to the Sugar Bowl committee, the governing body for one of the most prestigious college bowl games in the United States, would be a warm-up game before the Sugar Bowl, akin to an undercard in boxing. The committee rejected his offer, and Robinson's vision was not made real for another eight years, and even then was not carried out as he had imagined. The Sugar Cup Classic, played between Grambling and Bishop College, took place in City Park Stadium before only 2,000 fans. The game was played in a torrential downpour that made mud so deep that cars were stuck in the makeshift parking lot. While the field was muddy, Grambling had very little trouble moving the football, and defeated Bishop 42-6 in the first and last Sugar Cup Classic.

Though the 1964 Sugar Cup failed to attract a large crowd, Grambling-style football, complete with its high-powered offense, its shutdown defense, and its electrifying marching band, brought large crowds to stadium gates in major cities across the nation.

In 1966, Robinson received recognition for the successes he and his teams achieved on and off the field. With a steady stream of players finding their way onto the rosters of professional football teams and the accumulation of

championships and accolades, the College Football Writers of America recognized Robinson as the most important contributor to college football in over a
quarter of a century. Little did those writers know then that he had not yet reached
his stride as a coach and as an ambassador for the game of college football.

With the growing popularity of Grambling football, Robinson was often
interviewed live on national television. On one occasion in the late 1960s,
Howard Cosell welcomed Robinson to his show in New York City and wasted
little time by asking him one of the thorniest questions in American professional sports. He asked whether Robinson could prepare an athlete in only
four years to play football in NFL. Live on the air, and with a nation watching,
Robinson said, "Yes."

A black man had not played quarterback in a professional football game in
more than a decade. Willie Thrower, a standout player from Michigan State,
played quarterback in a game for the Chicago Bears in 1953, though no one
followed in his footsteps for years. With Cosell's prodding question still ring-
ing in his ears, Robinson flew from New York to Louisiana, where, rather
than return to campus, he went to visit James "Shack" Harris. Robinson told
Harris, a 6' 5", 210-pound quarterback, with direct words that carried implications broader than the game of football, "I am recruiting you to play quarterback in the NFL." Harris accepted the challenge and became a storied
collegiate and professional quarterback, drafted by the Buffalo Bills in 1969
and starting as quarterback in the NFL through most of the 1970s.

The September 1968 contest between Morgan State and Grambling was a
good measure of how far black college football had come in America. While
Dr. Martin Luther King had been assassinated earlier that year, Robinson and
his G-men did their part in the struggle for social equality. This game was
played in Yankee Stadium in the First Annual Whitney Young Classic, which
was a game designed to help promote adult education among African Americans. The game brought together two powerful and storied teams that had
not played one another since 1945. Robinson and Jones had pitted their
school against Morgan in the 1940s as one part of their earlier strategy to
make Grambling the black Notre Dame. The game did not go as planned, for
the Morgan State Bears beat the Tigers, 35-0. The game between Morgan
State and Grambling in September 1968 would be different.

By that year, only Notre Dame had more players in the professional ranks
than Grambling. Robinson's school was the defending black national champion, led by quarterback Harris. On the other side of the ball, the Morgan
State Bears had not lost a game since the 1964 season three years earlier. The
1968 game came down to a final goal-line stand. In the closing seconds of the
game, with Grambling down 9-7, Robinson saw the opportunity to kick a
field goal and secure a 10-9 Grambling victory. Instead, he decided to have the
team run the ball from Morgan's one-yard line.

This game was about pride, which runs deeper than winning. A field goal,
while securing a victory, would have also meant that Robinson did not believe

that his team could move the ball one yard against the Morgan State defense. Robinson believed in his team. On the game's final play, Harris handed the ball to 245-pound fullback Henry Jones. Jones fell short of the end zone as the Morgan defense held. Grambling lost 9-7. Years after the game, when asked if he would kick the field goal in that situation again, Robinson said, "I would go for the touchdown again because a man has to do what he believes in." Grambling's loss was still a win for the black community, as this clas-

*I was crying on the field because I remembered what it was like when blacks couldn't play in that stadium. For the players, it was a big game. For me, it was the walls falling down.*

sic, seen in person by 64,000 fans and broadcasted nationally on ABC, generated revenue to promote adult literacy among African Americans.

Robinson continued to seek ways to bring attention to Grambling's program. Buoyed by the success of the Whitney Young Classic, he began to reexamine the failure of the Sugar Cup Classic. He determined that Grambling did not make use of its rivalry with Southern, for this rivalry would guarantee a sell-out crowd in just about any stadium. Choosing the appropriate opponent was the first step. The next involved his approach. Rather than pitch the idea to the Sugar Bowl committee, he decided to first meet with the stadium committee, a group that would be interested in the amount of revenue the game would generate. As Robinson later noted, money is always important and powerful. So in 1974, Southern and Grambling met in Tulane Stadium in the first ever Bayou Classic before a sold-out crowd of 76,753 fans in New Orleans. The game was exciting and close, with Grambling winning over Southern, 19-14. Yet the real significance of the game cannot be determined from its final score.

The 1974 Bayou Classic was yet another indicator of the progress made by black people in American society. Robinson explained his own experience of that game, noting that it brought him to tears. Black people could not play in this stadium before, and Robinson believed that this game symbolized a powerful change for African Americans. Walls fell as Grambling, a small school in rural Louisiana, took its special brand of football and its marching band throughout the nation and beyond. The Grambling Tigers became the first college to host a football game abroad, playing Morgan State in Tokyo in 1976, the same year Robinson became president of the American Football Coaches Association.

Robinson and Grambling continued to change football through the 1970s. The coach explained their progress: "We were moving things forward in our own way. We weren't demonstrating in the streets, but we were demonstrating on the fields." Grambling produced three first-round draft picks, won five black national championships and eight SWAC titles, produced a legitimate Heisman Trophy candidate in Doug Williams, and won nearly 80 percent of its games during the 1970s. These accomplishments earned Robinson his first and only interview with an NFL team. He met with the Los Angeles Rams in 1978. Professional football had not had a black head coach since the early 1920s, when All-American quarterback Fritz Pollard from Brown University coached the Akron Pros. Robinson did not receive an offer from the Rams, though he was certain he would not have taken the job anyway. He had found his calling in the college game. In the next decade he, a black man of humble origins from rural Louisiana, became the winningest coach in the history of American football.

Entering his fourth decade of coaching in the 1980s, Robinson's name was mentioned in the same breath as the legends of his craft. He passed the records of legendary coach Amos Alonzo Stagg, one of the charter members of the College Football Hall of Fame and the coach who invented the huddle and the man in motion, with his 315th victory in 1984. This accomplishment put him second all-time, behind Paul "Bear" Bryant's 323 wins. Robinson surpassed Bryant on October 5, 1985. In their fourth game of the season, Robinson and his Tigers defeated Prairie View 27-7 in the State Fair Classic in Dallas, Texas. This victory made him the winningest coach in college football. Yet in his crowning moment, Robinson maintained his dignity, acknowledging that no one could approach the stature of Bear Bryant or erase what the Bear meant for college football. He later explained that what mattered most was not his achievement but his character: "Forty-four years at the same school, one job and one wife, that's the record." Robinson showed a deep and authentic humility, and a character that goes beyond the number of football games won. He understood that records can come and go, as someone better than him might come along. He cared, instead, about making a positive difference. In 2004, Trinidad native John Gagliardi, head football coach at St. John's in Minnesota, passed Coach Robinson for the number one spot. Records are made to be broken, as the saying goes, but legends are remembered. Such is the case with Eddie Robinson. In 1994, the Eddie Robinson Trophy was established and is awarded annually to the best player in black college football. In this way, Robinson's name will always be associated with excellence, and his memory will endure.

By his retirement in 1997, he had become a living legend, memorialized in multiple ways. The football stadium at Grambling and the street it's on both bear his name. A street in New Orleans, the home of Grambling's longtime rival Southern, is also named after Robinson. He was recognized by the NFL with a lifetime achievement award in 1998 and garnered four honorary doctorates. The only football coach from a historically black college to appear on the cover of *Sports Illustrated*, he was inducted into the College Football Hall of Fame two years after his retirement. The voting committee waived the three-year waiting period that typically separates football service from Hall of Fame induction. Today, the college football Coach of the Year award is named after Eddie Robinson. He has coached in the most games of any college coach with a total of 588. To this day he holds the longest tenure as a coach at any one school at an impressive 56 years.

Robinson's legacy extends far beyond his 408 career victories to reach the lives he touched. Coaching for more than a half century, he taught the game of football to over 4,000 men. Often concluding practices in the end zone, he spoke with his players about opportunities in life beyond the football field. He recruited players by promising their parents and guardians that their sons would go to church on Sundays and earn college degrees. He was true to his word: 85 percent of his players graduated, and those in his charge maintained strong moral values. He even ensured that his players rose from bed, ate breakfast, and prepared for their days of classes at the university.

Robinson, born, raised, and educated in the same state in which he coached, taught, and inspired, models consistency and excellence. His life shows us what is possible when we are true to our words and when we approach what we do with a sense of deep vocation and dedication. Reflecting on his 50-plus years of coaching, Robinson wrote:

> One of the best things that's happened to me in my lifetime is that I've heard the best coaches who have ever walked. From 1941, when I first went to coaching school, I've heard them all. You name them, and I have a piece of every one. . . . To paraphrase the late Alonzo Stagg: "The coaching profession is the most rewarding profession in the world, and no man is too good to coach in America." It's a great profession, and this is what you need to tell the young coaches. Work hard, and promotions will come. You can't work at one job, looking to go to another job. You've got to have commitment.

Robinson and his wife, Doris, had two children, five grandchildren, nine great grandchildren. He also touched generations of men, women, and children through his decades of work. He showed deep commitment, which he likened unto dancing with the girl he brought to the dance and no one else. Throughout his coaching career, he was known more for precision than innovation. Opposing coaches knew the plays Eddie Robinson would call, but his players achieved such a high level of precision and execution that it was nonetheless difficult to stop the G-men on game day or any given day.

More than football games, Robinson's unwavering patriotism and his belief in the founding principles of the United States will be his most enduring legacies. The closing stanza of his school's fight song captures much of his life:

> Fight for dear old Grambling,
> Fight, we're going to win.
> There's no doubt that we are
> The pride of the USA.

Throughout his life, Robinson wrestled deeply with the idea and the reality of being both black and American. Through his struggles and successes, he showed that the greatest injustice is not to be true to one's self. He became legendary through his commitment. Along with a great number of African Americans, their stories told or sometimes untold, Robinson and his Grambling Tigers made it through the crucible of racism to express their humanity.

When he retired, Robinson noted: "Racism is what made me work like hell. You remember when people used to hold hands and sing, 'We shall overcome?' I never did that. I always said, 'Anything you can do, I can do better.'" Ultimately, this belief in himself, and in those around him, makes Robinson an icon. He took the game of American football and made it a vehicle for expressing the strivings of African Americans: battling the odds in their collective search for promised lands and seeking to affirm their sense of worth and dignity through their actions, through their intelligence, their character, and indeed their very beings.

## FURTHER READING

Davis, O. K. *Grambling's Gridiron Glory: Eddie Robinson and the Tigers' Success Story*. Ruston, Louisiana: M & M Printing, 1983.

Hoffer, Richard. "Here's to You, Mr. Robinson," *Sports Illustrated* 87 (December 6, 1997): 106–108.

Hurd, Michael. "Grambling." *ESPN College Football Encyclopedia*. New York: ESPN, 2005.

Robinson, Eddie. "Fifty-Plus Years of Coaching Football." In *Football Coaching Strategies*. Champaign, IL: Human Kinetics, 1995.

Robinson, Eddie, and Richard Lapchick. *Never Before, Never Again: The Stirring Autobiography of Eddie Robinson, the Winningest Coach in the History of College Football*. New York: St. Martin's Press, 1999.

Rhoden, William C. "Robinson: Long Climb to the Top." *New York Times*, September 16, 1985: C1.

"This Week in Black History." *Jet* 106, no. 23 (December 6, 2004): 19.

Washington, Booker T. "Atlanta Exposition Address." Atlanta Cotton States and International Exposition. September 18, 1895.

AP Photo.

# Wilma Rudolph

*Rita M. Liberti*

Wilma Rudolph earned national and international recognition by winning three gold medals in the track and field competition of the 1960 Olympic Games. Her athletic achievements are important not only because she was an enormously skilled runner and the first American woman to win three gold medals at the Games, but also because her experiences provide an opportunity to better understand the relationship between sports and broader cultural issues, including race and gender inequality. Her story represents the distinct issues, concerns, and hardships faced by women of color as they attempted to succeed amidst racism and sexism in the United States.

Wilma Glodean Rudolph was born on June 23, 1940, in the northern Tennessee town of St. Bethelem. She was the sixth of Ed and Blanche Rudolph's eight children. Ed also had 14 children prior to his marriage to Blanche, thus considerably expanding the size of the family. Tennessee (and the entire South) were segregated during Rudolph's childhood. This reality was evident in the occupations of her parents. Her father worked as a porter for the railroad and also completed odd jobs to make ends meet. Like many other black women, her mother was a domestic worker who cleaned the homes of white families. Rudolph's parents had no formal education beyond elementary school, which reduced their occupational choices and economic opportunities. The family had little money but that didn't seem to matter, according to Rudolph, because of the close relationships she and her siblings enjoyed with each other and their parents.

Life in the South during the mid–twentieth century was surrounded by the realities of racism. Yet many African American parents, including Rudolph's, did their best to shield their children from the harshness of inequality and hatred. Their best efforts were not always successful, however. Rudolph realized when she was just four or five years old that black and white people not only led different lives but their experiences were unequal. She resented the fact, for example, that her mother had to clean white people's houses to make a living. Instead she wished that someone would serve her mother.

Rudolph's parents encouraged their children, despite the racism that surrounded them or maybe because of it, to be tenacious when achieving a goal. Born prematurely, Wilma suffered from a number of childhood illnesses that stressed her physically. These illnesses put to the test her ability to be steadfast in the face of adversity. By the time most children entered the second grade, she suffered from double pneumonia, whooping cough, scarlet fever, measles, and mumps. She also developed polio, which left one of her legs in a steel brace for several years from the age of five. She was tutored at home due to her chronic illnesses until the age of seven, when she was finally able to attend Cobb Elementary School in Clarksville. With the aid of her siblings and mother, as well as the medical staff at Meharry Hospital, the black medical college at Fisk University, she worked tirelessly to strengthen her frail leg. Although she didn't wear a leg brace past the age of 12, the emotional scars that developed when others called her a "cripple" remained with her for years.

Given Rudolph's physical ailments and limitations, her interest and ability to participate in athletic or physical activity were initially nonexistent. This changed, however, the summer before she entered Burt High School as a seventh-grade student in 1952. Though she became one of the strongest track athletes in history, it was her love affair with basketball that prompted her intrigue in movement and physical activity. The game's popularity among African Americans across the country, especially in the South, was firmly rooted in over a half-century of participation by the time she picked up a basketball in the early 1950s. On an individual level, the game suited her still-frail body quite well. She could shoot the ball from a stationary position and not have to move around much on her weak leg. Basketball's relatively inexpensive equipment and the fact that the game could be played outdoors most or all of the year in the temperate Southern climate made it an incredibly appealing activity to the broader African American community. Creativity and improvisation, on and off the court, were hallmarks of the basketball played among African Americans during this period. With little or no money, Rudolph and her childhood friends were forced to use their imaginations and creative energies to play the game. Old beach balls and tennis balls were sometimes used in place of standard basketballs, which weren't always available or affordable.

Rudolph did try out and make the girls' basketball team during the seventh and eighth grades at Burt High School, though she received few opportunities to play and display her skills. She used her time on the bench wisely, however, by studying the game and paying close attention to strategy and technique. Immediately following her eighth-grade basketball season, coach Clinton Gray invited the basketball members to try out for the newly formed girls' track team. Eager to stay in shape from one basketball season to the next, Rudolph signed up. Success in those early track events came easy for her as she outpaced her competition. Despite this success, she thought little of her achievements on the track because her energy and attention were concentrated on basketball. Track activities seemed far less organized and much more informal than the basketball games to which she was accustomed, which prevented her from approaching the sport as seriously as she did basketball. Her third season of basketball was as big a disappointment for her as the first two seasons. She remained on the bench for the majority of the year and had few chances to play. She entered her second track season more determined than ever to prove her worth as an athlete. Her success on the track continued as she won approximately 20 different races in her freshman year across five different events, including the 50-, 75-, 100-, and 200-meter runs as well as the relay. She did not lose one race.

The track meets between Rudolph's high school team and other schools in Tennessee resembled "play days," in that they deemphasized competition and promoted a spirit of cooperation among participants. Throughout the early to mid-twentieth century, play days were standard practice for girls' sports across the country, especially among athletic departments in the white community.

*Never underestimate the power of dreams and the influence of the human spirit. We are all the same in this notion: The potential for greatness lives within each of us.*

Educational officials feared, in part, that female participation in rigorous, competitive athletics was improper. Instead, they brought girls together in play day formats where they might engage in physical activity but in moderation. The extent to which this ideology of moderation was endorsed in black communities, including Rudolph's community in Clarksville, is debatable. On one hand, athletic leaders in the black community struggled with the tensions surrounding the perceived incompatibility of womanhood and athleticism. Some feared that athletic participation among girls and women might make them become "masculine" or mannish women. However, some in the African American community believed that womanhood and athleticism were not mutually exclusive. They actively supported female participation in sport. The idea that African American girls and women were too frail to participate in sport seemed at odds with the realities of their lives during this period. Within many black communities, women earned respect as wage earners and civic leaders, so their involvement in sport wasn't necessarily viewed with the same scorn as was women's athleticism in white communities in the United States.

Support for female athleticism also extended to historically black colleges and universities. Throughout the South, from the late 1920s onward, a number of these schools promoted competitive women's basketball programs. School officials believed athletic activities helped build qualities such as self-control and discipline in young black women that might help better prepare them for the trials they would face because they were black and female. Basketball courts and tracks at these institutions were laboratories to hone skills well beyond athletic aptitude.

Rudolph met new athletic success in her sophomore year. She grew to nearly 6' tall before the academic year began and blossomed as a basketball player. She was the key player leading her team to an 11–4 record and the Middle East Tennessee Conference championship. She set a state record for the most points scored in a season with 803 points in 25 games. Her track career changed course in her sophomore year as well. One meet in particular helped to steer her thinking toward the sport in a different direction, away from her disdain of the standard noncompetitive and loosely organized events she'd witnessed thus far. Burt High School was invited to participate in the Tuskegee Relays, hosted by the Tuskegee Institute, a historically black college in Alabama.

Tuskegee Institute officials, including director of Athletics and Physical Education Cleveland L. Abbott, wanted to create and promote an event similar to the prestigious Drake Relays, for historically black colleges. Tuskegee dominated women's track on a national level for decades, winning the Amateur Athletic Union (AAU) championship every year from 1937 to 1956. It was into this setting that Rudolph stepped as a sophomore in high school in 1955.

Young women throughout the South competed at the Tuskegee Relays. Rudolph did not fair well against such formidable opposition. She was devastated by the loss, in part because she had been so cocky prior to the event given her success in other track meets.

Fortunately, Rudolph's impressions of her performance at the Tuskegee Relays did not match observers' assessments. Ed Temple, the Tennessee State University women's track coach, was eager to invite the young athlete to his summer camp program. After taking over as the head women's track coach in 1953 at Tennessee State, Temple was anxious to move the program to the powerhouse status held by Tuskegee Institute for more than 20 years. He knew that a summer camp program would raise the level of high school female track talent as well as improve the profile of his program at Tennessee State. Initially, Rudolph's parents expressed some reservation about sending their daughter off to a camp away from home. The coach reassured them that he was a strict disciplinarian, however, who would keep a watchful eye over their daughter. Ultimately, the Rudolphs supported their daughter's wishes. They continued to encourage and support her athletic pursuits, in part because they believed it would secure her entrance into college. This was a fairly safe bet on their part, as 9 out of 10 young women who attended Temple's summer camp eventually enrolled at Tennessee State. If track was the path to a college education for Rudolph, then her parents enthusiastically supported her efforts. They understood very well that she might not have another opportunity to enter higher education because of their economic situation.

Rudolph's skills developed quickly that summer under the guidance of Ed Temple and the ever-present, high-quality competition of some of the best runners in the world. She was a member of the Tigerbelle squad, which won its first national AAU outdoor championship in the summer of 1955 in Ponca City, Oklahoma. The Tigerbelles were led by Mae Faggs, a veteran of two Olympic Games. Rudolph finished fourth behind three of her teammates in the 75-yard dash. Although she didn't win any events in Ponca City, the meet was a significant step in her career. It was her first national competition and her first racially integrated track event. The Tigerbelles' success at Ponca City helped propel them into the national sporting spotlight and soon the same type of attention was directed toward Wilma Rudolph.

In the summer of 1956, Rudolph returned to the Tennessee State campus to continue working with Temple. She joined fellow high school students Martha Hudson, Willye White, and Annette Anderson to form a junior relay team. Their talents grew steadily throughout the summer. Rudolph participated in the 75-yard dash, 100-yard dash, and the 440-yard relay in the girls' junior division at the Penn Relays in Philadelphia. She did not lose a race, thus leading the way for the team to win the national AAU meet in the junior division.

Rudolph's superb performance in Philadelphia prompted Temple to suggest that she was prepared to compete in the Olympic trials, scheduled to take place in Washington, D.C., just two weeks later. Still a high school student and only a handful of years out of her leg brace, Rudolph was going to compete for a spot to represent the United States at the 1956 Olympics in Melbourne, Australia. She and five other athletes, including mentor Mae Faggs, headed to Washington with Temple. Temple and Faggs believed that Rudolph often purposely held back in races, not wanting to beat her teammates and friends. In Washington, Faggs reminded Rudolph that the team depended on her to do well and win races. Rudolph's 200-meter trial dead heat with Faggs earned her a spot on the U.S. Olympic team and demonstrated that she had heeded her mentor's advice.

The success of the Tigerbelles represented the continuation of African American female dominance in U.S. track and field. Throughout the 1950s, African American women comprised more than 65 percent of the women who represented the United States at the sport's most elite levels. Public perception of female track and field athletes as "mannish" persisted through the middle decades of the century, however. African American coaches and other observers, including Temple, were quick to counter these dominant narratives. Temple and others worked to underscore the Tigerbelles' femininity and normalcy as women by pointing out that they dated men (and not other women). This was a delicate line for African American athletic officials to walk. They could not afford to inflame stereotypes of black women as hypersexual, regardless of sexual orientation. Well aware of public perception, Wilma also attempted to emphasize and reassure others of her femininity despite her athleticism. Amid these broader gender and racial tensions, the Tigerbelles continued to perform extremely well, dominating women's track and field just as Tuskegee Institute had done earlier in the century. The team held two consecutive AAU titles by 1956, and six members earned spots on the Olympic team.

The 1956 Olympic Games proved to be a challenge for Rudolph. Her team was remarkable in that it was the first to be coached by an African American woman in the Olympics. Nell Jackson, a former Olympic athlete, led the team. The two weeks of training in Australia leading up to Olympic competition did not go well for the Tigerbelles. Rudolph feared their sluggishness was a result of Temple's absence as their coach, which she thought had created a break in their routine. Unfortunately, the poor performance in practice remained with her during the actual Olympic competition. She was eliminated from the finals of the 200-meter race. Disappointed by such a poor showing, Rudolph hoped to salvage a medal in the 400-meter relay with teammates Margaret Mathews, Isabelle Daniels, and Faggs. The race went smoothly for the Tigerbelles, and they earned a bronze medal, finishing behind Australia and Great Britain. Interestingly, the relay was a very fast race, and all three teams had world record-breaking performances in this event. Moreover, Rudolph and her teammates were proud that five of the six medals won by the U.S. women's track team went to Tennessee State Tigerbelles. Australian sprinter Betty Cuthbert, who won three gold medals in Melbourne, had an especially profound impact on Rudolph. The icon vowed to work tirelessly over the next four years, return to the Olympics, and stand on the highest platform to collect a gold medal. In the meantime she returned home to a grand welcome from her classmates and soon resumed her routine as a high school student and basketball player.

Rudolph had numerous victories during her junior year. The Burt High School girls' basketball team had their most successful season to date. On more than one occasion the team scored over 100 points in one game (Rudolph, 1977, p. 101), a rarity in girls' or boys' basketball at the time. In addition, Rudolph averaged 35 points per game throughout the season, while best friend Nancy Bowen averaged 38. Tennessee State hosted the high school state championships in basketball, when Burt High faced off against Merry High School. Rudolph scored 25 points that night as Burt edged out Merry High to win the state title.

Rudolph also faced multiple challenges during her junior year of high school, however. She noticed that since returning from Melbourne her relationships with teammates, coaches, and opponents had changed. Some expected her to be perfect, given her standing as a world-class athlete. In track, some opponents chose simply not to compete against her, seeing their efforts as pointless. Despite these setbacks, she was not discouraged and instead looked forward to the end of her junior year, the school's junior/senior prom, and another summer at Tennessee State. Rudolph attended the prom with longtime boyfriend Robert Eldridge, who played on the football and boys' basketball teams at Burt High. On the evening of the prom, her best friend, Bowen, was killed in a car accident. The emotional impact of the tragedy stayed with Rudolph for years, and was especially intense as she tried her best to focus on her running at Tennessee State that summer. Her strength as a runner continued to improve, however. At the national outdoor AAU championship in Cleveland, Ohio, she set records in the 75-yard dash, the 100-yard dash, and the 300-yard relay. With her first AAU records under her belt, Rudolph was eager to start her senior year.

Rudolph's relationship with her boyfriend deepened during her senior year. During a routine physical examination for basketball, a doctor told her that she was pregnant. Naive about the implications of having sex, she was shocked and in disbelief. Coach Temple forbade women with children to participate in his program. Fearful of her parents' response as well as what Temple might say, she kept her pregnancy secret for a while. Using her sister Yvonne as an intermediary, she eventually told her parents and Temple of the pregnancy. Fortunately, they were supportive of her during this trying time. Within the local black community of Clarksville, out-of-wedlock teenage pregnancy did not receive the scorn it might have in other localities. However, wider white public perception of black unwed mothers saw the pregnancies as transgressions that reinforced stereotypes of the entire race's moral failings. It consequently isn't surprising that some accounts of Rudolph's life fail to mention her pregnancy and instead simply note that the athlete was ill for most of 1958.

*[I know poor black women] who don't listen to the women's liberation rhetoric because they know that it's nothing but a bunch of [middle-class] white women who want to change their life-styles. They say things like they don't want men opening doors for them anymore, and they don't want men lighting their cigarettes for them anymore. Big deal. Black women have been opening doors for themselves and lighting their own cigarettes for a couple centuries in this country. Black women don't quibble about things that are not important.*

Rudolph graduated from Burt High School in May 1958 and two months later gave birth to her first child, whom she named Yolanda. Initially, Rudolph, her sister Yvonne, and her mother decided that Yvonne would care for Yolanda in St. Louis so that the athlete could attend Tennessee State and run track. The effort by the Rudolphs, though not easy, wasn't an unusual occurrence—poor African American families during this period devised creative, collective solutions to problems in order to raise and educate their children. Soon, however, Rudolph realized that the separation of miles between her and her daughter was far too great. Her mother agreed to care for Yolanda in Clarksville, much closer to the Tennessee State campus.

Rudolph joined an ensemble of many of the best female track athletes in the world when she entered Tennessee State as a freshman. Although Faggs was gone, Isabelle Daniels, Margaret Matthews, and Barbara Jones, all holders of AAU championship titles, were present to push her past established athletic boundaries. As a freshman, her efforts helped propel her team to the national indoor AAU championship in Washington, D.C. The Tennessee State Tigerbelles devastated the competition, finishing the meet with 61.5 total points while their closest challenger was held to 18 points. In the summer of 1959, her winning ways continued as she won the AAU title in the 100-yard dash. Faggs's wise words a few years earlier—that her team does well when she does well—rang true as Rudolph helped carry the team to even greater heights. She set American records as a sophomore in the 100-yard dash at 11.1 seconds and in the 220-yard dash at 25.7 seconds in the indoor championships in Chicago in the spring of 1960. Her feats catapulted Tennessee State to its sixth consecutive national indoor title.

The 1960 Olympic Games in Rome were now within Rudolph's sights. She directed her energy and attention even more deliberately toward making the team and winning a gold medal. At the Olympic trials on the campus of Texas Christian University, she competed in the 100-meter and 200-meter races as well as the 400-meter relay. With an incredible time of 22.9 seconds in the 200-meter final, Rudolph became the first American woman to set a world record in a running event. Her Tigerbelle teammates did well too, with nearly half of the 18 female athletes on the U.S. track and field team hailing from Tennessee State. Temple was named the coach of the team, which helped establish a solid and comfortable routine for the Tigerbelles as they edged closer to Rome.

Rudolph's second Olympic competition was very successful. Now an Olympic veteran, she felt far more at ease than she had at the start of the Melbourne Games in 1956. Her confidence showed in the heats leading up to the finals of the 100-meter dash. She ran well and in the fourth heat set a world record with a time of 11 seconds. Unfortunately, Olympic officials dismissed the record. At the time of the race, the wind was blowing at 2.2 miles per hour, giving the runners a slight wind at their backs and thus a perceived unnatural advantage. Regardless, Rudolph was confident about her chances in the finals of the 100-meter race, and she again outpaced her opponents with an 11 second time to win the gold medal. Despite a second refusal by Olympic officials to allow her record-setting time to stand because of the wind, she now had a gold medal. She stood on the highest platform of the medal stand and became the first American woman in 24 years to win a gold medal in the 100-meter dash. Though disappointed in her 24-second time in the 200-meter finals, she out-distanced West Germany's Jutta Heine and Britain's Dorothy Hyman to win her second gold medal. In an attempt to win her third gold medal of the Games, she ran the anchor leg of the 400-meter relay, behind Tigerbelle team-mates Martha Hudson, Barbara Jones, and Lucinda Williams. Rudolph bobbled the baton handoff from Williams. This fumble provided the Germans, Australians, and Soviets with split seconds to take or maintain their leads over the U.S. squad as she began the anchor leg. Working with the kind of determination her parents had impressed upon her as a youngster, she charged ahead, coming alongside and then ahead of her opponents to win her third gold medal of the Olympics. Wilma Rudolph was the first American woman to win three gold medals in track and field in Olympic history and the first athlete, male or female, to win three gold medals at the 1960 Games.

The increasing prominence of television technology throughout the 1950s brought the 1960 Rome Olympics, as well as the performances of athletes such as Rudolph, into more homes in the United States and around the world than ever before. More people were able to watch athletic competition unfold as it happened, which heightened the excitement and anticipation surrounding the events. In addition, athletic competition was used during this era to supply cold war rhetoric between the Soviet Union and the United States, with each side using feats of athletic excellence as an indication of political supremacy. U.S. officials also used the prominence of black athletes in international competition as proof of its democratic ideals and practices. Of course, the presence of black athletes on the U.S. Olympic team did not prove racial equality in the country, since segregationist policies and laws remained firmly entrenched.

Prior to the competition, Rudolph had confided in Temple that she was angry to have not received more pre-Olympic press coverage. Her performance changed that immediately, as she became a celebrity in the United States and across the globe. Unfortunately, media seemed as preoccupied with her light skin color and femininity as it was with her athleticism. By highlighting and privileging her skin and femininity, journalists made her a palatable commodity for a white American public that still felt uneasy about the place of African Americans in society and women in sport. To some, at least in terms of gender, Rudolph's embodiment of more traditional notions of femininity was used as an exception to prove the rule that track and field athletes were unfeminine, unwomanly, and thus unnatural. The media often described her as a "gazelle," which was a racialized term that also depicted her running style and physical stature. Representations such as these, though they may have been well meaning, played upon broader, deeply rooted stereotypes of blacks as animal-like and reinforced dominant perceptions of blacks' natural place in sport and society.

Rudolph's opinion of the characterization of gazelle was mixed. Upon her return from Rome, in a meeting with President Kennedy, she noted that she did not like the nicknames assigned to her in the press. However, years later she commented that the descriptions were wonderful.

Public attention stayed upon Rudolph when she returned to the United States. The town of Clarksville held an enormous celebration for her that carried with it racial implications. Rudolph told state officials she would not take part in any event that was not integrated. As a result, her welcoming was the first integrated event in Clarksville. Black and white citizens lined the parade route that began two miles outside of town. All-white organizations joined with black leaders and institutions to participate in the parade itself. Over 1,000 people, black and white, gathered for a banquet that evening in the Clarkville armory to celebrate the hometown heroine. The historical significance of this integrated space is enormous given that segregation was lawful and widely practiced in the South in 1960. Rudolph's call for an integrated homecoming was a courageous act of deviance, challenging the white status quo. Three years later, in 1963, she joined with other black leaders from Clarksville to protest a restaurant's segregationist practices. As these actions illustrate, she stood up to challenges both on and off the track to better her own situation and those within the broader society.

In the months immediately following her homecoming, Rudolph made dozens of appearances across the country, with numerous national and international awards bestowed upon her. Notable among the accolades was the Associated Press Female Athlete of the Year Award in 1960, Italy's Christopher Columbus Award, which was given to the most outstanding international sports figure of the year, and the 1960 Helms World Trophy for North America, which honored the best athlete on each continent of the globe.

In the two or three years following the Olympics, Rudolph continued to compete in track and field events. She won the AAU 100-yard dash, her third consecutive win in that race. At a race in Stuttgart, Germany, in July 1961, she set a new world record in the 100-meter dash with a very fast 11.2 seconds. That fall, she surprised many with her marriage to Tennessee State student William Ward. However, their marriage didn't last long, and the couple was divorced the following year. Throughout 1961, she participated in a number of events and collected multiple honors, including the prestigious Sullivan Award, which was given to the top amateur athlete in the United States. She continued to race until her graduation from Tennessee State in May 1963, when she made her decision to retire from track.

Rudolph was eager to settle down and think about life after track. At the end of July 1963, she married Robert Eldridge, her high school sweetheart and the father of Yolanda. She took a teaching job at Cobb Elementary, the school she attended as a young girl. She also accepted a position as track coach at her former high school. During this first year of teaching, she became pregnant and gave birth to Djuanna, her second child. Rudolph and her husband had their third child, Robert, Jr. in August 1965. Feeling the need to move her family away from Tennessee, Rudolph moved several times over the next few years. She took a variety of jobs, but none fulfilled her and thus each was short-lived. She gave birth to her second son, Xurry, in 1971. In the 1970s, she did some work in television and was part of a magazine ad for Geritol in 1976. She finished her autobiography in 1977, and the book was turned into a movie for television. In 1980, she ended her marriage to Eldridge and never remarried. She continued to find various positions in a number of occupations during the 1980s, including teacher, coach, artist, and consultant. In July 1994, Rudolph was diagnosed with a brain tumor. She died on November 12, 1994 at the very young age of 54.

In the years since her death, Wilma Rudolph has been memorialized in a number of ways. Clarksville commemorated her life with the construction of a life-size statue. ESPN ranked her as the 41st greatest athlete of the twentieth century, and the U.S. Postal Service created a postage stamp in her honor in 2004. These and other markers in her honor are notable because they represent and underscore the historical significance of her life. Her experiences, on and off the track, were a testament to her individual desire to thrive and the collective will of the black community to help her succeed in the face of intense marginalization as a female athlete of color. She helped lay the foundation on which track and field athletes today are able to claim fame and riches. However, her legacy reaches far beyond the gold medals, world records, and the track and field arena. Wilma Rudolph's gift to us lies within the way she negotiated the realities of racism, sexism, and class inequality to achieve greatness.

## FURTHER READING

Cahn, Susan K. *Coming on Strong: Gender and Sexuality in Twentieth-Century Women's Sport.* New York: Free Press, 1994.

Davis, Michael D. *Black American Women in Olympic Track and Field.* Jefferson, NC: McFarland & Company, 1992.

Only hours after winning the gold and bronze medals in the 1968 Olympic 200-meter race, Tommie Smith and John Carlos made history again. As "The Star-Spangled Banner" played to honor the two athletes and their nation during their award ceremony, the athletes removed their shoes, turned to their left to face the U.S. flag, and each thrust one fist into the air. Australian Peter Norman, who won the silver medal in the same race, wore an Olympic Project for Human Rights (OPHR) pin to demonstrate his support. Smith and Carlos remained silent as the U.S. anthem played, allowing the symbolism of their actions to communicate for them. Their removed shoes represented black poverty, which was and still is a hidden embarrassment in a nation that prides itself on freedom and equality. Smith wore a black scarf around his neck to represent black pride, and Carlos wore a string of beads to commemorate black people who had been lynched. Their heads were bowed in prayer, as their raised, gloved fists represented Black Power.

Their protest was unwelcome to many. As the athletes left the podium, the crowd booed the Olympians. The two young, accomplished athletes used their Olympic victory as a platform to challenge racism within the United States and beyond. Their decision to demonstrate at the Olympic Games was unprecedented. It shocked many throughout the world. Though numerous black athletes from the United States discussed the possibility of a boycott or protest at the Games, no organized action was planned prior to the 1968 Olympics. Smith and Carlos devised their protest themselves, believing that they were obligated to use their athletic skill and the international attention it drew to help their communities and others. The men's raised fists received unforeseen criticism, however, and deeply affected the athletes' lives in the ensuing decades. Yet neither has expressed regret for their protest. Instead, they note that they acted in the interest of their communities when they raced in Mexico City in 1968. The young men risked their medals, futures, and even their lives in their effort to give voice to marginalized and oppressed African Americans, particularly black athletes. Smith and Carlos left an indelible mark on the history of sports and the struggle for equality. The bravery and passion they exhibited on one of the world's largest and most celebrated stages truly make them icons, just as their superior skill and discipline made them Olympians and leading athletes of track and field.

Though Smith and Carlos acted together at the Olympics, their lives before and after the race were separate and distinct. The two men were raised in different areas of the United States; their backgrounds informed their opinions about their place in the world. The similarities and differences between them worked to bring them together for that race on October 16, 1968.

Smith was born in Clarksville, Texas, on June 6, 1944. His birth occurred on D-day, the day the Battle of Normandy began in World War II. He grew up in nearby Acworth, which was a town that boasted a population of approximately twenty people. While his hometown was small, his family was not: He had 13 siblings, 11 of whom survived infancy. His parents were sharecroppers, and the Smith children helped them work long, arduous hours in the fields. His parents valued work and education and attempted to instill these values in their children. Smith's early educational opportunities were limited. He attended a racially segregated, one-room school in Acworth.

The Smith family moved from Texas to California while Tommie was still young. The family's transportation was paid by their future employers, who put the Smiths and many other families in a labor camp and subjected them to continued agricultural work. California's integrated schools provided new opportunities, however. Here Smith developed his burgeoning athletic talent and raced his older sister Sally through the fields their family worked and later in physical education classes at school. One of his white teachers took the young student under his wing, teaching him to develop confidence in his academic and athletic abilities.

*In those days reputation was a big thing. If you could win a game before you went out, win it. That could mean winning it in the papers by saying certain things or by not saying certain things. You got very crafty at the game.*

Tommie Smith

As a high school student, Smith became a successful athlete. He played football and basketball, ran track, and lettered in all three sports every year of high school for a total of 12 letters. He did well as a receiver in football and was his school's all-time leading scorer. He did particularly well in track, however, participating in jumps, all races, and all relays available at his school. His specialty was the 220-yard race, but Smith particularly made a name for himself with a different event. His junior year, he ran the 440-yard race in 47.7 seconds at a meet on his first try, which was the best time in the United States that year. The physical conditioning that he developed by working with his family in the fields provided both strength and endurance; the difficult work he'd performed with his family also gave him the discipline necessary to improve his game.

Smith demonstrated his developing political consciousness at this time as well. His athletic success, combined with his pleasant demeanor, prompted his peers to elect him student body vice president. He discussed the nature and effects of racism during one speech he delivered for that office. His high school was unprepared to hear this message, however, and did not receive it well. He later noted that the student body, as well as the faculty of his school, felt betrayed by his comments. Smith had not expected his audience to express such discomfort with his opinion on racism and was surprised by their reaction.

Smith's athletic success provided him with the opportunity to attend college. Though many schools solicited the icon in the making, San Jose State University proved to be his best option because it offered him a scholarship while also keeping him close to home and to his older siblings. At San Jose State, Smith had opportunities to play football, basketball, or track and field because his scholarship allowed him to choose between the three sports. After trying collegiate basketball for a season, he moved to track and field. Lloyd "Bud"

Winter coached San Jose State's team; his aptitude for coaching and the talent he fostered at the school earned the team the nickname "Speed City." Though Smith injured his hamstring and spent most of his first season in college in recovery, he was still named athlete of the year by the USA Track and Field Foundation. His athletic success continued. He was far larger than his contemporary sprinters at 6' 4" and 180 pounds. His size might have been a burden in such a short race, but his strength and the lessons he learned at Speed City allowed him to use his size, and strides measuring at nine feet or more, to his advantage. He set numerous world records during his subsequent years at San Jose State. At one point he held 11 world records, placing him at the ready for the upcoming 1968 Olympic Games.

John Carlos's childhood and adolescence also brought him to the Olympic Games. He was born in Harlem, New York, on June 5, 1945. He understood poverty just as well as Smith, though his childhood was not consumed by sharecropping. The experiences of the two men were informed by different perspectives; both experienced racism, but the opportunities available to African Americans in Harlem were different from those available in Texas and California. Carlos recalled breaking into freight trains by Yankee Stadium in his youth, for example; Smith, in contrast, remembered picking cotton with his family. Racism and poverty dictated the circumstances of both athletes, but the regions in which they lived also affected their experiences.

Carlos's academic and athletic talents provided him the opportunity to escape his circumstances, however. In high school, he realized that he was a powerful student; he was gifted academically as well as athletically. He graduated from Machine Trade and Medal High School, and secured admission to East Texas State University (ETSU) on a full track and field scholarship. He led his collegiate team to win the track and field Lone Star Conference championship, providing the school with its first and only championship from this competition. After studying at ETSU for one year, the athlete transferred to San Jose State, the same school Smith attended. Carlos ran track at his new school under the guidance of Winter.

Smith and Carlos made history together, but circumstances and personality kept the men apart in many ways. Though they both studied at San Jose State University, they did not run for the school's team during the same years. By the time that Carlos, a transfer student, qualified to run at Speed City, Smith was no longer eligible to participate in the school's athletic programs. Their different backgrounds also provided them with contrasting perspectives; Smith's childhood in Texas and California shaped his opinions just as strongly as Carlos's childhood in Harlem shaped his. Carlos later explained that in many ways, the differences between him and Smith were similar to the differences between the philosophies of Malcolm X and Martin Luther King Jr. Their personalities were similarly different; where Smith is calm and understated, Carlos is boisterous and exuberant. Smith's personality shone forth during his races, for example. He wore sunglasses in most of them, in part to protect his eyes from the sun but also due to shyness: he wished to hide his face from spectators even as he seized their attention and set world records. Carlos, in contrast, felt comfortable with attention. Smith expressed jealousy regarding his teammate's ease with others decades after the Olympic Games, writing, "Don't ever think John Carlos doesn't know what to do when he has a stage" (Smith, p. 14).

There was much for Smith and Carlos to learn. The two emerged during a period of intense change in the United States. The Civil Rights Movement, and the individuals who labored to provide equal opportunities to all citizens, fought for the majority of the two athletes' young lives. That movement reached a turning point by the time Smith and Carlos entered San Jose State University. Malcolm X was assassinated in February 1965, shortly after Smith entered college. Race riots broke out throughout the United States later that summer as African Americans vented their feelings of outrage and hopelessness. Dr. King was assassinated in April 1968. The 1968 Olympics occurred during a time of great upheaval, and the activist sentiments held by Smith and Carlos did not develop in isolation.

Smith and Carlos participated in political activism through their years at San Jose State, just as they labored in Speed City to perfect the craft of track. Smith and teammate Lee Evans, a 400-meter sprinter, created the United Black Students for Action (UBSA) and became members of the organization's executive committee. Together with Carlos, they also studied under Dr. Harry Edwards, a sociology professor. Edwards, who had attended San Jose State himself on an athletic scholarship as an undergraduate, was Smith's first African American professor. He challenged his students, through courses on race relations and black leadership and also through interactions outside of the classroom, to recognize that their opinions mattered, even if many of their peers believed that they were only valuable for their physical abilities as athletes. Edwards became their primary advisor and political teacher during their final years at San Jose State.

The political expression of African American athletes shifted prior to the 1968 Olympic Games. Muhammad Ali made international news when he changed his name from Cassius Clay in 1964. He again shocked many throughout the United States when he refused to fight for the country in the Vietnam War in 1966. His political resistance allowed athletes such as Smith and Carlos to recognize that they, and not just politicians and traditional activists, possess political views and have opinions that can make a difference. Ali's actions were part of a changing climate in which athletes realized that they were valuable for their athletic prowess and discipline, but also for their minds. Carlos explained, "Athletes are human beings. We have feelings too. How can you ask someone to live in the world, to exist in the world, and not have something to say about injustice?" (Zirin, "Living Legacy"). Athletes also have political views and opinions of value. African American athletes throughout the United States discovered their power during this era, and used the attention they received

*Athletes are human beings. We have feelings too. How can you ask someone to live in the world, to exist in the world, and not have something to say about injustice?*

John Carlos

through athletics to change their sports as well as the nation. Smith and Carlos learned, by watching Muhammad Ali and listening to Dr. Harry Edwards, that their thoughts mattered, regardless of their chosen profession.

Smith and Carlos, as well as many of their contemporaries, believed that their identity as men was a particularly compelling reason for their activism. Carlos later described his protest at the Olympics as a "revolt of the black men," rather than a revolt of athletes. He explained, "I raised my voice in protest as a man" (Zirin, "Living Legacy"). Smith and Carlos closely linked their dignity and sense of worth to their ability to fulfill the duties they believed that men held.

The African American athletes preparing for the 1968 Olympics soon began meeting with one another, and these meetings attracted the interest of journalists. As the Games neared, the media also speculated on the athletes' plans. During a competition in Tokyo in September 1967, a Japanese reporter spoke to Smith. The icon, when questioned by the reporter, explained that he did not believe that African Americans were treated fairly in the United States. The reporter next asked him if he and other African American athletes planned to boycott the Olympics. Smith responded, "Depending upon the situation, you cannot rule out the possibility that we Negro athletes might boycott the Olympic Games" (Drake). Smith's comments fueled the fears of those in the United States who already suspected that plans were in place to disrupt the 1968 Olympics. They believed that any protest or boycott on the part of African American athletes representing the United States would be a disruption to the proceedings and an embarrassment to the nation.

African American athletes continued to prepare for the Games and deliberate upon possible political action. They did not prepare for the upcoming Olympics in isolation, however. They formally created the OPHR in October 1967, under the guidance of Edwards, to organize together and determine whether they should take formal action in the upcoming Games. Smith and Evans were the athletic spokespeople for the organization. The goals of the OPHR were ambitious; Edwards and the athletes involved wished to use the Olympic Games and their notoriety in sports to fundamentally challenge the racism African Americans faced in the United States. The organization's founding statement read, in part,

> We must no longer allow this country to use a few so-called Negroes to point out to the world how much progress she has made in solving her racial problems when the oppression of Afro-Americans is greater than it ever was. We must no longer allow the sports world to pat itself on the back as a citadel of racial justice when the racial injustices of the sports world are infamously legendary. . . . Any black person who allows himself to be used in the above matter is a traitor

because he allows racist whites the luxury of resting assured that those black people in the ghettos are there because that is where they want to be. So we ask why should we run in Mexico only to crawl home? (Zirin, *What's My Name, Fool?*, p. 74)

The OPHR wished to prevent the United States and sports institutions from using African American success in sports as proof that racism did not exist, or as evidence that African Americans were happy with their status and able to reach economic success. The men in the OPHR believed that their actions would demonstrate that even those few black people who were able to reach some level of financial or social success through sports were unhappy with the state of civil rights in the United States. The primary aims of the OPHR were threefold: to reinstate Muhammad Ali as the heavyweight champion of the world, remove Avery Brundage as head of the U.S. Olympic Committee (USOC), and remove South Africa and Rhodesia from the Games.

The OPHR was ultimately unable to decide on a formal action that all athletes were willing to take. Some feared that a boycott would ruin their only chance to play in the Olympics. Others were concerned that participating in a boycott or protest would limit their opportunities to play professional sports or prevent them from finding endorsements after the Games. Others were unconvinced that a formal protest was necessary, or worried about the harassment they believed they would face if they participated. In the end, the OPHR decided that no formal boycott would be organized. Each athlete was left to decide his best individual course of action.

The 1968 Olympic Trials provided Smith and Carlos an opportunity to again prove their physical abilities. Carlos finished the 200-meter dash in 19.7 seconds and broke the world record for the race. His time was not recognized as a world record, however, because he wore spiked shoes that were not allowed. Smith had a good showing as well, finishing the race in 19.9 seconds. Public speculation surrounding the athletes focused not only on political actions they might take before or during the Games but also on their physical prowess and the upcoming 200-meter race.

October 16, the day of the 200-meter race, proved trying for both athletes. At the end of the semifinal heat, Smith pulled his left abductor muscle. His thoughts concerning how he might stage a protest after the race, in addition to his nervousness, distracted him, and he slowed down too quickly crossing the finish line. He fell and was carried from the field. Winters, as well as Carlos and Evans, tended to Smith in the waiting room, icing the injury, until the final was less than one hour away. They took Smith back to the training field so that he could practice walking and running on the injury. He jogged briefly, finding that he could still maintain mobility despite the injury.

The race itself inevitably neared, giving Smith and Carlos the opportunity for which they'd trained for years. The lanes for this race were drawn by lot; Smith was placed in lane 3 and Carlos in lane 4, which are among the better lanes from which to race. The runners positioned themselves in their starting blocks. Carlos was ahead of Smith in position. The two men prepared to race, and soon heard the starter's whistles. The gun fired next, and Smith, Carlos, and the other runners took off. Smith intentionally held back through most of the race, as he feared that he could not run the entire race at full power due to his injury. Believing he had 15 full strides available to him before he might re-injure himself or collapse, Smith waited until the last 60 meters of the race before running at full capacity. Carlos was about three meters ahead of him, but Smith almost immediately surpassed him as he thundered by with his long strides. Carlos seemed to slow down, perhaps due to his surprise that his injured teammate had suddenly entered his field of vision. Smith, elated to near the finish line first, triumphantly raised his arms in the air. This slowed his progress in the race's final meters, but even so he finished the race at 19.83 seconds, winning the gold and setting his personal best in the event despite his injury. Norman and Carlos followed immediately thereafter, at 20 seconds, with Norman just beating Carlos for the silver.

The infamous protest soon followed. Immediately following the race, the runners were escorted back to their dressing room. Smith and Carlos finalized their plans for the protest in these underground rooms. Hours later, they staged their infamous protest during their medal ceremony. When the U.S. anthem played, the athletes turned toward their flag and enacted the protest they'd prepared together earlier that day. Though both believed that this protest was necessary and that it communicated the struggles of African Americans to the United States and the world, neither man realized the full consequences of the protest that day. They both faced death threats in the months leading up to the 1968 Games, as had other members of the OPHR. Edwards even chose not to attend the Games, despite his earlier efforts to serve as a mentor to the two athletes prior to the competition. Smith believes that Edwards failed to come to Mexico City because he feared the death threats that they each received. The icons' protest meant that the two would receive more death threats, as well as other repercussions.

Smith and Carlos were punished for their protest almost immediately. Brundage suspended them from the U.S. team and banned them from the Olympic Village. When the USOC refused to follow his orders, Brundage threatened to ban the entire U.S. track team. Smith and Carlos were subsequently expelled from the Games. Criticism met the two athletes before they even returned from Mexico City. Their salute was described as "Nazi-like," "childish," and "angry." Few in the media were willing to acknowledge the motivation behind the gesture, and instead only focused on the fact that their protest embarrassed the image of the United States as a bastion of freedom and equality.

Both athletes faced difficulty returning to their normal lives as well. Few people seemed to agree with their protest, and fewer still were able to help the two men secure employment or find peaceful ways to live with the greater white communities of California. Smith and Carlos experienced periods of stressful unemployment and faced harassment for their decision to become politically active.

Smith faced harassment upon his return to the United States. He believes that he also had difficulty securing employment and finding the means to support his family due to his politics. He worried about how he would be able to support his wife, Denise, and their son, Kevin, and believes that the difficulties he and Denise faced during this time ultimately led to their divorce. His extended family also faced pressure after his protest. His mother died of a heart attack in 1970, which he blames on the stress she experienced after receiving death threats and harassment for more than a year. Smith notes that the farmers for whom she still worked sent her manure and dead rats in the mail. These deliveries were messages intended to frighten her and punish her for raising a son who would challenge his place in the world by becoming successful and protesting institutionalized racism.

Smith continued his career in sports, however. The few doors that did open to him following his protest were provided through the world of sports. He played professional football with the Cincinnati Bengals for three years after graduating from college. Following his last season of professional football, he petitioned the National Collegiate Athletic Association to return to track. The NCAA rejected his request because he had become a professional athlete already. (Boundaries between professional and amateur athletes are less rigid now.) This ruling did not entirely keep Smith away from his sport of choice, however. He coached track at Oberlin College instead. Having earned a master's degree, he also taught sociology. In 1995, he coached the U.S. team at Barcelona's World Indoor Championships. More recently, he taught sociology at Santa Monica College in California.

Smith received eventual acclaim for his athleticism. He was inducted into the National Track and Field Hall of Fame in 1978 and the California Black Sports Hall of Fame in 1996. Smith held 11 world records during his career and set all-time bests, including 10.1 seconds for the 100-meter dash, his Olympic 19.83 seconds for the 200, and 44.5 seconds for the 400.

Carlos similarly faced great difficulty following the Olympics. Immediately after the Games, he continued to pursue his talent in track and field. In 1969, he ran the 100-meter race and tied the existing world record. He also had to support his family, however, and found that he faced harassment and threats similar to those that met Smith, as well as trouble finding employment. He did not finish his academic training at San Jose State; his lack of an advanced degree compounded his problems finding a meaningful job. He played football with the Philadelphia Eagles, but a knee injury prematurely ended his career.

Carlos's hard times grew even worse. His wife committed suicide in 1977. Carlos believes that the stress she faced from their economic hardship as they tried to raise four children, combined with the fear created by the death threats they continued to receive, led her to end her life. Though these struggles appeared insurmountable, he did not give up and continued to search for a place in which he belonged.

Carlos did find a job assisting a Los Angeles city councilperson, which turned his attention again toward helping and representing others. He founded the John Carlos Youth Development Program in 1977 in Los Angeles. Funding the program was a struggle, however; despite his success in the 1968 Games, the controversy surrounding his protest, coupled with the fact that he founded a program long before later athletes found financial success and corporate sponsorship, limited his opportunities to grow the program. He used a marketing position he landed with Puma to fund the program, though his consultant work with the sport goods company was of limited duration.

Carlos's connection to sports continued, however. In 1982, he was hired by the Los Angeles Olympic Organizing Committee to bring inner-city organizations to the city's efforts to prepare for the 1984 Games. He continued to run competitively as well, though age and lack of time to train limited his success. He also became a counselor, in-school suspension supervisor, and track and field coach at a high school in Palm Springs in 1985.

Though Smith and Carlos eventually found some measure of stability and success, this safety took them more than a decade to secure. The icons still communicate frustration over the loneliness they experienced during those years. Carlos described his experience as a time of great isolation, "I don't feel embraced, I feel like a survivor, like I survived cancer. It's like if you are sick and no one wants to be around you, and when you're well everyone who thought you would go down for good doesn't even want to make eye contact. It was almost like we were on a deserted island" (Zirin, "Living Legacy"). Fortunately, the tides finally changed for the two men in recent years. Though the honors they now receive cannot make up for the years in which they were left in fear of death threats or the time they believed no one else wished to help them, these awards do allow the athletes to realize that their protest and courage are remembered and celebrated. The National Track and Field Hall of Fame inducted Carlos in 2003. That same year, students at San Jose State University announced plans to erect a statue to honor the two athletes at their alma mater. Political artist Rigo 23 was commissioned for the task, and in 2005 created a 20-foot-high statue commemorating the protest at the athletes' alma mater. Smith was particularly heartened that students, 35 years removed from his own years at the school, would take such efforts to recognize his activism, protest, and life.

The two men continue to accrue acclaim for their protest and the powerful athleticism with which they graced the Olympic stage. An exhibit about Speed City in 2007 honored San Jose State's former prowess in track and field, the efforts of coach Winter, and the talent of the students who pursued the sport under his guidance. Carlos was recently honored at the Trumpet Awards in Las Vegas in 2007. His connection to athletics also continued when he trained Charles Barkley, a former NBA star, to race in a somewhat staged competition against Dick Bavetta, one of the NBA's most popular, experienced, and well-conditioned referees, at the 2007 NBA All-Star Weekend.

Smith and Carlos were remarkable athletes. Just as remarkably, they helped change the connection between U.S. athletes and politics by demonstrating that athletes have political opinions of their own and the opportunities to communicate them. Though both men paid dearly for their activism, the courage and will that led them to win the Olympics and stage their protest also allowed them to survive the threats, criticism, and isolation they experienced in the ensuing years. Their history and lives stand as testaments to the influence and longevity of icons, as their talent, discipline, bravery, and commitment to something larger than themselves helped changed the world for the better.

## FURTHER READING

Drake, Dick. "Tommie Smith and Lee Evans Discuss Potential Olympic Boycott." *Track & Field News* (November 1967). http://www.trackandfieldnews.com/display_article.php?id=1605 (accessed March 27, 2007).

Hartmann, Douglas. *Race, Culture, and the Revolt of the Black Athlete: The 1968 Olympic Protests and Their Aftermath*. Chicago: University of Chicago Press, 2003.

Maese, Rick. "A Courageous Act of Defiance," *Montreal Gazette*, August 20, 2004, C4.

Smith, Tommie, with David Steele. *Silent Gesture: The Autobiography of Tommie Smith*. Philadelphia: Temple University Press, 2007.

Zirin, Dave. "The Living Legacy of Mexico City: An Interview with John Carlos." *Counterpunch* (November 1/2, 2003). http://www.counterpunch.org/zirin11012003.html (accessed March 14, 2007).

Zirin, Dave. *What's My Name, Fool? Sports and Resistance in the United States*. Chicago: Haymarket Books, 2005.

AP Photo/Darron Cummings.

AP Photo/Amy Sancetta.

# Venus and Serena Williams

*Matthew C. Whitaker*

Since 1994, Venus and Serena Williams have stood at the vanguard of professional athletic achievement, advocacy for racial and gender equality, and innovation in the business, interior design, and fashion worlds. The Williams sisters stunned the world with their domination of professional tennis. Their physical strength and will to win set them apart from their peers. The key to their games are fast serves and strong returns that exhaust their opponents; these skills, and their desire to excel, fueled their rise in the rankings in both women's singles and women's doubles competitions. Still in their 20s, speculation abounds as to which of the sisters will ultimately prove to be the most successful player in the long term. No matter who registers the most victories, garners the most awards, or makes their mark in the world beyond the tennis court, the Williams sisters have already cemented their collective, unsurpassed legacy of excellence and achievement.

The sisters' path into professional tennis and celebrity status was plotted before their birth. Their father, Richard, loved to watch tennis on television, and he envisioned a time during which his yet-to-be-born children would compete at the highest levels of professional tennis. His first three daughters did not become tennis players, but Venus and Serena took to the game almost immediately. Venus Ebone Starr Williams was born on June 17, 1980, in Lynwood, California, and Serena Jameka Williams was born on September 26, 1981, in Saginaw, Michigan. When the sisters were still toddlers, their father and Oracene (Brandi) Williams, their mother, introduced them to tennis. For six hours a day they played with shabby rackets and useless balls against a wall or on a pot-holed court. They were subjected to a grueling regimen as their father dissected his tennis manual and shouted instructions. They learned well and began to compete before the age of five.

Venus and Serena were not yet teenagers when invitations to national training camps began arriving in their Compton, Los Angeles, post office box. By the time the pair became teenagers, their father withdrew them from the junior circuit, but he later enrolled them in the professional tour after a brief hiatus. He was criticized for taking them out of school, but he justified his actions by saying that they would be best served by concentrating on the most important area in which they were straight-A students. The two initially played in private professional events because they were too young to compete in World Tennis Association (WTA) events. Nevertheless, their games improved dramatically.

Venus was the first to come of age and make her mark in professional tennis in October 1994. After 1994, the WTA did not allow 14-year-olds to compete in all tour events, although "phase-in" clauses allowed some to play in a limited number of events. The elder sister turned pro before the new rule went into effect, so the new limit did not affect her opportunities to play. Her first tournament was the Bank of the West Classic in Oakland, California, where she showed a good deal of promise in a loss to Arantxa Sanchez-Vicario, who was then ranked number two in the world. For her first two years on the pro tour, Williams stayed out of the limelight and kept up with her high school studies, not making her debut at a Grand Slam until the 1997 French Open.

Venus was a success that year. She became the first unseeded woman ever to reach the final of the U.S. Open in 1997 and the first African American woman to do so since Althea Gibson won back-to-back championships in 1957 and 1958. Though she lost in the finals to Switzerland's Martina Hingis, the 17-year-old number one player in the world, she saw her own ranking shoot up from number 66 to number 25 in only one day. The highlight of that tournament and the year, however, was the infamous "bump" that occurred during the Irina Spirlea and Williams semifinal. The two collided during a changeover. Williams's father later said that the incident was initiated by Spirlea and racially motivated. He described his daughters as "the ghetto Cinderellas of the lily-white tennis world," in part because the bump would not be the first or last time that he and his daughters called attention to what they considered to be racist treatment on the circuit.

Despite the racism and on-court challenges that they faced in 1997, the Williams sisters flourished. Venus started out the 1998 season well, beating Hingis in a tournament in Sydney, Australia, and reaching the quarterfinals of the Australian Open after defeating her younger sister in the tournament. Though she lost to Lindsay Davenport in the singles draw, the elder sister teamed up with Justin Gimelstob to win the mixed doubles championship. She won her first WTA singles title at the IGA Tennis Classic in March and went on to score a big win at the Lipton International, defeating Anna Kournikova of Russia (another of tennis's highly touted up-and-comers) and Hingis. The Lipton win propelled Venus into the top 10. She finished 1998 with a great record in the Grand Slams, reaching the quarterfinals of the French Open and Wimbledon and the semifinals of the U.S. Open. She also set the record for the fastest serve ever recorded by a female player in a main draw match at 129 mph.

Despite her impressive record and growing confidence, Venus had yet to achieve the accolade she dreamed about her whole life: a Grand Slam victory. Serena, who the sisters' father once claimed would be the better player of the two, became a pro four years earlier in her first, non-WTA event, the Bell Challenge in Vanier, Quebec, in October 1995. She reached her sister's goal first, however, when she won the 1999 U.S. Open. Serena had played sporadically and did not meet with much individual success until 1997, when her ranking shot up from number 453 to 304. After beating Mary Pierce and Monica Seles at the Ameritech Cup in Chicago, she jumped to number 100 in the world. In July 1998, she won the mixed doubles title at Wimbledon with Max Mirnyi, and by August she improved to number 21. In October 1998, Serena beat her sister for the first time in the finals of the Grand Slam Cup in Munich, Germany.

Serena won her first WTA tour singles victory in early 1999 at the Open Gaz de France in Paris. That win began an incredible season of five singles titles in 48 matches. In September 1999, the 17-year-old athlete defeated Hingis in the finals of the U.S. Open, becoming the first African American woman to capture a Grand Slam singles title since Gibson, who won five Slam events in the late 1950s. The following day, Serena and Venus, who reached the semifinals of the singles draw before losing to Hingis, teamed up to win the doubles title. Both victories took place at the Arthur Ashe Stadium in Flushing Meadows, New York, which was named for the last African American to win a major tennis title in 1975 at Wimbledon. The sisters also teamed up to win the doubles titles at the French Open and the U.S. Open in 1999, becoming the first and only sister team to win a Grand Slam doubles title in the twentieth century.

The Williams sisters finished the 1999 season ranked in the top five in the world. Still, the higher-ranked Venus finished off the 1999 season ranked number 3 in the world and was the second highest-paid player in terms of prize with career earnings of nearly $4.6 million. Serena finished the season well, too, as the third highest-paid player. The next year the glory belonged to her sister, although it did not appear that way initially. Both women got off to a slow start in 2000 due to injuries, and in April Richard Williams announced that his older daughter was contemplating retirement. Just a few months later, however, Venus began a winning streak that took her all the way to Wimbledon, where she grabbed a Grand Slam title of her own, beating both Hingis and her younger sister in an emotional semifinal match, before dominating defending champion Davenport in the finals. Just one day later, the icons teamed up to win the Wimbledon doubles title.

The sisters' success continued. On September 9, 2000, Venus met Davenport again in the finals of the U.S. Open, where she won her twenty-sixth straight match and became the first woman to win two Grand Slam titles in one year since Hingis did in 1997. Venus and Serena also captured the doubles title. In the fall of 2000, both athletes represented the United States at the Olympic Games in Sydney, Australia, alongside Davenport and Monica Seles. Continuing her amazing winning streak, Venus became the only other woman besides Helen Wills Moody in 1924 to capture gold in both singles and doubles in the same Olympiad. The sisters won their twenty-second straight doubles match in the finals at the Olympic Games.

As their celebrity grew, they were reminded, however, that many people still viewed them as inferior by virtue of their race. Early in 2001, in Indian Wells, California, an injured Venus withdrew from her semifinal against her younger sister 10 minutes before the match began. During the tournament's final against Belgium's Kim Clijsters, crowds jeered and booed Serena. She believed that this reception was racially motivated. Their father also noted that he and Venus were called "niggers" by members of the crowd as they made their way to their seats at the 2001 tournament. He explained, "When Venus and I were walking down the stairs to our seats, people kept calling me nigger. One guy said: 'I wish it was '65 [a reference to the 1965 Los Angeles race riots]; we'd skin you alive'" (Hodgkinson, 2007). The pain created by this tournament lives on; the Williams sisters have boycotted Indian Wells ever since.

Venus and Serena did not let such racist behavior deter them, however, and they remained a remarkable force in the tennis world. In July 2001, Venus successfully defended her Wimbledon title, beating Davenport in the semifinal and Belgian player Justine Henin in the finals. She had an even more eventful U.S. Open, beating the resurgent Jennifer Capriati in the semifinals before facing Serena in the finals in the first meeting of sisters in a Grand Slam final since 1884. The elder athlete's maturity served her well in the all-Williams match, as she beat Serena in two sets to win her second consecutive Open title. The younger Williams sister handled an up-and-down season in 2001, but still reached a high point at the U.S. Open in September, where she had commanding victories over Davenport and Hingis in the quarter- and semifinals, respectively.

The year 2002, however, belonged to Serena. She opened the year by defeating Henin to win the Gold Coast tournament. The icon reached the quarterfinals of the Australian Open, and defeated Venus in the finals of the French Open, Wimbledon, and U.S. Open. The string of victories catapulted Serena to the top of WTA tour rankings, while her sister dropped to second. Serena won seven singles titles in 2002, a career best, and in February 2002, she became the top-ranked player in the world and the first African American player to secure that spot since the computer rankings began in 1975. Despite Venus's fall in the international rankings, she and her sister won the 2002 Wimbledon doubles title for the second time.

The sisters' professional and personal lives were not without challenges, however. Venus started the year by losing to her sister in the 2003 Australian Open final. During a semifinal match against Clijsters at Wimbledon in 2003, she suffered a severe abdominal injury that required medical attention during the match. She rebounded to win that match, but lost the final to Serena. The sisters also experienced personal tragedy in 2003, when older sister Yetunde Price was murdered in Compton, California, on the morning of September 14. The era of domination by the Williams sisters appeared to close out after their sister's murder. Following Wimbledon, both suffered injuries that kept them out of competition for the last half of the year.

The sisters returned to the tour somewhat rusty and were inconsistent on the court. Venus rebounded from a tough start to reach the 2004 Wimbledon final. She lost a controversial second round match to Croatian Karolina Sprem. The umpire of the match, Ted Watts, awarded Sprem an unearned point in the second set tiebreak, casting a cloud of doubt over Sprem's victory and putting his job security on the line. (He was fired immediately after the match.)

The sisters improved the following year. At Wimbledon in 2005, Venus defeated defending champion Maria Sharapova in a semifinal. This marked the sixth consecutive year that at least one of the Williams sisters reached the final, and it was the elder sister's fifth appearance in the Wimbledon final in the past six years. In the longest Wimbledon final in history, Venus was down match point at 6-4, 6-7(4), 5-4 (40-30) before coming back to defeat top-seeded Davenport. This was Venus's third Wimbledon singles title, and the first time in 70 years that a player won after being down match point during the women's final. In addition, as the fourteenth seed, she was the lowest seed to win the women' singles title in Wimbledon history. She also reached the quarterfinals at the 2005 U.S. Open. In the fourth round, she defeated Serena for the second consecutive time. In the quarterfinals, she lost to Clijsters, who went on to win the tournament. *Tennis Magazine* ranked Venus twenty-fifth and Serena seventeenth on their list of the 40 Greatest Players of the Tennis era that year.

Serena cemented her own championship legacy between 1999 and 2007. After suffering a series of setbacks and facing limited success against a series of opponents, she logged some remarkable victories and returned to full form at the 2007 Australian Open, where she was unseeded and defeated fifth-seeded Nadia Petrova of Russia in the third round. This was her first win over a top 10 player since her defeat of Davenport in the 2005 Australian Open final. In the fourth round, the icon defeated the eleventh-seeded Jelena Jankovic of Serbia. She then defeated sixteenth-seeded Shahar Pe'er in the quarter-finals and tenth-seeded Nicole Vaidisova in the semifinals. In the final, Serena dominated top-seeded and then second-ranked Sharapova in just 63 minutes to take her third Australian Open singles title. The victory elevated her ranking from eighty-first to fourteenth in the world. It also marked the first time either Williams sister won a Grand Slam singles title in the absence of the other's participation in the same tournament. Serena dedicated the win to her deceased sister. This return to success was her sixteenth career Grand Slam title, pushing her career totals to six women's doubles titles, three mixed doubles titles, and eight singles titles.

By 2006, Venus also established herself as one of the all-time greats of professional tennis. Playing with a white Wilson (K) Factor limited-edition racket featuring 22-carat gold leaf laid into the frame, a resurgent Venus won her first six singles matches at Wimbledon in 2006 and reached the final for the sixth time. She clinched her fourth Wimbledon title on July 7, 2007, with a decisive, unreturned 124 mph serve into the body of her opponent, Marion Bartoli. Seeded number 23, Williams beat her own 2005 record as the lowest women's seed to win Wimbledon. During the ceremony, she said that her little sister inspired her to win. By claiming her fourth Wimbledon title, Venus joined an elite group of champion tennis players, including Billie Jean King, Martina Navratilova, and Steffi Graf as the only women to win four or more Wimbledon ladies' singles titles in the open era.

Despite their dominance, Venus and Serena continue to face racism and sexism on and off of the court. As recently as March 2007, the sports world was rocked by news that Serena was subjected to racist heckling by a male spectator at the Sony Ericsson Open. The individual shouted to Williams to "hit the ball into the net like any nigger would." She reported the abuse to the umpire during her third-round victory against Czech Lucie Safarova, and the racist heckler was eventually removed from stadium. She later explained, "I was shocked. I couldn't believe it. It threw me off. I shouldn't have let it bother me because growing up in Compton, in Los Angeles, we had drive-by shootings, and I guess that's what my dad prepared me for, but I'm not going to stand for it" (Hodgkinson, 2007). Zina Garrison, a former Wimbledon finalist with close links to the Williams family, also suffered occasional racist abuse during her playing days. Garrison said that, even for someone as mentally strong as Serena, racist insults are still extremely hurtful.

> *I was shocked. I couldn't believe it. It threw me off. I shouldn't have let it bother me because growing up in Compton, in Los Angeles, we had drive-by shootings, and I guess that's what my dad prepared me for, but I'm not going to stand for [racist behavior].*
>
> Serena Williams

The mistreatment that Venus and Serena face on the court is unfortunately not unique. Women of color who enter sports that are usually considered nontraditional for people of their race and gender are often confronted by social conventions that limited their access and opportunities. Their physical appearance, intelligence, intentions, and commitment are often questioned. Women of color, through their very existence, also force others to rethink conceptions of race, gender roles, and femininity. Inflexible definitions and conventions for race and femininity limit opportunities for women such as the Williams sisters. Women of color who enter a nontraditional sport are often criticized for not conforming to norms and patterns established by a society dominated by whites and men. Women who decide to participate in traditionally male sports, or female athletes whose physical appearances diverge from the norm, risk being stereotyped as less feminine or lesbian. For example, Venus and Serena are regularly described as very muscular or "masculine" in build. The force with which they play has been likened to that of their male peers. Descriptions of the sisters frequently comment on their gender, even when journalists are not masculinizing them by describing their build. Venus and Serena are not identified as athletes in some descriptions, but instead as female players. Their skills and athleticism alone are insufficient for these journalists, who instead insist on comparing the sisters to men in their sport.

To be the "other" in contemporary society is to be nonwhite, working-class, or nonmale. Insinuated, built-in preferences for members of the dominant community are nearly invisible to the very people who benefit from them. As a result, they help fuel a cycle of racial, gender, and class discrimination under a veneer of ignorance and altruism in some of the most powerful institutions in American culture that play large roles in reflecting and shaping popular culture and stereotypes. The media, in particular, acts as a unifying agent by fostering one-dimensional classifications of race, gender, and class, in addition to its tendency to turn its back on and misrepresent specific groups. The U.S. institution of sports also exhibits a problematic history with race, gender, and class. Even though the sports industry explicitly highlights the masculine ideal, it also creates race and class disparities with the help of the media.

The media's coverage of Venus and Serena does not reflect the women's dominance and celebrity. The tennis stars receive fewer endorsements than many other tennis players, particularly their blonde (and blue- and green-eyed) counterparts. Their dark and muscular appearances stand in stark contrast to Western notions of beauty and femininity, which have changed little since the Middle Ages. Ironically, when female athletes of color are complimented for deploying their physique and strength, commentators often cite their "natural" or "inherent" ability. These compliments suggest that their race, as opposed to their knowledge of the game and work ethic, are responsible for their success.

Serena and Venus have devoted a great deal of time and energy to refuting negative stereotypes about African Americans and women, and they have fought to eradicate institutional inequities within professional tennis. Like Billie Jean King who came before them, the Williams sisters were not content to work only as ambassadors for athletic excellence. They also revealed themselves to be crusaders for equality and justice. The icons long objected to the unequal prize money awarded to men and women at Wimbledon and the French Open. Despite decades of lobbying by tennis pioneer King and others, in 2005 the French Open and Wimbledon still refused to pay women's and men's players equally through all rounds. Venus met with officials from both tournaments in 2005 to argue that female tennis players should be paid as much as males. Although WTA tour President Larry Scott listened to her demands, he refused to reverse the policy. The turning point for female tennis players came on the eve of the 2006 Wimbledon championship, when Venus published an essay in the *New York Times*. She accused Wimbledon of standing on the "wrong side of history." She felt that their stance devalued the principle of meritocracy and the years of hard work that women on the tour put into becoming professional tennis players.

She wrote,

> I [would] like to convey to women and girls across the globe that there is no glass ceiling. My fear is that Wimbledon is loudly and clearly sending the opposite message. . . . Wimbledon has argued that . . . they [men] work harder for their prize money. . . . In the eyes of the general public the men's and women's games have the same value. . . . I intend to keep doing everything I can until Billie Jean's original dream of equality is made real. It's a shame that the name of the greatest tournament in tennis, an event that should be a positive symbol for the sport, is tarnished. (Williams, June 26, 2006)

Many listened to Williams's comments. British Prime Minister Tony Blair and members of Parliament publicly endorsed the further arguments that she made in her essay. Later that year, the Women's Tennis Association and UNESCO teamed for a campaign to promote gender equality in sports, asking Venus to lead the campaign.

Efforts to secure gender equality in tennis, led by Venus, produced change. Under enormous pressure, Wimbledon announced in February 2007 that it would award equal prize money to all competitors in all rounds. The French Open followed suit a day later. In the aftermath, French Tennis Federation president Christian Bimes admitted he was "particularly sensitive" to Williams's remarks. Venus ultimately became the first woman to benefit from the equalization of prize money at Wimbledon by winning the 2007 tournament. Wimbledon awarded her the same amount as the male winner. After winning her second-round match at Wimbledon in 2007, Venus responded to critics' claims that she was the sixth most likely woman to win Wimbledon. She explained that it was okay, because, if she were to have listened to critics, she never would have made it out of Compton to the posh Palm Beach Gardens area of Miami.

> *I believe that athletes, especially female athletes in the world's leading sport for women, should serve as role models. The message I like to convey to women and girls across the globe is that there is no glass ceiling.*
> Venus Williams

Venus and Serena Williams diversified their professional endeavors and made their mark in business, interior design, and the world of fashion. Venus is a businesswoman and CEO of interior design firm V Starr Interiors, located in Jupiter, Florida. Her company garnered prominence by designing the set of the *Tavis Smiley Show* on PBS, the Olympic athletes' apartments as a part of the U.S. bid package for New York to host the 2012 Games, and the interiors for residences and businesses in the Palm Beach area. Most recently she partnered with retailer Steve & Barry's to launch her own fashion line, EleVen. Her business success, coupled with her athletic victories, make her a force in multiple fields. It is no surprise that the *Ladies' Home Journal* named her one of the 30 most powerful women in America.

For her part, Serena also established herself as an icon. She transcended the success and notoriety of the sports world to garner fame and power in business and fashion. She is well known for her distinct, colorful outfits on and off the court. In 2002, she created an on-court stir when she wore what appeared to be a leather catsuit at the U.S. Open. She stunned onlookers at the 2004 U.S. Open when she wore a denim skirt and boots. She soon developed her own special line of shoes and clothing with athletic apparel giant Puma. Currently she has her own brand with Nike.

The Williams sisters also made their presence known through entertainment. Serena became the center of attention and reached a new level of exposure at the London premiere of Pierce Brosnan's film *After the Sunset* in November 2004. She wore a candy apple red dress with sheer fabric over her chest that created a nearly topless effect to the gala. The younger sister also oversees the production of her own line of designer clothing called Aneres (her first name spelled backward), which she plans to sell in boutiques in Miami and Los Angeles. In 2001, the sisters appeared on *The Simpsons*. Serena also posed for a *Sports Illustrated* swimsuit issue and has a lucrative career in advertisements. MTV announced in April 2005 plans to broadcast a reality show around the lives of the sisters, but the show was ultimately aired on ABC Family. Serena also appeared on a number of television shows, including *My Wife and Kids, ER*, and *Law & Order: Special Victims Unit*.

Despite their inevitable rivalry and busy schedules, the Williams sisters remain close friends. Raised as devout Jehovah's Witnesses, both were home-schooled by their mother and received their high school diplomas. They are also graduates of the Art Institute of Florida, where they studied fashion design. Their love for tennis and their competitive spirit brought them closer together rather than driving them apart. When Venus won her first Wimbledon title in 2000 against Lindsay Davenport, the sisters sat up until 2 a.m. celebrating, and then went on to win the women's doubles the next day. Their affection for each other has also contributed to allegations of match fixing against their high-profile, image-conscious father; critics accused Richard Williams of orchestrating his daughters' careers to maximize their collective financial potential and titles. This accusation has never been substantiated.

Such intense scrutiny by critics, combined with the sisters' struggles against racism and sexism, do not cause them as much pain as witnessing the losses and disappointments of their own family. The violent murder of their sister Yetunde, and the sadness they feel when they witness one another's professional tennis losses, are in some ways more taxing than attacks they face from those outside their family. For example, when Venus won the Wimbledon title for the second time in 2001 and returned during the same season to defend her U.S. Open title in a historic sibling showdown, her victory was bittersweet. She explained her mixed feelings regarding the title win, "I don't feel like I've won. I just hate to see Serena lose, even against me. I'm the big sister. I make sure she has everything, even if I don't have anything. I love her and it's hard" (Donaldson, 2003).

By 2007, although still experienced and intimidating players on the circuit, the siblings seem to be slowing down. Their father suggested that the pair were losing interest in the sport. Despite this, Serena secured her third Australian Open singles title and her eighth Grand Slam singles title in 2007. For her part, Venus said of her last major win, "I knew my destiny was to be in the winner's circle." On the tennis court and beyond, Venus and Serena Williams emerged as towering championship athletes, adroit businesswomen, and international celebrities. They are truly African American icons of sport.

## FURTHER READING

Beard, Hilary, Venus Williams, and Serena Williams. *Venus and Serena: Serving from the Hip: 10 Rules for Living, Loving, and Winning*. Boston: Houghton Mifflin, 2005.

Donaldson, Madeline. *Venus and Serena Williams*. New York: First Avenue Editions, 2003.

Hodgkinson, Mark. "Serena 'Shocked' by More Racist Abuse," http://www.telegraph.co.uk. (March 4, 2007) (accessed September 10, 2007).

"Little Sister, Big Hit: Williams Family Surprise-Serena Williams Wins the U.S. Open," *Sports Illustrated* (September 20, 1999).

"Party Crasher: Venus Williams Shakes up Tennis," *Sports Illustrated* (September 15, 1997).

Schafer, A. R. *Serena and Venus Williams*. Kentwood, LA: Edge Books, 2002.

"Serena Williams—Awesome: The Next Target the French Open," *Sports Illustrated* (May 28, 2003).

Williams, Venus, "Wimbledon has sent me a message: I'm only a second-class champion," *New York Times* (June 26, 2006).

Photofest.

# Tiger Woods

*Maureen Margaret Smith*

Only weeks after missing the cut of the U.S. Open Championship that ended his record streak of 39 consecutive majors, golfer Tiger Woods marked his return to dominance. He won the 2006 British Open only one month after his father died of cancer. After putting in at the eighteenth hole, he broke down crying in the arms of Steve Williams, his caddy of seven years. Minutes later, under the glare of the television cameras, he sobbed with wife Elin. Undoubtedly, the absence of his father on the final hole only served to remind him of his father's passing. In accepting the trophy, Woods paid tribute to his father and to the lessons he learned that were instrumental to his success on the golf course.

The British golf course was dry the day he won this tournament, which made the bounce of the golf ball unpredictable. In adjusting his game to the course, Woods used a variety of clubs in his assault, making his victory one of admirable strategy. He attributed his strategic approach to the course to years of learning the game from his late father. Fans were moved by this uncharacteristic display of emotion. This British Open title was his eleventh major; he was only eight behind Jack Nicklaus's record of 19 major titles. In the weeks that followed, Woods won the next four tournaments, including another major at the Professional Golfers Association (PGA) Championship. By the end of the summer, he was only four behind Nicklaus and appeared to be unstoppable.

Clearly, Woods's success on the golf course makes him a notable athlete. He has achieved iconic status in a sport that rarely favors an individual player. From his exceptional beginnings as a three-year-old who shot nine holes to his three U.S. amateur titles and other professional championships, his athletic achievements alone merit such status. His position as an American sporting icon is, however, largely the result of his image. His successes and subsequent endorsements, in combination with his multiethnic heritage, created an image of an American athlete recognizable around the globe. Woods's fame places him among the likes of former heavyweight champion boxer Muhammad Ali and NBA star Michael Jordan.

Eldrick Woods was born on December 30, 1975, in Cypress, California, to Earl and Kutilda Woods. Earl was a retired lieutenant colonel in the U.S. Army. He gave his son the name Tiger in honor of his friend, Vuong Dang Phong, a Vietnamese soldier who Earl had also nicknamed Tiger. His first marriage of 18 years to Barbara Woods Gary resulted in three children, who are the golfer's older half-siblings: Earl Jr., Kevin, and Royce. Cheyenne Woods, one of Tiger's nieces, is also a golfer. Earl was of mixed ethnic heritage; his ancestry was a combination of black, Chinese, and Native American. Kutilda Woods is a native of Thailand and is Thai, Chinese, and Dutch. Tiger has referred to his own multiethnic identity as Cablinasian, a term he coined to describe his Caucasian, black, Native American, and Asian ancestry. Woods's father also golfed and was instrumental in developing the budding golfer's talent. Earl died on May 3, 2006.

According to family stories, Woods began imitating his father's golf swing at the precocious age of six months. He made his first television appearance at the age of two on the *Mike Douglas Show*, where he putted golf balls with entertainer Bob Hope. When he has three years old, Woods shot 48 for nine holes. Two years later he was featured in *Golf Digest* and appeared on the television show *That's Incredible*. His childhood ambition was to beat his father in a game of golf.

Woods's success continued throughout his childhood and adolescence. As an amateur golfer, he won the Optimist International Junior Tournament six times. He first won the tournament as an 8-year-old against 9- and 10-year-old competitors. At the age of 15, he won his first of three U.S. Junior Amateur titles and became the title's youngest winner. The next year, he became the first to win the title a second time. He is the only amateur golfer to win the U.S. Junior Amateur title in three consecutive years, 1991, 1992, and 1993. Despite his amateur status, he also regularly competed in professional tournaments. His debut at a professional tournament came in 1992, when he entered the Nissan Los Angeles Open as a 16-year-old. He entered three PGA Tour events in 1993, and in 1994 tied for thirty-fourth place at the Johnny Walker Asian Classic in Thailand.

Woods continued his amateur career as a college student. He played at Stanford University, where he majored in economics. He soon won the William Tucker Invitational, his first collegiate event. He was named Stanford's Male Freshman Athlete of the Year. He was also voted Pac-10 Player of the Year and named a National Collegiate Athletic Association (NCAA) First Team All-American. In two years at Stanford, he won 10 collegiate events, including the NCAA title as a sophomore.

After completing his second year of college, Woods entered major championship play. He entered the Masters and British Open in 1995. The only amateur to make the cut for the Masters that year, Woods tied tying for forty-first place overall. A year later, he finished eighty-second at the U.S. Open and improved to twenty-second place at the British Open by tying the amateur record with a score of 281. His career as an amateur golfer brought him numerous awards and much acclaim. He was named *Golf Digest* Player of the Year in 1991 and 1992, *Golf World* Player of the Year in 1992 and 1993, *Golfweek* National Amateur of the Year in 1992, and *Golf World* Man of the Year in 1994, and he received the Fred Haskins and Jack Nicklaus College Player of the Year awards in 1996.

One week after winning his third U.S. amateur title in 1996, Woods began his career as a professional golfer. He entered the Greater Milwaukee Open on August 27, 1996. In his rookie season, Woods won the Las Vegas Invitational and the Walt Disney World/Oldsmobile Classic and qualified for the Tour Championship. He also finished twenty-fifth on the year's money list, earning a total of $790,594, or $940,420 including international tournaments. *Sports Illustrated* named him Sportsman of the Year in 1996 to honor his rookie season and commemorate the hype surrounding his entrance into professional golf. He began 1997 well, beating Tom Lehman in a playoff to win the season-opening Mercedes Championship.

Woods won the 1997 Masters Tournament, becoming the first champion of the tournament of either African or Asian heritage. He won by a record margin of 12 strokes and was the youngest Masters champion ever at age 21. His achievement was all the more remarkable given the tournament's history on race. The Masters tournament did not include a black player until 1975, and the Augusta National Golf Club, which hosts the Masters Tournament every year, did not admit a black member until 1990. Woods knew this history and paid tribute to those who had paved the way for his entrance into golf. He recognized that while he may have been the first African American golfer to win the tournament, he owed a debt to others whom he identified as pioneers of the sport, including Charlie Sifford, Lee Elder, and Teddy Rhodes. These pioneers in turn praised Woods's success. Elder believed that Woods's victory was meaningful for minorities and thought it would have an impact on the future of golf. Sifford felt that Woods's win was wonderful for golf regardless of the emerging athlete's race. Sports commentators including Paul Delany also considered Woods's decision to recognize his predecessors as important. Delany argued that the young golfer understood that he was not the first athlete to ever perform, and realized that he was one of many golfers who played the game. Delaney compared the golfer favorably to Jackie Robinson, but noted that whites would not receive Woods as poorly as they had received Robinson.

Some believed that Woods's tribute to his predecessors was inadequate, however. He did not participate in a celebration of the fiftieth anniversary of Jackie Robinson's integration of baseball, which took place shortly after the Masters Tournament victory. Invited to appear at the Shea Stadium extravaganza in Robinson's honor, the golfer declined the trip, which included a private helicopter from former President Bill Clinton. He had already made plans to head to Mexico with college friends. His decision to not attend the event disappointed many; some suggested that it belied his claims to honor older black athletes who had made his career possible. Sports fans and commentators had wanted to witness the spectacle of the new legend of golf paying tribute to the old legend of baseball.

The timing of Woods's victory with Robinson's anniversary added to the national discussion of race and ethnicity. Many sports fans saw the color of Woods's skin and considered him black, though the golfer does not identity himself black. Reporters described him as an African American golfer and wondered about the impact of his victory on minority access to the sport of golf. Others compared the significance of his barrier-breaking victory to Robinson's career from a half century earlier.

The media and devotees of the sport paid strict attention to Woods's ethnic makeup following his victory in the 1997 Masters Tournament. Hate mail awaited his return to the clubhouse the first time he played the Augusta course. Newspapers quoted one letter addressed to the golfer, "Just what we don't need another nigger in sports." Though Woods is of mixed parentage, the media, Nike, and most sport fans described him as a black golfer. Only a year earlier, Woods had argued that his racial identity should not matter. Regardless of his race, he was American. Few seemed to share this belief that his racial identity didn't matter, though some did not focus on identity solely so they could send the golfer hate mail. One reporter, who described Woods as "African-Asian-Native-American," credited his multicultural heritage with his ability to bring new fans to a sport that previously interested few. Woods's victory was seen as a breakthrough in the traditionally white sport.

Woods's peers also focused on his race. Fellow golfer Fuzzy Zoeller made remarks in an interview that were widely interpreted as racist, though he maintained that he was joking. In a CNN interview, Zoeller referred to Woods as a "little boy" and then asked him not to request fried chicken and collard greens at next year's Champions Dinner at the Augusta National Club. Zoeller's comments cost him a contract with Kmart as the company's golf spokesman. He faced criticism in the press and even dropped out of the Greater Greensboro Classic to restore his image.

Woods's Masters Tournament victory and Zoeller's remarks occurred during the fiftieth anniversary celebration of Jackie Robinson's integration of baseball. This timing was both ironic and compelling. It forced Americans, many of whom are otherwise silent in the discussion or even the contemplation of skin color, to become aware of race. Zoeller's remarks did not occur in isolation but were the latest in a string of comments made by public figures in sports. A month earlier, New Jersey Nets coach John Calipari called a reporter a "Mexican idiot." In addition, David Halberstam, a Miami Heat radio announcer, made a bizarre connection between basketball and Thomas Jefferson's slaves just prior to Zoeller's CNN interview. These comments sustained a pattern of racism in U.S. sports, despite the victories achieved by Woods and other athletes.

Shortly after Woods's triumph, the young golfer starred in a controversial Nike commercial that introduced the element of race to American sport fans in a way no other commercial endorsement had done before. In the ad, Woods explained, "There are still golf courses in the United States that I cannot play because of the color of my skin. I'm told that I'm not ready for you. Are you ready for me?" Responses to the ad were varied, but many disliked the commercial since it attempted to sell something more than footwear. The loudest critiques suggested that it struck a nerve and left some, particularly those who play golf, feeling threatened. Reporters mocked the ad, correctly reporting that Woods could probably play on any course he wanted. Others noted that while he could play on any course, most people who looked like him could not; this lack of access was the crux of the whole commercial. Woods bravely spoke out on a social issue, taking an action that most contemporary athletes

*There are still golf courses in the United States that I cannot play because of the color of my skin. I'm told that I'm not ready for you. Are you ready for me?*

avoid in fear of losing their jobs and endorsement contracts. He liked Nike's ads and said that they made people think. Nike and Woods both faced criticism for the ad, however. Nike was accused of using Woods to sell its products, specifically golf gear, to African Americans. The athlete's first attempt to engage in serious dialogue by bringing up an issue worthy of discussion resulted in chastisement from reporters and sport fans.

Fellow golfers also responded negatively to the Nike ad. Vijay Singh, dark-skinned and of Indian descent, did not support Woods's decision to identify skin color as an issue in golf. Singh recalled that when he first started playing tournaments in the United States, reporters tried to make an issue of his skin color; he believes that he did not allow them to do so, however. He instead explained that he simply wished to play golf. Singh did not view himself as colored but as a foreigner. He told reporters to stop commenting on his race, and instead view him only as a "foreigner." African American sports reporter William Rhoden rightly noted that Woods did not have the luxury of a foreign identity. He also recognized that though Woods initially identified as African and Asian, "when lucrative advertising dollars met reality, dollars triumphed" and the golfer focused upon his African American heritage. Rhoden thought Nike played up Woods's black roots with advertisements discussing race and segregation. Singh resented Woods's emphasis on race as the latter golfer established himself in the endorsement and professional golf scenes. Singh focused instead upon talent and meritocracy, saying that the media should pay attention to Woods's athletic abilities rather than to his racial identity.

The Nike commercial and the controversy surrounding it did not hurt Woods's popularity. The young golfer was named the second most popular American in 1997 by an NBC poll, placing behind only General Colin Powell and just ahead of world-famous Michael Jordan. All three African Americans were identified as more popular than political leaders, including the president. Notably, the three most popular Americans were African Americans, and two of the three were also male athletes.

Still, others could not help but notice the wide impact the young golfer had on black and white, young and old, male and female. Like Michael Jordan, Woods was a "black" athlete who transcended race. One journalist noted that he was "accepted by Blacks as a brother and by Whites as a lot more than that." The golfer's multicultural background was part of a growing trend in the United States in which individuals identify as biracial; in the past, these same individuals would have been labeled "black." Woods still had an impact on African Americans, however. In the United States, the athlete was "quite clearly black." John Merchant, CEO of the National Minority Golf Association, predicted that black kids' awareness of golf would quadruple by the time Woods turned 30.

The icon's success, which has had a lasting influence on numerous fans, did not develop by accident. Earl Woods, who was visible in his son's amateur career and Masters victory, had engineered the young golfer's career for decades. The father knew that his son's racial makeup was different from that of golfers of the past, but he also understood that his son's mindset was different. He described his son as "the first intuitive golfer," and argued that Woods was so successful at the sport because he played it from early childhood. Woods's career rose in the midst of the Nike ad controversy and continued discussions about his racial identity. Including his Masters victory, he won four PGA Tour events in 1997. He was also awarded the Arnold Palmer Award, which is given to the Tour's leading money earner, for winning a record $2,066,833. On June 15, 1997, in his forty-second week as a professional, Woods became the youngest golfer to climb the ranks to the position of number 1 on the Official World Golf Ranking at the age of 21.

Woods continued to find success on the golf course over the next several years. He won the Bell South Classic, a PGA Tour event, the Johnnie Walker Classic, and the PGA Grand Slam of Golf in 1998. His successes at these tournaments earned him a total of $2,927,005. A year later, Woods established his dominance on golf courses around the world, winning eight PGA Tour tournaments (including the Buick Invitational, Memorial Tournament, Motorola Western Open, WGC-NEC Invitational, National Car Rental Golf Classic/Disney, the Tour Championship, WGC-American Express Championship), including one major, the PGA Championship. His record earnings in 1999 totaled $6,615,585, nearly $3 million more than runner-up David Duval's earnings. Woods's eight PGA victories were the most won in a single year by an individual since 1974, when Johnny Miller won eight as well. The icon won six tournaments in a streak of consecutive victories between 1999 and 2000. Two of these wins were suspenseful surprises in which Woods won despite being several strokes behind during part of the tournament. Such comebacks contributed to his growing reputation as a tough competitor. He won nine more tournaments in 2000, including three majors, the U.S. Open, the British Open, and the PGA Championship. His nine wins in 2000 earned him another record; this total was the fifth highest number of victories in one year and the most a golfer had won in one year since 1950, when Sam Snead won 11. Woods also matched Ben Hogan's record, set in 1953, of winning three professional major championships in the same year. The young icon became the first golfer to win the PGA Championship two years in a row since 1937. When he won the British Open in 2000, he became only the fifth golfer to complete the career Grand Slam, which means that he had won each major once. This amazing accomplishment placed him among golfing greats Ben Hogan, Gene Sarazen, Gary Player, and Jack Nicklaus. The 2000 season was another record-breaking year at the bank for Woods, who won $9,188,321 on the PGA Tour and a total of $11,034,530 worldwide. He also teamed with Duval to win the World Cup team title for the United States. Closing out a successful year, Woods won the World Sportsman of the Year award at the Laureus World Sports Awards and became the first two-time winner of *Sports Illustrated*'s Sportsman of the Year award.

Woods followed his successful 2000 campaign with an encore performance in 2001. He won five PGA Tour events and eight international tournaments. He became the first golfer to ever hold all four major titles at once when he won the Masters in 2001. This achievement has since become known as the Tiger Slam. He was also victorious at the Bay Hill Invitational, the Players Championship, Memorial Tournament, and WGC-NEC Invitational. In 2002, for the fourth consecutive year, he was at the top of the PGA money list, winning $6,912,625 on the tour through five victories, including two majors, and more than $1 million through seven international wins.

Woods's dominance on the golf course often discouraged his competitors. At times, he seemed unbeatable. Some courses even lengthened the distances of their courses as a means of "Tiger proofing." Journalists suggested that his abilities were bad for the sport. His long drives were of such concern to tournament directors that courses, including Augusta, added yardage to their tees in an effort to slow him down. Woods began to play fewer tournaments a year, limiting himself to between 20 and 23 tournaments and working to peak at the major championship events. Still, he revealed weaknesses in his game and experienced periodic slumps. He failed to win a major in either 2003 or 2004, although he only fell to second on the money list in 2003 and to fourth in 2004. In September 2004, Woods lost his number one ranking, after holding it for a record 264 consecutive weeks, to rival Vijay Singh.

This lag did not by any means signify an end to Woods's career. The golfer described this time as one in which he focused on changing his game and working on his swing. He expected that soon he would return to top form. He also changed his driver, switching to a titanium clubhead and graphite shaft. He hired a new coach, ending his relationship with Butch Harmon and working instead with Hank Haney. Others suspected that he was distracted by his October 2004 marriage to Elin Nordegren and their $1.5 million wedding ceremony in Barbados. He met Nordegren, a Swedish model, through Swedish golfer Jesper Parnevik when she worked as a nanny for his children. When asked how he thought marriage would affect his golf game, Woods suggested that his talent would improve.

Woods seemed to get back to his winning ways in 2005. That year, he beat Phil Mickelson to win the Ford Championship and reclaimed his number one ranking. He won his third Masters title, his first major win in two years, in April 2005. His victory at the Masters was a dramatic playoff that solidified his number one position. He traded this ranking back and forth with Singh for weeks until July, when he won his second major of the year and the tenth of his career at the British Open. He went on to win six additional PGA Tour events in 2005 and topped the money list once again.

Woods holds many records. He is currently second on the list of major victories on the PGA Tour, behind Jack Nicklaus. He won each major at least twice, which is also a record he shares with Nicklaus; he holds four Masters titles, three British Open titles, and three PGA Championship titles. He has 18 top five finishes and 22 top 10 finishes. He won the Associated Press Male Athlete of the Year award in 1997, 1999, and 2000, joining Michael Jordan as the only two three-time winners. ESPN selected him as Male Athlete of the Year in 1997, 1999, and 2000. He was also selected by the PGA Tour, the PGA of America, and the Golf Writers Association of America as the Player of the Year in 1997, 1999, 2000, 2001, and 2003. He holds the record for the lowest 72-hole score in relation to par in two of the majors and shares the record in the other two majors. For the Masters, his –18 (270) in 1997 earned him the outright to-par and low 72-holes record. He shares the U.S. Open low 72-holes record of –12 (272), which he accomplished in 2000, with Jack Nicklaus, Lee Janzen, and Jim Furyk and owns the outright record. At the British Open, Woods's 2000 score of –19 (269) gave him the outright to-par record, and he shares the low 72-holes record with Greg Norman. He shares the to-par record with Bob May at the PGA Championship, where he scored –18 (270) in 2000, also giving him a share of the low 72-holes record with David Toms. His performances earned him two additional records for victory margin at the Masters, which he won by 12 strokes in 1997, and the U.S. Open, which he won in 2000 by 15 strokes. This U.S. Open victory set a record margin for all four of the majors and broke a record no one had touched since 1862.

Consistency has always been one of Woods's strengths. At the 2003 Tour Championship, he set a record for the most consecutive cuts made at 114, passing Byron Nelson. He extended his record to 142 cuts before missing the cut at the EDS Byron Nelson Championship. Along with owning the lowest career scoring average in PGA Tour history, he has the most career earnings of any golfer in PGA history. He is the only currently active golfer among the top 20 major champion winners and has more victories on the PGA Tour than any other active golfer.

Though Woods is the career money leader on the PGA Tour, he earns additional income from his various endorsements deals. In fact, he earns more every year from his endorsements with Nike, General Motors, General Mills, Accenture, and American Express than he does from playing golf. In 2005, *Forbes* magazine listed Woods as the highest-earning professional athlete, given his annual income of $87 million. His five-year $100 million contract with Nike was the largest endorsement deal made by any athlete at the time of his signing. Nike was especially active in marketing the golfer in a number of popular television commercials. One campaign, titled "I am Tiger Woods," showed children of all racial and ethnic groups claiming to be Tiger Woods. Another advertisement featured the icon doing a golf club trick where he

*From early childhood I dreamed of being the world's best golfer. I worked hard and applied my family's values to everything I did. Integrity, honesty, discipline, responsibility and fun; I learned these values at home and in school, each one pushing me further toward my dream. . . . As a result, I've learned that success on the course was only part of what I wanted to achieve. In 1996, my father and I established the Tiger Woods Foundation to inspire dreams in America's youth because I believe in passing on the values I received from my parents and teachers.*

bounced the golf ball on his club over and over. After his father's death, Nike created a Father's Day advertisement featuring home movie footage of Woods and his dad on the golf course. The company dedicated the commercial to Earl Woods and fathers around the world. Woods's endorsements have brought him both money and greater fame. Golfer Arnold Palmer and NBA star Michael Jordan are the only two athletes to have made more money from endorsements.

Woods contributes much of his money to charitable foundations. He specifically gives to one organization that is very personal to the young golfer. With the help of his father, he created the Tiger Woods Foundation after turning professional. The foundation offers programs including golf clinics for disadvantaged youth, scholarship programs, and the Start Something character development program. Woods's philosophy for the foundation connects his youth to the experiences of those his organization helps.

In February 2006, Woods christened the new Tiger Woods Learning Center in Anaheim, California. The center provides a day program for fourth- through sixth-graders, as well as an after-school program for middle school students. At the opening ceremonies for the center, political figures including Bill Clinton and California First Lady Maria Shriver praised Woods's effort and the education facility. He also works with the Target World Challenge, a charity golf tournament, the Tiger Woods Foundation National Junior Golf Team, and the Tiger Jam, a fundraising concert.

Woods has already established himself, at the relatively early age of 30, as one of history's greatest golfers. His impact on the game has been immeasurable. Thanks to him, young children pick up golf clubs, new fans come to watch tournaments, and competitors are challenged to be better athletes. When *Sports Illustrated* named him their Sportsman of the Year in 1996, the athlete's father said that his son was "qualified through his ethnicity to do more than any other man in history to change the course of humanity." Woods's mother was in agreement with her husband, noting that her son's multiethnic ancestry made him a universal child who could hold everyone together. Woods's parents were not shy about recognizing the gifts of their child, and believed that his greatness in golf will extend into the rest of society. While he has already established himself as one of the greatest golfers, his legacy in society remains to be seen. At this writing, Tiger Woods seems poised to continue as a dominant athlete for years to come. He remains a generous philanthropist and thoughtful citizen of the world.

## FURTHER READING

Andrisani, John. *The Tiger Woods Way: An Analysis of Tiger Woods' Power-Swing Technique.* New York: Three Rivers Press, 1990.

Bonk, Thomas. "The Driving Force of Tiger Woods," *Los Angeles Times* (August 29, 1996).

Delaney, Paul. "Rooting for What Really Mattered," *New York Times* (April 20, 1997).

Dorman, Larry. "'We'll Be Right Back, after This Hip and Distorted Commercial Break,'" *New York Times* (September 1, 1996).

Dorman, Larry. "Woods Tears up Augusta and Tears down Barriers," *New York Times* (April 14 1997): C7.

Lapchick, Richard E. "Lessons of Tiger Woods Will Not Be Easy Ones," *New York Times* (May 18 1997): S9.

Rhoden, William C. "What If Color Were a Choice?" *New York Times* (August 16, 1997): 37.

Rosaforte, Tim. *Raising the Bar: The Championship Years of Tiger Woods.* Canbury, NJ: Bedford St. Martin's Press, 2000.

Sandomir, Richard. "Zoeller Learns Race Remarks Carry a Price," *New York Times* (April 24, 1997): C29.

"Tiger Woods' Triumph," *Washington Post* (April 15, 1997): A18.

# Selected Bibliography

Aasang, Nathan. *Florence Griffith Joyner: Dazzling Olympian*. Minneapolis: Lerner Publications, 1989.

Ali, Muhammad, and Richard Durham. *The Greatest: My Own Story*. New York: Random House, 1975.

American Express Magic Johnson 2004 All Star Game Tribute. http://www.nba.com/allstar2004/magic_tribute.

Andrews, D. L., ed. *Michael Jordan, Inc.: Corporate Sport, Media Culture and late Modern America*. Albany: State University of New York Press, 2001.

———. "The Facts of Michael Jordan's Blackness: Excavating a Floating Racial Signifier." *Sociology of Sport Journal* 13:2 (1996): 125–158.

Andrisani, John. *The Tiger Woods Way: An Analysis of Tiger Woods' Power-Swing Technique*. New York: Three Rivers Press, 1990.

Ardell, Jean Hastings. "Baseball Annies, Jack Johnson, and Kenesaw Mountain Landis: How Groupies Influenced the Lengthy Ban on Blacks in Organized Baseball." *Nine* (Spring 2005): 103.

Ashe, Arthur R., Jr. *A Hard Road to Glory: A History of the African-American Athlete*. New York: Amistad Press, 1988.

Ashe, Arthur R., and Arnold Rampersad. *Days of Grace: A Memoir*. New York: Ballantine Books, 1993.

Ashe, Arthur R., with Frank DeFord. *Arthur Ashe: Portrait in Motion*. Boston: Houghton Mifflin Company, 1975.

Ashe, Arthur R., with Alexander McNab. *Arthur Ashe on Tennis*. London: Aurum Press, 1995.

Ashe, Arthur R., with Neil Amdur. *Off the Court*. New York: New American Library, 1981.

Bak, Richard. *Joe Louis: the Great Black Hope*. New York: Da Capo Press, 1998.

Baker, William J. *Jesse Owens: An American Life*. New York: Free Press, 1986.

Barkley, Charles. *I May Be Wrong but I Doubt It*. New York: Random House, 2003.

———. *Outrageous!* New York: Random House, 1994.

———. *Sir Charles: The Wit and Wisdom of Charles Barkley*. New York: Warner Books, 1994.

———. *Who's Afraid of a Large Black Man?* New York: Penguin Press, 2005.

Beard, Hilary, Venus Williams, and Serena Williams. *Venus and Serena: Serving from the Hip: 10 Rules for Living, Loving, and Winning.* Boston: Houghton Mifflin, 2005.

Bingham, Howard L., and Max Wallace. *Muhammad Ali's Greatest Fight: Cassius Clay vs. The United States of America.* New York: M. Evans, 2000.

Biography. *The Harlem Globetrotters: America's Court Jesters.* A&E Television Networks, 2005.

Biracree, Tom. *Althea Gibson.* New York: Chelsea House Publishers, 1989.

Bloom, Barry M. "Bonds Reflects on'01, Dad's Influence," October 5, 2005, MLB .com, http://barrybonds.mlb.com/NASApp/mlb/news/article.jsp?ymd=20051004 &content_id=1237223&vkey=news_sf&fext=.jsp&c_id=sf (accessed August 1, 2006).

Bogle, Donald. *Toms, Coons, Mulattoes, Mammies, and Bucks: An Interpretive History of Blacks in American Films.* New York: Continuum, 2001.

Bonk, Thomas. "The Driving Force of Tiger Woods," *Los Angeles Times* (August 29, 1996).

Boskin, Joseph. *Sambo: The Rise & Demise of an American Jester.* Oxford: Oxford University Press, 1988.

Brashler, William. *Josh Gibson: A Life in the Negro Leagues.* New York: Harper and Row, 1978.

Brown, Jim, with Myron Cope. *Off My Chest.* New York: Double Day, 1964.

Brown, Jim, with Steve Delsohn. *Out of Bounds.* New York: Kensington Publishing, 1989.

Brunt, Stephen. *Facing Ali: 15 Fighters, 15 Stories.* New York: Lions Press, 2002.

Cahn, Susan K. *Coming on Strong: Gender and Sexuality in Twentieth-Century Women's Sport.* New York: Free Press, 1994.

Capeci, Dominic J., and Martha Wilkerson. "Multifarious Hero: Joe Louis, American Society and Race Relations during World Crisis, 1935–1945." *Journal of Sport History* 10:3 (Winter 1983): 5–25.

Chadwin, Dean. *Those Damn Yankees: The Secret Life of America's Greatest Franchise.* New York and London: Verso, 2000.

Chamberlain, Wilton Norman. *A View from Above.* New York: Random House, 1991.

———. *Wilt: Just Like Any Other 7-Foot Black Millionaire Who Lives Next Door.* New York: Macmillan, 1973.

Cherry, Robert. *Wilt: Larger than Life.* Chicago: Triumph Books, 2004.

Christgau, John. *Tricksters in the Madhouse: Lakers vs Globetrotters, 1948.* Lincoln: University of Nebraska Press, 2004.

CNN, "Arthur Ashe," CNN/SI, http://sportsillustrated.cnn.com/tennis/features/1997/ arthurashe/biography.html (accessed October 5, 2006).

Davidson, Sue. *Changing the Game: The Stories of Tennis Champions Alice Marble and Althea Gibson.* Seattle: Seal Press, 1997.

Davis, Michael D. *Black American Women in Olympic Track and Field.* Jefferson, NC: McFarland, 1992.

Davis, O.K. *Grambling's Gridiron Glory: Eddie Robinson and the Tigers' Success Story.* Ruston, LA: M & M Printing, 1983.

Deardorff, Donald, II. "World Boxing Champion Jack Johnson, Contemptuous and Irritating, Taunted Whites." *St. Louis Journalism Review* 8:3 (October 1995).

Delaney, Paul. "Rooting for What Really Mattered," *New York Times* (April 20, 1997).

Donaldson, Madeline. *Venus and Serena Williams*. New York: First Avenue Editions, 2003.

Dorman, Larry. "We'll Be Right Back, after This Hip and Distorted Commercial Break," *New York Times* (September 1, 1996).

———. "Woods Tears up Augusta and Tears down Barriers," *New York Times* (April 14 1997): C7.

Drake, Dick. "Tommie Smith & Lee Evans Discuss Potential Olympic Boycott." *Track & Field News* (November 1967). http://www.trackandfieldnews.com/display_ article.php?id=1605 (accessed March 27, 2007).

Du Bois, W. E. B. *The Souls of Black Folk*. New York: Knopf, 1903.

Dyson, Michael Eric. "Be Like Mike?: Michael Jordan and the Pedagogy of Desire." *Cultural Studies* 7:1 (1993): 64–72.

Early, Gerald, ed. *The Muhammad Ali Reader*. Hopewell, NJ: Ecco Press, 1998.

Edwards, Harry. *The Struggle That Must Be: An Autobiography*. New York: Macmillan, 1980.

Eichhorn, Dennis. *Shaq*. Seattle: Turman Publishing, 1995.

ESPN. "Author Ashe." ESPN Sportcentury, ESPN Classic (February 2001).

Euchner, Charles. *The Last Nine Innings*. Napierville, IL: Sourcebooks, 2006.

Evans, Art. "Joe Louis as a Key Functionary: White Reactions towards a Black Champion." *Journal of Black Studies* 16:1 (September 1985): 95–111.

Fainaru-Wada, Mark. "The Truth: Barry Bonds and Steroids," *Sports Illustrated* (March 13, 2006).

Fainaru-Wada, Mark, and Lance Williams. *Games of Shadows: Barry Bonds, BALCO, and the Steroids Scandal that Rocked Professional Sports*. New York: Gotham, 2006.

Festle, Mary Jo. *Playing Nice: Politics and Apologies in Women's Sports*. New York: Columbia University Press, 1996.

Foreman, George, and Joel Engel. *By George: The Autobiography of George Foreman*. New York: Villard Books, 1995.

Freeman, Mike. *Jim Brown: The Fierce Life of an American Hero*. New York: William Morrow, 2006.

Gates, Henry Louis, Jr., and Evelyn Brooks Higginbotham, eds. "Jim Brown." In *African American Lives*. New York: Oxford University Press, 2004, pp. 115–116.

Gibson, Althea, and Richard Curtis. *So Much to Live For*. New York: G. P. Putnam's Sons, 1968.

Gibson, Althea, and Ed Fitzgerald. *I Always Wanted to Be Somebody*. New York: Harper & Brothers, 1958.

Gilmore, Al-Tony. "Jack Johnson and White Women: The National Impact." *Journal of Negro History* 58:1 (January 1973): 18–38.

Gray, Frances Clayton, and Yanick Rice Lamb. *Born to Win: The Authorized Biography of Althea Gibson*. Hoboken, NJ: Wiley, 2004.

Green, Ben. *Spinning the Globe: The Rise, Fall, and Return to Greatness of the Harlem Globetrotters*. New York: Amistad, 2005.

Griffith Joyner, Florence. *Running for Dummies*. Foster City, CA: IDG Books, 1999.

Halberstam, David. *Playing for Keeps: Michael Jordan and the World He Made*. New York: Random House, 1999.

Hamrahi, Joe, with Bill James. "Being Barry Bonds." *Baseball Digest* (May 29, 2006).

Hanes, Bailey. *Bill Picket, Bulldogger: The Biography of a Black Cowboy.* Norman: University of Oklahoma Press, 1977.

Hartmann, Douglas. *Race, Culture, and the Revolt of the Black Athlete: The 1968 Olympic Protests and Their Aftermath.* Chicago: University of Chicago Press, 2003.

Hatch, Robert, and William Hatch. "Florence Griffith Joyner." *The Hero Project: How We Met Our Greatest Heroes; Two Teens, One Notebook, Thirteen Extraordinary Interviews.* New York: McGraw-Hill, 2006.

Hauser, Thomas. *Muhammad Ali: His Life and Times.* New York: Simon and Schuster, 1991.

Hietala, Thomas R. *The Fight of the Century: Jack Johnson, Joe Louis, and the Struggle for Racial Equality.* Armonk, NY: M.E. Sharpe, 2002.

Himes Gissendanner, Cindy. "African American Women Olympians: The Impact of Race, Gender, and Class Ideologies, 1932–1968." *Research Quarterly for Exercise and Sport* 67 (June 1996): 172–182.

Hodgkinson, Mark. "Serena 'Shocked' by More Racist Abuse," http://www.telegraph.co.uk. (March 4, 2007) (accessed September 10, 2007).

Hoffer, Richard. "Here's to You, Mr. Robinson." *Sports Illustrated* 87 (December 6, 1997): 106–108.

Hogan, Lawrence D. *A Black National News Service: The Associated Negro Press and Claude Barnett, 1919–1945.* Rutherford: Farleigh Dickinson University Press, 1984.

Holway, John. *Black Diamonds: Life in the Negro Leagues from the Men Who Lived It.* West Port, CT: Meckler Publishing, 1989.

———. *Blackball Stars: Negro League Pioneers.* West Port, CT: Meckler Publishing, 1988.

———. *Voices from the Great Black Baseball Leagues.* New York: Da Capo Press, 1992.

Hurd, Michael. "Grambling." *ESPN College Football Encyclopedia.* New York: ESPN, 2005.

Jeter, Derek, with Jack Curry. *The Life You Imagine: Life Lessons for Achieving Your Dreams.* New York: Three Rivers Press, 2000.

Johnson, Cecil. *Guts: Legendary Black Rodeo Cowboy Bill Pickett.* Ft. Worth, TX: Summit Group, 1994.

Johnson, Earvin "Magic," with William Novak. *My Life.* New York: Random House, 1992.

Johnson, Jack. *In the Ring and Out.* Chicago: National Sports Publishing Company, 1927.

Jordan, Michael, and David Halberstam. *Driven from Within.* New York: Atria, 2006.

Jordan, Michael, and W. Iooss. *Rare Air: Michael on Michael.* New York: Harper Collins, 1993.

Kline, Johnny. *Never Lose: From Globetrotter to Addict to Ph.D.: An Autobiography.* New York: Papa Joe's Book Company, 1996.

Knight, Athelia. "Track Star Griffith Joyner Dies at 38." *Washington Post Company,* 1998. http://www.mmjp.or.jp/amlang.atc/di&legends/flojo/aboutflojo.htm (accessed October 28, 2006).

Koral, April. *Florence Griffith Joyner: Track and Field Star*. New York: F. Watts, 1992.

Kuska, Bob. *Hot Potato: How Washington and New York Gave Birth to Black Basketball and Changed America's Game Forever*. Charlottesville: University of Virginia Press, 2004.

Lansbury, Jennifer H. "The Tuskegee Flash and the Slender Harlem Stroker: Black Women Athletes on the Margin." *Journal of Sport History* 28:2 (Summer 2001): 233–252.

Lapchick, Richard E. "Lessons of Tiger Woods Will Not Be Easy Ones," *New York Times* (May 18, 1997): S9.

Lauderdale, Pat. "Racism, Racialization and American Indian Sports." In *Native Americans in Sports*, edited by C. Richard King. New York: M.E. Sharpe, 2005: 248–252

Lazenby, Roland. *The Show: The Inside Story of the Spectacular Los Angeles Lakers in the Words of Those Who Lived It*. New York: McGraw-Hill, 2005.

Lee, Spike. *Jim Brown: All-American*. Home Box Office, Inc., 2004.

———. *That's My Story and I'm Sticking to It (as told to Kaleem Aftab)*. New York: W.W. Norton, 2006.

Lewis, Dwight, and Susan Thomas. A *Will to Win*. Mt. Juliet, TN: Cumberland Press, 1983.

"Little Sister, Big Hit: Williams Family Surprise—Serena Williams Wins the U.S. Open," *Sports Illustrated* (September 20, 1999).

Lois, George, ed. *Ali Rap: Muhammad Ali, The First Heavy Weight Champion of Rap*. New York: ESPN Books, 2006.

Louis, Joe. *Joe Louis, My Life*. New York: Harcourt Brace Jovanovich, 1997.

MacAloon, John J. *This Great Symbol: Pierre de Coubertin and the Origins of the Modern Olympic Games*. Chicago: University of Chicago Press, 1981.

Maese, Rick. "A Courageous Act of Defiance," *Montreal Gazette* (August 20, 2004): C4+.

Mailer, Norman. *The Fight*. New York: Vintage, 1997.

Maiorana, Sal. *A Lifetime of Yankee Octobers*. Chelsea, MI: Sleeping Bear Press, 2002.

Mandell, Richard D. *The Nazi Olympics*. Urbana: University of Illinois Press, 1987.

Margolick, David. *Beyond Glory: Joe Louis vs. Max Schmeling, and a World on the Brink*. New York: Knopf, 2005.

Marqusee, Mike. *Redemption Song: Muhammad Ali and the Spirit of the Sixties*. New York: Verso Books, 2004.

Massey, Sara. *Black Cowboys of Texas*. College Station: Texas A&M University Press, 2000.

McCallum, Jack. "The Desire Is Not There," *Sports Illustrated* 79 (1993): 28–35.

McCoyd, Ed. *To Live and Dream: The Incredible Story of George Foreman*. New York: New Street Publishing, 1997.

McDonald, M. G. "Michael Jordan's Family Values: Marketing, Meaning and Post Reagan America." *Sociology of Sport Journal* 13 (1996): 344–365.

McDonald, M. G., and D. L. Andrews. "Michael Jordan: Corporate Sport and Post-modern Celebrityhood." In *Sport Stars: The Cultural Politics of Sporting Celebrity*, D. L. Andrews and S. J. Jackson, eds. London: Routledge, 2001, pp. 20–35.

McRae, Donald. *Heroes without a Country: America's Betrayal of Joe Louis and Jesse Owens*. New York: HarperCollins, 2002.

McRae, Donald. *In Black and White: The Untold Story of Joe Louis and Jesse Owens*. New York: Simon & Schuster, 1997.

Mead, Chris. *Champion Joe Louis: A Biography*. New York: Scribner's, 1985.

Moore, Kenny. "Getup and Go: Florence Griffith Joyner's Dramatic Garb Made Her a Colorful Blur as She Smashed the World Record in the 100 Meters at the Olympic Trials," *Sports Illustrated* (July 25, 1998). http://sportsillustrated.cnn.com/olympics/features/joyner/flashback2.html (accessed October 14, 2006).

———. "Go, Flo, Go: Florence Griffith Joyner Did Just That in Blazing to Victory in the 100 Meters," *Sports Illustrated* (October 3, 1988). http://sportsillustrated.cnn.com/olympics/features/joyner/flashback3.html (accessed October 14, 2006).

———. "Very Fast, Very Fast: U.S. Sprinter Florence Griffith Joyner Is Certainly Eye-Catching—If, That Is, You Can Catch Her," *Sports Illustrated* (September 14, 1998). http://sportsillustrated.cnn.com/olympics/features/joyner/flashback1.html (accessed October 14, 2006).

Nagel, Rob. "The Joyners." *Epic Lives: One Hundred Black Women Who Made a Difference*. Detroit: Visible Ink Press, 1993.

NBA @ 50 interview with Magic Johnson, http://www.nba.com/history/players/magic_johnson_nba50_pt1.html; http://www.nba.com/history/players/magic_johnson_nba50_pt2.html.

Noden, Merrell. "FloJo Lived Her Life in Fast-Forward," *Sports Illustrated* (September 22, 1998). http://sportsillustrated.cnn.com/olympics/features/joyner/flojo_noden.html (accessed October 14, 2006).

Norment, L. "Michael and Juanita Jordan Talk about Love, Marriage, and Life after Basketball." *Ebony* 47 (November 1991): 68–76.

O'Neal, Shaquille. *Shaq and the Beanstalk and Other Very Tall Tales*. New York: Jump at the Sun, 1999.

———. *Shaq Talks Back: The Uncensored Word on My Life and Winning in the NBA*. New York: St. Martin's Press, 2001.

O'Neal, Shaquille, and Jack McCallum. *ShaqAttaq!: My Rookie Year*. New York: Hyperion Books, 1993.

Onley, Buster. *The Last Night of the Yankee Dynasty*. New York: Ecco, 2004.

Owens, Jesse, with Paul G. Neimark. *Blackthink: My Life as Black Man and White Man*. New York: William Morrow, 1970.

———. *I Have Changed*. New York: William Morrow, 1972.

"Party Crasher: Venus Williams Shakes up Tennis," *Sports Illustrated* (September 15, 1997).

Pearlman, Jeff. *Love Me, Hate Me: Barry Bonds and the Making on an Anti-Hero*. New York: HarperCollins, 2006.

Peterson, Robert W. *Only the Ball Was White*. New York: McGraw-Hill, 1984.

Remnick, David. *King of the World*. New York: Vintage Books, 1998.

Rhoden, William C. *Forty Million Dollar Slaves: The Rise, Fall and Redemption of the Black Athlete*. New York: Random House, 2006.

———. "Robinson: Long Climb to the Top," *New York Times* (September 16, 1985): C1.

———. "What If Color Were a Choice?," *New York Times* (August 16, 1997): 37.

Riley, James A. *The Biographical Encyclopedia of the Negro Baseball Leagues*. New York: Carroll & Graf, 1994.

Robinson, Eddie. "Fifty-Plus Years of Coaching Football." In *Football Coaching Strategies*. Champaign, IL: Human Kinetics, 1995.

Robinson, Eddie, and Richard Lapchick. *Never Before, Never Again: The Stirring Autobiography of Eddie Robinson, the Winningest Coach in the History of College Football*. New York: St. Martin's Press, 1999.

Robinson, Frazier "Slow," and Paul Bauer. *Catching Dreams: My Life in the Negro Baseball Leagues*. Syracuse: Syracuse University Press, 1999.

Rosaforte, Tim. *Raising the Bar: The Championship Years of Tiger Woods*. Canbury, NJ: Bedford St. Martin's Press, 2000.

Ruck, Rob. *Sandlot Seasons: Sport in Black Pittsburgh*. Urbana: University of Illinois Press, 1987.

Rudolph, Wilma, with Martin Ralbovsky. *Wilma: The Story of Wilma Rudolph*. New York: Signet, 1977.

Rurup, Reinhard. *1936 The Olympic Games and National Socialism*, 2nd edition. USZ, Wien: Institute F. Sportwissenschaften, 1996.

Sandomir, Richard. "Zoeller Learns Race Remarks Carry a Price," *New York Times* (April 24, 1997): C29.

Sanford, William, and Carl Green. *Bill Pickett: African-American Rodeo Star*. Springfield, NJ: Enslow Publishers, 1997.

Schafer, A. R. *Serena and Venus Williams*. Kentwood, LA: Edge Books, 2002.

Schoenfeld, Bruce. *The Match: Althea Gibson and Angela Buxton*. New York: HarperCollins Publishers, 2004.

Schwartz, Larry. "Jim Brown Was Hard to Bring Down." Sportscentury Biography. http://espn.go.com/classic/biography/s/Brown_Jim.html (accessed February 10, 2008).

Sears, Edward S. *Running through the Ages*. Jefferson, NC: McFarland, 2001.

"Serena Williams—Awesome: The Next Target the French Open," *Sports Illustrated* (May 28, 2003).

Sharman, Jay, Mike Sear, David Houle, and Mannie Jackson (executive producers). *Harlem Globetrotters: The Team that Changed the World*. Burbank, CA: Warner Bros., 2005.

Sherman, Joel. *Birth of a Dynasty: Behind the Pinstripes with the 1996 Yankees*. New York: Rodale, 2006.

Sklaroff, Lauren Rebecca. "Constructing G.I. Joe Louis: Cultural Solutions to the 'Negro Problem' during World War II." *Journal of American History* 89:3 (December 2002): 958–983.

Smith, Maureen. *Wilma Rudolph: A Biography*. Westport, CT: Greenwood Press, 2006.

Smith, Tommie, with David Steele. *Silent Gesture: The Autobiography of Tommie Smith*. Philadelphia: Temple University Press, 2007.

Stout, Glenn, and Richard A. Johnson. *Yankees Century*. Boston and New York: Houghton Mifflin, 2002.

Sullivan, Michael J. *Sports Great Shaquille O'Neal*. Berkeley Heights, NJ: Enslow Publishers, 1998.

Thomas, Ron. *They Cleared the Lane: The NBA's Black Pioneers*. Lincoln: University of Nebraska Press, 2002.

Taylor, Phil. "Unstoppable," *Sports Illustrated* (June 4, 2001).

"This Week in Black History." *Jet* 106:23 (December 6, 2004): 19.

"Tiger Woods' Triumph," *Washington Post* (April 15, 1997): A18.

Ungs, Tim. *Shaquille O'Neal.* New York: Chelsea House Publishers, 1996.

Ward, Geoffrey. *Unforgivable Blackness: The Rise and Fall of Jack Johnson.* New York: Norton, 2004.

Washington, Booker T. "Atlanta Exposition Address." Atlanta Cotton States and International Exposition. September 18, 1895.

Zirin, Dave. "The Living Legacy of Mexico City: An Interview with John Carlos." *Counterpunch* (November 1/2, 2003). http://www.counterpunch.org/zirin 11012003.html (accessed March 14, 2007).

———. *What's My Name, Fool? Sports and Resistance in the United States.* Chicago: Haymarket Books, 2005.

# About the Editor and Contributors

**Matthew C. Whitaker**, the editor, is Associate Professor of History at Arizona State University–Tempe. He is also an affiliate faculty in African and African American Studies and the School of Justice and Social Inquiry at ASU. He specializes in American history, African American history, the African Diaspora, civil and human rights, sports history, popular culture, and the American West. He is a member of the International Advisory Board of the Muhammad Ali Center in Louisville, Kentucky, and the author of *Race Work: The Rise of Civil Rights in the Urban West* (University of Nebraska Press). He is also the author of the forthcoming *Over Jordan: A History of African Americans in the Twentieth Century* (Harlan Davidson) and coeditor of *Hurricane Katrina: America's Unnatural Disaster* (University of Nebraska).

**Scott Bowman** is currently Assistant Professor of Criminal Justice at Texas State University–San Marcos. He earned a Ph.D. in Justice and Social Inquiry, an M.S. in Justice and Social Inquiry, a B.A. in Psychology, and a B.S. in Justice Studies from Arizona State University. With an educational background from an interdisciplinary department, he holds diverse interests and affiliations in the fields of sociology and criminology. He is currently preparing forthcoming publications on the topics of the ritual of Southern lynchings, African American middle-class wealth and asset attainment, and the African American construction of the police function.

**James R. Coates** is Associate Professor of Education at the University of Wisconsin–Green Bay, where he has also served as a diversity liaison to the UW-Green Bay Athletic Department. He specializes in American sports history, African American sports history, coaching, African American history, culture, and multicultural education.

**Brian S. Collier** is Assistant Professor of History at Grand Valley State University in Allendale, Michigan. He is completing a book titled *Steve Gachupin: Native American Runner and King of the Mountain*. He specializes in indigenous history, the history of education, and the intersection of race, class, gender, and religion in American history.

**Pero Gaglo Dagbovie** is Assistant Professor of History at Michigan State University. He specializes in American history and African American history and life. His articles include "Black Women, Carter G. Woodson, and the Association for the Study of Negro Life and History, 1915–1950" (*Journal of African American History*), and his recently published book is *The Early Black History Movement, Carter G. Woodson, and Lorenzo Johnston Greene* (University of Illinois Press). His forthcoming books include *African Americans and the Clinton Presidency: The Need for a Third Reconstruction*, with Darlene Clark Hine (University of Illinois Press).

**Megan Falater** earned her Bachelor of Arts in History from Arizona State University and will begin graduate studies in history in Fall 2008. She also works as a freelance copyeditor and independent historian. She has presented a number of papers and participated in various panels and roundtable discussions at critical religious symposia and professional historical conferences in the United States. Her research interests emphasize race, gender, and religion in United States.

**Elyssa Ford** is a Ph.D. student in the Department of History at Arizona State University where she also earned an M.A. in History and a certificate in Museum Studies. She has worked at museums in Maryland, Texas, and Arizona and has been involved in numerous public history projects, including the Arizona Women's Heritage Trail and the Eastland County Oral History Project. Her research looks at race, gender, and identity in the American rodeo.

**Delano Greenidge-Copprue** is currently teaching at Columbia University, Fordham University, and the Manhattan School of Music. He is writing a novel about baseball and jazz, along with a nonfiction narrative that examines leadership and professional football, particularly African American leadership. He completed his undergraduate work in literature at Rutgers College before studying at Columbia University, where he completed two master's degrees and a doctorate. His doctoral thesis examines the jazz cadence of nineteenth- and twentieth-century American literature, from Herman Melville to Toni Morrison. He has published writings on Zora Neale Hurston, Mark Twain, and nineteenth-century African American history.

**Victoria Jackson** holds a master's degree in history from Arizona State University. She specializes in indigenous history, African American history, the history of education, and the intersections of race, class, and gender in United States history. Jackson, a summa cum laude history graduate of the University of North

Carolina—Chapel Hill, is also an accomplished athlete who distinguished herself as a championship runner on the nationally ranked Arizona State University cross country and track and field teams and as a rising star among professional long-distance runners worldwide. A 2006 NCAA national champion at 10,000-meters, Jackson coaches and trains with Arizona State University and plans to continue her studies and writing.

**David J. Johns** is a recent graduate of Columbia University's Teachers College, where he received a Master's Degree in Sociology and Education Policy. Johns, a former fellow with the Congressional Black Caucus, has research interests in black masculine identity, intersections of race, gender, class, socioeconomic status, and education, and critical policy analysis. His most recent articles are encyclopedic entries about Langston Hughes, the Dance Theatre of Harlem, and Kappa Alpha Psi Fraternity (Florida International University Press). He was born in Los Angeles and received his B.A. in English, African American Studies, and Creative Writing from Columbia College, Columbia University.

**Shawn Ladda** is Chairperson and Associate Professor in the Department of Physical Education and Human Performance at Manhattan College located in the Bronx, New York. Prior to teaching at Manhattan College, she taught and coached at Columbia University and the Massachusetts Institute of Technology. Shawn has served on the executive board for the National Association for Girls and Women in Sport and currently is the Chair of the National Pathfinder Award Committee. In addition, she has presented on the state, district, national, and international level on a variety of topics. She has a variety of publications, including writings related to quality physical education, historical pieces, and technology. She earned her B.S. from Penn State, M.S. from Springfield College, and a M.Ed. and Ed.D. at Columbia University, Teacher's College.

**Pat Lauderdale** is Professor of Justice and Social Inquiry and Adjunct Professor of Law at Arizona State University–Tempe. He specializes in the comparative sociology of law—political trials, diversity and deviance, terrorism, world systems, global inequity, social movements, protest, dispute negotiation, Indigenous jurisprudence, and justice theory. He is the author, coauthor, or editor of a number of books, including *Terrorism: A New Testament* (Sage), *Globalization and Post-Apartheid South Africa* (de Sitter), *A Political Analysis of Deviance*, new edition (de Sitter), *Terror and Crisis in the Horn of Africa: Autopsy of Democracy, Human Rights, and Freedom* (Ashgate), and *Terrorism: A New Testament* (de Sitter, 2005) with Annamarie Oliverio.

**Jeremy I. Levitt** is Associate Professor of Law and Director of the Program on International Law and Policy in the Developing World at Florida International College of Law. He is also an affiliate faculty of the Africa New World Studies Program at Florida International University. He teaches international and comparative law, international human rights, and the international law of the use of force and armed conflict. He published a number of articles, authored *The Evolution of Deadly Conflict in Liberia: From "Paternaltarianism" to State Collapse* (Carolina Academic Press) and is the editor of *Africa: Selected Documents on Constitutive, Conflict and Security, Humanitarian, and Judicial Issues* (Transnational Publishers).

**Rita M. Liberti** is Associate Professor of History and Philosophy of Sport in the Department of Kinesiology and Physical Education at California State University–East Bay. She teaches gender and sport, history of sport and physical education, philosophical foundations of sport, and sport in society. Her publications include "Fostering Community Consciousness: Women's Basketball at Black Colleges and Universities, 1900–1950," in Charles Ross (ed.), *Race and Sport in the American South* (University of Mississippi Press) and the forthcoming "Ruth Glover Mullen," in *African American Lives* (Oxford University Press), edited by Henry Louis Gates Jr. and Evelyn Brooks Higginbotham.

**Mary G. McDonald** is Associate Professor of Kinesiology and Health at Miami University in Oxford, Ohio. She is also an affiliate faculty member in Women's Studies at Miami and a former assistant basketball coach at Xavier University in Cincinnati, Ohio, and Indiana University in Bloomington. Her published work includes articles on gender and racial politics in sports, third wave feminism, and the intersections of gender, race, class, and sexuality in sport and American culture. She is the editor (with S. Birrell) of *Reading Sport: Critical Essays on Power and Representation* (Northwestern University Press).

**Susan Rayl** is an Associate Professor in the Department of Kinesiology at the State University of New York at Cortland. She directs the Sport Studies major and teaches courses on the history of sport and physical activity. Her primary research and teaching interests focus on the history of sport. Her research focuses on the African American experience and her forthcoming book on the New York Renaissance professional basketball team will be published by Syracuse University Press.

**Brooks D. Simpson** is Professor of History at Arizona State University–Tempe. Simpson's primary area of expertise is nineteenth-century American political and military history, especially the Civil War and Reconstruction era, and the American presidency. He is also interested in sports history, and the intersections of race, class, and gender in American history. His books include studies of Ulysses S. Grant, Henry Adams, and Reconstruction policy and politics, as well as several documentary editions and shorter works. His publications include *Let Us Have Peace: Ulysses S. Grant and the Politics of War and Reconstruction* (University of North Carolina Press), *Ulysses S. Grant: Triumph over Adversity, 1822–1865* (Houghton Mifflin), and *The Reconstruction Presidents* (University Press of Kansas). Dr. Simpson was assisted by his daughter, **Rebecca Simpson**, as he prepared his chapter on Derek Jeter. Rebecca Simpson is a sports enthusiast and aspiring scholar.

**Maureen Margaret Smith** is a Professor in the Department of Kinesiology and Health Science at California State University–Sacramento. Raised in Norwich, New York, Smith earned her Bachelor of Science and Master of Science degrees in Physical Education from Ithaca College. At Ohio State University, Smith completed a Master of Arts degree in Black Studies and her Ph.D. in Cultural Studies of Sport. She has written widely on gender, masculinity, race, and religion and sports and is the author of "Muhammad Speaks and Muhammad Ali: Intersections of the Nation of Islam and Sport in the 1960s," in *With God on Their Side: Sport in the Service of Religion*, edited by Tara Magdalinski and Tim Chandler (Routledge).

**Amaris J. White** is a Ph.D. student in the Department of History at Michigan State University. She earned her B.A. in History from the University of Florida. Her major field of study is twentieth-century African American history. Her research and teaching focus primarily on African American and Jewish relations and African American social movements and resistance in Florida.

**Ying Wushanley** is an Associate Professor of Wellness and Sport Sciences at Millersville University in Pennsylvania. He is a member of the publications board and a former council member of the North American Society for Sport History. He is an internationally recognized historian of women and sport and has published in numerous journals and encyclopedias. His most recent book is *Playing Nice and Losing: The Struggle for Control of Women's Intercollegiate Athletics, 1960–2000* (Syracuse University Press). He was born in Shanghai, China, and he received his Ph.D. at Penn State University, his M.S. at Washington State University, and his B.S at Shanghai Teachers' University.

**Neil A. Wynn** is Professor of Twentieth-Century American History at the University of Gloucestershire in England. He is a graduate of Edinburgh University (Scotland) and the Open University (England). A former ACLS research fellow in Washington, DC, Wynn is also a founding member and director of the Maastricht Centre for Transatlantic Studies. He is the author of *The Afro American and the Second World War* (Holmes & Meier), *From Progressivism to Prosperity: World War I and American Society* (Holmes & Meier), and co-editor of *America's Century: Perspectives on U.S. History since 1900* (Holmes & Meier). He has contributed chapters to various books and written a number of journal articles and reviews on African American and American history. He specializes in American race relations, as well as African American and popular culture.

# Index

Chamberlain, Wilton Norman, 28, 61–71, 105
Charity, Ron, 14, 15
Charles, Ezzard, 174
Charleston, Oscar, xix
Charlotte Bobcats, 152
Chattanooga Black Lookouts, 183
Chevrolet, 150
Cheyenne Frontier Days rodeo, 210, 212
Chez Paree, 39
Chicago American Giants, 179, 183–84
Chicago Bears, 226
Chicago Boys and Girls Club, 150, 206
Chicago Bulls, 28, 124, 146, 147, 148, 152, 188, 193, 194
Chicago Columbia Giants, 179
*Chicago Defender*, 173
*Chicago Herald*, 101–2
Chicago White Sox, 36
Childs, Frank, 134
Choynski, Joseph Bartlett, 133
Christian Club, 96
Christopher Columbus Award, 240
Churchill, Winston, 140
Church of the Holy Redeemer, 17
Cincinnati Bengals, 251
"Cincinnati Cobra," 174
Cincinnati Reds, 40
Cinderella Man, 169
Civil Rights Act, 18
Civil Rights Movement, 6, 11, 27, 50, 56, 57, 58, 175, 206, 247
Clarett, Maurice, 60
Clark, Lamar, 2
Clark, Monte, 56
Clark, Sterling, 14
Clay, Cassius Marcellus, Jr. *See* Ali, Muhammad
Clay, Cassius Marcellus, Sr., 2
Clemens, Roger, 111
Cleveland Browns, 50, 54–55
Cleveland Cubs, 183
Cleveland Indians, 110
Clifton, Nat "Sweetwater," 103, 104–5
Clijsters, Kim, 258, 259, 260
Clinton, Bill, 31, 164, 270, 276
CNN, 14, 271
Coach of the Year Award, 228
Cobb, Ty, 182
*The Cobbler*, 63
Coca-Cola, 150, 153
Cody, Buffalo Bill, 213–14
Cold War, 104

Coliseum (Chicago), 102
College All-Star team (basketball), 102, 104
College Football Hall of Fame, 220, 228
College Football Writers of America, 226
College Player of the Year (basketball), 147
College World Series, 38
Collier, Blanton, 55–56
Collier, Brian, xix
Collins, Bud, 19
Collins, Dr., 53
Colorado Rockies, 44
Colored Base Ball Leagues, 178, 180
Colored Intercollegiate Athletic Association Tennis championships, 14
*Conan the Destroyer*, 71
Cone, David, 112
Congressional Medal of Honor, 175
Conn, Billy, 142, 171, 173, 175
Conner, Johnny, 132
Connors, Jimmy, 19, 20
Cooke, Jack Kent, 119
Cooper, Chuck, 104–5
Cooper, Henry, 2, 3, 5
Cornerstone Schools, 33
Cosby, Bill, 101, 105, 150
Cosell, Howard, 4, 77, 226
Cotton Bowl, 53
Cowboys, 209–18
Cowgirls, 214
*A Crash Course on Calcium*, 165
Cuban Giants, 178, 179
Cuban X-Giants, 179
Cunningham, Mattie Cordell, 14, 20
Cuthbert, Betty, 236
Cy Young Award, 184

Dabney, Milton, 178
Dallas Cowboys, xv
Dallas Mavericks, 188, 196
Daniels, Isabelle, 236, 238
Dapper Dan Classic, 190
Dart, Greta, 118
Dart, Jim, 118
Daughtry, Nora P., 51, 59
Davenport, Lindsay, 257, 260, 264
Davis, Ambrose, 179
Davis, Mattie, 84
Davis, Sammie, Jr., 174
Day, Guy, 178
*Days of Grace* (Ashe), 22
Decathlon, 50
"Dee-Dee." *See* Joyner, Florence Griffith